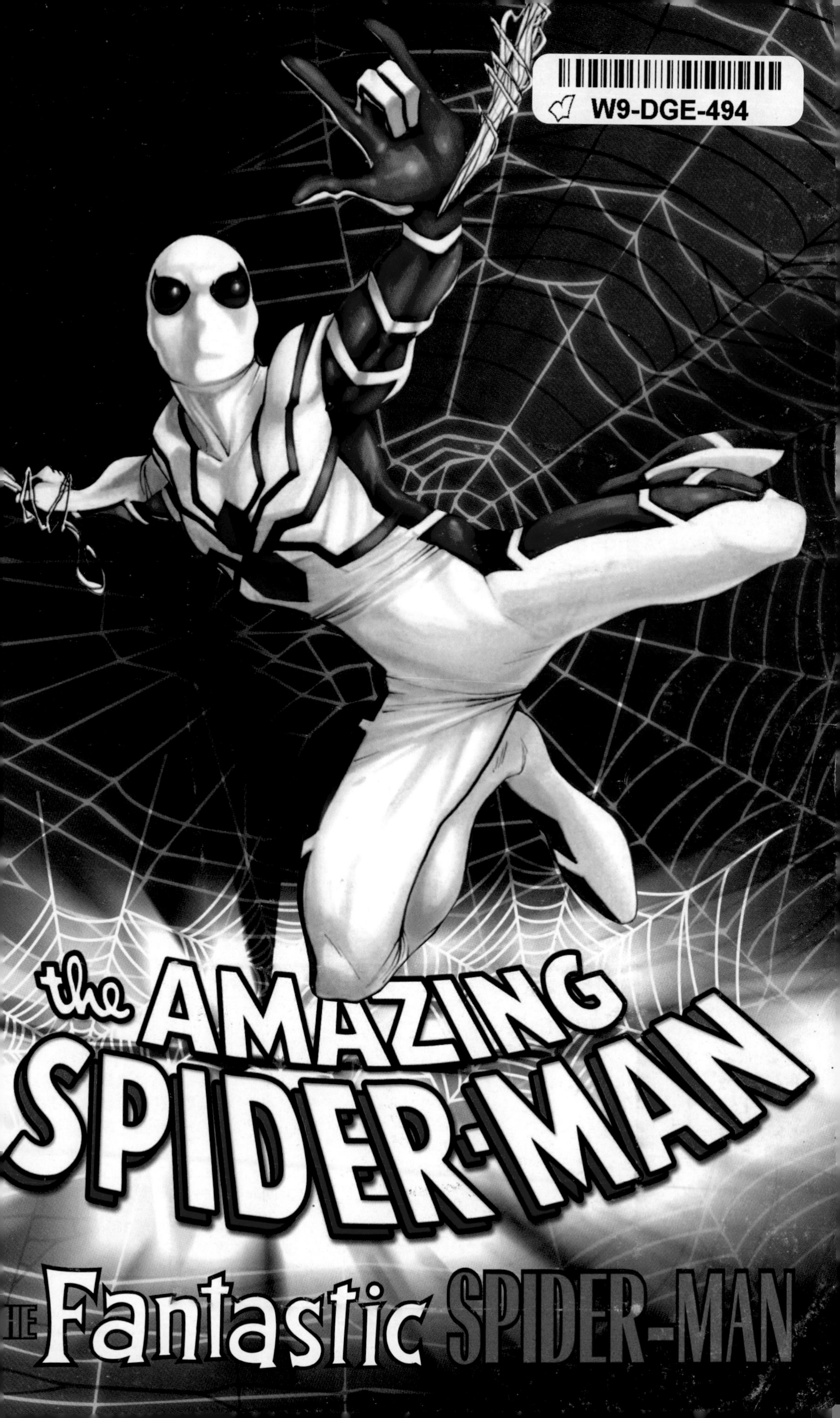
the AMAZING
SPIDER-MAN
HE Fantastic SPIDER-MAN

the AMAZING SPIDER-MAN

THE FANTASTIC SPIDER-MAN

ISSUE #658
Writer: **DAN SLOTT**
Artist: **JAVIER PULIDO**
Colorists: **MUNSTA VICENTE** (PP. 1-17) & **JAVIER RODRIQUEZ** (PP. 18-23)
Cover Art: **MARKO DJURDJEVIC**

ISSUES #659-660
Writers: **DAN SLOTT** & **FRED VAN LENTE**
Artists: **STEFANO CASELLI** (#659 & #660, PP. 18-20) & **MIKE MCKONE** (#660, PP. 1-17)
Colorist: **MARTE GRACIA**
Cover Art: **STEFANO CASELLI** & **LORENZO DE FELICI**

ISSUES #661-662
Writer: **CHRISTOS GAGE**
Penciler: **REILLY BROWN**
Inker: **VICTOR OLAZABA**
Colorist: **JOHN RAUCH**
Cover Art: **ED MCGUINNESS** & **MORRY HOLLOWELL**
Cover Letterer: **VC'S CHRIS ELIOPOULOS**

"JUST ANOTHER DAY"
Writer: **PAUL BENJAMIN**
Artist: **JAVIER PULIDO**
Colorist: **MATT HOLLINGSWORTH**

"THE CHOICE"
Writer: **FRANK TIERI**
Artist: **JAVIER RODRIGUEZ**

"CAN'T GET THE SERVICE
Writer: **ROB WILLIAM**
Penciler: **LEE GARBET**
Inker: **ALEJANDRO SICA**
Colorist: **FABIO D'AURI**
Cover Art: **ROBERTO DE LA TORR**
& **MATT HOLLINGSWORT**

Letterer: **VC'S JOE CARAMAGNA** • Assistant Editor: **ELLIE PYLE** • Senior Editor: **STEPHEN WACKER**

Collection Editor: **JENNIFER GRÜNWALD** • Assistant Editors: **ALEX STARBUCK** & **NELSON RIBEIRO**
Editor, Special Projects: **MARK D. BEAZLEY** • Senior Editor, Special Projects: **JEFF YOUNGQUIST**
Senior Vice President of Sales: **DAVID GABRIEL** • SVP of Brand Planning & Communications: **MICHAEL PASCIULL**

Editor in Chief: **AXEL ALONSO** • Chief Creative Officer: **JOE QUESADA** • Publisher: **DAN BUCKLEY** • Executive Producer: **ALAN FIN**

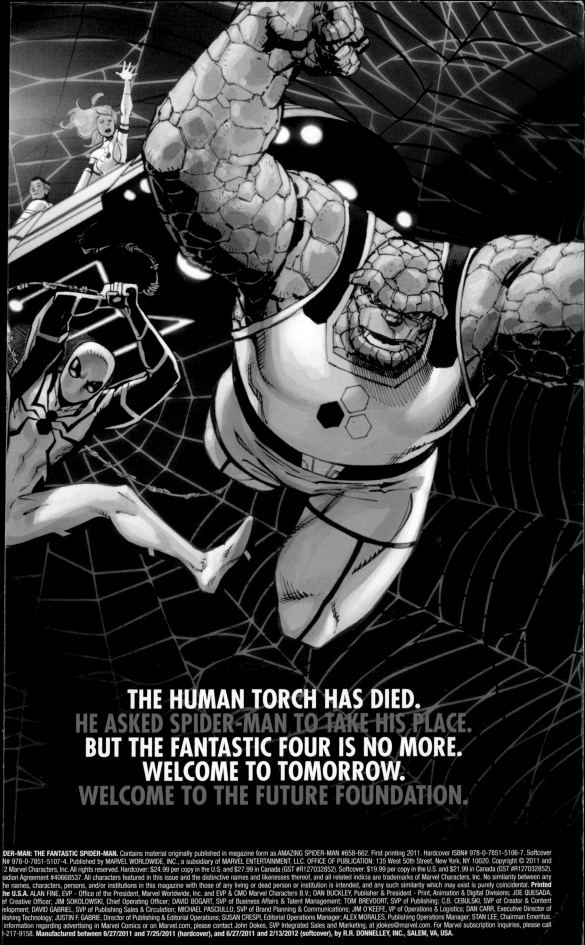

THE HUMAN TORCH HAS DIED.
HE ASKED SPIDER-MAN TO TAKE HIS PLACE.
BUT THE FANTASTIC FOUR IS NO MORE.
WELCOME TO TOMORROW.
WELCOME TO THE FUTURE FOUNDATION.

DER-MAN: THE FANTASTIC SPIDER-MAN. Contains material originally published in magazine form as AMAZING SPIDER-MAN #658-662. First printing 2011. Hardcover ISBN# 978-0-7851-5106-7. Softcover N# 978-0-7851-5107-4. Published by MARVEL WORLDWIDE, INC., a subsidiary of MARVEL ENTERTAINMENT, LLC. OFFICE OF PUBLICATION: 135 West 50th Street, New York, NY 10020. Copyright © 2011 and 2 Marvel Characters, Inc. All rights reserved. Hardcover: $24.99 per copy in the U.S. and $27.99 in Canada (GST #R127032852). Softcover: $19.99 per copy in the U.S. and $21.99 in Canada (GST #R127032852). adian Agreement #40668537. All characters featured in this issue and the distinctive names and likenesses thereof, and all related indicia are trademarks of Marvel Characters, Inc. No similarity between any he names, characters, persons, and/or institutions in this magazine with those of any living or dead person or institution is intended, and any such similarity which may exist is purely coincidental. **Printed** he U.S.A. ALAN FINE, EVP - Office of the President, Marvel Worldwide, Inc. and EVP & CMO Marvel Characters B.V.; DAN BUCKLEY, Publisher & President - Print, Animation & Digital Divisions; JOE QUESADA, ef Creative Officer; JIM SOKOLOWSKI, Chief Operating Officer; DAVID BOGART, SVP of Business Affairs & Talent Management; TOM BREVOORT, SVP of Publishing; C.B. CEBULSKI, SVP of Creator & Content velopment; DAVID GABRIEL, SVP of Publishing Sales & Circulation; MICHAEL PASCIULLO, SVP of Brand Planning & Communications; JIM O'KEEFE, VP of Operations & Logistics; DAN CARR, Executive Director of lishing Technology; JUSTIN F. GABRIE, Director of Publishing & Editorial Operations; SUSAN CRESPI, Editorial Operations Manager; ALEX MORALES, Publishing Operations Manager; STAN LEE, Chairman Emeritus. information regarding advertising in Marvel Comics or on Marvel.com, please contact John Dokes, SVP Integrated Sales and Marketing, at jdokes@marvel.com. For Marvel subscription inquiries, please call)-217-9158. **Manufactured between 6/27/2011 and 7/25/2011 (hardcover), and 6/27/2011 and 2/13/2012 (softcover), by R.R. DONNELLEY, INC., SALEM, VA, USA.**

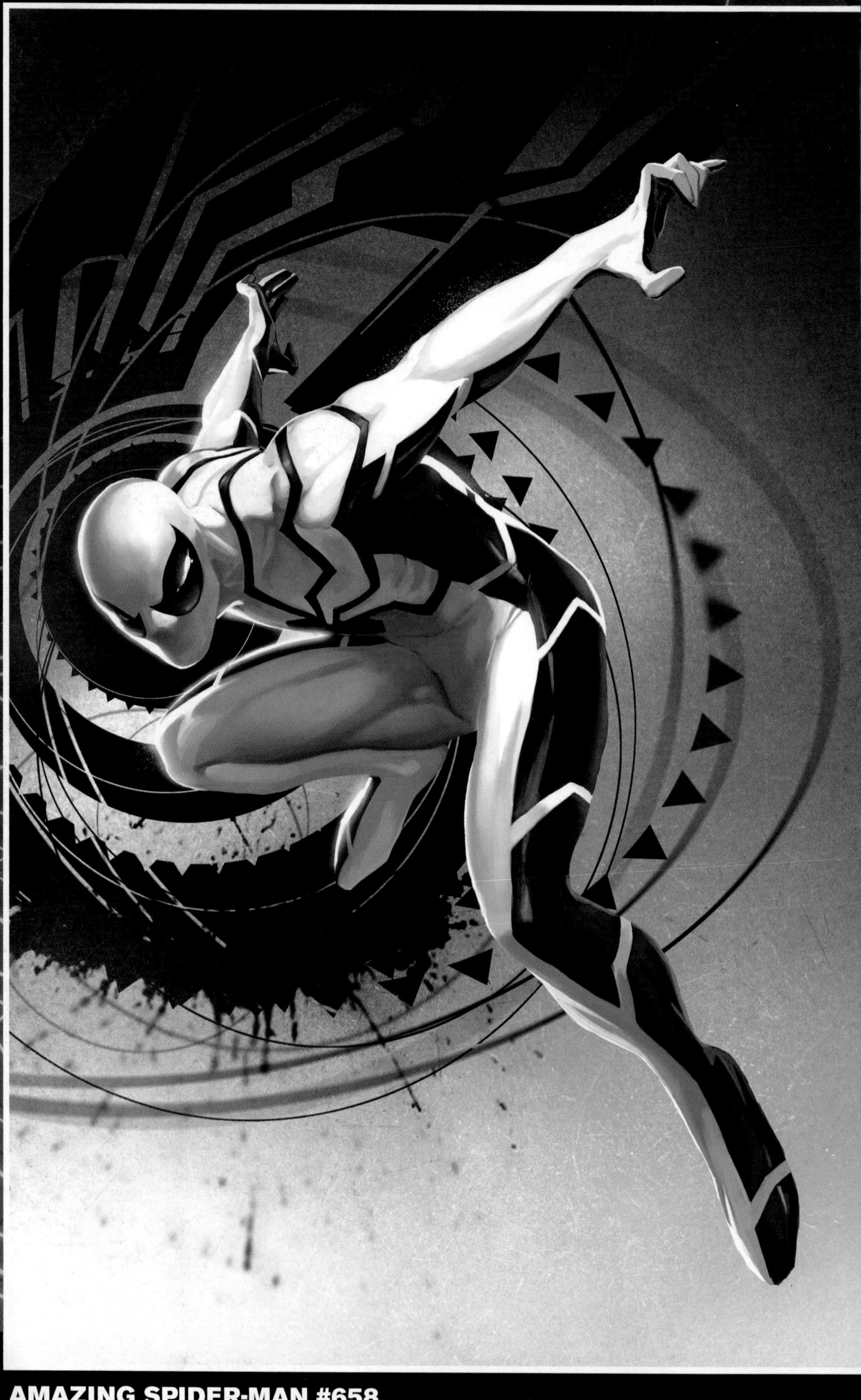

AMAZING SPIDER-MAN #658
COVER BY MARKO DJURDJEVIC

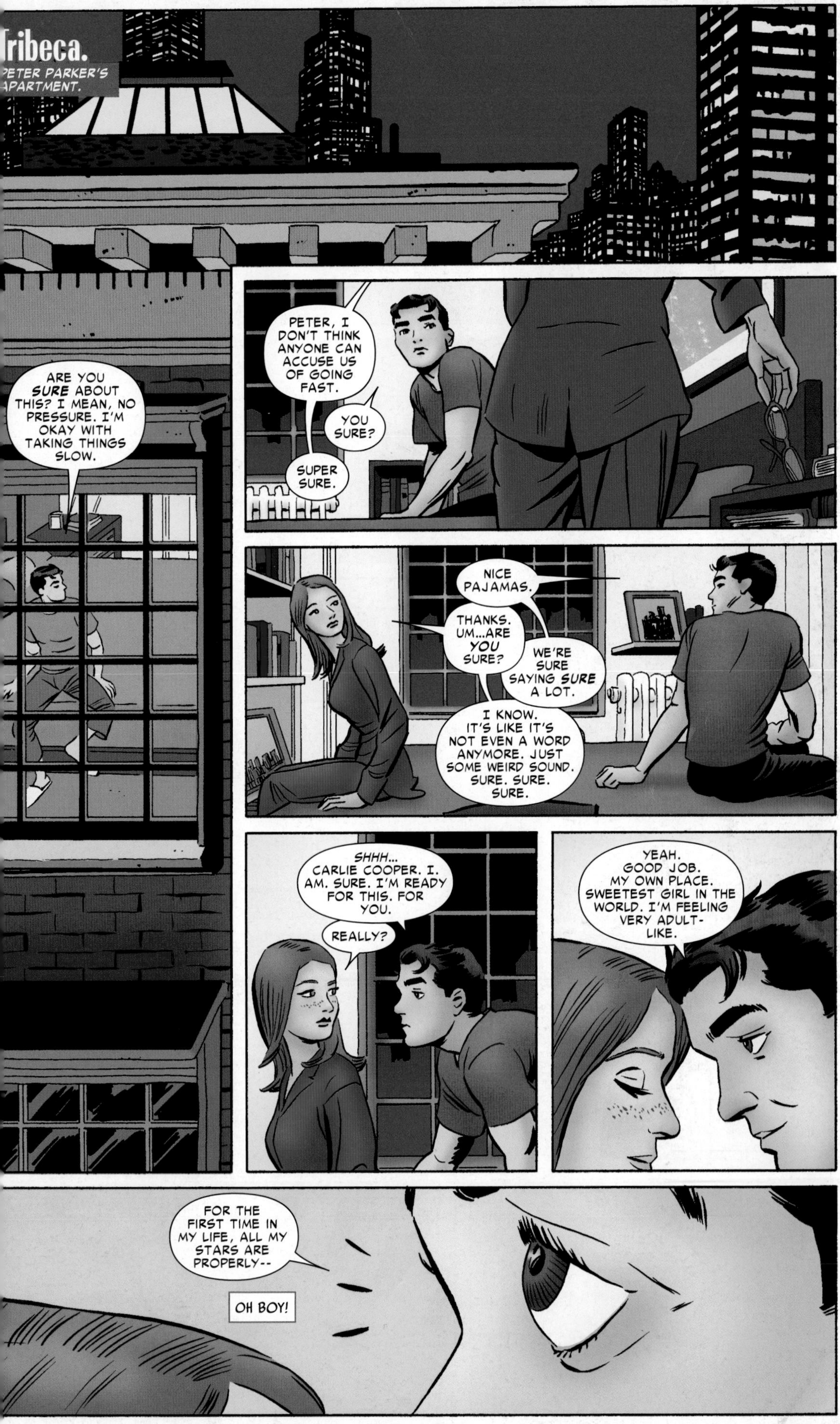
Tribeca.
PETER PARKER'S APARTMENT.
ARE YOU SURE ABOUT THIS? I MEAN, NO PRESSURE. I'M OKAY WITH TAKING THINGS SLOW.
PETER, I DON'T THINK ANYONE CAN ACCUSE US OF GOING FAST.
YOU SURE?
SUPER SURE.
NICE PAJAMAS.
THANKS. UM...ARE YOU SURE?
WE'RE SURE SAYING SURE A LOT.
I KNOW. IT'S LIKE IT'S NOT EVEN A WORD ANYMORE. JUST SOME WEIRD SOUND. SURE. SURE. SURE.
SHHH... CARLIE COOPER. I. AM. SURE. I'M READY FOR THIS. FOR YOU.
REALLY?
YEAH. GOOD JOB. MY OWN PLACE. SWEETEST GIRL IN THE WORLD. I'M FEELING VERY ADULT-LIKE.
FOR THE FIRST TIME IN MY LIFE, ALL MY STARS ARE PROPERLY--
OH BOY!

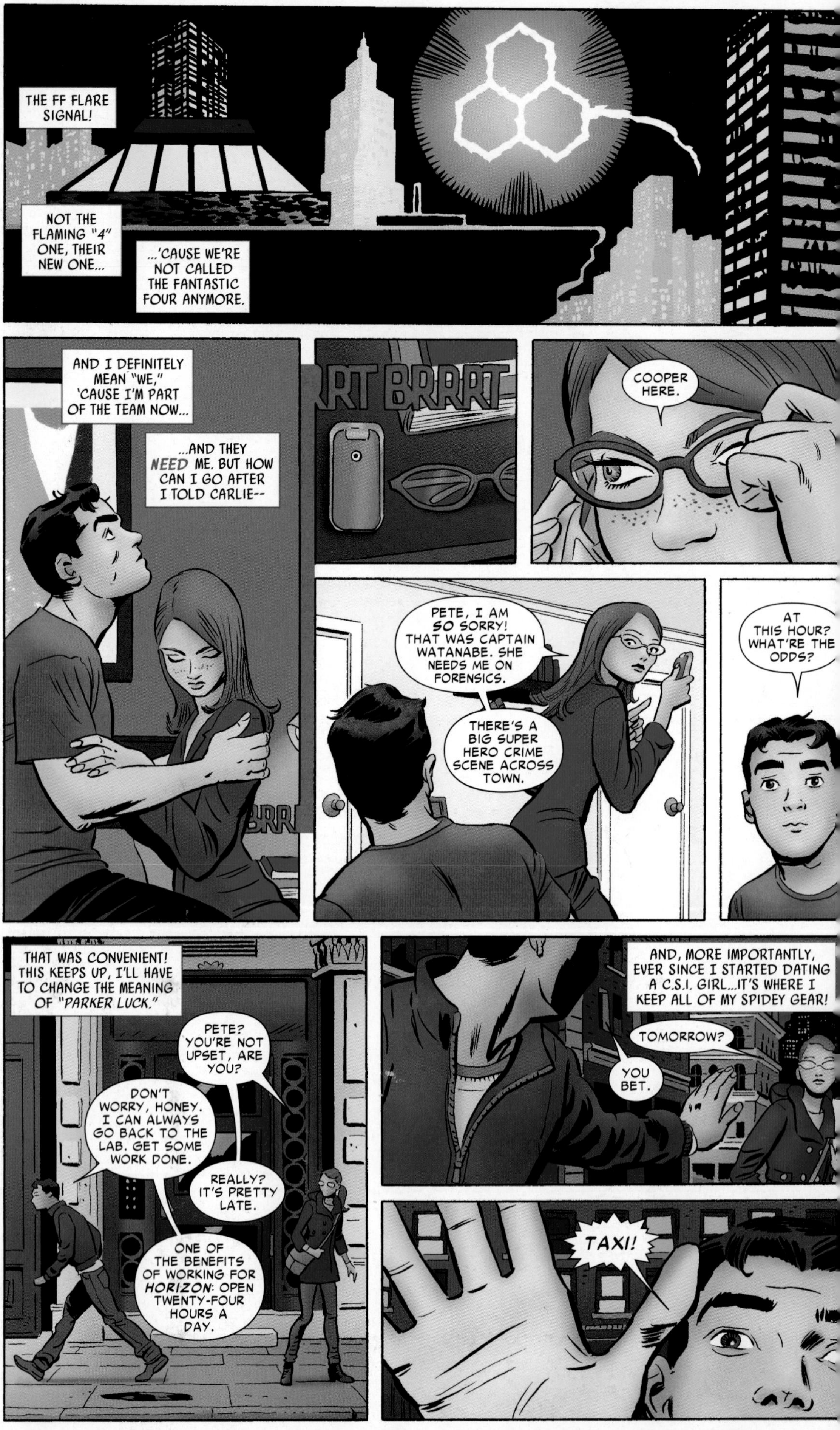

THE FF FLARE SIGNAL!
NOT THE FLAMING "4" ONE, THEIR NEW ONE...
...'CAUSE WE'RE NOT CALLED THE FANTASTIC FOUR ANYMORE.
AND I DEFINITELY MEAN "WE," 'CAUSE I'M PART OF THE TEAM NOW...
...AND THEY NEED ME. BUT HOW CAN I GO AFTER I TOLD CARLIE--
BRRRT BRRRT
COOPER HERE.
PETE, I AM SO SORRY! THAT WAS CAPTAIN WATANABE. SHE NEEDS ME ON FORENSICS.
THERE'S A BIG SUPER HERO CRIME SCENE ACROSS TOWN.
AT THIS HOUR? WHAT'RE THE ODDS?
THAT WAS CONVENIENT! THIS KEEPS UP, I'LL HAVE TO CHANGE THE MEANING OF "PARKER LUCK."
PETE? YOU'RE NOT UPSET, ARE YOU?
DON'T WORRY, HONEY. I CAN ALWAYS GO BACK TO THE LAB. GET SOME WORK DONE.
REALLY? IT'S PRETTY LATE.
ONE OF THE BENEFITS OF WORKING FOR HORIZON: OPEN TWENTY-FOUR HOURS A DAY.
AND, MORE IMPORTANTLY, EVER SINCE I STARTED DATING A C.S.I. GIRL...IT'S WHERE I KEEP ALL OF MY SPIDEY GEAR!
TOMORROW?
YOU BET.
TAXI!

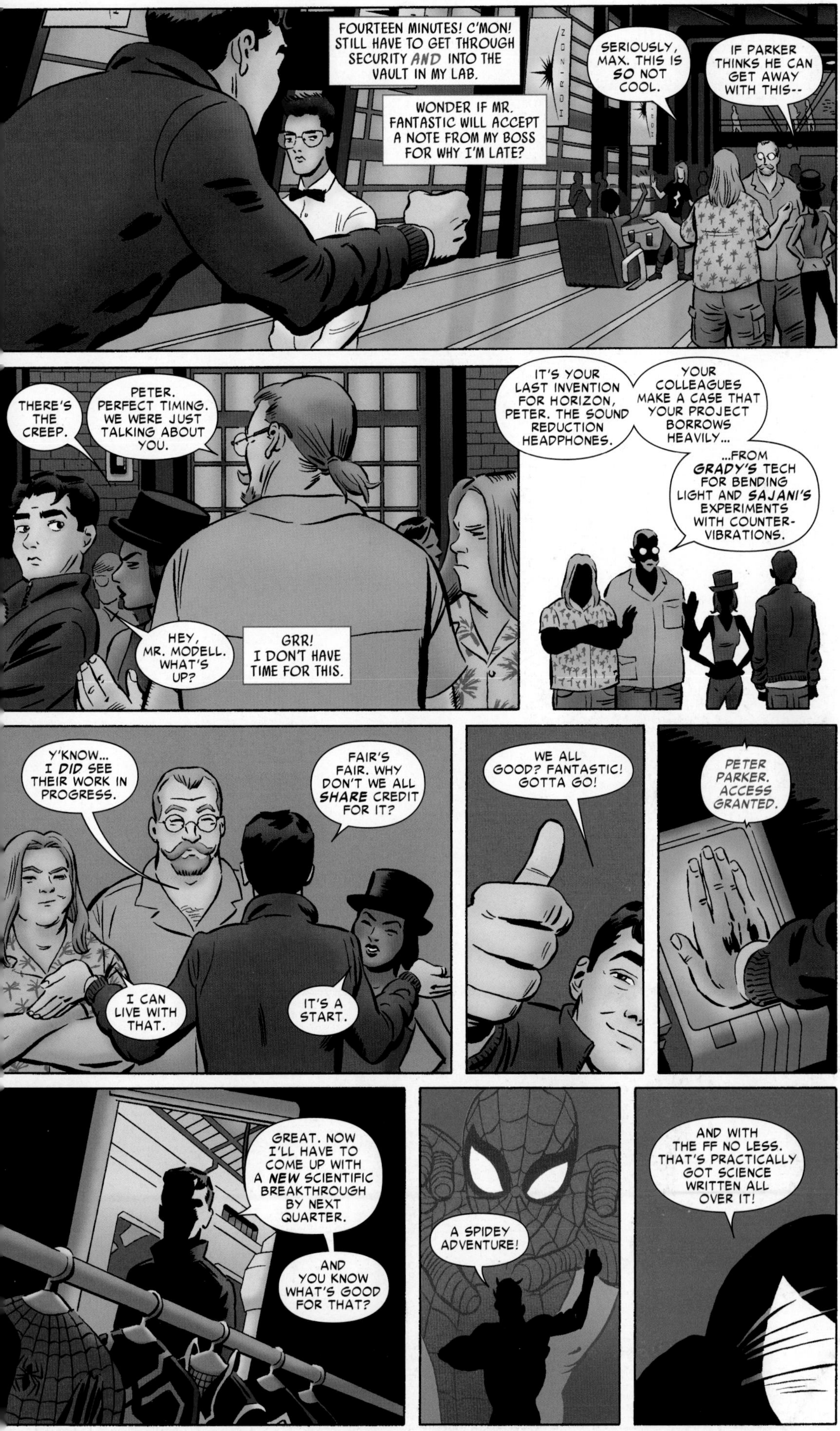
FOURTEEN MINUTES! C'MON! STILL HAVE TO GET THROUGH SECURITY AND INTO THE VAULT IN MY LAB.
WONDER IF MR. FANTASTIC WILL ACCEPT A NOTE FROM MY BOSS FOR WHY I'M LATE?
SERIOUSLY, MAX. THIS IS SO NOT COOL.
IF PARKER THINKS HE CAN GET AWAY WITH THIS--
THERE'S THE CREEP.
PETER. PERFECT TIMING. WE WERE JUST TALKING ABOUT YOU.
HEY, MR. MODELL. WHAT'S UP?
GRR! I DON'T HAVE TIME FOR THIS.
IT'S YOUR LAST INVENTION FOR HORIZON, PETER. THE SOUND REDUCTION HEADPHONES.
YOUR COLLEAGUES MAKE A CASE THAT YOUR PROJECT BORROWS HEAVILY...
...FROM GRADY'S TECH FOR BENDING LIGHT AND SAJANI'S EXPERIMENTS WITH COUNTER-VIBRATIONS.
Y'KNOW... I DID SEE THEIR WORK IN PROGRESS.
FAIR'S FAIR. WHY DON'T WE ALL SHARE CREDIT FOR IT?
I CAN LIVE WITH THAT.
IT'S A START.
WE ALL GOOD? FANTASTIC! GOTTA GO!
PETER PARKER. ACCESS GRANTED.
GREAT. NOW I'LL HAVE TO COME UP WITH A NEW SCIENTIFIC BREAKTHROUGH BY NEXT QUARTER.
AND YOU KNOW WHAT'S GOOD FOR THAT?
A SPIDEY ADVENTURE!
AND WITH THE FF NO LESS. THAT'S PRACTICALLY GOT SCIENCE WRITTEN ALL OVER IT!

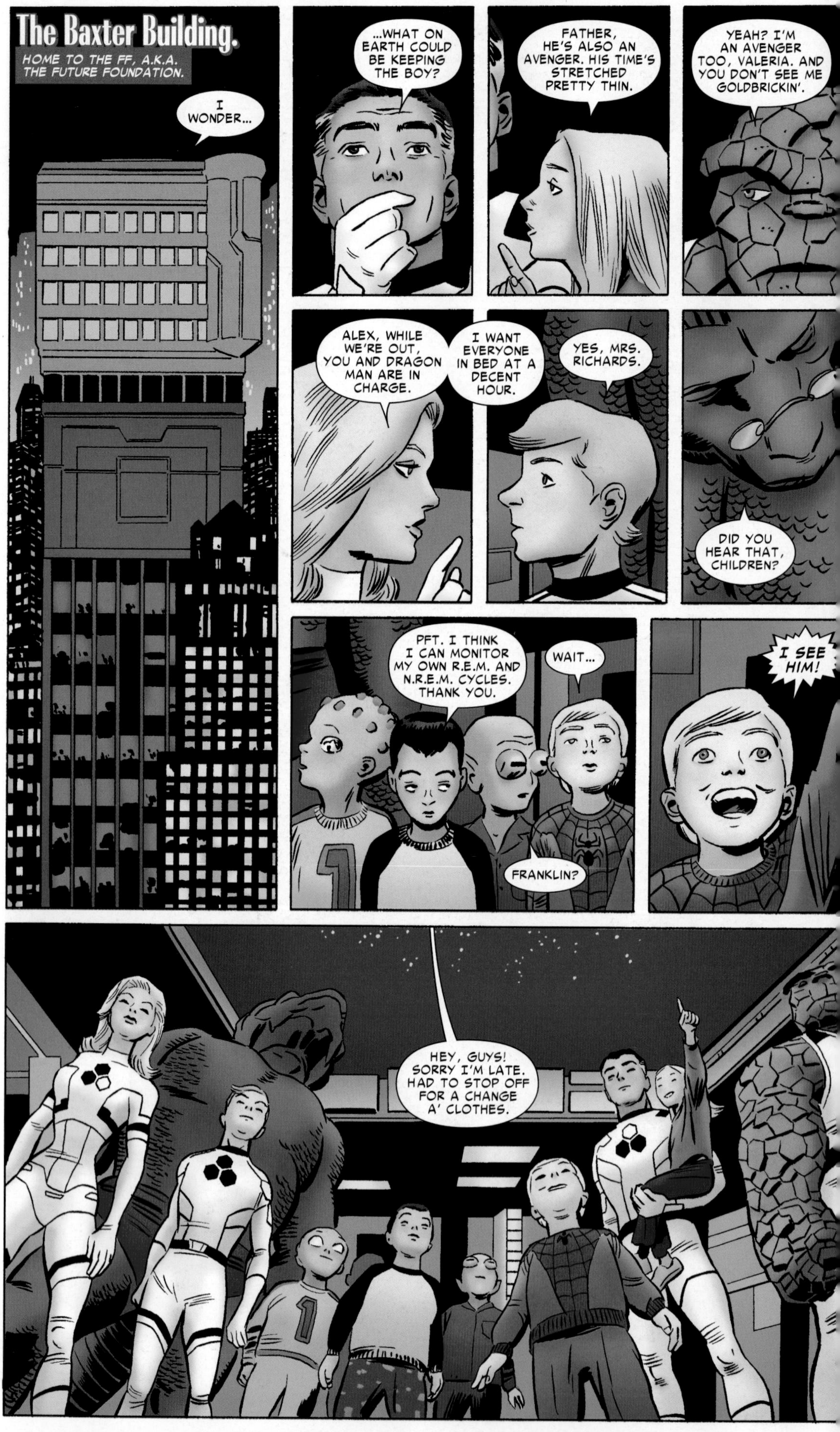
The Baxter Building.
HOME TO THE FF, A.K.A. THE FUTURE FOUNDATION.
I WONDER...
...WHAT ON EARTH COULD BE KEEPING THE BOY?
FATHER, HE'S ALSO AN AVENGER. HIS TIME'S STRETCHED PRETTY THIN.
YEAH? I'M AN AVENGER TOO, VALERIA. AND YOU DON'T SEE ME GOLDBRICKIN'.
ALEX, WHILE WE'RE OUT, YOU AND DRAGON MAN ARE IN CHARGE.
I WANT EVERYONE IN BED AT A DECENT HOUR.
YES, MRS. RICHARDS.
DID YOU HEAR THAT, CHILDREN?
PFT. I THINK I CAN MONITOR MY OWN R.E.M. AND N.R.E.M. CYCLES. THANK YOU.
WAIT...
FRANKLIN?
I SEE HIM!
HEY, GUYS! SORRY I'M LATE. HAD TO STOP OFF FOR A CHANGE A' CLOTHES.

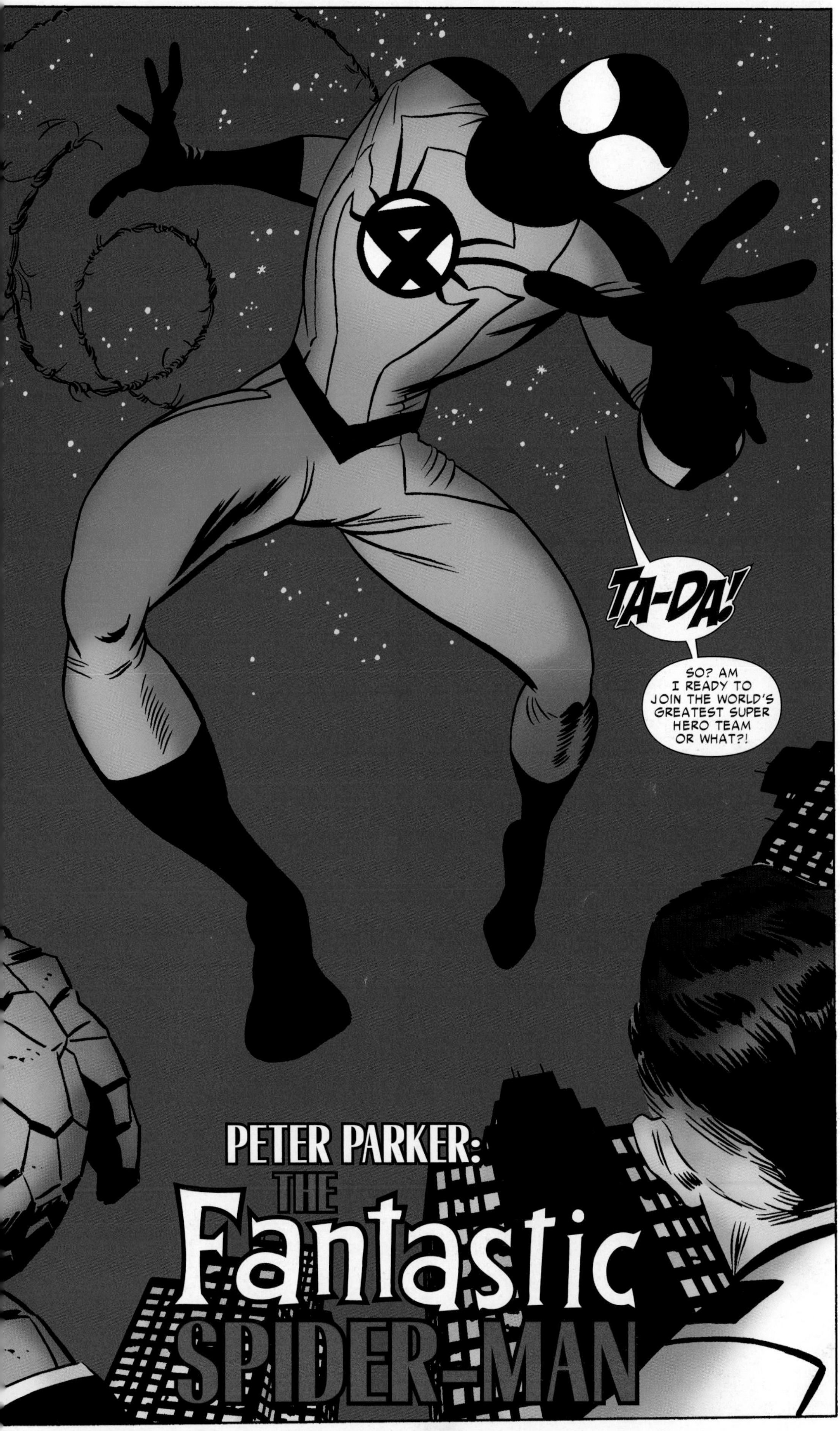
TA-DA!
SO? AM I READY TO JOIN THE WORLD'S GREATEST SUPER HERO TEAM OR WHAT?!
PETER PARKER: THE Fantastic SPIDER-MAN

OF ALL THE INSENSITIVE--

YEAH! OUT WITH IT, WEBS! WHATTYA DOIN' IN THAT COCKAMAMIE GETUP?!

WHAT? THIS? I ALWAYS WANTED TO BE ON THIS TEAM.

I HAD MY TAILOR, LEO, MAKE THIS UP SPECIAL. IT'S COOL, RIGHT?

NO! TAKE IT OFF.

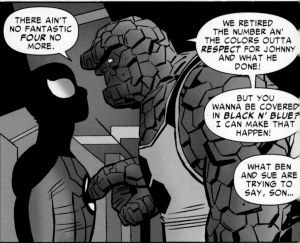

THERE AIN'T NO FANTASTIC FOUR NO MORE.

WE RETIRED THE NUMBER AN' THE COLORS OUTTA RESPECT FOR JOHNNY AND WHAT HE DONE!

BUT YOU WANNA BE COVERED IN BLACK N' BLUE? I CAN MAKE THAT HAPPEN!

WHAT BEN AND SUE ARE TRYING TO SAY, SON...

...IS THAT WE'RE HONORED TO HAVE YOU ON OUR TEAM AND IN OUR FAMILY.

WE JUST HOPE THAT YOU'RE PROUD TO BE PART OF THE FUTURE FOUNDATION AS WELL.

HERE. YOU LEFT YOUR UNIFORM LAST TIME.

OY. WITH THE GUILT. FINE!

WHAT? OH, WE'RE THE FUTURE FOUNDATION NOW.

WANNA BE IN THE FANTASTIC FOUR, SPIDEY? SURE.

BAIT N' SWITCH IF YOU ASK ME. RAZZIN' FRAZZIN'...

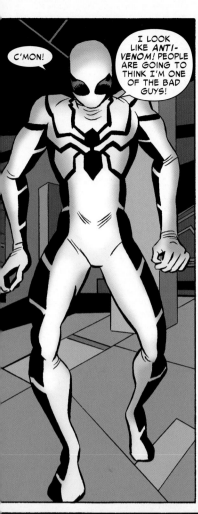

C'MON!

I LOOK LIKE *ANTI-VENOM!* PEOPLE ARE GOING TO THINK I'M ONE OF THE BAD GUYS!

OH, NO THEY WON'T. GET OVER IT.

SUE! HOW CAN YOU *NOT* SEE THIS?

WHITE SUIT. BLACK SPIDER. *ANTI-VENOM!*

BENTLEY, I AM CONFUSED. ACCORDING TO FRANKLIN THIS SPIDER-MAN IS AN ADULT. YET HE BEHAVES LIKE AN INFANT.

CORRECT. HE'S A BIG BABY.

ALL RIGHT. I LOVE IT. BEST SUIT EVER.

CAN WE *GO* NOW?

BYE!

SO? WHAT'S THE BIG MISSION?

WE'VE DETECTED THREE RIFTS IN THE SPACE-TIME CONTINUUM.

IN THE MICROVERSE, THE DISTANT FUTURE, AND ONE RIGHT HERE ON EARTH.

IF WE DON'T SEAL ALL THREE, THERE'S A DANGER REALITY COULD COLLAPSE IN ON ITSELF.

WOW. NEVER ANYTHING SMALL WITH YOU GUYS, IS IT?

WELL? WHERE TO FIRST? LATVERIA? WAKANDA? OOH-- ATLANTIS?

FRANCE.

FRANCE?!

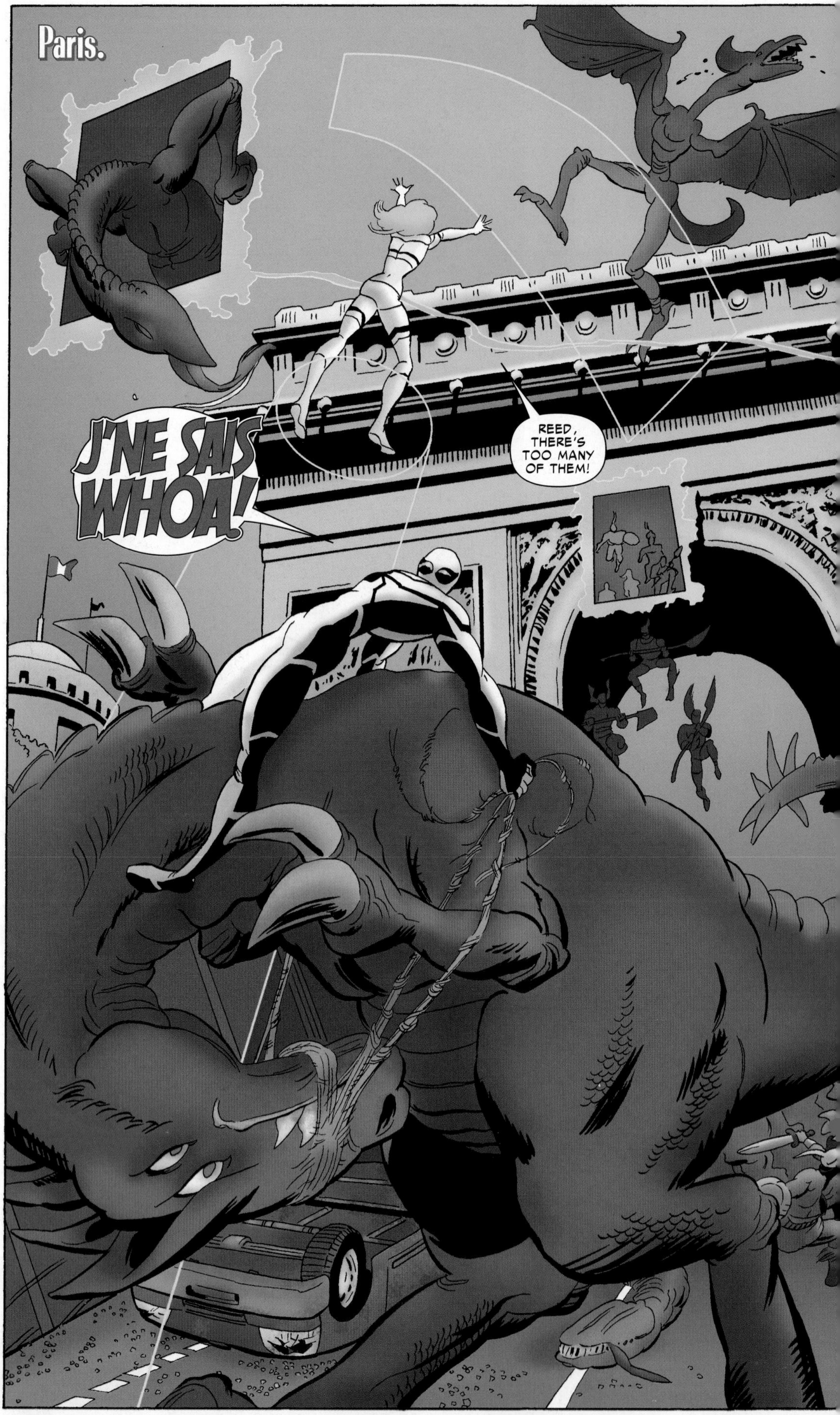
Paris.
J'NE SAIS WHOA!
REED, THERE'S TOO MANY OF THEM!

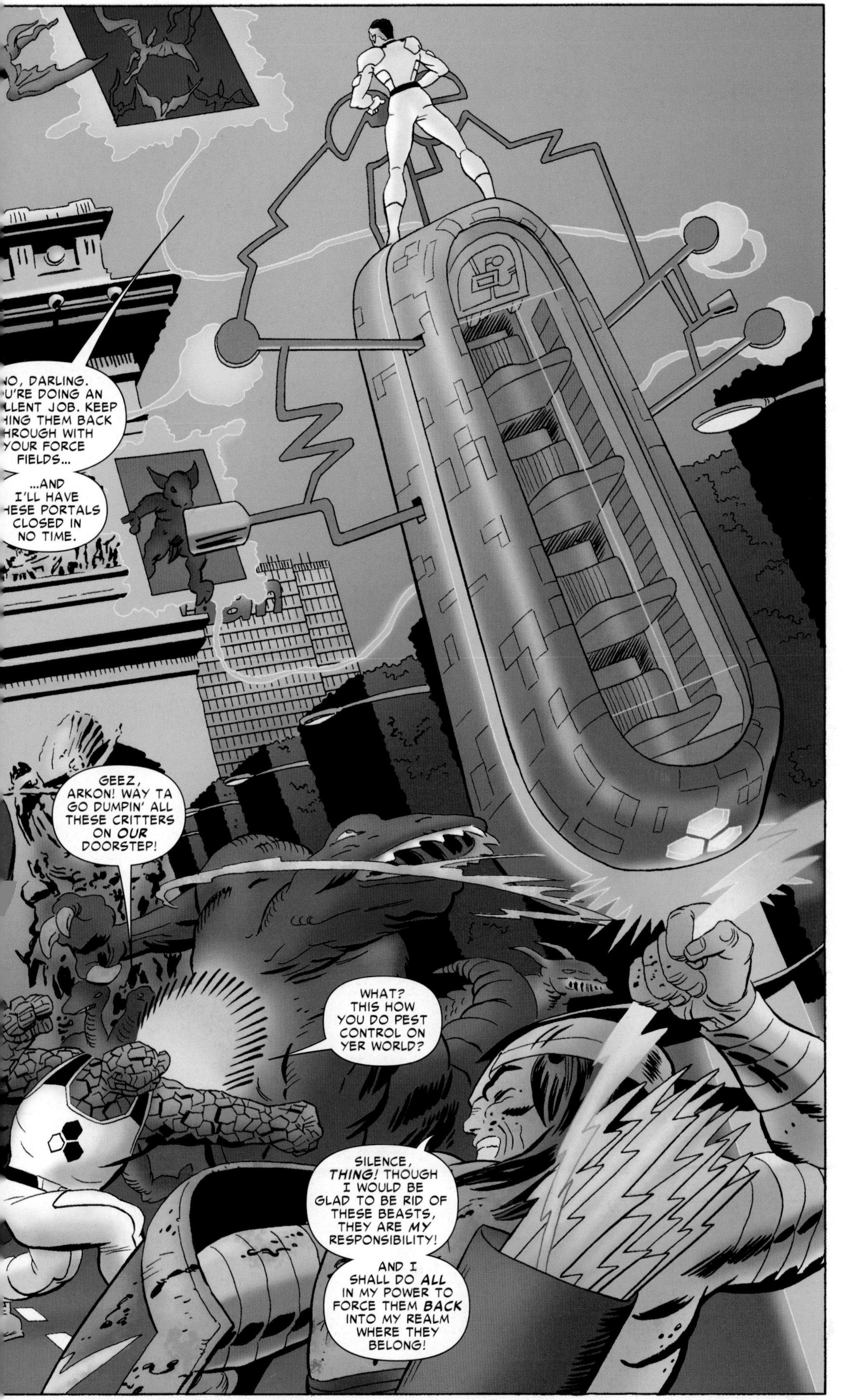
O, DARLING. U'RE DOING AN LLENT JOB. KEEP HING THEM BACK HROUGH WITH YOUR FORCE FIELDS...
...AND I'LL HAVE HESE PORTALS CLOSED IN NO TIME.
GEEZ, ARKON! WAY TA GO DUMPIN' ALL THESE CRITTERS ON *OUR* DOORSTEP!
WHAT? THIS HOW YOU DO PEST CONTROL ON YER WORLD?
SILENCE, *THING!* THOUGH I WOULD BE GLAD TO BE RID OF THESE BEASTS, THEY ARE *MY* RESPONSIBILITY!
AND I SHALL DO *ALL* IN MY POWER TO FORCE THEM *BACK* INTO MY REALM WHERE THEY BELONG!

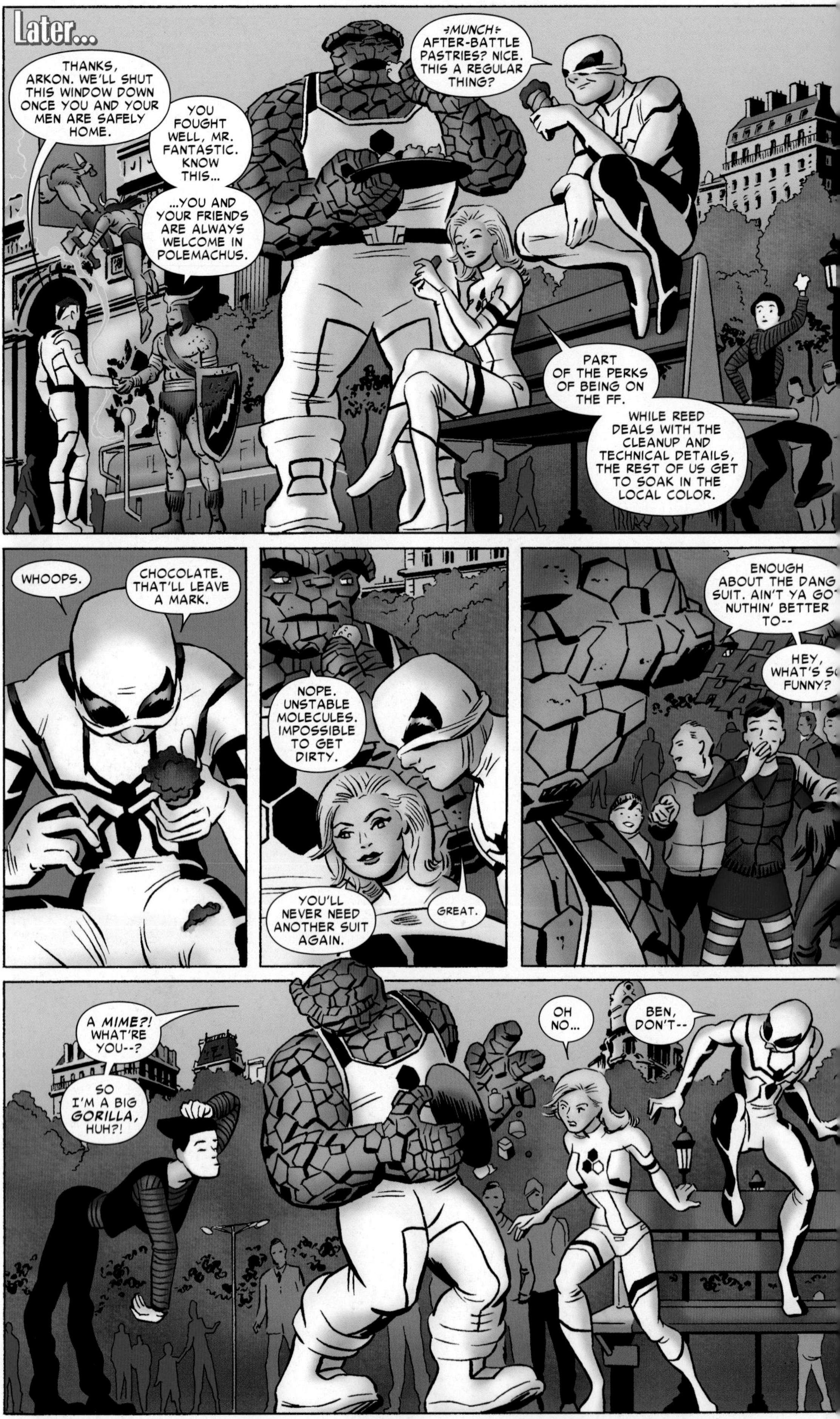
Later...
THANKS, ARKON. WE'LL SHUT THIS WINDOW DOWN ONCE YOU AND YOUR MEN ARE SAFELY HOME.
YOU FOUGHT WELL, MR. FANTASTIC. KNOW THIS...
...YOU AND YOUR FRIENDS ARE ALWAYS WELCOME IN POLEMACHUS.
MUNCH
AFTER-BATTLE PASTRIES? NICE. THIS A REGULAR THING?
PART OF THE PERKS OF BEING ON THE FF.
WHILE REED DEALS WITH THE CLEANUP AND TECHNICAL DETAILS, THE REST OF US GET TO SOAK IN THE LOCAL COLOR.
WHOOPS.
CHOCOLATE. THAT'LL LEAVE A MARK.
NOPE. UNSTABLE MOLECULES. IMPOSSIBLE TO GET DIRTY.
YOU'LL NEVER NEED ANOTHER SUIT AGAIN.
GREAT.
ENOUGH ABOUT THE DANG SUIT. AIN'T YA GOT NUTHIN' BETTER TO--
HEY, WHAT'S S FUNNY?
A *MIME?!* WHAT'RE YOU--?
SO I'M A BIG *GORILLA,* HUH?!
OH NO...
BEN, DON'T--

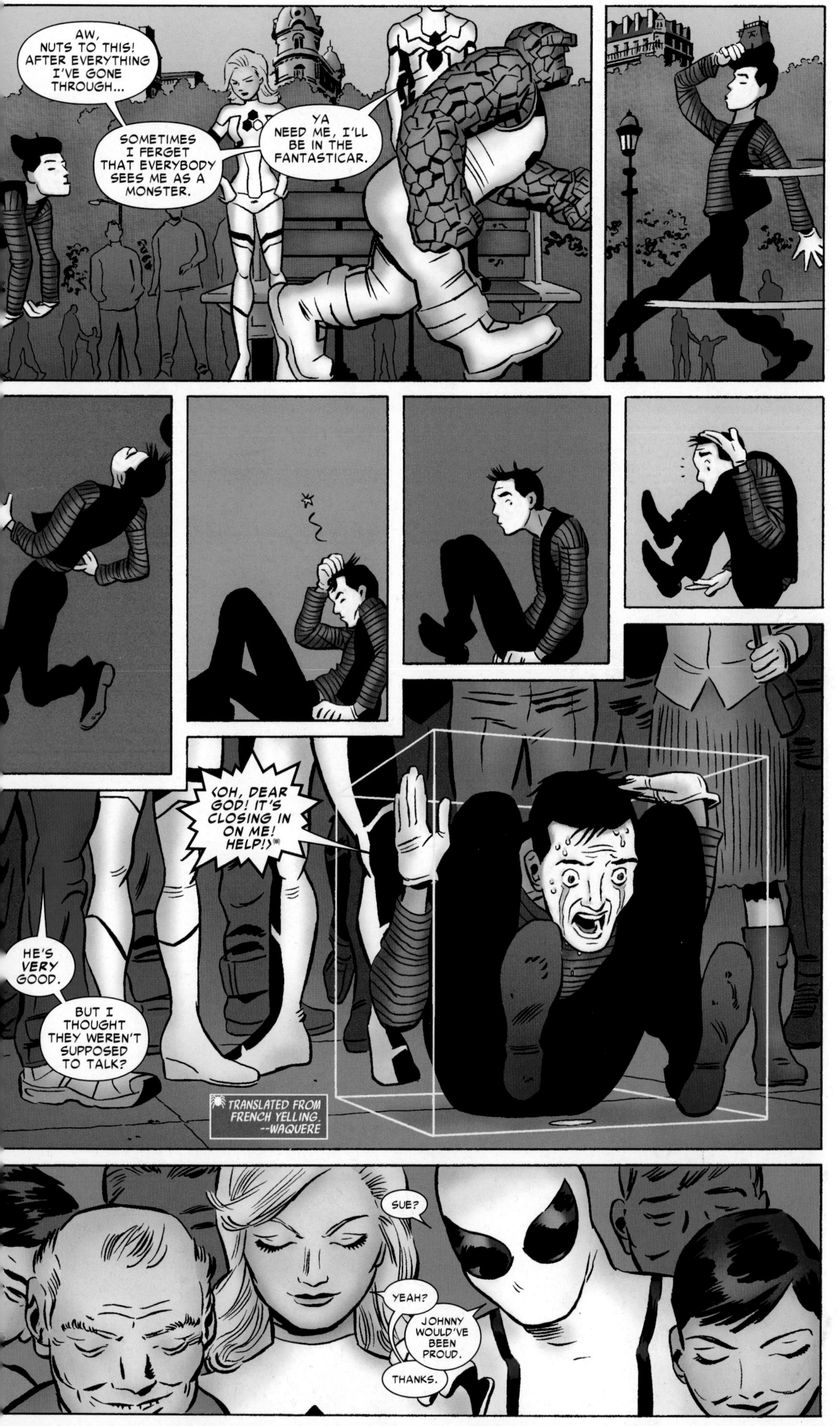
AW, NUTS TO THIS! AFTER EVERYTHING I'VE GONE THROUGH...
SOMETIMES I FERGET THAT EVERYBODY SEES ME AS A MONSTER.
YA NEED ME, I'LL BE IN THE FANTASTICAR.
‹OH, DEAR GOD! IT'S CLOSING IN ON ME! HELP!›
HE'S *VERY* GOOD.
BUT I THOUGHT THEY WEREN'T SUPPOSED TO TALK?
TRANSLATED FROM FRENCH YELLING. --WAQUERE
SUE?
YEAH?
JOHNNY WOULD'VE BEEN PROUD.
THANKS.

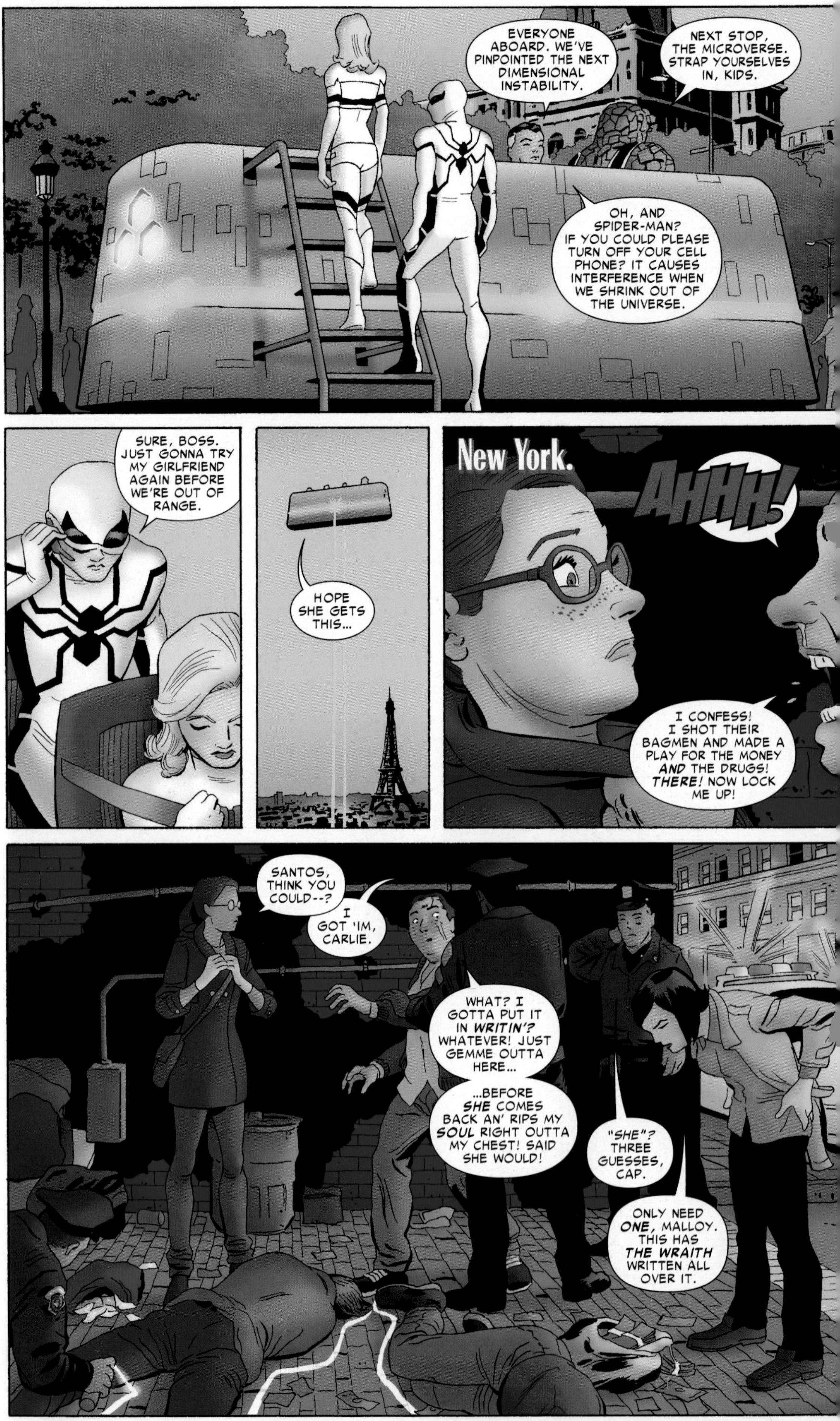
EVERYONE ABOARD. WE'VE PINPOINTED THE NEXT DIMENSIONAL INSTABILITY.
NEXT STOP, THE MICROVERSE. STRAP YOURSELVES IN, KIDS.
OH, AND SPIDER-MAN? IF YOU COULD PLEASE TURN OFF YOUR CELL PHONE? IT CAUSES INTERFERENCE WHEN WE SHRINK OUT OF THE UNIVERSE.
SURE, BOSS. JUST GONNA TRY MY GIRLFRIEND AGAIN BEFORE WE'RE OUT OF RANGE.
HOPE SHE GETS THIS...
New York.
AHHH!
I CONFESS! I SHOT THEIR BAGMEN AND MADE A PLAY FOR THE MONEY AND THE DRUGS! THERE! NOW LOCK ME UP!
SANTOS, THINK YOU COULD--?
I GOT 'IM, CARLIE.
WHAT? I GOTTA PUT IT IN WRITIN'? WHATEVER! JUST GEMME OUTTA HERE...
...BEFORE SHE COMES BACK AN' RIPS MY SOUL RIGHT OUTTA MY CHEST! SAID SHE WOULD!
"SHE"? THREE GUESSES, CAP.
ONLY NEED ONE, MALLOY. THIS HAS THE WRAITH WRITTEN ALL OVER IT.

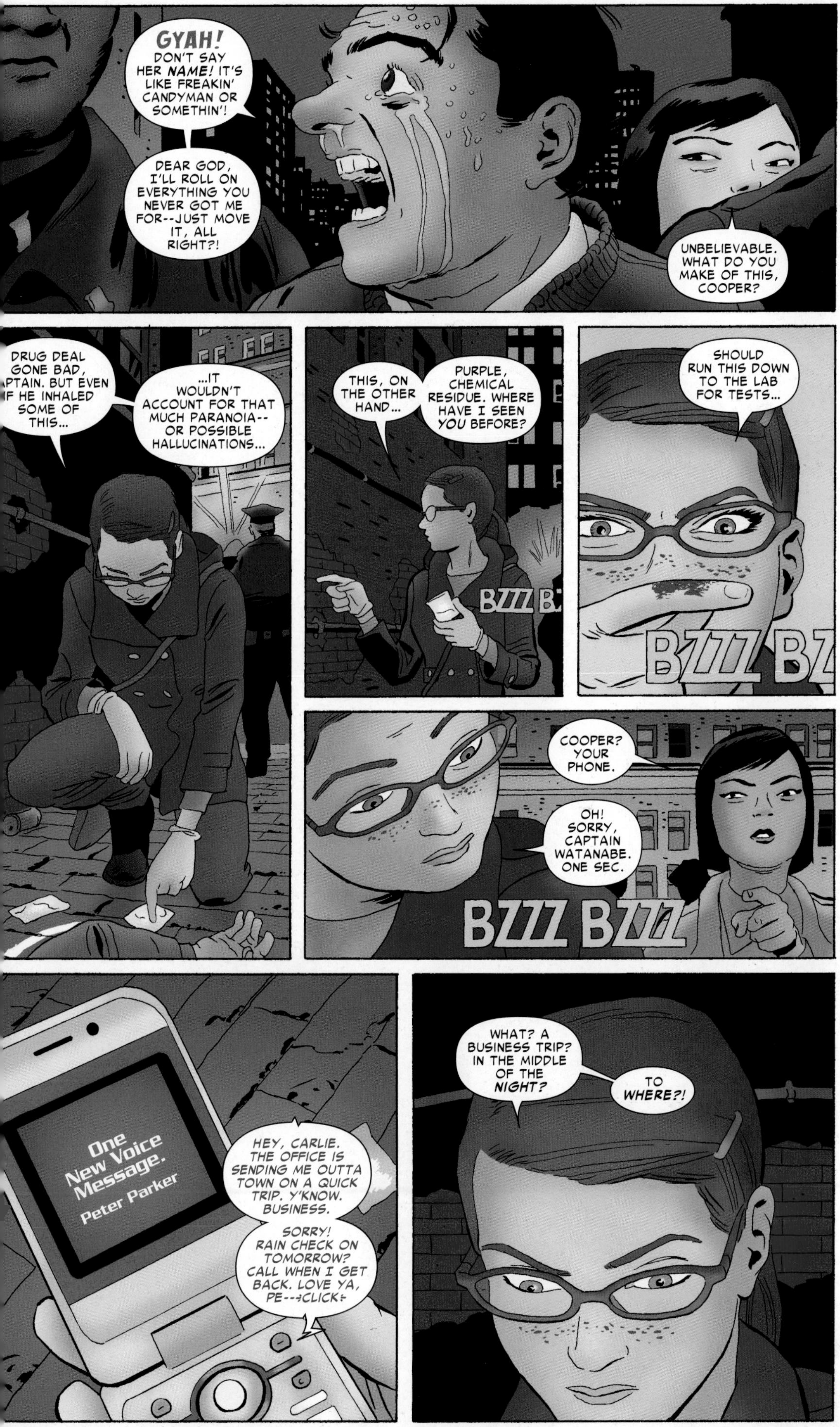

GYAH! DON'T SAY HER NAME! IT'S LIKE FREAKIN' CANDYMAN OR SOMETHIN'!
DEAR GOD, I'LL ROLL ON EVERYTHING YOU NEVER GOT ME FOR--JUST MOVE IT, ALL RIGHT?!
UNBELIEVABLE. WHAT DO YOU MAKE OF THIS, COOPER?
DRUG DEAL GONE BAD, PTAIN. BUT EVEN F HE INHALED SOME OF THIS...
...IT WOULDN'T ACCOUNT FOR THAT MUCH PARANOIA-- OR POSSIBLE HALLUCINATIONS...
THIS, ON THE OTHER HAND...
PURPLE, CHEMICAL RESIDUE. WHERE HAVE I SEEN YOU BEFORE?
BZZZ B
SHOULD RUN THIS DOWN TO THE LAB FOR TESTS...
BZZZ BZ
COOPER? YOUR PHONE.
OH! SORRY, CAPTAIN WATANABE. ONE SEC.
BZZZ BZZZ
One New Voice Message.
Peter Parker
HEY, CARLIE. THE OFFICE IS SENDING ME OUTTA TOWN ON A QUICK TRIP. Y'KNOW. BUSINESS.
SORRY! RAIN CHECK ON TOMORROW? CALL WHEN I GET BACK. LOVE YA, PE--CLICK
WHAT? A BUSINESS TRIP? IN THE MIDDLE OF THE NIGHT?
TO WHERE?!

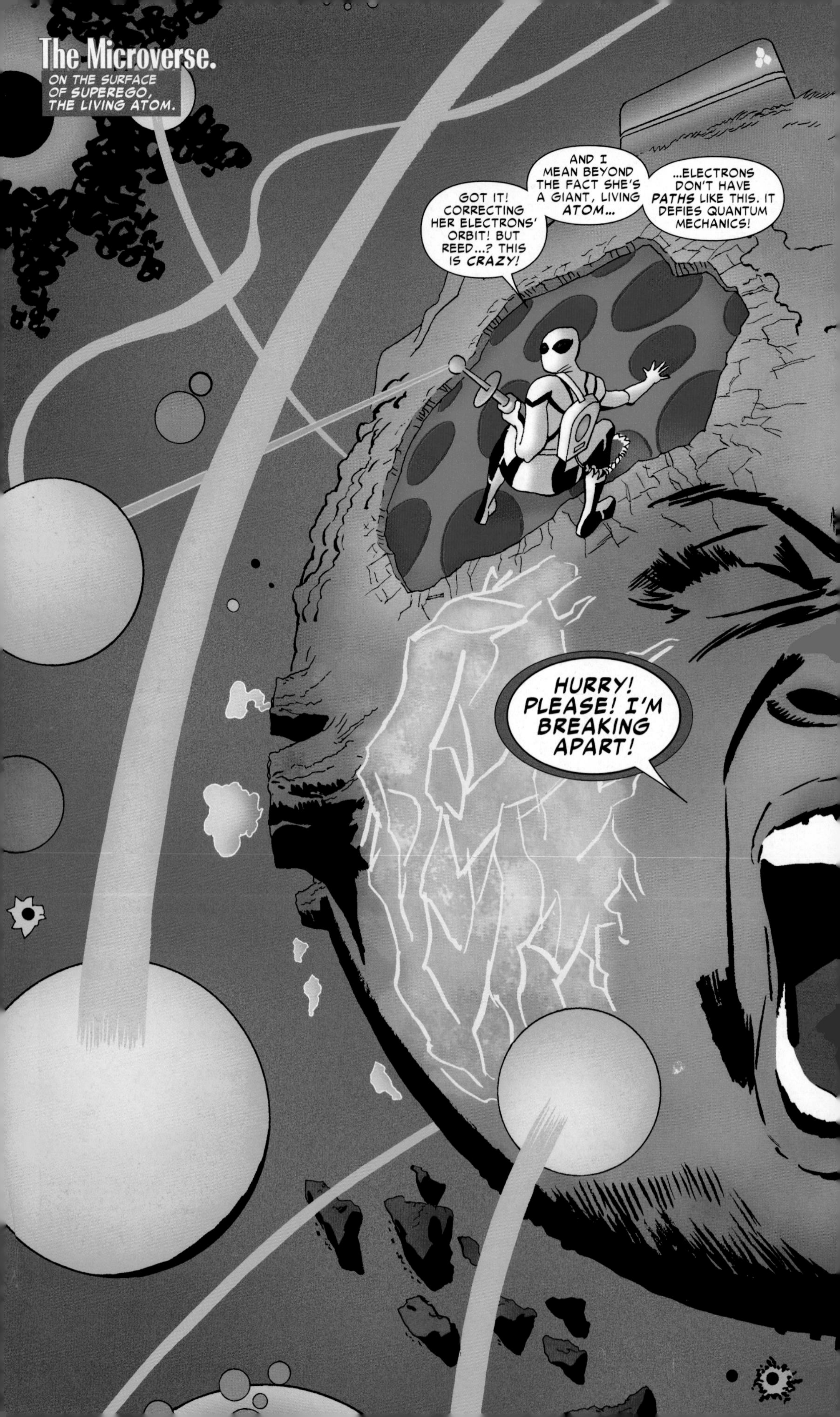
The Microverse.
ON THE SURFACE OF SUPEREGO, THE LIVING ATOM.
GOT IT! CORRECTING HER ELECTRONS' ORBIT! BUT REED...? THIS IS CRAZY!
AND I MEAN BEYOND THE FACT SHE'S A GIANT, LIVING ATOM...
...ELECTRONS DON'T HAVE PATHS LIKE THIS. IT DEFIES QUANTUM MECHANICS!
HURRY! PLEASE! I'M BREAKING APART!

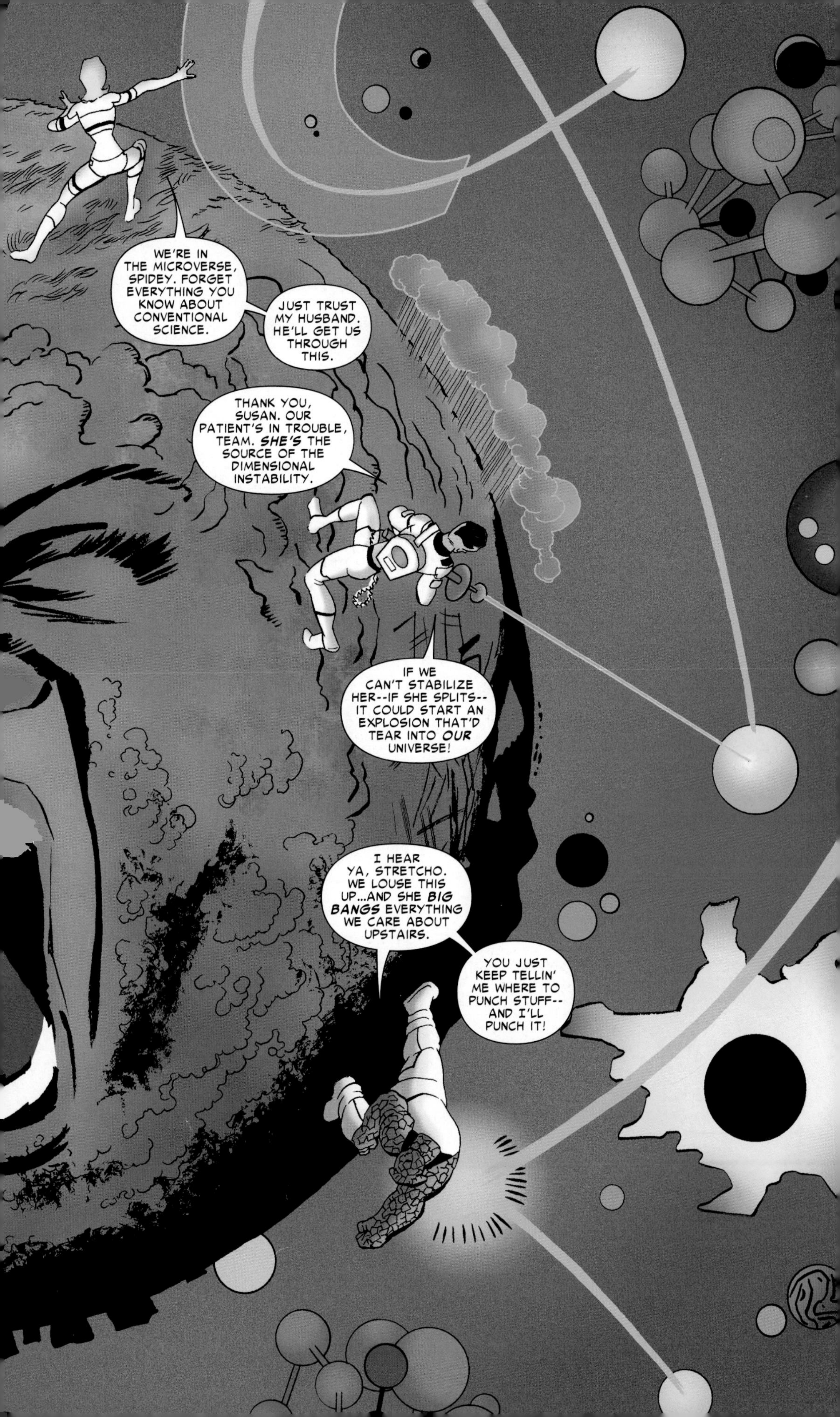
WE'RE IN THE MICROVERSE, SPIDEY. FORGET EVERYTHING YOU KNOW ABOUT CONVENTIONAL SCIENCE.
JUST TRUST MY HUSBAND. HE'LL GET US THROUGH THIS.
THANK YOU, SUSAN. OUR PATIENT'S IN TROUBLE, TEAM. *SHE'S* THE SOURCE OF THE DIMENSIONAL INSTABILITY.
IF WE CAN'T STABILIZE HER--IF SHE SPLITS-- IT COULD START AN EXPLOSION THAT'D TEAR INTO *OUR* UNIVERSE!
I HEAR YA, STRETCHO. WE LOUSE THIS UP...AND SHE *BIG BANGS* EVERYTHING WE CARE ABOUT UPSTAIRS.
YOU JUST KEEP TELLIN' ME WHERE TO PUNCH STUFF-- AND I'LL PUNCH IT!

THAT SHOULD DO IT. THOUGH DON'T EVEN ASK ME WHY.

DON'T SELL YOURSELF SHORT, SPIDER-MAN. YOU'VE TAKEN A BIG STEP TODAY...

...INTO AREAS OF META-SCIENCE FEW MINDS CAN GRASP.

"META-SCIENCE"?

HERE WE GO.

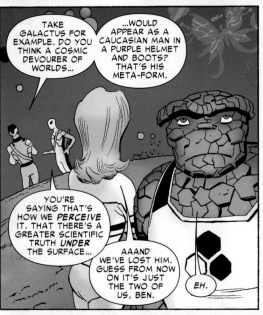

TAKE GALACTUS FOR EXAMPLE. DO YOU THINK A COSMIC DEVOURER OF WORLDS...

...WOULD APPEAR AS A CAUCASIAN MAN IN A PURPLE HELMET AND BOOTS? THAT'S HIS META-FORM.

YOU'RE SAYING THAT'S HOW WE PERCEIVE IT. THAT THERE'S A GREATER SCIENTIFIC TRUTH UNDER THE SURFACE...

AAAND WE'VE LOST HIM. GUESS FROM NOW ON IT'S JUST THE TWO OF US, BEN.

EH.

SO REED'S GOT HIMSELF A NEW PLAYMATE FOR THE BIG BRAIN STUFF. FINE BY ME.

LOOK, COSMIC BUTTERFLIES. WANNA BRING SOME BACK FER VAL AND THE--

HUH?

WHAT'S THE MATTER?

SOMETHIN' AIN'T RIGHT. LET'S JUST SAY MY GRIMM-SENSE IS TINGLIN'.

IT'S THE STRANGEST FEELIN'. LIKE WE WUZ BEIN' WATCHED...

THANK YOU, FF! BLESSINGS AND PROPORTIONAL MASS BE UPON YOU!

FOR SOMEONE SURROUNDED WITH NEGATIVELY CHARGED PARTICLES, SHE'S VERY UPBEAT.

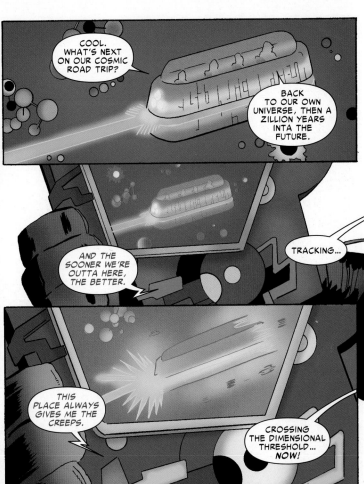

COOL. WHAT'S NEXT ON OUR COSMIC ROAD TRIP?

BACK TO OUR OWN UNIVERSE, THEN A ZILLION YEARS INTA THE FUTURE.

AND THE SOONER WE'RE OUTTA HERE, THE BETTER.

TRACKING...

THIS PLACE ALWAYS GIVES ME THE CREEPS.

CROSSING THE DIMENSIONAL THRESHOLD... NOW!

THE EXPANSION FREQUENCY! I HAVE IT!

THE KEY WHICH WILL ALLOW ME INGRESS INTO THE HEAVENS ABOVE!

HA HA! SOON! A WHOLE WORLD FOR THE PSYCHO-MAN TO TORMENT!

OH, THANK YOU, RICHARDS! YOU'VE GIVEN ME QUITE THE GIFT. AN ENTIRE DIMENSION AS MY OWN PERSONAL PLAYGROUND!

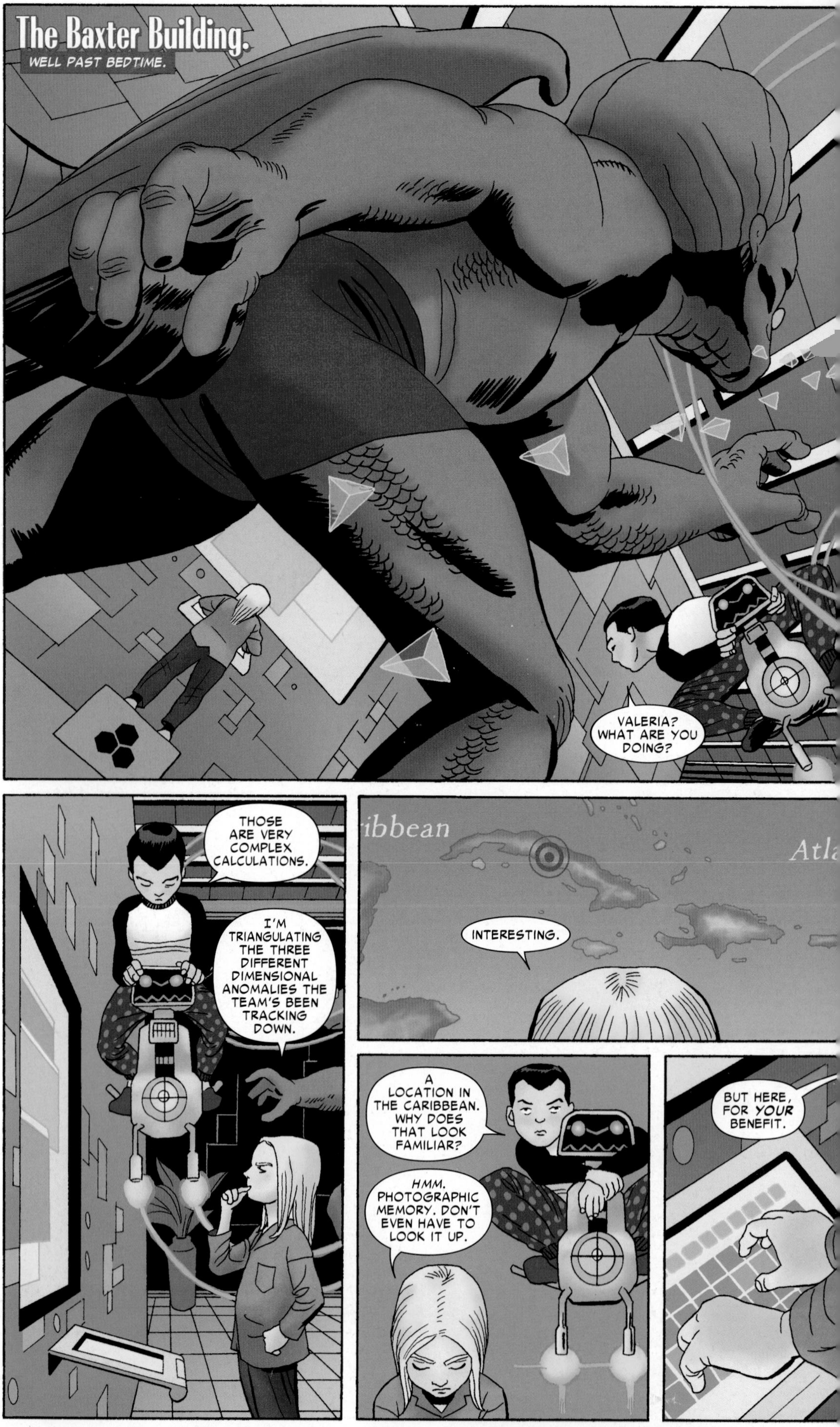
The Baxter Building.
WELL PAST BEDTIME.
VALERIA? WHAT ARE YOU DOING?
THOSE ARE VERY COMPLEX CALCULATIONS.
I'M TRIANGULATING THE THREE DIFFERENT DIMENSIONAL ANOMALIES THE TEAM'S BEEN TRACKING DOWN.
ribbean
Atla
INTERESTING.
A LOCATION IN THE CARIBBEAN. WHY DOES THAT LOOK FAMILIAR?
HMM. PHOTOGRAPHIC MEMORY. DON'T EVEN HAVE TO LOOK IT UP.
BUT HERE, FOR YOUR BENEFIT.

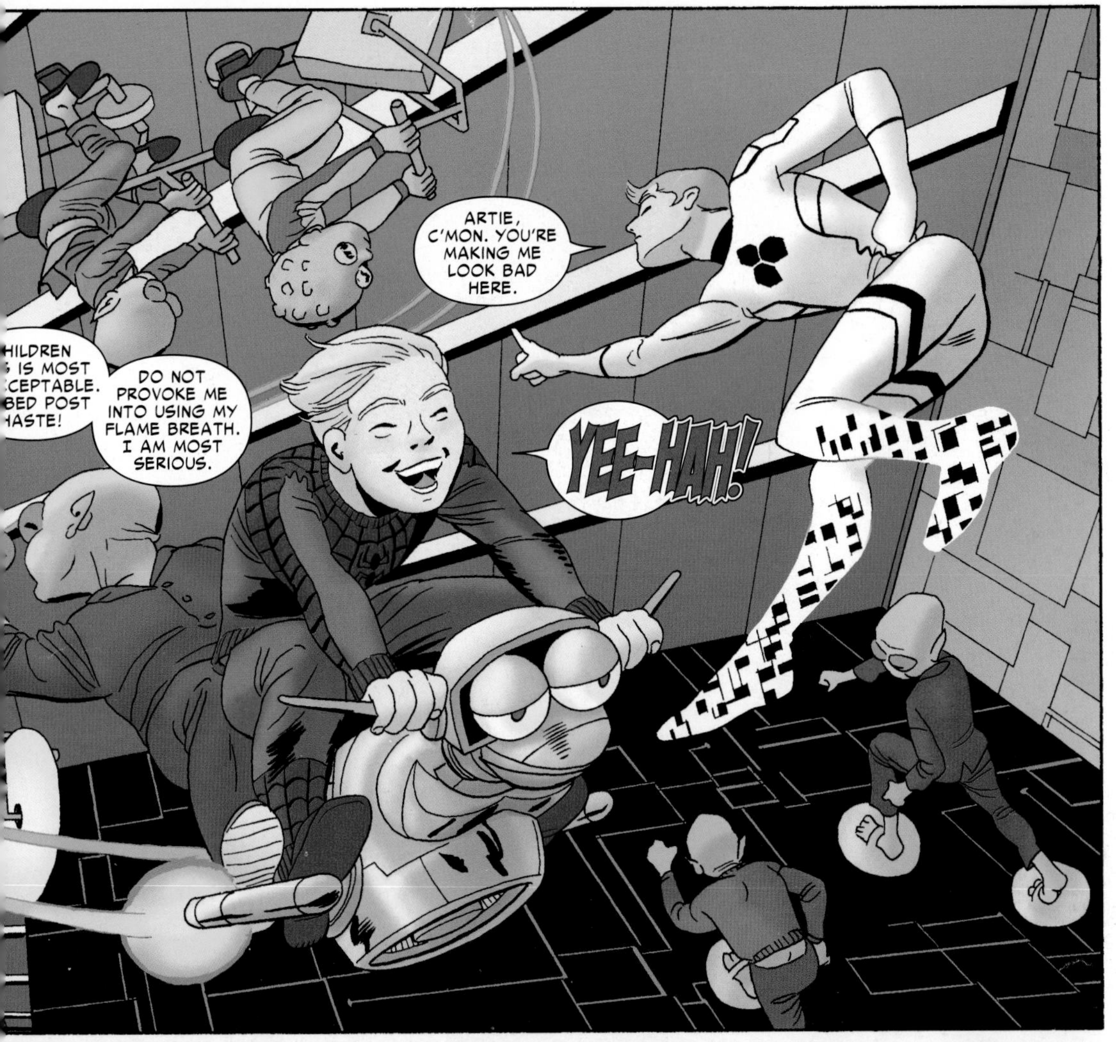
HILDREN
IS MOST
CEPTABLE.
BED POST
HASTE!
DO NOT PROVOKE ME INTO USING MY FLAME BREATH. I AM MOST SERIOUS.
ARTIE, C'MON. YOU'RE MAKING ME LOOK BAD HERE.
YEE-HAH!

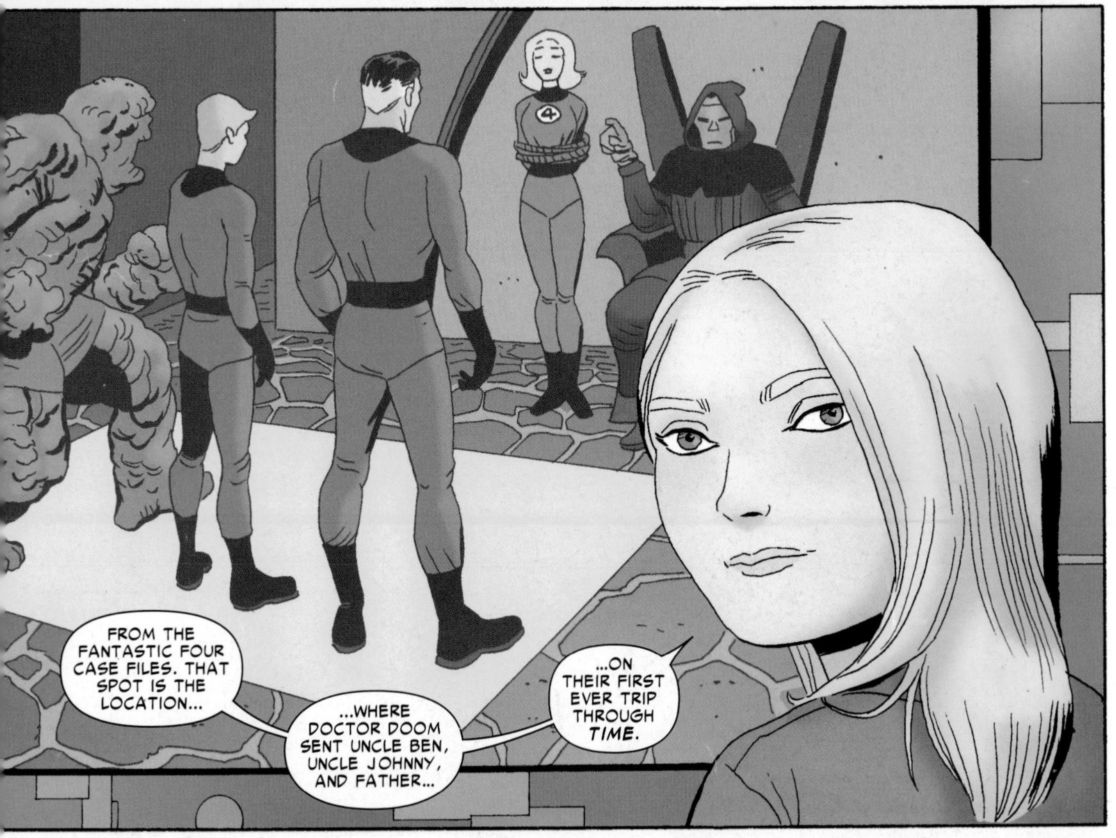
FROM THE FANTASTIC FOUR CASE FILES. THAT SPOT IS THE LOCATION...
...WHERE DOCTOR DOOM SENT UNCLE BEN, UNCLE JOHNNY, AND FATHER...
...ON THEIR FIRST EVER TRIP THROUGH *TIME*.

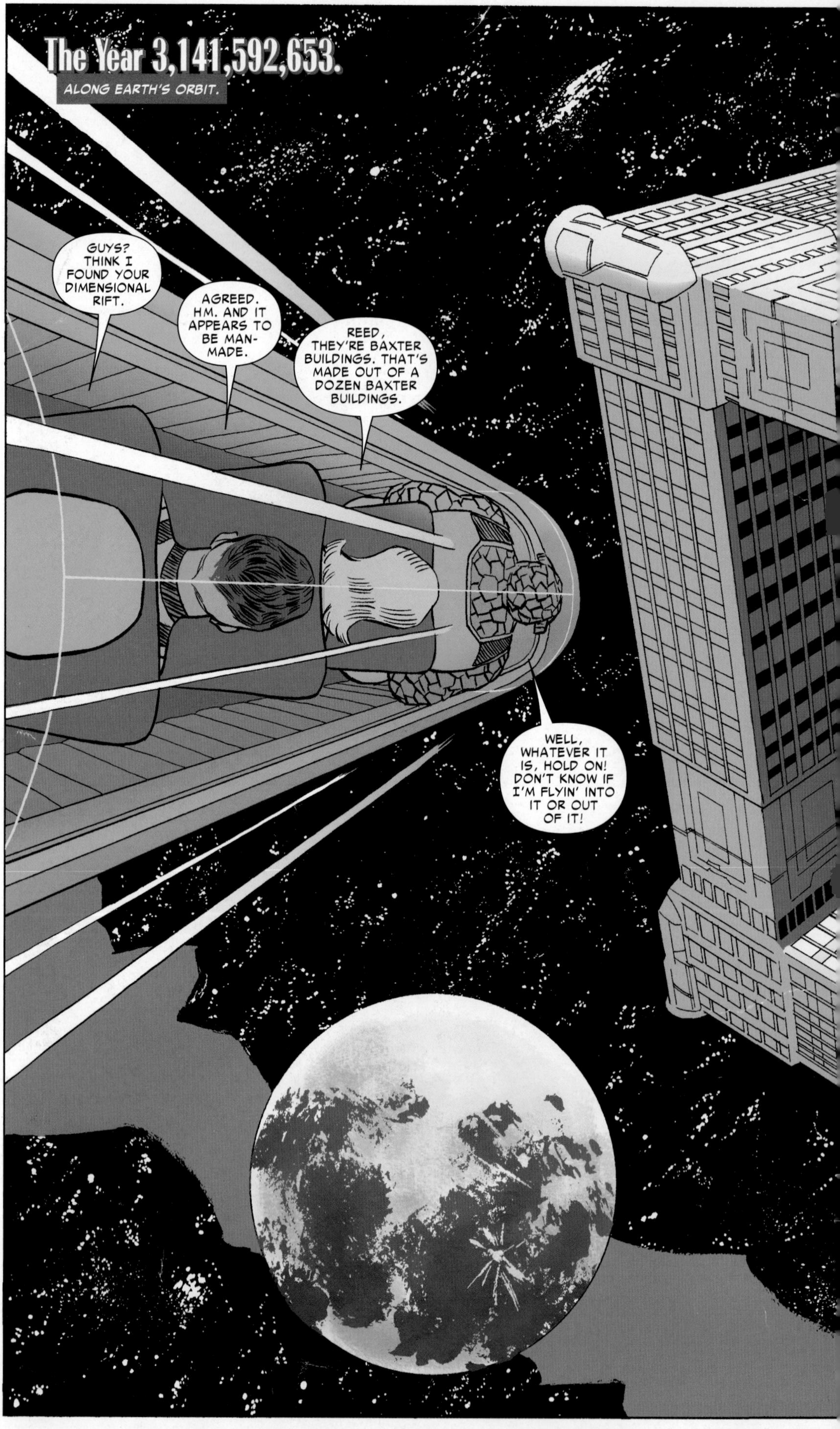
The Year 3,141,592,653.
ALONG EARTH'S ORBIT.
GUYS? THINK I FOUND YOUR DIMENSIONAL RIFT.
AGREED. HM. AND IT APPEARS TO BE MAN-MADE.
REED, THEY'RE BAXTER BUILDINGS. THAT'S MADE OUT OF A DOZEN BAXTER BUILDINGS.
WELL, WHATEVER IT IS, HOLD ON! DON'T KNOW IF I'M FLYIN' INTO IT OR OUT OF IT!

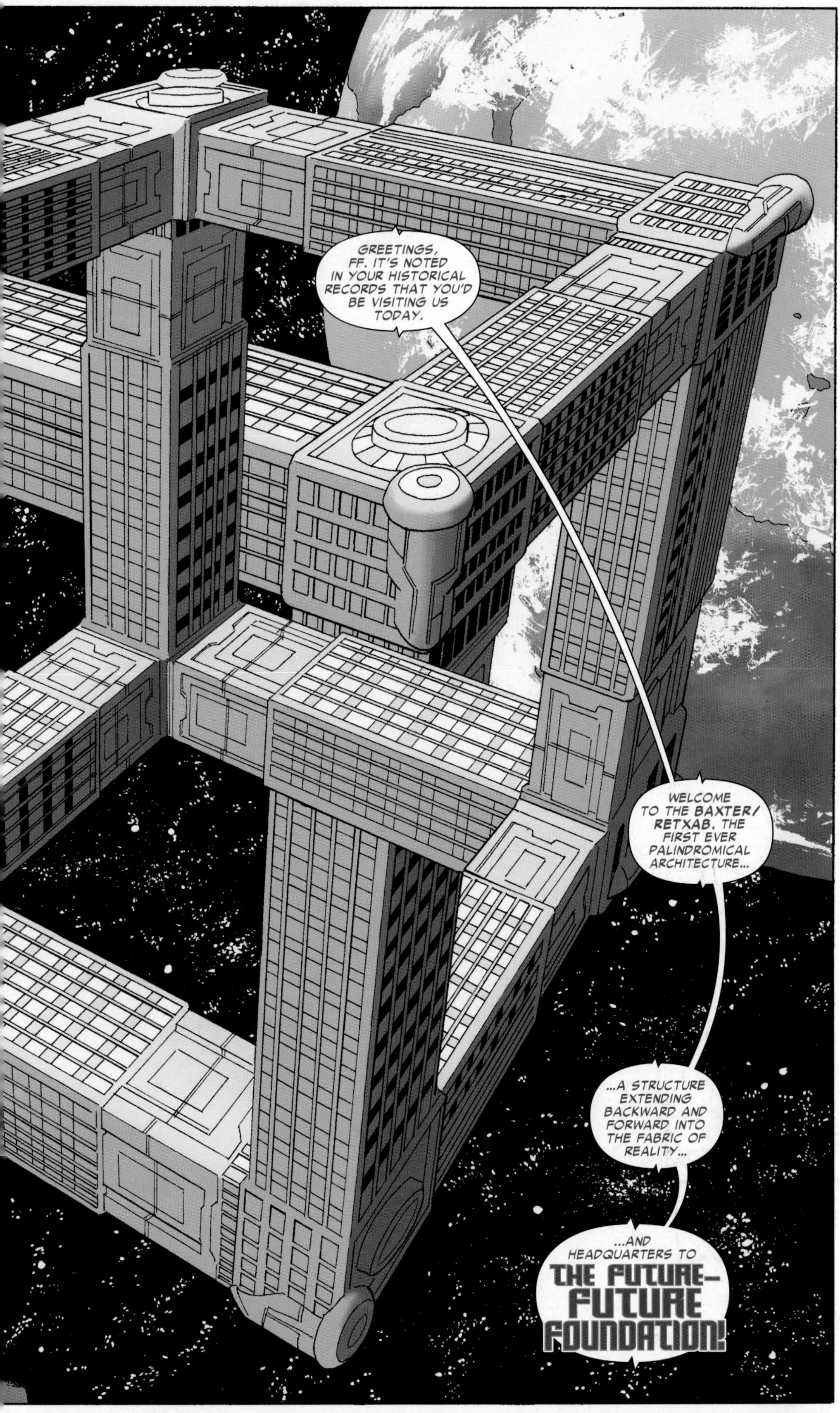
GREETINGS, FF. IT'S NOTED IN YOUR HISTORICAL RECORDS THAT YOU'D BE VISITING US TODAY.
WELCOME TO THE BAXTER/ RETXAB. THE FIRST EVER PALINDROMICAL ARCHITECTURE...
...A STRUCTURE EXTENDING BACKWARD AND FORWARD INTO THE FABRIC OF REALITY...
...AND HEADQUARTERS TO THE FUTURE-FUTURE FOUNDATION!

THIS IS MEGA-STORM, SUPREMO, XANDAR, YANCY...

...AND I'M THEIR LEADER, CAPTAIN WAKANDA. WE'RE GLAD YOU'RE HERE. WE COULD USE YOUR HELP.

OF COURSE, WE'LL DO WHATEVER WE CAN.

WHICH IS WHAT EXACTLY? LOOK AT THIS. YOU'RE FUTURE-FUTURE GUYS. WE'RE JUST PRESENT-PRESENT PEOPLE.

EXACTLY.

THE DIMENSIONAL CIRCUITS IN OUR BASE ARE FAILING, FOLDING IN ON THEMSELVES. AND WE CAN'T FIGURE OUT WHY.

IT'S THE TECHNOLOGY. IT'S SO ANCIENT, ITS SECRETS HAVE BEEN LOST TO TIME.

WHOA! BUT IT'S STILL LIGHT YEARS AHEAD OF US.

WAIT. THIS LOOKS FAMILIAR.

IT'S A HIGHLY ADVANCED VERSION OF HANK PYM'S DIMENSIONAL WAVE INDUCER.

NOT BAD. JUST LOOKING AT THIS STUFF IS GIVING ME ALL KINDS OF IDEAS FOR MY JOB BACK HOME--

FOR HORIZON LABS?

UM. YEAH.

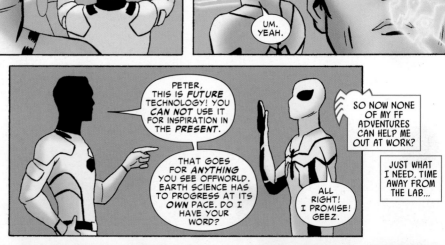

PETER, THIS IS FUTURE TECHNOLOGY! YOU CAN NOT USE IT FOR INSPIRATION IN THE PRESENT.

THAT GOES FOR ANYTHING YOU SEE OFFWORLD. EARTH SCIENCE HAS TO PROGRESS AT ITS OWN PACE. DO I HAVE YOUR WORD?

ALL RIGHT! I PROMISE! GEEZ.

SO NOW NONE OF MY FF ADVENTURES CAN HELP ME OUT AT WORK?

JUST WHAT I NEED. TIME AWAY FROM THE LAB...

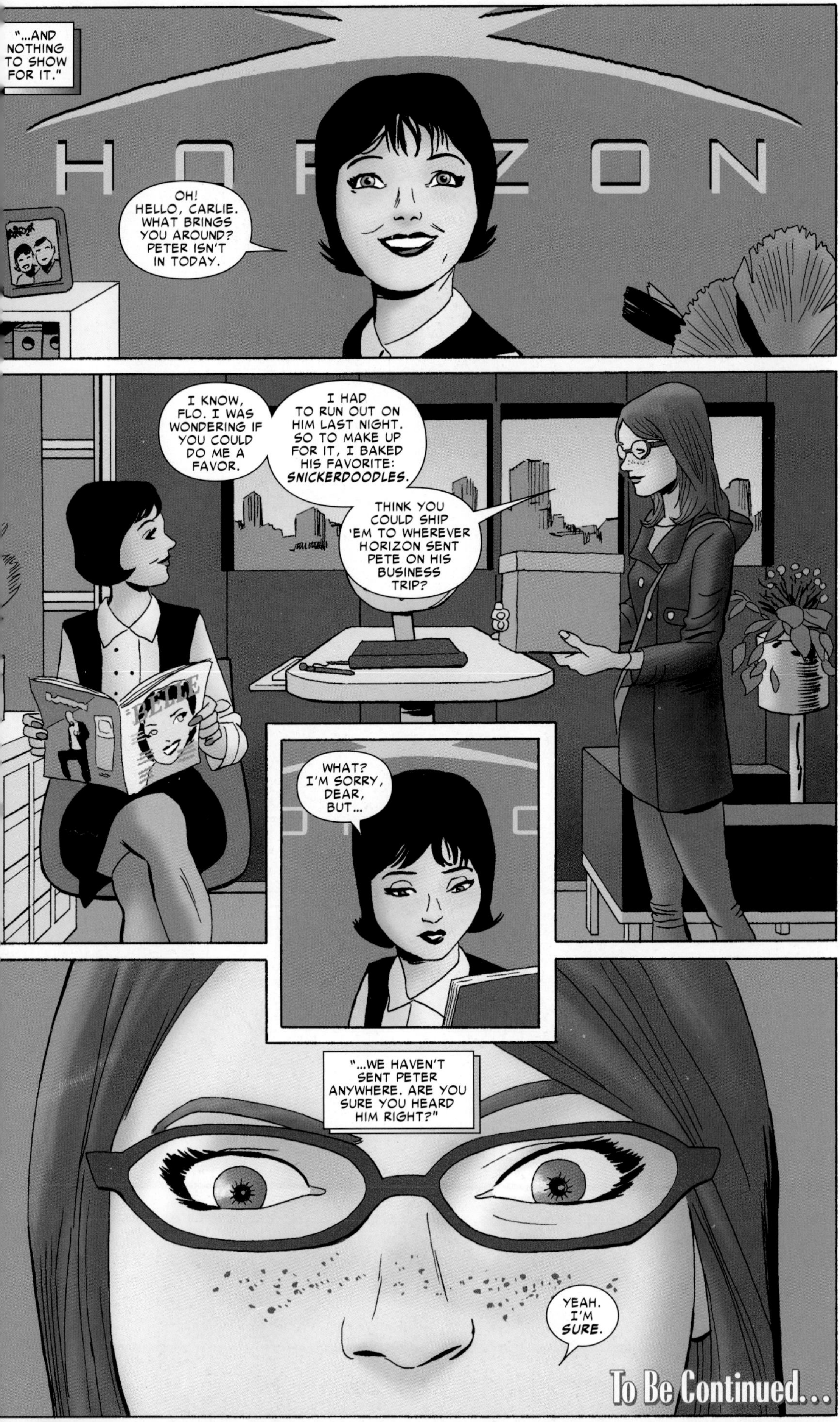
"...AND NOTHING TO SHOW FOR IT."
HORIZON
OH! HELLO, CARLIE. WHAT BRINGS YOU AROUND? PETER ISN'T IN TODAY.
I KNOW, FLO. I WAS WONDERING IF YOU COULD DO ME A FAVOR.
I HAD TO RUN OUT ON HIM LAST NIGHT. SO TO MAKE UP FOR IT, I BAKED HIS FAVORITE: *SNICKERDOODLES*.
THINK YOU COULD SHIP 'EM TO WHEREVER HORIZON SENT PETE ON HIS BUSINESS TRIP?
BELLE
WHAT? I'M SORRY, DEAR, BUT...
"...WE HAVEN'T SENT PETER ANYWHERE. ARE YOU SURE YOU HEARD HIM RIGHT?"
YEAH. I'M *SURE*.
To Be Continued...

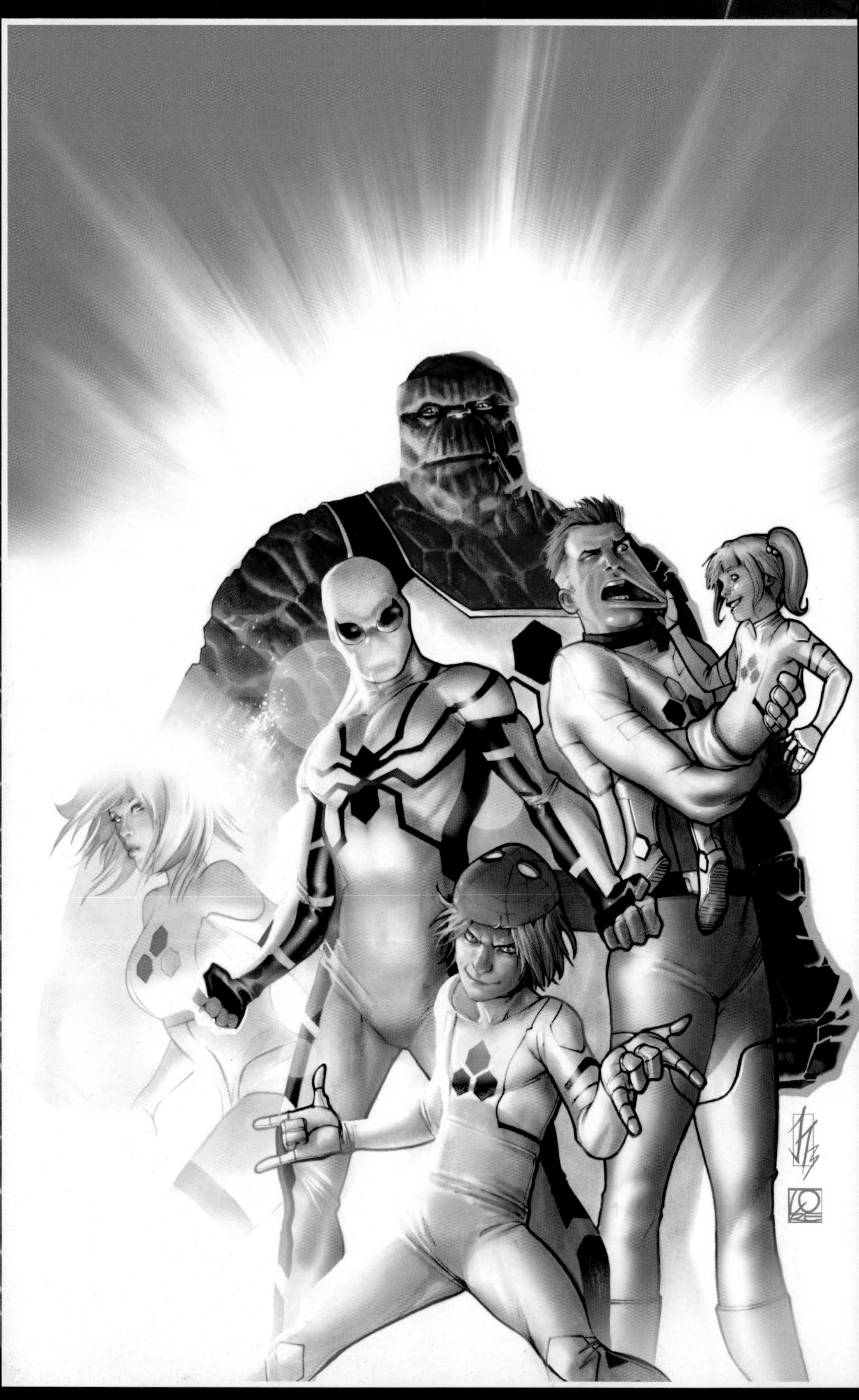

AMAZING SPIDER-MAN #653
COVER BY STEFANO CASELLI & LORENZO DE FELICI

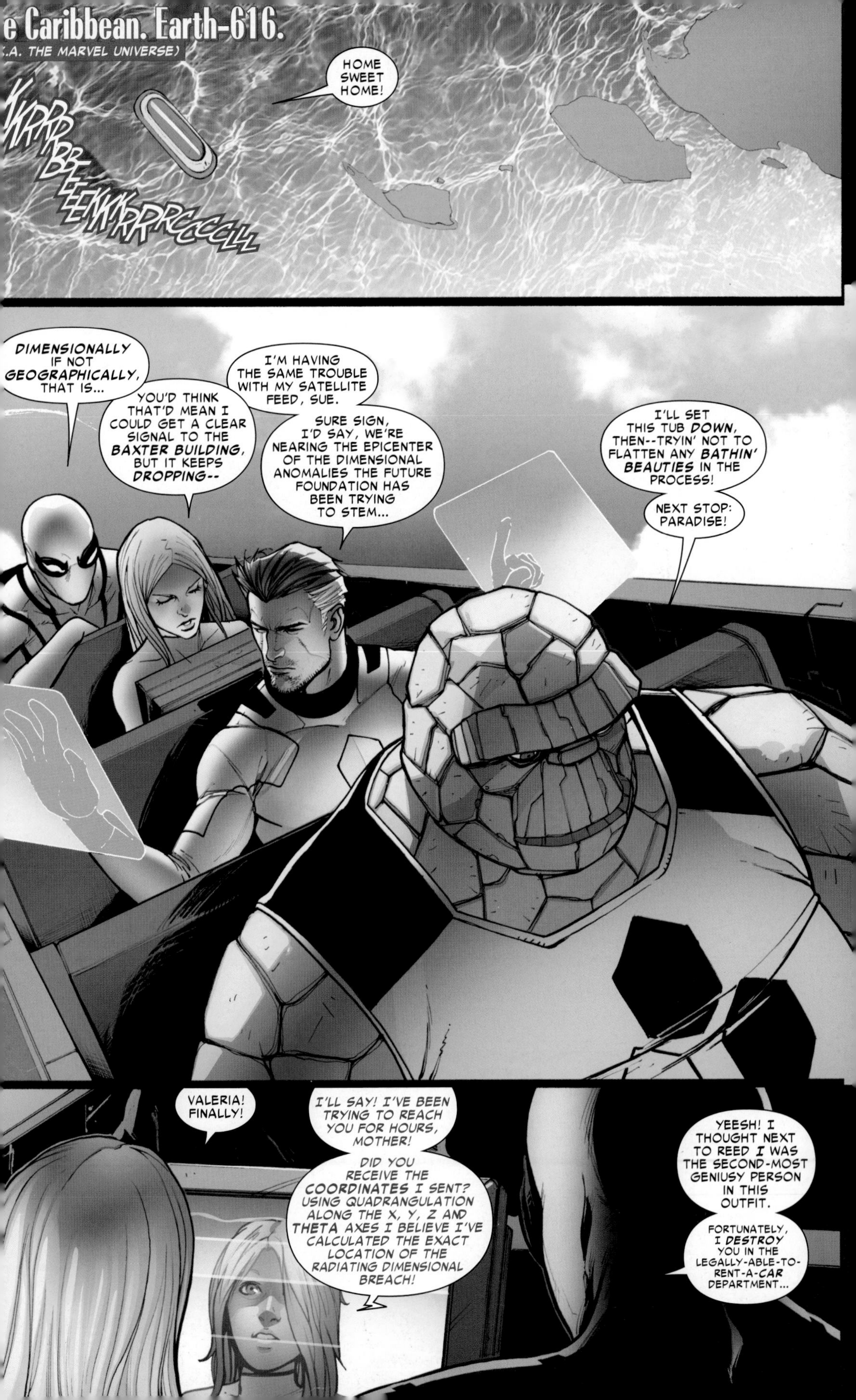
e Caribbean. Earth-616.
.A. THE MARVEL UNIVERSE)
HOME SWEET HOME!
KKRRRBBEEKKKRRRRCCCLLL
DIMENSIONALLY IF NOT GEOGRAPHICALLY, THAT IS...
YOU'D THINK THAT'D MEAN I COULD GET A CLEAR SIGNAL TO THE BAXTER BUILDING, BUT IT KEEPS DROPPING--
I'M HAVING THE SAME TROUBLE WITH MY SATELLITE FEED, SUE.
SURE SIGN, I'D SAY, WE'RE NEARING THE EPICENTER OF THE DIMENSIONAL ANOMALIES THE FUTURE FOUNDATION HAS BEEN TRYING TO STEM...
I'LL SET THIS TUB DOWN, THEN--TRYIN' NOT TO FLATTEN ANY BATHIN' BEAUTIES IN THE PROCESS!
NEXT STOP: PARADISE!
VALERIA! FINALLY!
I'LL SAY! I'VE BEEN TRYING TO REACH YOU FOR HOURS, MOTHER!
DID YOU RECEIVE THE COORDINATES I SENT? USING QUADRANGULATION ALONG THE X, Y, Z AND THETA AXES I BELIEVE I'VE CALCULATED THE EXACT LOCATION OF THE RADIATING DIMENSIONAL BREACH!
YEESH! I THOUGHT NEXT TO REED I WAS THE SECOND-MOST GENIUSY PERSON IN THIS OUTFIT.
FORTUNATELY, I DESTROY YOU IN THE LEGALLY-ABLE-TO-RENT-A-CAR DEPARTMENT...

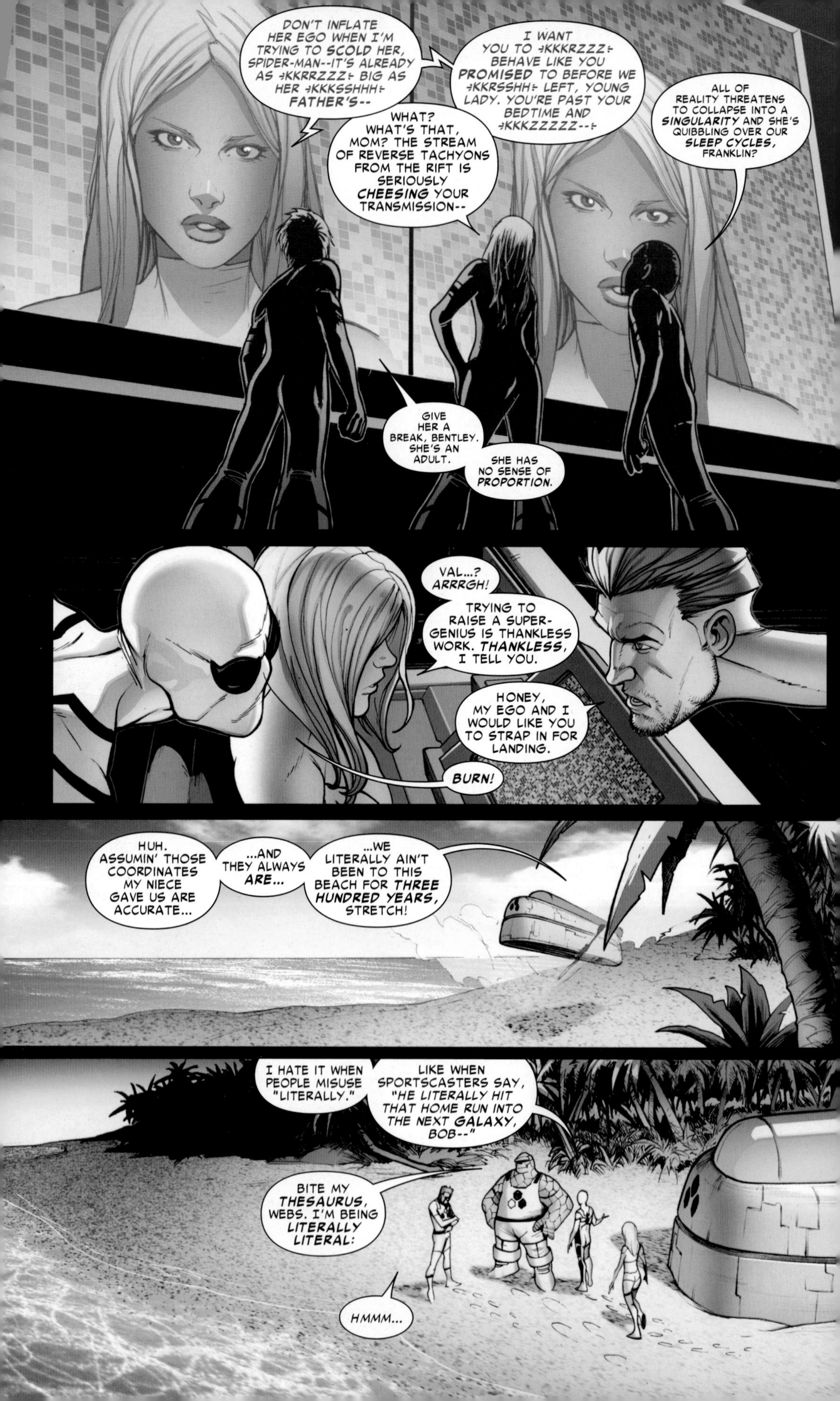

DON'T INFLATE HER EGO WHEN I'M TRYING TO SCOLD HER, SPIDER-MAN--IT'S ALREADY AS ⊰KKRZZZ⊱ BIG AS HER ⊰KKKSSHHH⊱ FATHER'S--
I WANT YOU TO ⊰KKKRZZZ⊱ BEHAVE LIKE YOU PROMISED TO BEFORE WE ⊰KKRSSHH⊱ LEFT, YOUNG LADY. YOU'RE PAST YOUR BEDTIME AND ⊰KKKZZZZZ--⊱
WHAT? WHAT'S THAT, MOM? THE STREAM OF REVERSE TACHYONS FROM THE RIFT IS SERIOUSLY CHEESING YOUR TRANSMISSION--
ALL OF REALITY THREATENS TO COLLAPSE INTO A SINGULARITY AND SHE'S QUIBBLING OVER OUR SLEEP CYCLES, FRANKLIN?
GIVE HER A BREAK, BENTLEY. SHE'S AN ADULT.
SHE HAS NO SENSE OF PROPORTION.
VAL...? ARRRGH!
TRYING TO RAISE A SUPER-GENIUS IS THANKLESS WORK. THANKLESS, I TELL YOU.
HONEY, MY EGO AND I WOULD LIKE YOU TO STRAP IN FOR LANDING.
BURN!
HUH. ASSUMIN' THOSE COORDINATES MY NIECE GAVE US ARE ACCURATE...
...AND THEY ALWAYS ARE...
...WE LITERALLY AIN'T BEEN TO THIS BEACH FOR THREE HUNDRED YEARS, STRETCH!
I HATE IT WHEN PEOPLE MISUSE "LITERALLY."
LIKE WHEN SPORTSCASTERS SAY, "HE LITERALLY HIT THAT HOME RUN INTO THE NEXT GALAXY, BOB--"
BITE MY THESAURUS, WEBS. I'M BEING LITERALLY LITERAL:
HMMM...

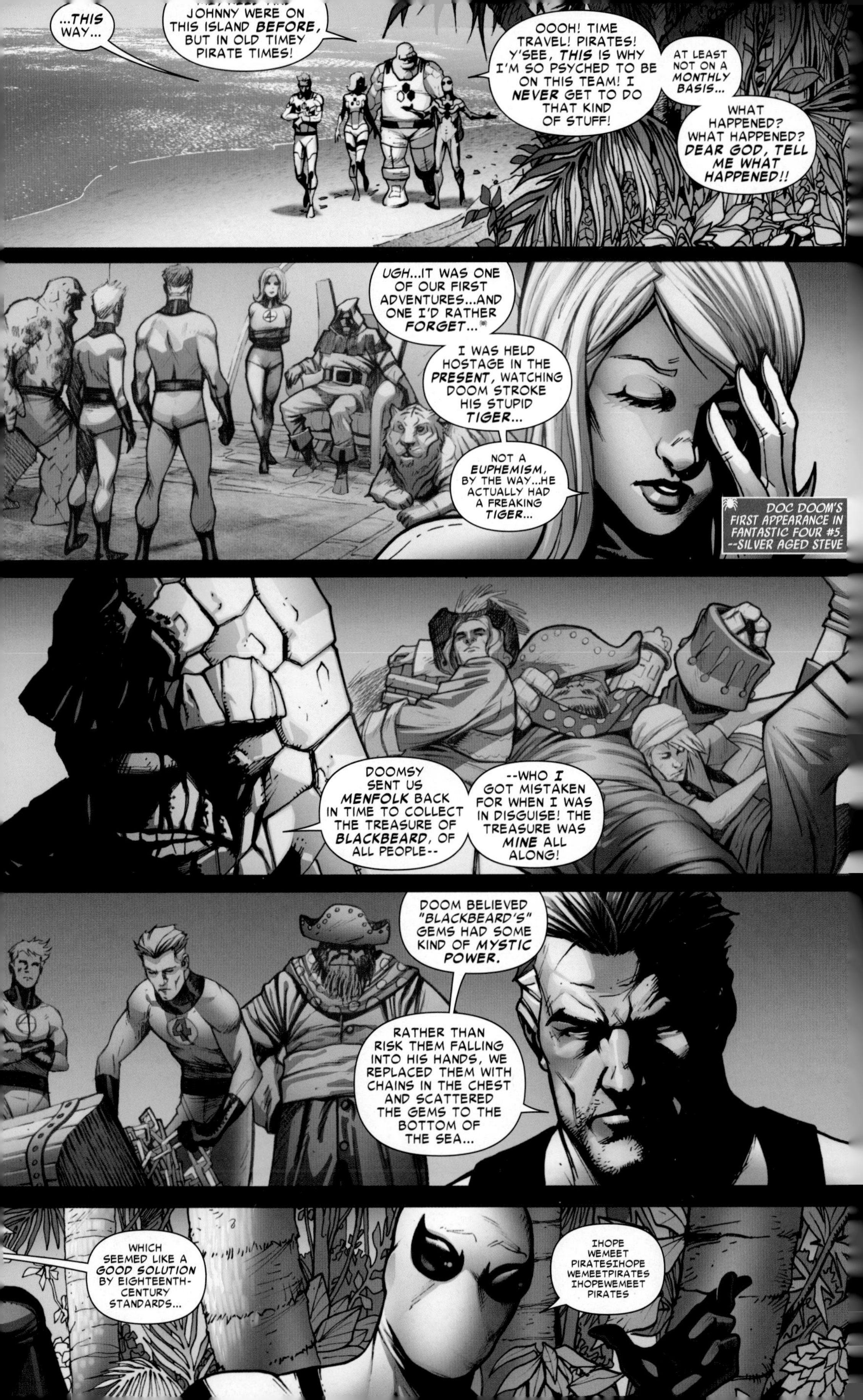
...THIS WAY...
JOHNNY WERE ON THIS ISLAND BEFORE, BUT IN OLD TIMEY PIRATE TIMES!
OOOH! TIME TRAVEL! PIRATES! Y'SEE, THIS IS WHY I'M SO PSYCHED TO BE ON THIS TEAM! I NEVER GET TO DO THAT KIND OF STUFF!
AT LEAST NOT ON A MONTHLY BASIS...
WHAT HAPPENED? WHAT HAPPENED? DEAR GOD, TELL ME WHAT HAPPENED!!
UGH...IT WAS ONE OF OUR FIRST ADVENTURES...AND ONE I'D RATHER FORGET...
I WAS HELD HOSTAGE IN THE PRESENT, WATCHING DOOM STROKE HIS STUPID TIGER...
NOT A EUPHEMISM, BY THE WAY...HE ACTUALLY HAD A FREAKING TIGER...
DOC DOOM'S FIRST APPEARANCE IN FANTASTIC FOUR #5. --SILVER AGED STEVE
DOOMSY SENT US MENFOLK BACK IN TIME TO COLLECT THE TREASURE OF BLACKBEARD, OF ALL PEOPLE--
--WHO I GOT MISTAKEN FOR WHEN I WAS IN DISGUISE! THE TREASURE WAS MINE ALL ALONG!
DOOM BELIEVED "BLACKBEARD'S" GEMS HAD SOME KIND OF MYSTIC POWER.
RATHER THAN RISK THEM FALLING INTO HIS HANDS, WE REPLACED THEM WITH CHAINS IN THE CHEST AND SCATTERED THE GEMS TO THE BOTTOM OF THE SEA...
WHICH SEEMED LIKE A GOOD SOLUTION BY EIGHTEENTH-CENTURY STANDARDS...
IHOPE WEMEET PIRATESIHOPE WEMEETPIRATES IHOPEWEMEET PIRATES

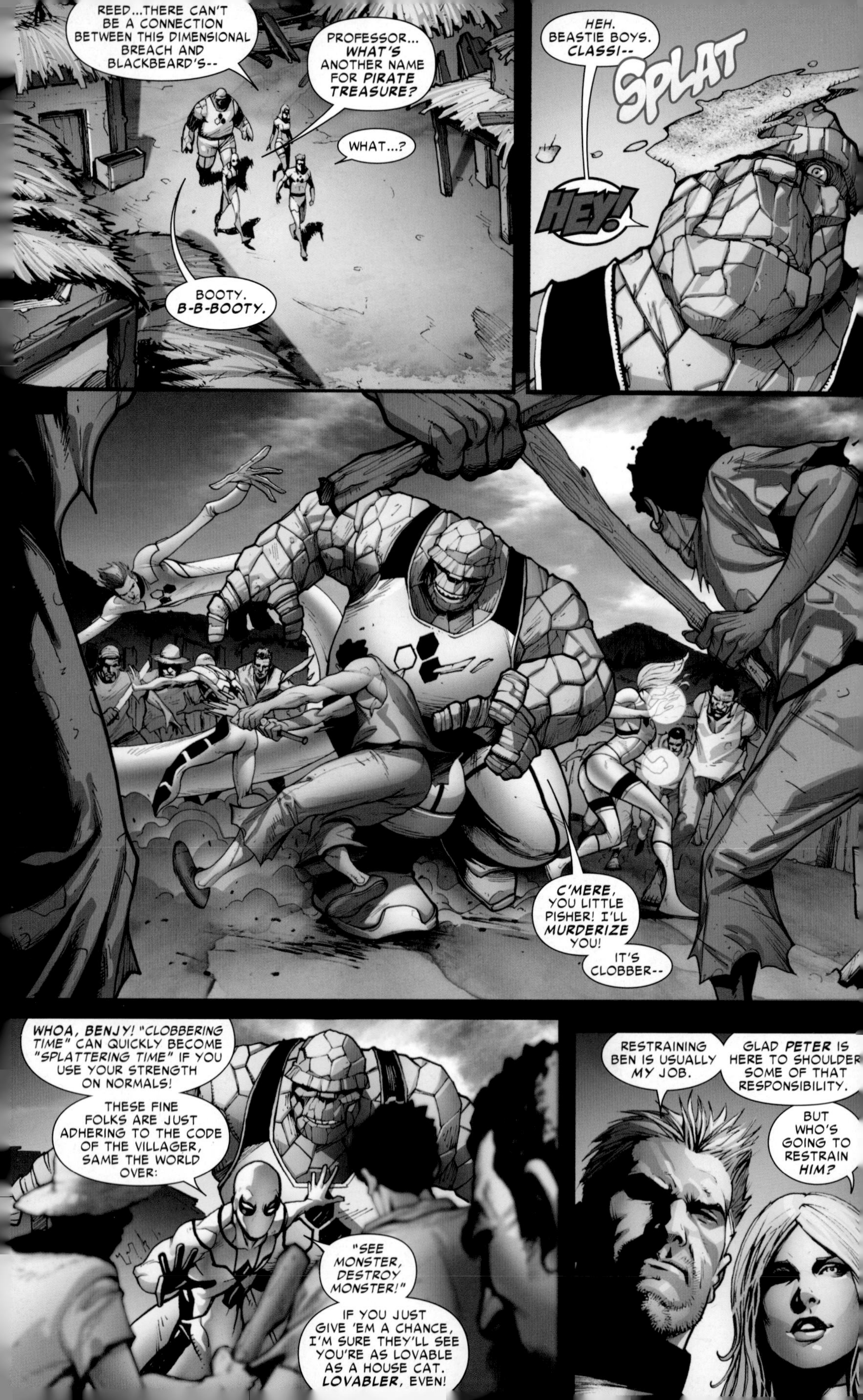
REED...THERE CAN'T BE A CONNECTION BETWEEN THIS DIMENSIONAL BREACH AND BLACKBEARD'S--
PROFESSOR... WHAT'S ANOTHER NAME FOR PIRATE TREASURE?
WHAT...?
BOOTY. B-B-BOOTY.
HEH. BEASTIE BOYS. CLASSI--
SPLAT
HEY!
C'MERE, YOU LITTLE PISHER! I'LL MURDERIZE YOU!
IT'S CLOBBER--
WHOA, BENJY! "CLOBBERING TIME" CAN QUICKLY BECOME "SPLATTERING TIME" IF YOU USE YOUR STRENGTH ON NORMALS!
THESE FINE FOLKS ARE JUST ADHERING TO THE CODE OF THE VILLAGER, SAME THE WORLD OVER:
"SEE MONSTER, DESTROY MONSTER!"
IF YOU JUST GIVE 'EM A CHANCE, I'M SURE THEY'LL SEE YOU'RE AS LOVABLE AS A HOUSE CAT. LOVABLER, EVEN!
RESTRAINING BEN IS USUALLY MY JOB.
GLAD PETER IS HERE TO SHOULDER SOME OF THAT RESPONSIBILITY.
BUT WHO'S GOING TO RESTRAIN HIM?

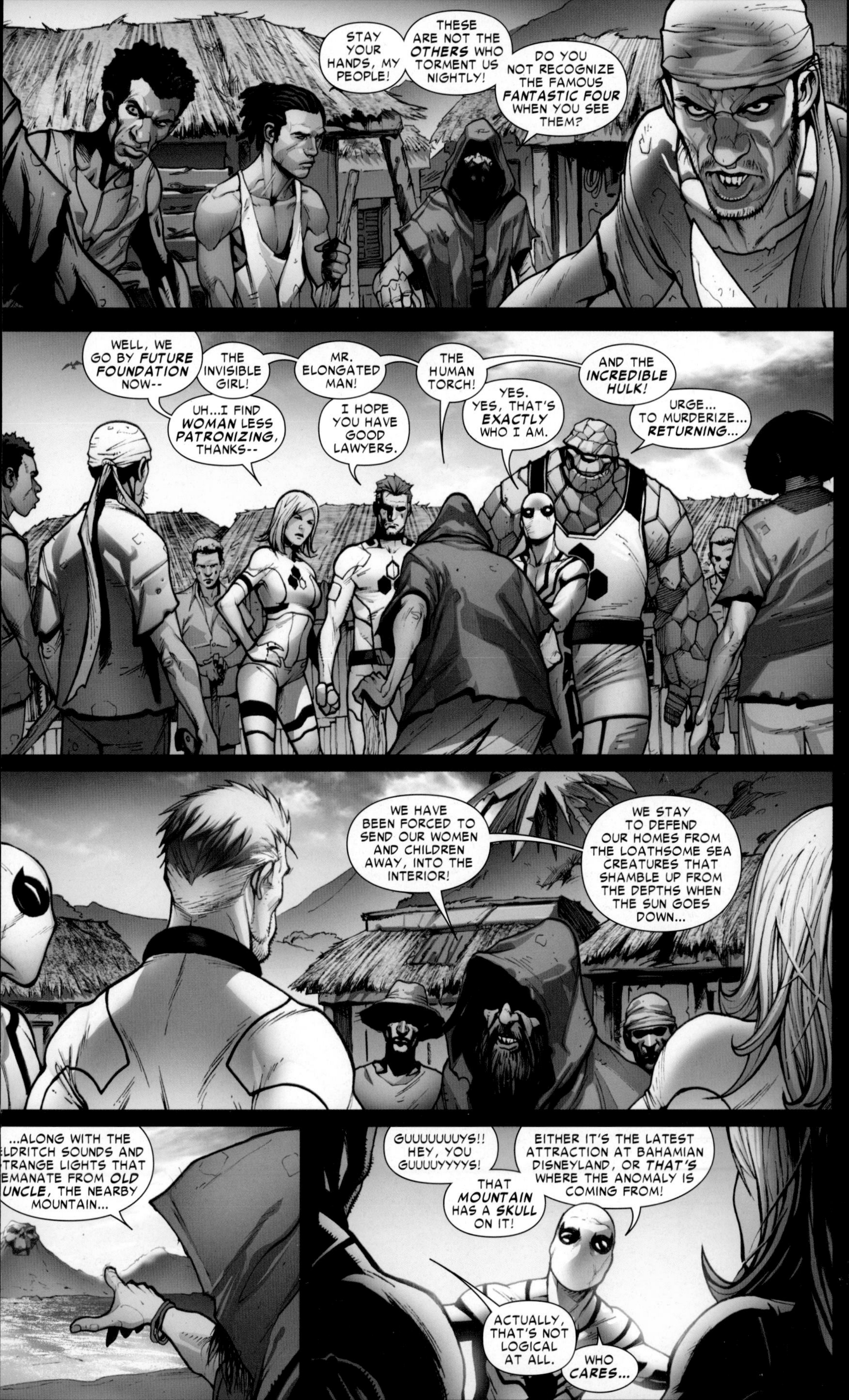
STAY YOUR HANDS, MY PEOPLE!
THESE ARE NOT THE OTHERS WHO TORMENT US NIGHTLY!
DO YOU NOT RECOGNIZE THE FAMOUS FANTASTIC FOUR WHEN YOU SEE THEM?
WELL, WE GO BY FUTURE FOUNDATION NOW--
THE INVISIBLE GIRL!
UH...I FIND WOMAN LESS PATRONIZING, THANKS--
MR. ELONGATED MAN!
I HOPE YOU HAVE GOOD LAWYERS.
THE HUMAN TORCH!
YES. YES, THAT'S EXACTLY WHO I AM.
AND THE INCREDIBLE HULK!
URGE... TO MURDERIZE... RETURNING...
WE HAVE BEEN FORCED TO SEND OUR WOMEN AND CHILDREN AWAY, INTO THE INTERIOR!
WE STAY TO DEFEND OUR HOMES FROM THE LOATHSOME SEA CREATURES THAT SHAMBLE UP FROM THE DEPTHS WHEN THE SUN GOES DOWN...
...ALONG WITH THE ELDRITCH SOUNDS AND STRANGE LIGHTS THAT EMANATE FROM OLD UNCLE, THE NEARBY MOUNTAIN...
GUUUUUUUYS!! HEY, YOU GUUUUYYYYS!
THAT MOUNTAIN HAS A SKULL ON IT!
EITHER IT'S THE LATEST ATTRACTION AT BAHAMIAN DISNEYLAND, OR THAT'S WHERE THE ANOMALY IS COMING FROM!
ACTUALLY, THAT'S NOT LOGICAL AT ALL.
WHO CARES...

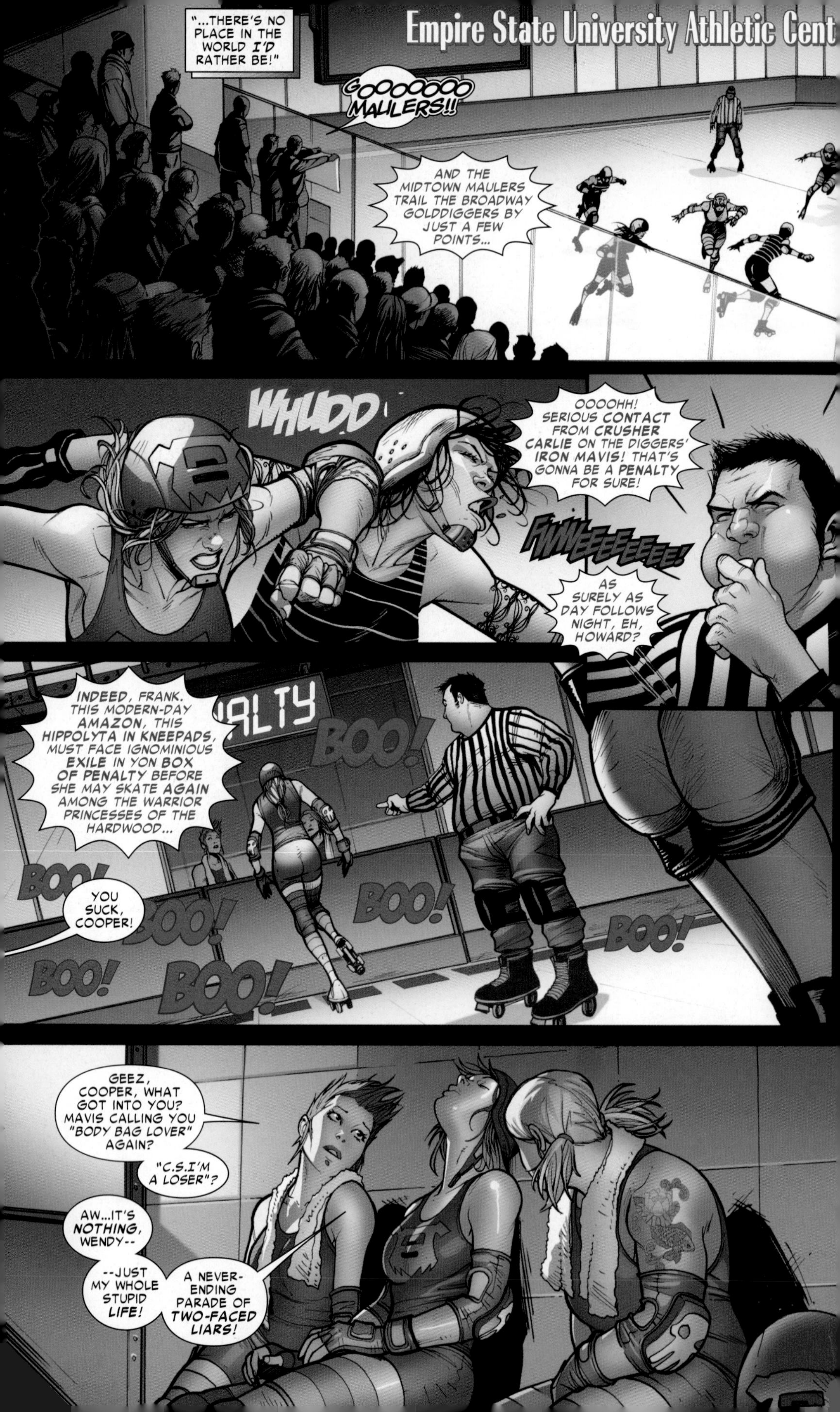
Empire State University Athletic Cent
"...THERE'S NO PLACE IN THE WORLD I'D RATHER BE!"
GOOOOOOO MAULERS!!
AND THE MIDTOWN MAULERS TRAIL THE BROADWAY GOLDDIGGERS BY JUST A FEW POINTS...
WHUDD
OOOOHH! SERIOUS CONTACT FROM CRUSHER CARLIE ON THE DIGGERS' IRON MAVIS! THAT'S GONNA BE A PENALTY FOR SURE!
FWWEEEEEEEE!
AS SURELY AS DAY FOLLOWS NIGHT, EH, HOWARD?
INDEED, FRANK. THIS MODERN-DAY AMAZON, THIS HIPPOLYTA IN KNEEPADS, MUST FACE IGNOMINIOUS EXILE IN YON BOX OF PENALTY BEFORE SHE MAY SKATE AGAIN AMONG THE WARRIOR PRINCESSES OF THE HARDWOOD...
ALTY
BOO!
BOO!
YOU SUCK, COOPER!
BOO!
BOO!
BOO!
BOO!
BOO!
GEEZ, COOPER, WHAT GOT INTO YOU? MAVIS CALLING YOU "BODY BAG LOVER" AGAIN?
"C.S.I'M A LOSER"?
AW...IT'S NOTHING, WENDY--
--JUST MY WHOLE STUPID LIFE!
A NEVER-ENDING PARADE OF TWO-FACED LIARS!

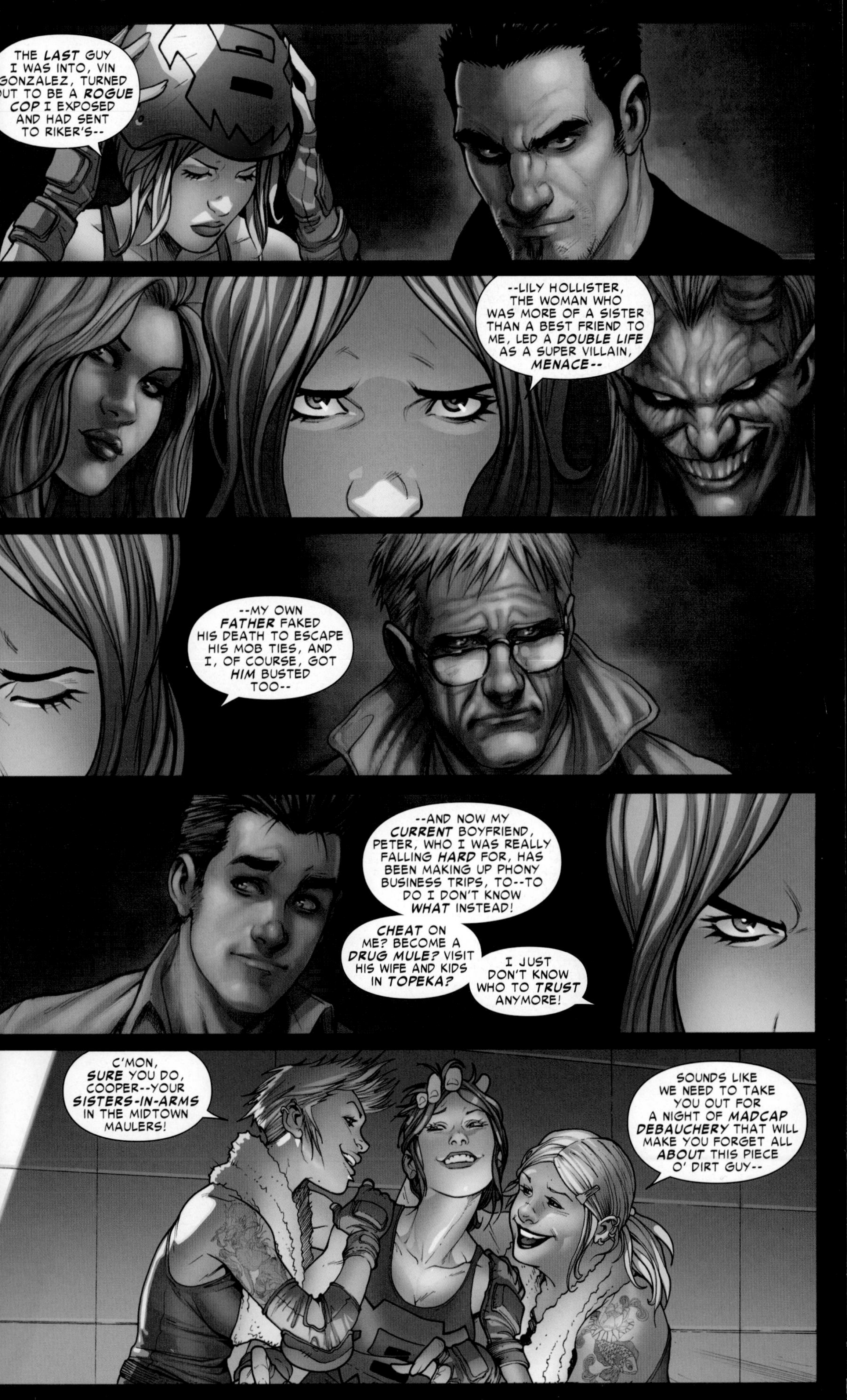
THE LAST GUY I WAS INTO, VIN GONZALEZ, TURNED OUT TO BE A ROGUE COP I EXPOSED AND HAD SENT TO RIKER'S--
--LILY HOLLISTER, THE WOMAN WHO WAS MORE OF A SISTER THAN A BEST FRIEND TO ME, LED A DOUBLE LIFE AS A SUPER VILLAIN, MENACE--
--MY OWN FATHER FAKED HIS DEATH TO ESCAPE HIS MOB TIES, AND I, OF COURSE, GOT HIM BUSTED TOO--
--AND NOW MY CURRENT BOYFRIEND, PETER, WHO I WAS REALLY FALLING HARD FOR, HAS BEEN MAKING UP PHONY BUSINESS TRIPS, TO--TO DO I DON'T KNOW WHAT INSTEAD!
CHEAT ON ME? BECOME A DRUG MULE? VISIT HIS WIFE AND KIDS IN TOPEKA?
I JUST DON'T KNOW WHO TO TRUST ANYMORE!
C'MON, SURE YOU DO, COOPER--YOUR SISTERS-IN-ARMS IN THE MIDTOWN MAULERS!
SOUNDS LIKE WE NEED TO TAKE YOU OUT FOR A NIGHT OF MADCAP DEBAUCHERY THAT WILL MAKE YOU FORGET ALL ABOUT THIS PIECE O' DIRT GUY--

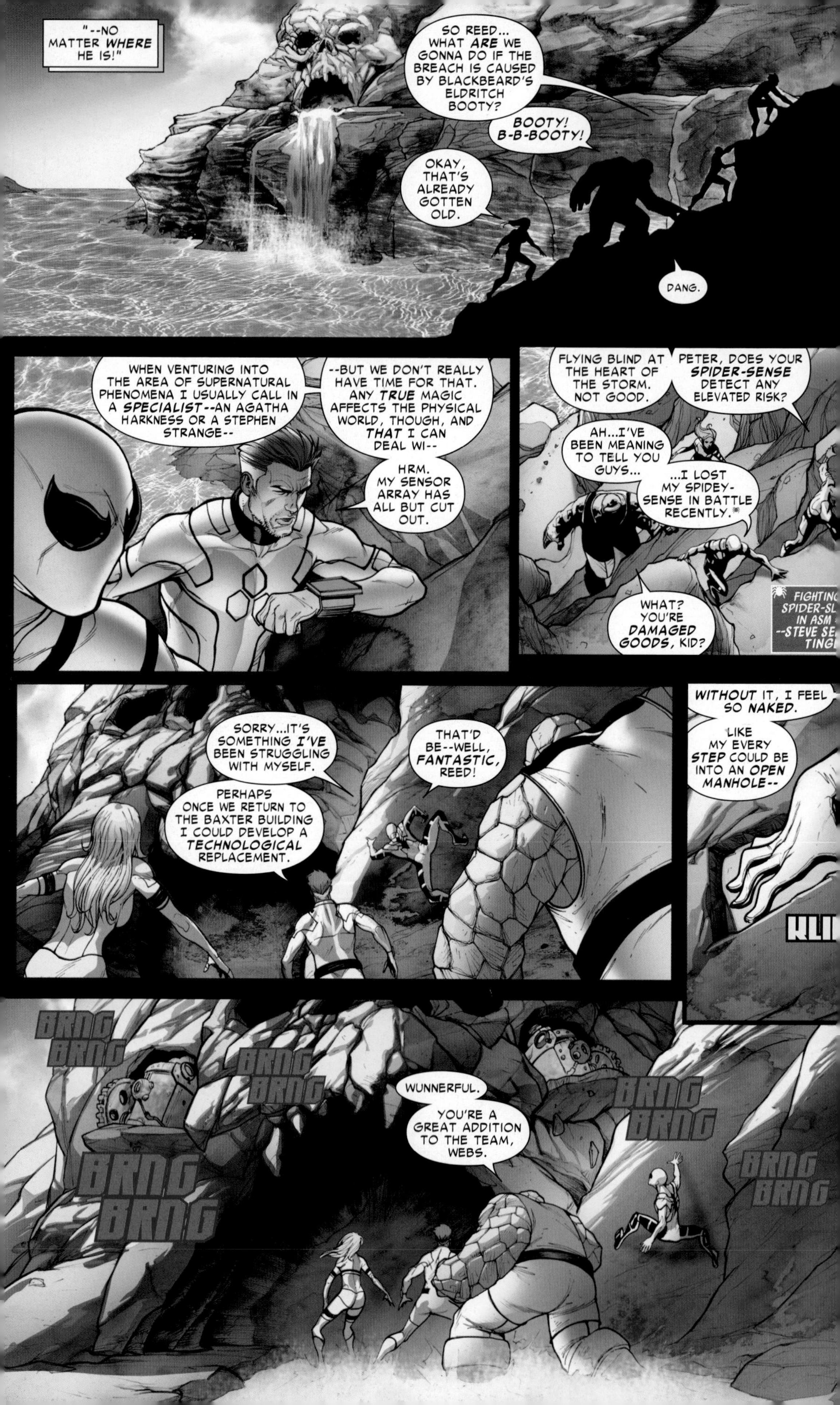
"--NO MATTER WHERE HE IS!"
SO REED... WHAT ARE WE GONNA DO IF THE BREACH IS CAUSED BY BLACKBEARD'S ELDRITCH BOOTY?
BOOTY! B-B-BOOTY!
OKAY, THAT'S ALREADY GOTTEN OLD.
DANG.
WHEN VENTURING INTO THE AREA OF SUPERNATURAL PHENOMENA I USUALLY CALL IN A SPECIALIST--AN AGATHA HARKNESS OR A STEPHEN STRANGE--
--BUT WE DON'T REALLY HAVE TIME FOR THAT. ANY TRUE MAGIC AFFECTS THE PHYSICAL WORLD, THOUGH, AND THAT I CAN DEAL WI--
HRM. MY SENSOR ARRAY HAS ALL BUT CUT OUT.
FLYING BLIND AT THE HEART OF THE STORM. NOT GOOD.
PETER, DOES YOUR SPIDER-SENSE DETECT ANY ELEVATED RISK?
AH...I'VE BEEN MEANING TO TELL YOU GUYS...
...I LOST MY SPIDEY-SENSE IN BATTLE RECENTLY.*
WHAT? YOU'RE DAMAGED GOODS, KID?
SORRY...IT'S SOMETHING I'VE BEEN STRUGGLING WITH MYSELF.
PERHAPS ONCE WE RETURN TO THE BAXTER BUILDING I COULD DEVELOP A TECHNOLOGICAL REPLACEMENT.
THAT'D BE--WELL, FANTASTIC, REED!
WITHOUT IT, I FEEL SO NAKED.
LIKE MY EVERY STEP COULD BE INTO AN OPEN MANHOLE--
KLI
BRNG BRNG
BRNG BRNG
BRNG BRNG
WUNNERFUL.
YOU'RE A GREAT ADDITION TO THE TEAM, WEBS.
BRNG BRNG
BRNG BRNG

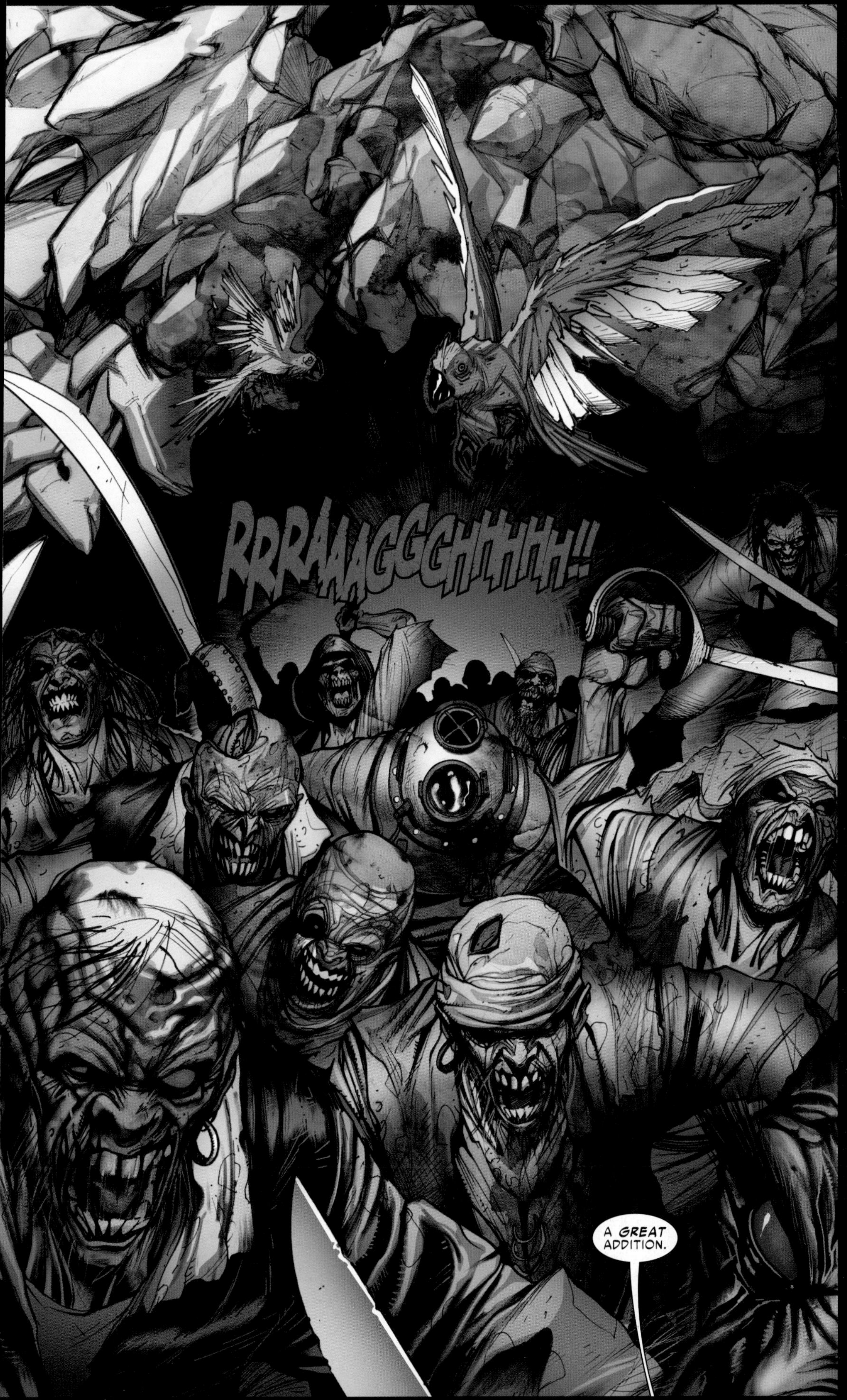
RRRAAAGGGHHHHH!!
A GREAT ADDITION.

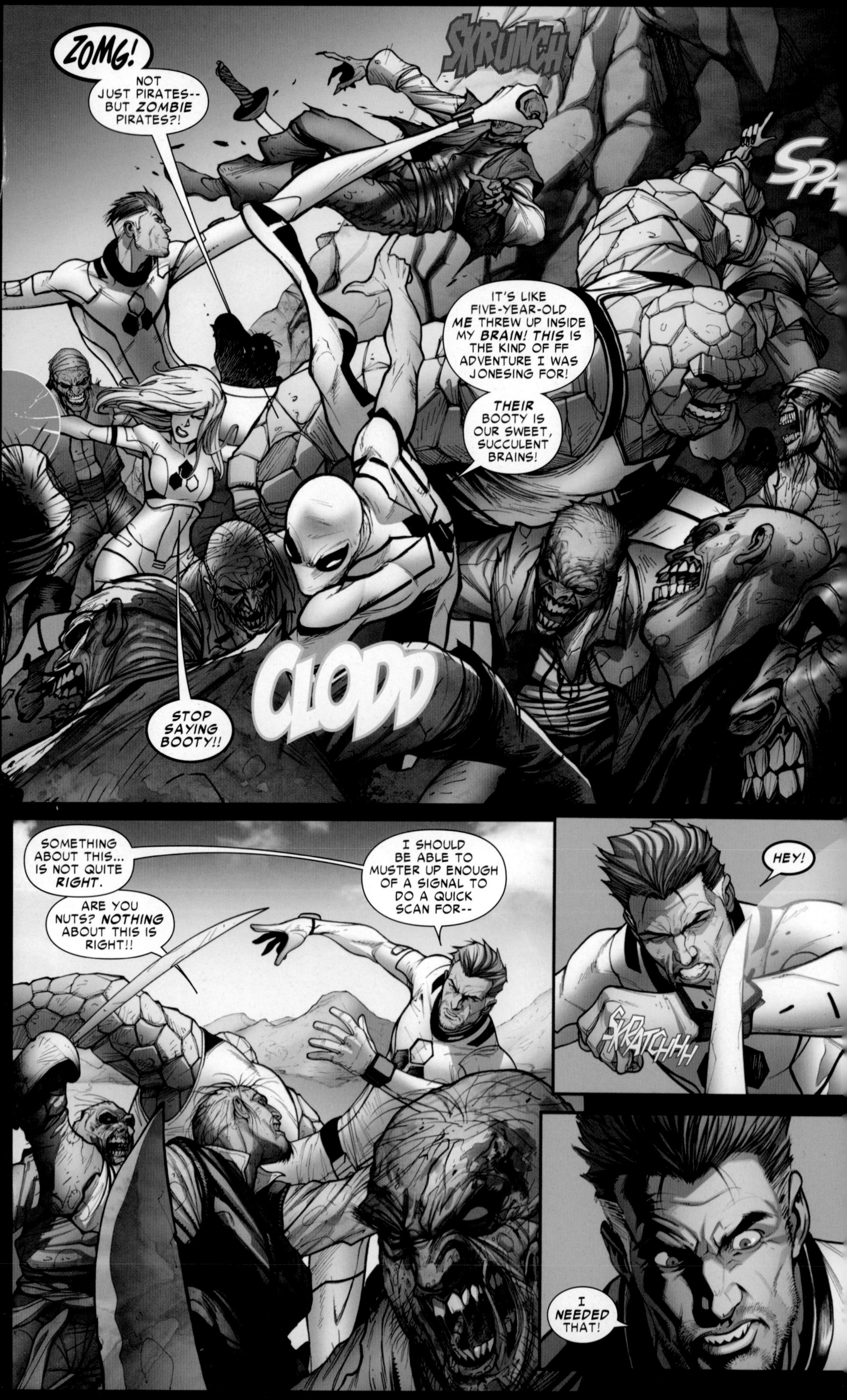
ZOMG!
NOT JUST PIRATES-- BUT ZOMBIE PIRATES?!
SKRUNCH
SPA
IT'S LIKE FIVE-YEAR-OLD ME THREW UP INSIDE MY BRAIN! THIS IS THE KIND OF FF ADVENTURE I WAS JONESING FOR!
THEIR BOOTY IS OUR SWEET, SUCCULENT BRAINS!
CLODD
STOP SAYING BOOTY!!
SOMETHING ABOUT THIS... IS NOT QUITE RIGHT.
ARE YOU NUTS? NOTHING ABOUT THIS IS RIGHT!!
I SHOULD BE ABLE TO MUSTER UP ENOUGH OF A SIGNAL TO DO A QUICK SCAN FOR--
HEY!
SKRATCHHH
I NEEDED THAT!

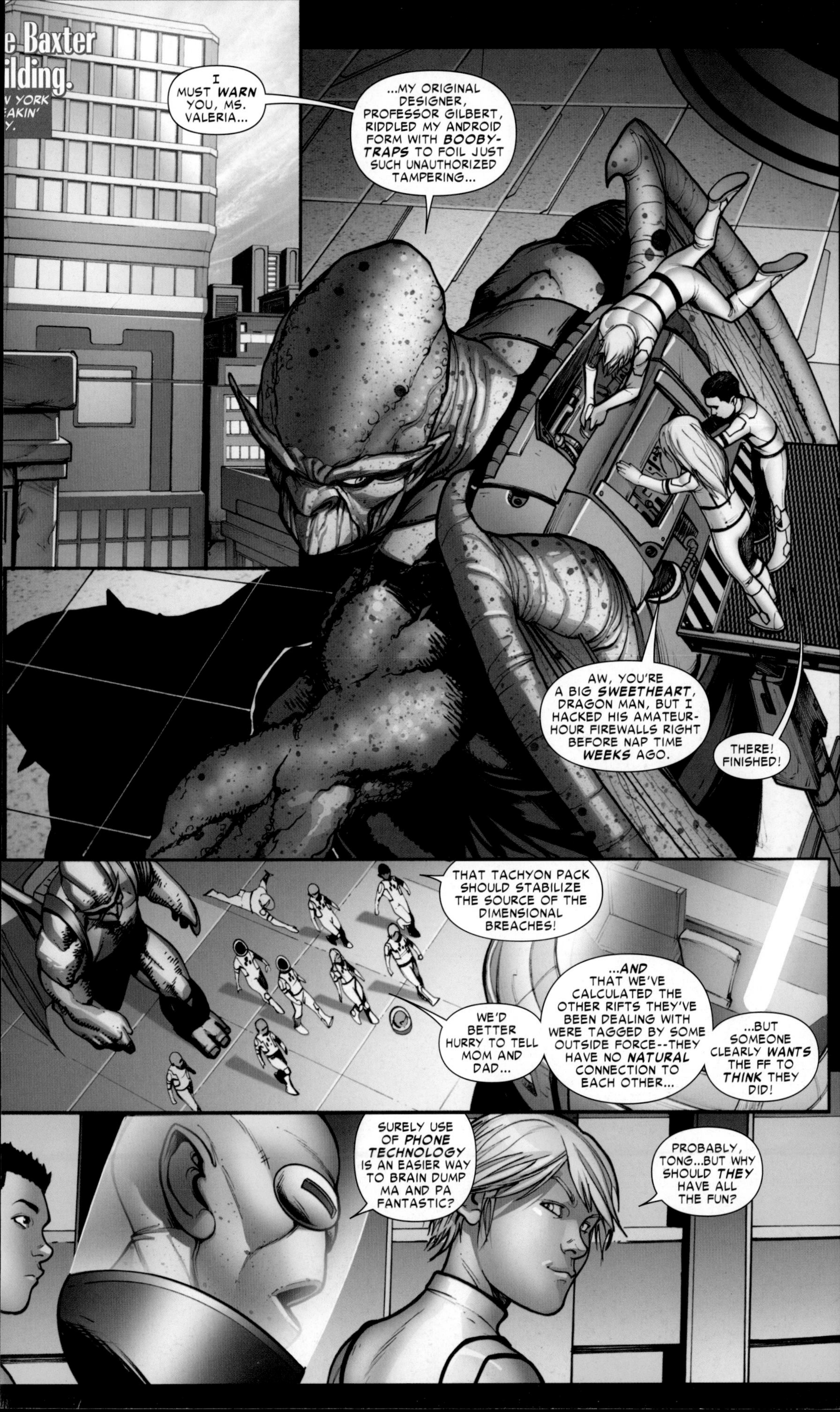

e Baxter
ilding.
w York
eakin'
y.
I MUST WARN YOU, MS. VALERIA...
...MY ORIGINAL DESIGNER, PROFESSOR GILBERT, RIDDLED MY ANDROID FORM WITH BOOBY-TRAPS TO FOIL JUST SUCH UNAUTHORIZED TAMPERING...
AW, YOU'RE A BIG SWEETHEART, DRAGON MAN, BUT I HACKED HIS AMATEUR-HOUR FIREWALLS RIGHT BEFORE NAP TIME WEEKS AGO.
THERE! FINISHED!
THAT TACHYON PACK SHOULD STABILIZE THE SOURCE OF THE DIMENSIONAL BREACHES!
...AND THAT WE'VE CALCULATED THE OTHER RIFTS THEY'VE BEEN DEALING WITH WERE TAGGED BY SOME OUTSIDE FORCE--THEY HAVE NO NATURAL CONNECTION TO EACH OTHER...
...BUT SOMEONE CLEARLY WANTS THE FF TO THINK THEY DID!
WE'D BETTER HURRY TO TELL MOM AND DAD...
SURELY USE OF PHONE TECHNOLOGY IS AN EASIER WAY TO BRAIN DUMP MA AND PA FANTASTIC?
PROBABLY, TONG...BUT WHY SHOULD THEY HAVE ALL THE FUN?

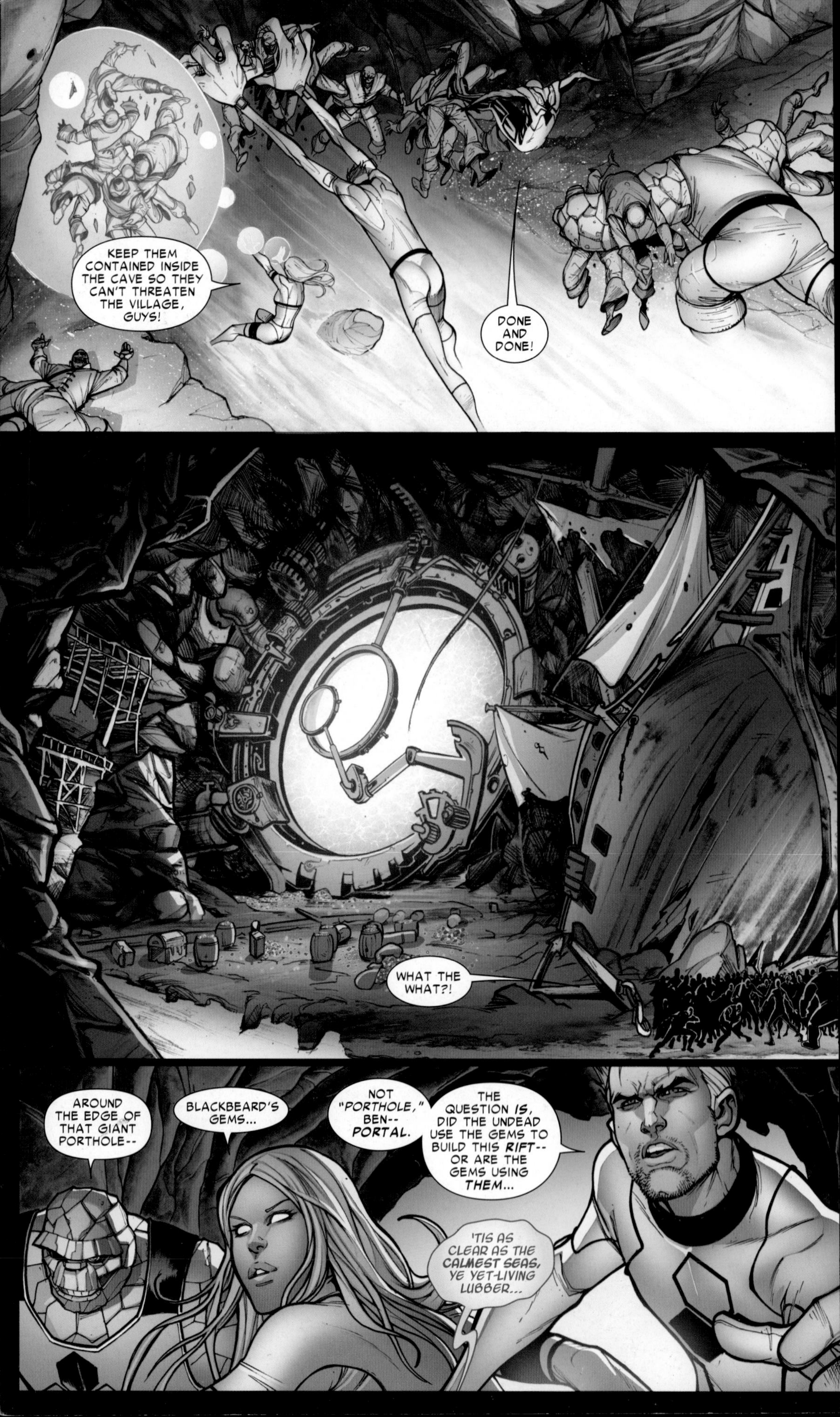
KEEP THEM CONTAINED INSIDE THE CAVE SO THEY CAN'T THREATEN THE VILLAGE, GUYS!
DONE AND DONE!
WHAT THE WHAT?!
AROUND THE EDGE OF THAT GIANT PORTHOLE--
BLACKBEARD'S GEMS...
NOT "PORTHOLE," BEN-- PORTAL.
THE QUESTION IS, DID THE UNDEAD USE THE GEMS TO BUILD THIS RIFT-- OR ARE THE GEMS USING THEM...
'TIS AS CLEAR AS THE CALMEST SEAS, YE YET-LIVING LUBBER...

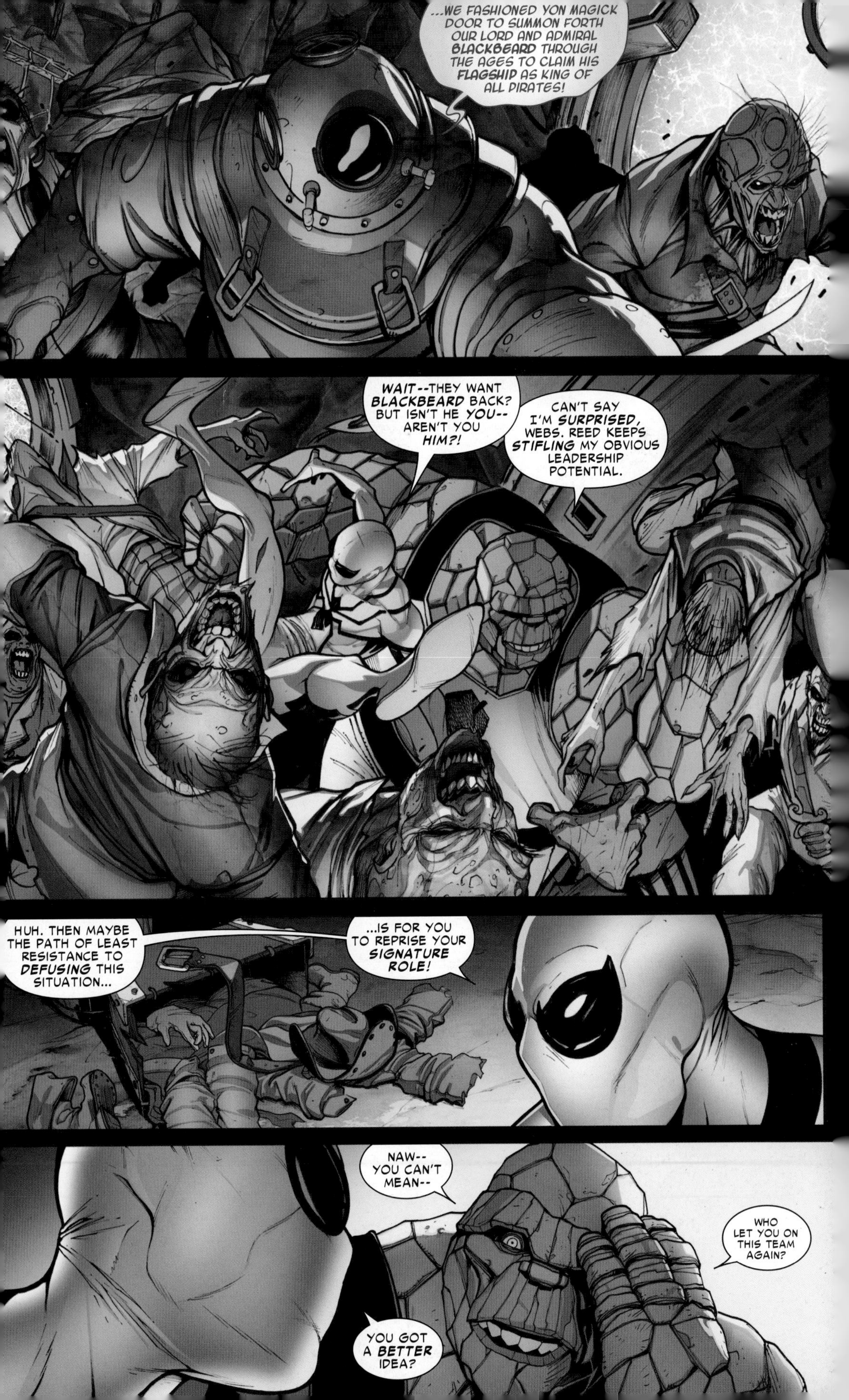
...WE FASHIONED YON MAGICK DOOR TO SUMMON FORTH OUR LORD AND ADMIRAL BLACKBEARD THROUGH THE AGES TO CLAIM HIS FLAGSHIP AS KING OF ALL PIRATES!
WAIT--THEY WANT BLACKBEARD BACK? BUT ISN'T HE YOU--AREN'T YOU HIM?!
CAN'T SAY I'M SURPRISED, WEBS. REED KEEPS STIFLING MY OBVIOUS LEADERSHIP POTENTIAL.
HUH. THEN MAYBE THE PATH OF LEAST RESISTANCE TO DEFUSING THIS SITUATION...
...IS FOR YOU TO REPRISE YOUR SIGNATURE ROLE!
NAW--YOU CAN'T MEAN--
WHO LET YOU ON THIS TEAM AGAIN?
YOU GOT A BETTER IDEA?

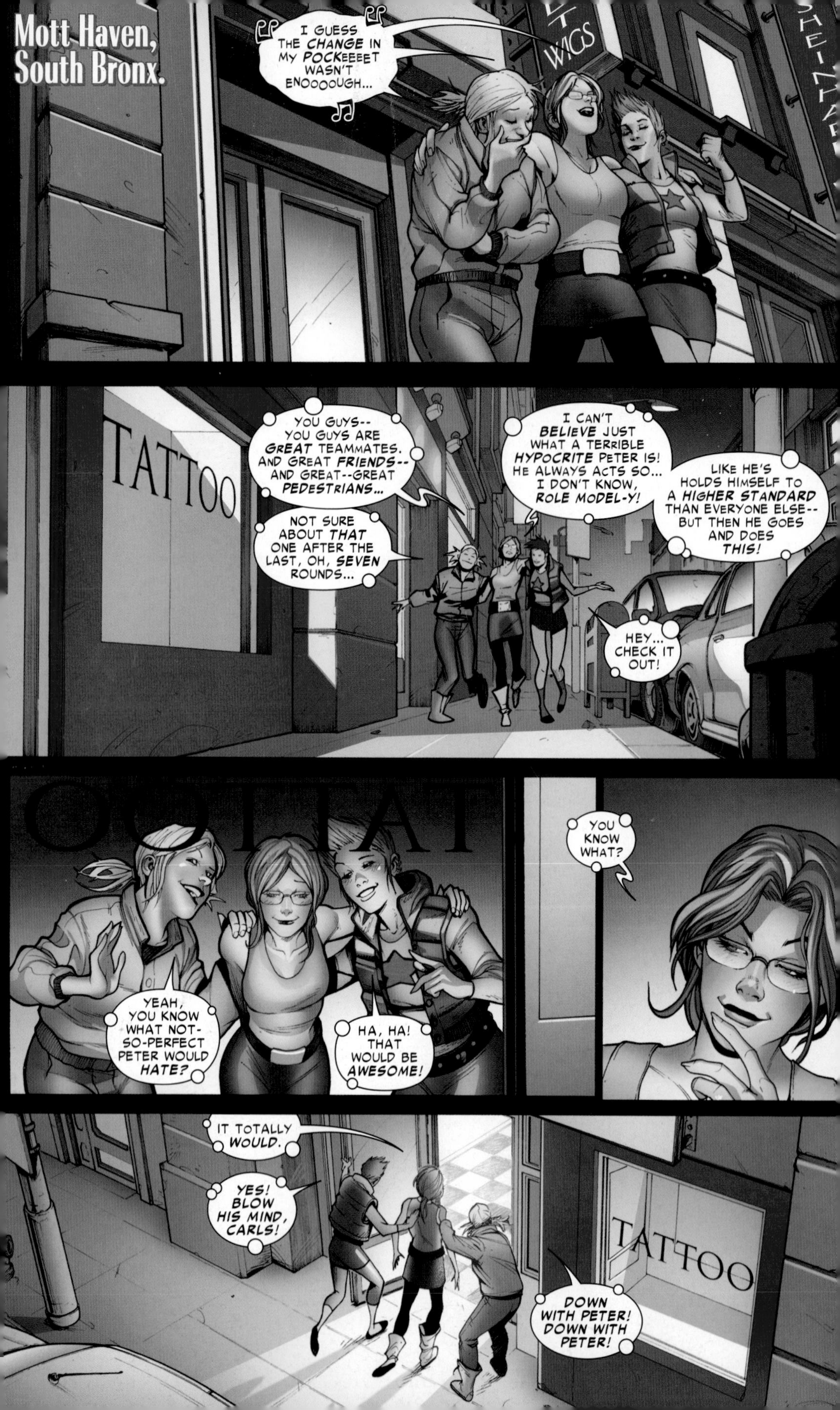

Mott Haven, South Bronx.
I GUESS THE CHANGE IN MY POCKEEEEET WASN'T ENOOOOUGH...
LT WIGS
TATTOO
YOU GUYS-- YOU GUYS ARE GREAT TEAMMATES. AND GREAT FRIENDS-- AND GREAT--GREAT PEDESTRIANS...
NOT SURE ABOUT THAT ONE AFTER THE LAST, OH, SEVEN ROUNDS...
I CAN'T BELIEVE JUST WHAT A TERRIBLE HYPOCRITE PETER IS! HE ALWAYS ACTS SO... I DON'T KNOW, ROLE MODEL-Y!
LIKE HE'S HOLDS HIMSELF TO A HIGHER STANDARD THAN EVERYONE ELSE-- BUT THEN HE GOES AND DOES THIS!
HEY... CHECK IT OUT!
YEAH, YOU KNOW WHAT NOT-SO-PERFECT PETER WOULD HATE?
HA, HA! THAT WOULD BE AWESOME!
YOU KNOW WHAT?
IT TOTALLY WOULD.
YES! BLOW HIS MIND, CARLS!
TATTOO
DOWN WITH PETER! DOWN WITH PETER!

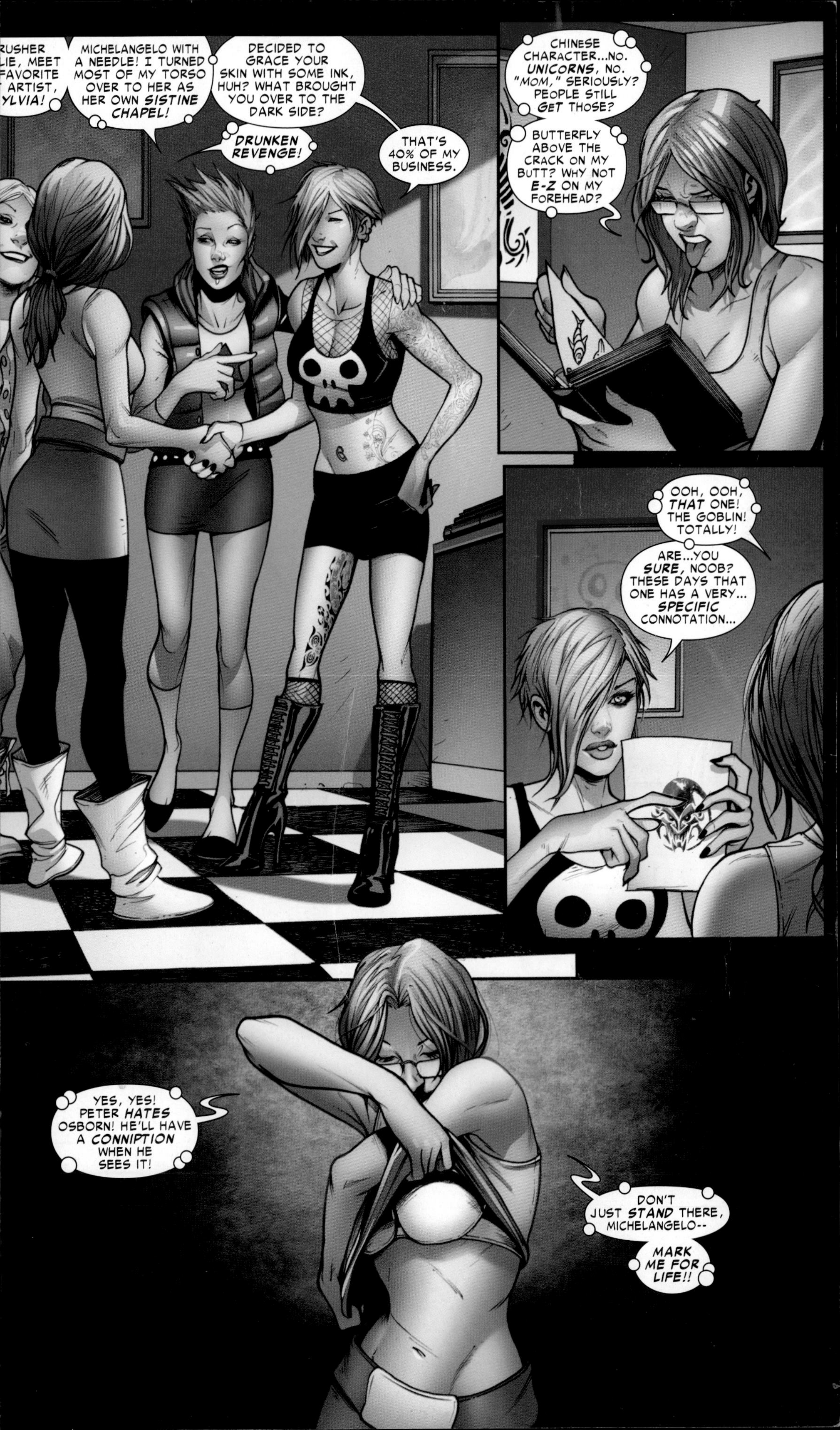

RUSHER
LIE, MEET
FAVORITE
ARTIST,
YLVIA!
MICHELANGELO WITH A NEEDLE! I TURNED MOST OF MY TORSO OVER TO HER AS HER OWN SISTINE CHAPEL!
DECIDED TO GRACE YOUR SKIN WITH SOME INK, HUH? WHAT BROUGHT YOU OVER TO THE DARK SIDE?
DRUNKEN REVENGE!
THAT'S 40% OF MY BUSINESS.
CHINESE CHARACTER...NO. UNICORNS, NO. "MOM," SERIOUSLY? PEOPLE STILL GET THOSE?
BUTTERFLY ABOVE THE CRACK ON MY BUTT? WHY NOT E-Z ON MY FOREHEAD?
OOH, OOH, THAT ONE! THE GOBLIN! TOTALLY!
ARE...YOU SURE, NOOB? THESE DAYS THAT ONE HAS A VERY... SPECIFIC CONNOTATION...
YES, YES! PETER HATES OSBORN! HE'LL HAVE A CONNIPTION WHEN HE SEES IT!
DON'T JUST STAND THERE, MICHELANGELO--
MARK ME FOR LIFE!!

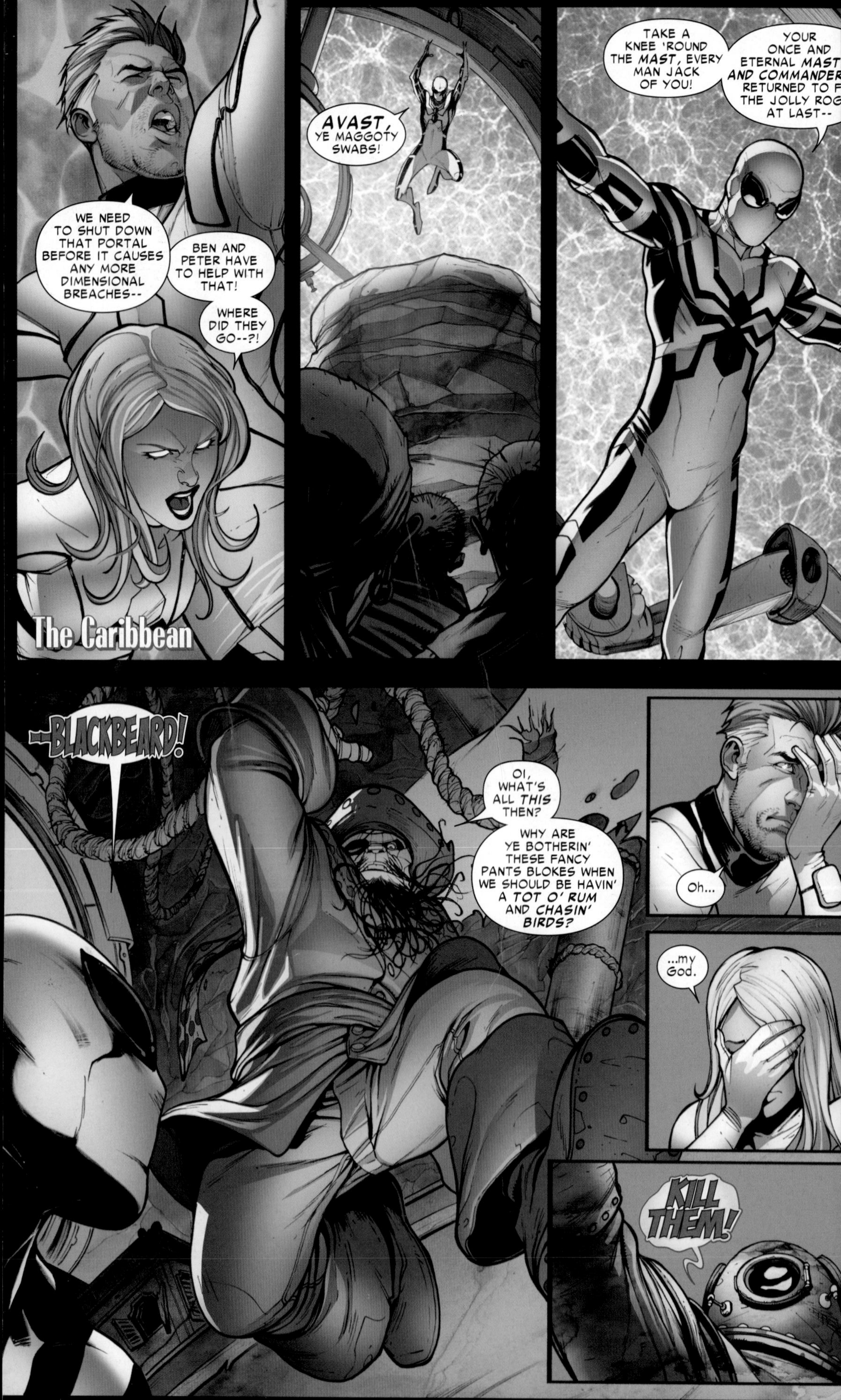
WE NEED TO SHUT DOWN THAT PORTAL BEFORE IT CAUSES ANY MORE DIMENSIONAL BREACHES--
BEN AND PETER HAVE TO HELP WITH THAT!
WHERE DID THEY GO--?!
The Caribbean
AVAST, YE MAGGOTY SWABS!
TAKE A KNEE 'ROUND THE MAST, EVERY MAN JACK OF YOU!
YOUR ONCE AND ETERNAL MAST AND COMMANDER RETURNED TO THE JOLLY ROG AT LAST--
--BLACKBEARD!
OI, WHAT'S ALL THIS THEN?
WHY ARE YE BOTHERIN' THESE FANCY PANTS BLOKES WHEN WE SHOULD BE HAVIN' A TOT O' RUM AND CHASIN' BIRDS?
Oh...
...my God.
KILL THEM!

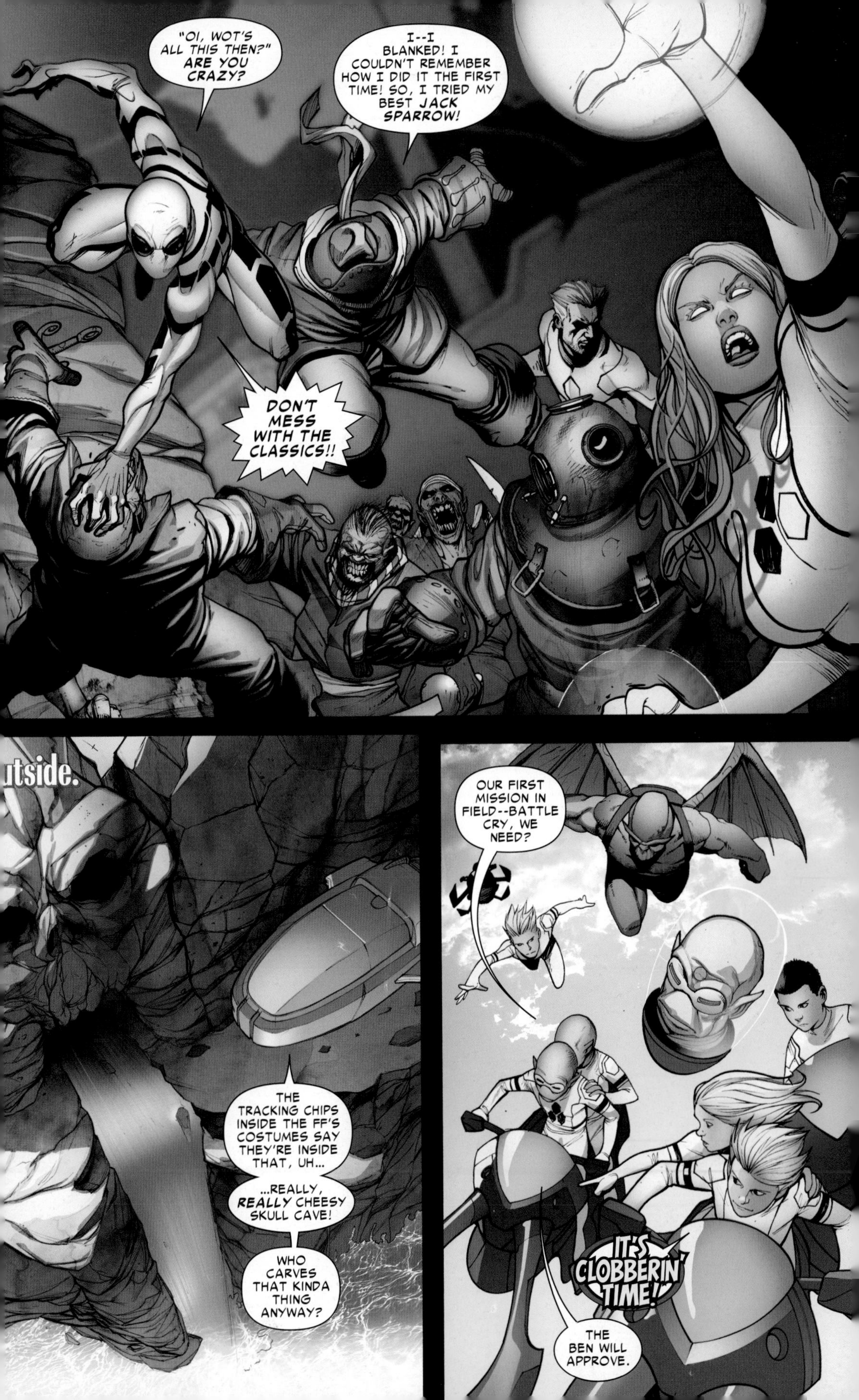
"OI, WOT'S ALL THIS THEN?" ARE YOU CRAZY?
I--I BLANKED! I COULDN'T REMEMBER HOW I DID IT THE FIRST TIME! SO, I TRIED MY BEST JACK SPARROW!
DON'T MESS WITH THE CLASSICS!!
...tside.
THE TRACKING CHIPS INSIDE THE FF'S COSTUMES SAY THEY'RE INSIDE THAT, UH...
...REALLY, REALLY CHEESY SKULL CAVE!
WHO CARVES THAT KINDA THING ANYWAY?
OUR FIRST MISSION IN FIELD--BATTLE CRY, WE NEED?
IT'S CLOBBERIN' TIME!
THE BEN WILL APPROVE.

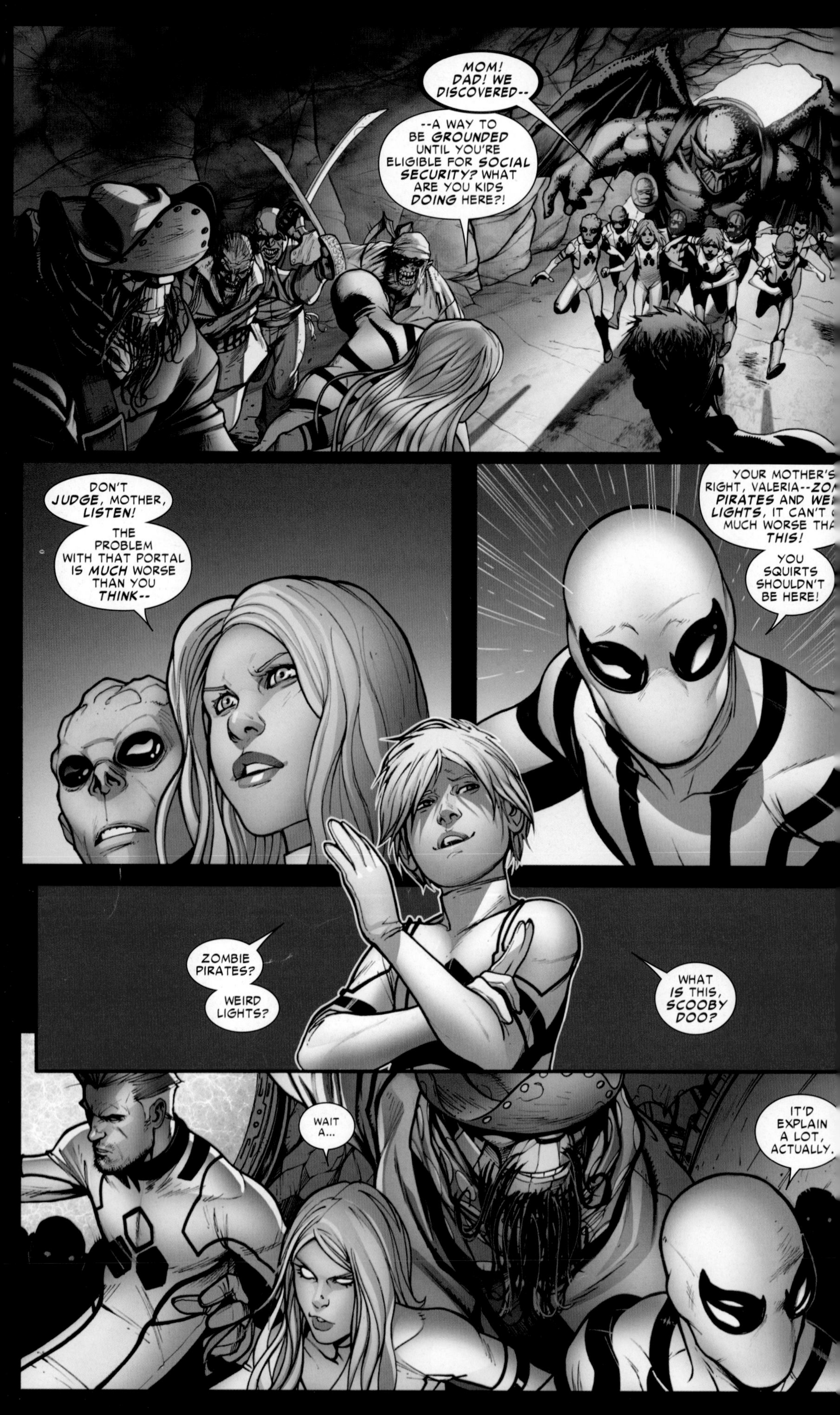
MOM! DAD! WE DISCOVERED--
--A WAY TO BE GROUNDED UNTIL YOU'RE ELIGIBLE FOR SOCIAL SECURITY? WHAT ARE YOU KIDS DOING HERE?!
DON'T JUDGE, MOTHER, LISTEN!
THE PROBLEM WITH THAT PORTAL IS MUCH WORSE THAN YOU THINK--
YOUR MOTHER'S RIGHT, VALERIA--ZOM PIRATES AND WE LIGHTS, IT CAN'T MUCH WORSE THA THIS!
YOU SQUIRTS SHOULDN'T BE HERE!
ZOMBIE PIRATES?
WEIRD LIGHTS?
WHAT IS THIS, SCOOBY DOO?
WAIT A...
IT'D EXPLAIN A LOT, ACTUALLY.

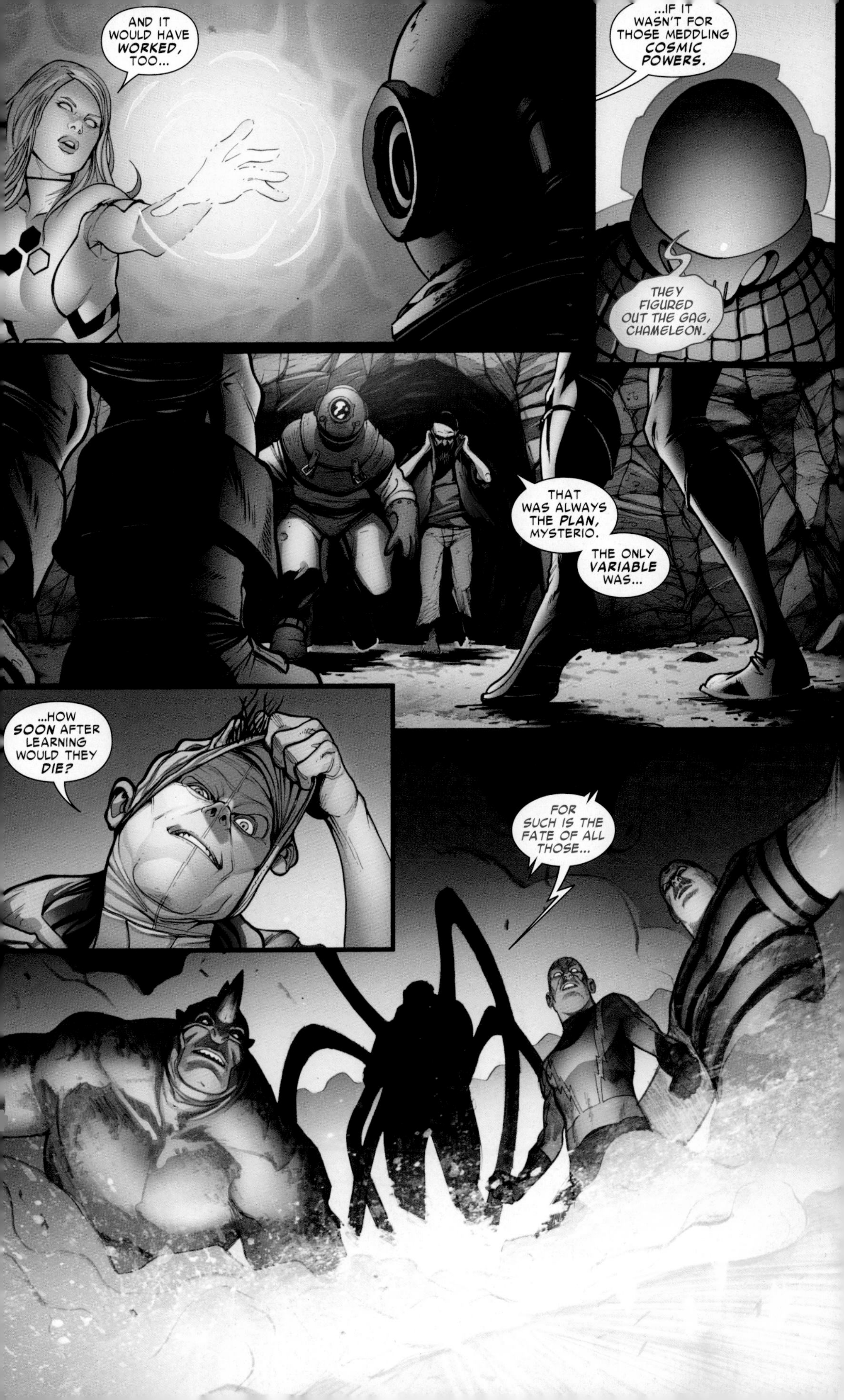
AND IT WOULD HAVE WORKED, TOO...
...IF IT WASN'T FOR THOSE MEDDLING COSMIC POWERS.
THEY FIGURED OUT THE GAG, CHAMELEON.
THAT WAS ALWAYS THE PLAN, MYSTERIO.
THE ONLY VARIABLE WAS...
...HOW SOON AFTER LEARNING WOULD THEY DIE?
FOR SUCH IS THE FATE OF ALL THOSE...

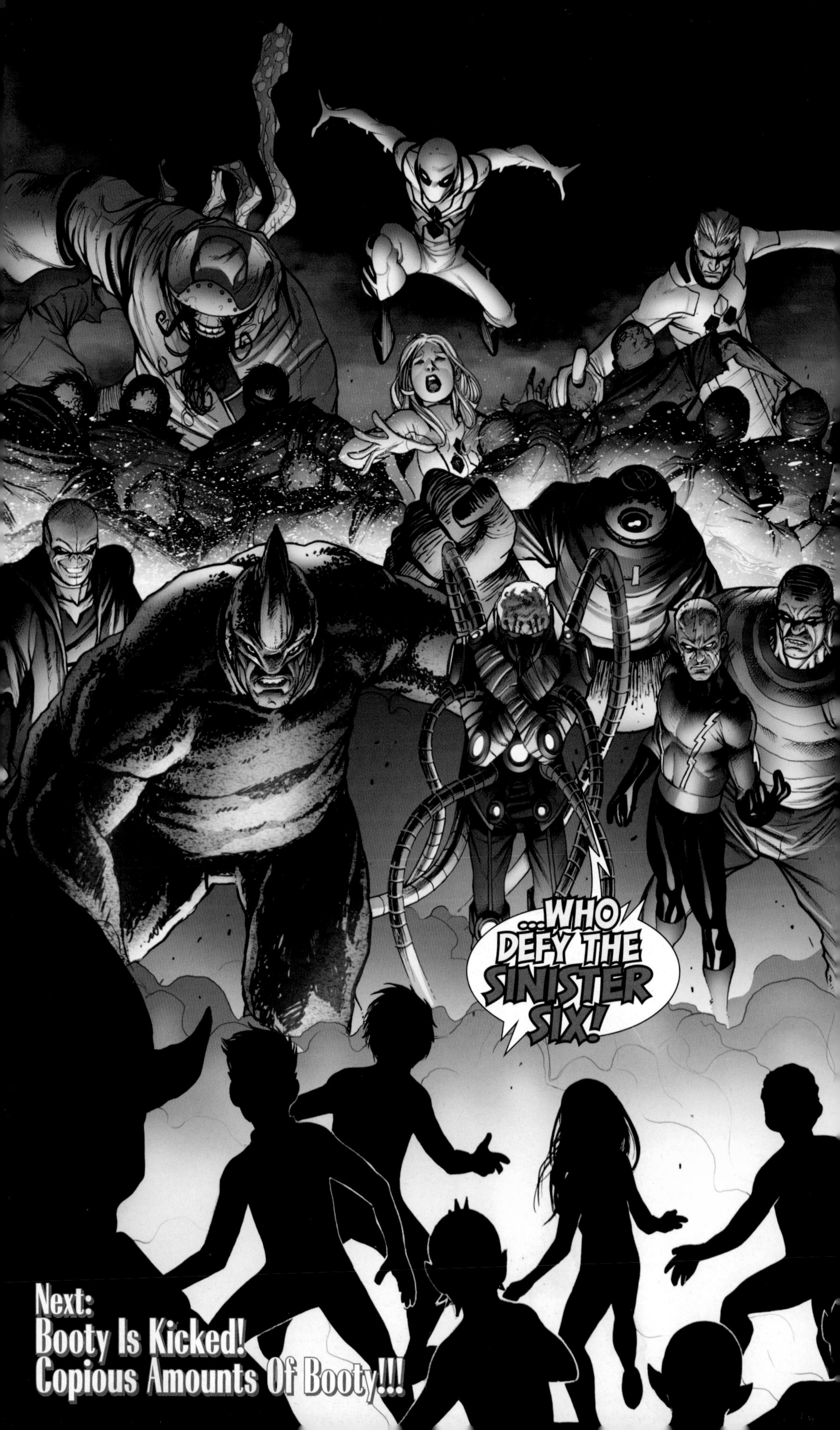
...WHO DEFY THE SINISTER SIX!
Next:
Booty Is Kicked!
Copious Amounts Of Booty!!!

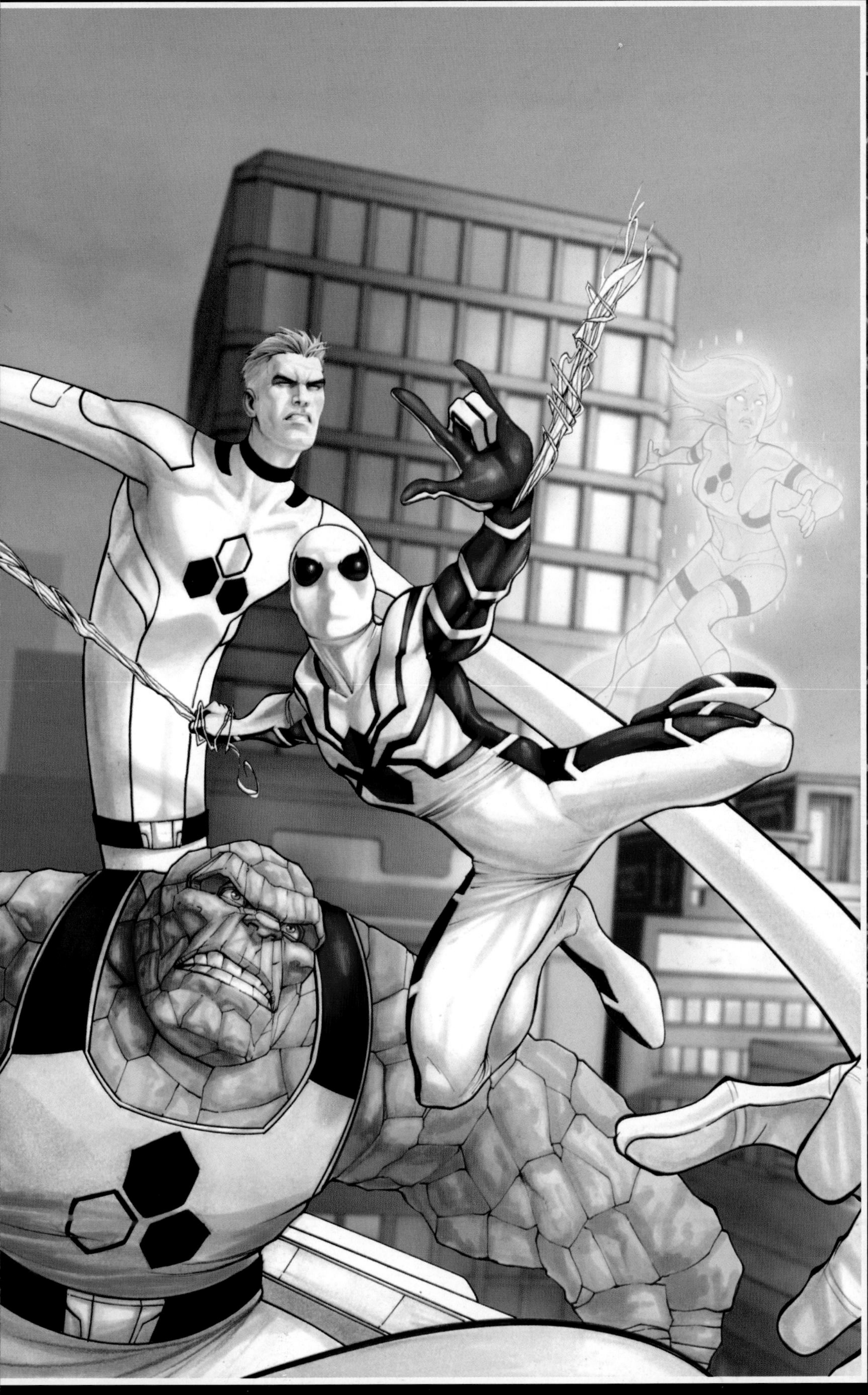

AMAZING SPIDER-MAN #660
COVER BY STEFANO CASELLI & LORENZO DE FELICI

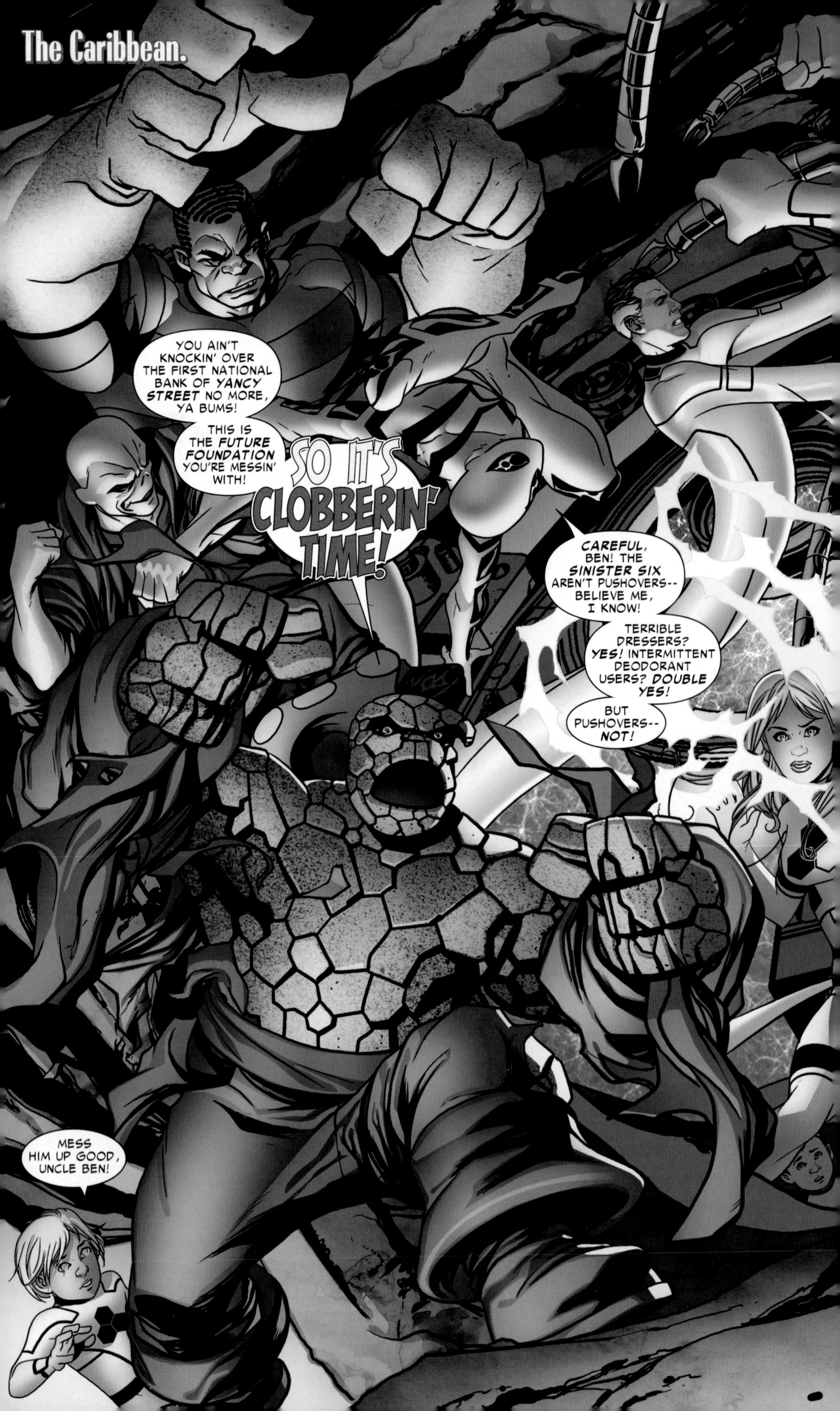
The Caribbean.
YOU AIN'T KNOCKIN' OVER THE FIRST NATIONAL BANK OF YANCY STREET NO MORE, YA BUMS!
THIS IS THE FUTURE FOUNDATION YOU'RE MESSIN' WITH!
SO IT'S CLOBBERIN' TIME!
CAREFUL, BEN! THE SINISTER SIX AREN'T PUSHOVERS-- BELIEVE ME, I KNOW!
TERRIBLE DRESSERS? YES! INTERMITTENT DEODORANT USERS? DOUBLE YES!
BUT PUSHOVERS-- NOT!
MESS HIM UP GOOD, UNCLE BEN!

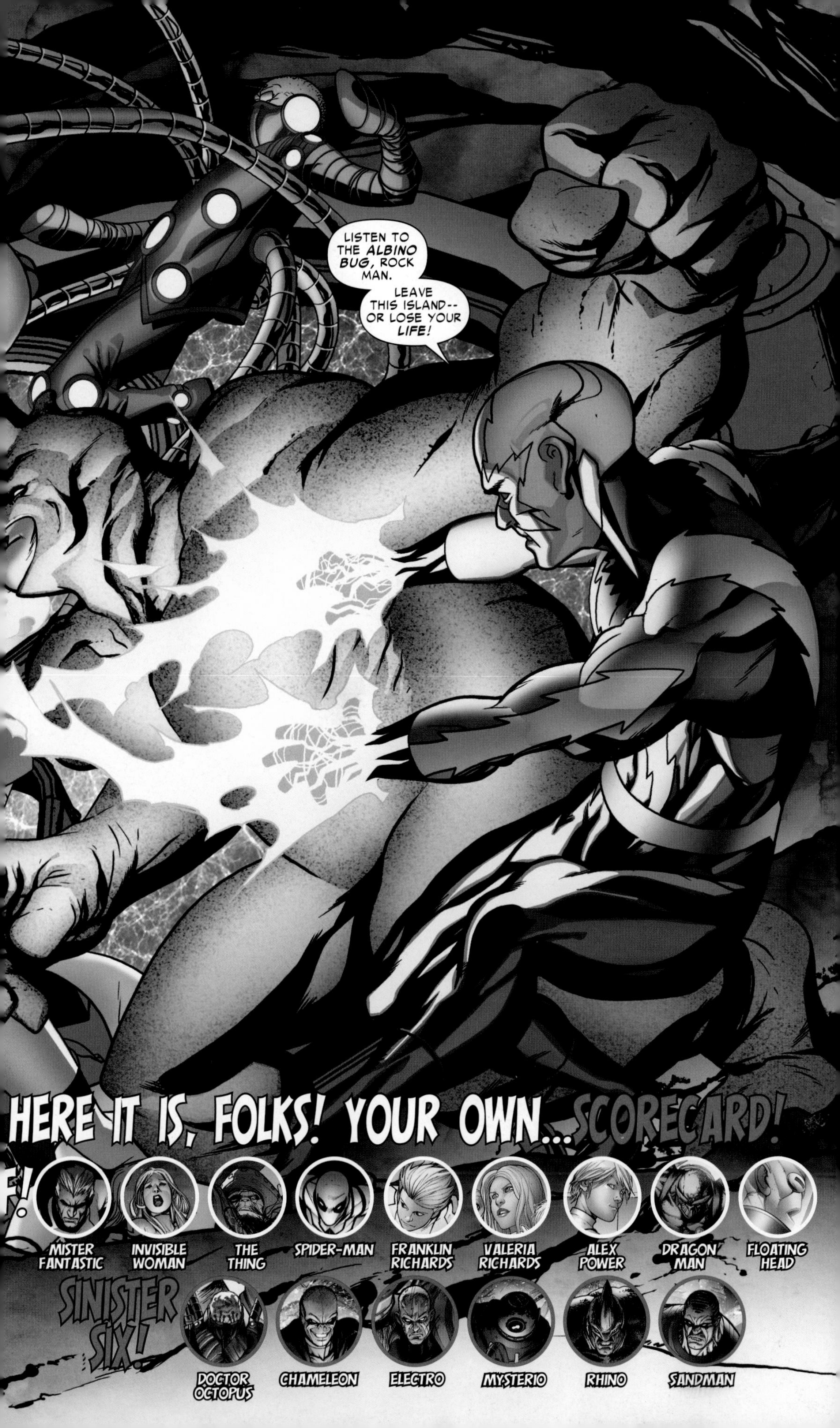
LISTEN TO THE ALBINO BUG, ROCK MAN.
LEAVE THIS ISLAND-- OR LOSE YOUR LIFE!
HERE IT IS, FOLKS! YOUR OWN... SCORECARD!
MISTER FANTASTIC
INVISIBLE WOMAN
THE THING
SPIDER-MAN
FRANKLIN RICHARDS
VALERIA RICHARDS
ALEX POWER
DRAGON MAN
FLOATING HEAD
SINISTER SIX!
DOCTOR OCTOPUS
CHAMELEON
ELECTRO
MYSTERIO
RHINO
SANDMAN

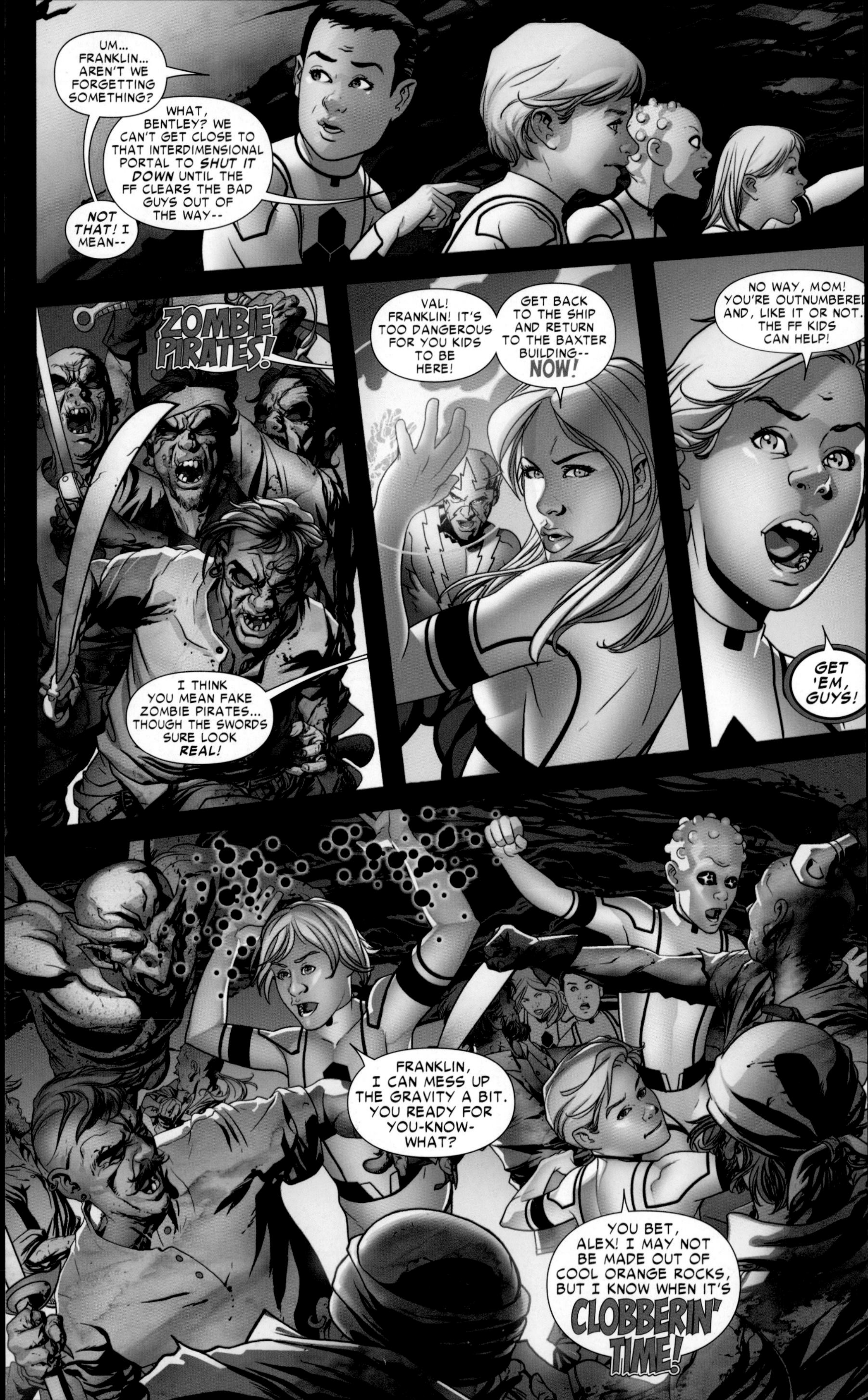

UM... FRANKLIN... AREN'T WE FORGETTING SOMETHING?
WHAT, BENTLEY? WE CAN'T GET CLOSE TO THAT INTERDIMENSIONAL PORTAL TO SHUT IT DOWN UNTIL THE FF CLEARS THE BAD GUYS OUT OF THE WAY--
NOT THAT! I MEAN--
ZOMBIE PIRATES!
I THINK YOU MEAN FAKE ZOMBIE PIRATES... THOUGH THE SWORDS SURE LOOK REAL!
VAL! FRANKLIN! IT'S TOO DANGEROUS FOR YOU KIDS TO BE HERE!
GET BACK TO THE SHIP AND RETURN TO THE BAXTER BUILDING-- NOW!
NO WAY, MOM! YOU'RE OUTNUMBERED AND, LIKE IT OR NOT, THE FF KIDS CAN HELP!
GET 'EM, GUYS!
FRANKLIN, I CAN MESS UP THE GRAVITY A BIT. YOU READY FOR YOU-KNOW-WHAT?
YOU BET, ALEX! I MAY NOT BE MADE OUT OF COOL ORANGE ROCKS, BUT I KNOW WHEN IT'S CLOBBERIN' TIME!

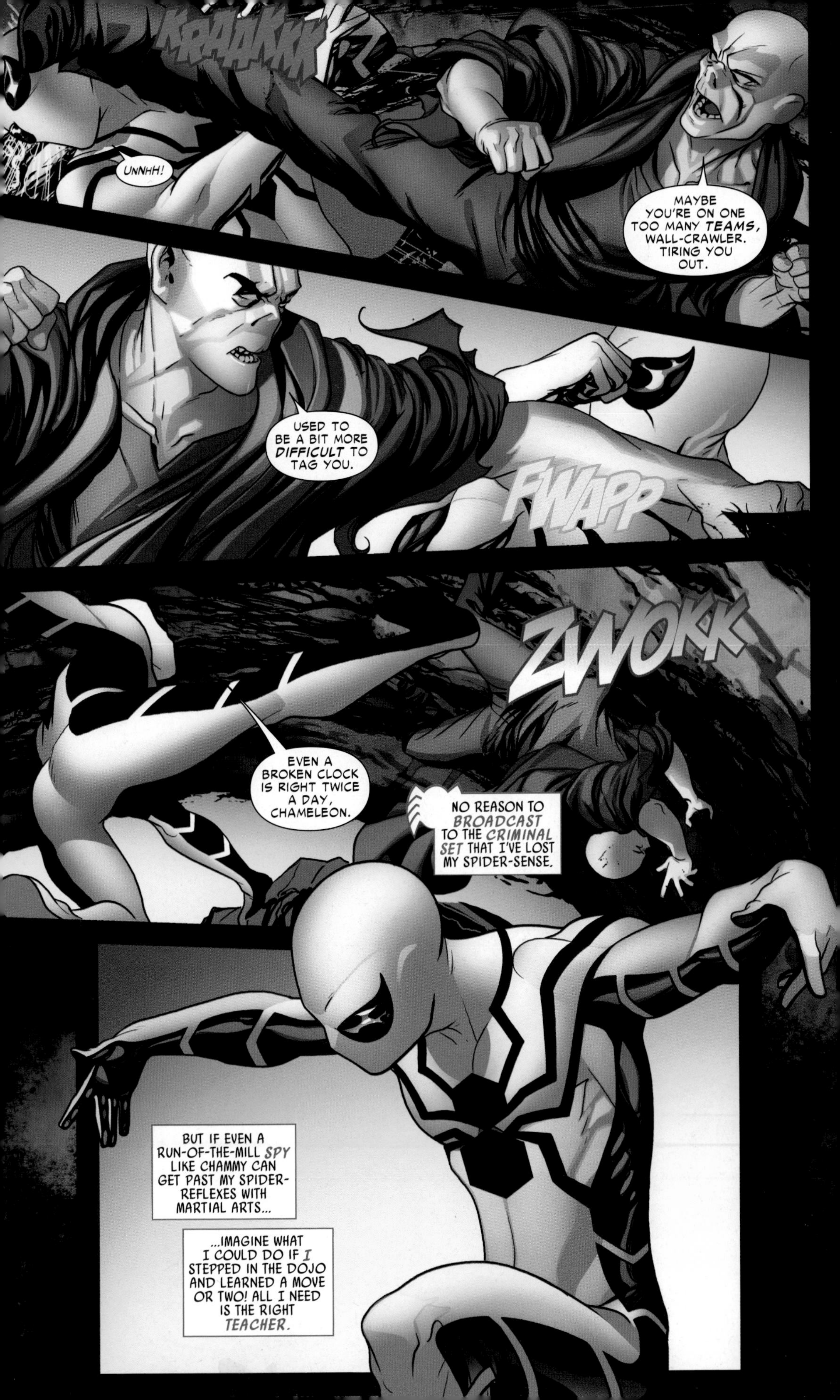

KRAAKKK
UNNHH!
MAYBE YOU'RE ON ONE TOO MANY TEAMS, WALL-CRAWLER. TIRING YOU OUT.
USED TO BE A BIT MORE DIFFICULT TO TAG YOU.
FWAPP
ZWOKK
EVEN A BROKEN CLOCK IS RIGHT TWICE A DAY, CHAMELEON.
NO REASON TO BROADCAST TO THE CRIMINAL SET THAT I'VE LOST MY SPIDER-SENSE.
BUT IF EVEN A RUN-OF-THE-MILL SPY LIKE CHAMMY CAN GET PAST MY SPIDER-REFLEXES WITH MARTIAL ARTS...
...IMAGINE WHAT I COULD DO IF I STEPPED IN THE DOJO AND LEARNED A MOVE OR TWO! ALL I NEED IS THE RIGHT TEACHER.

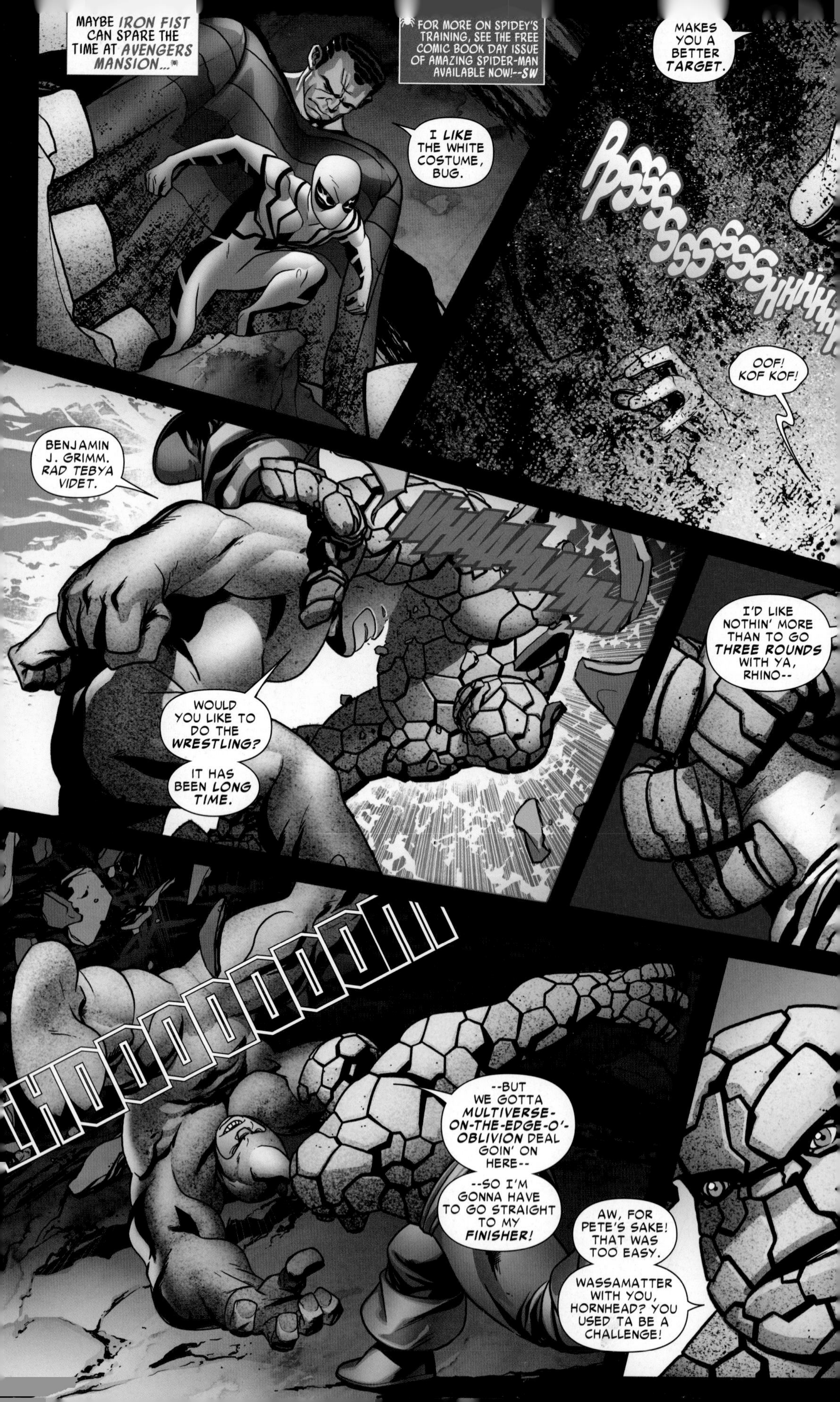
MAYBE IRON FIST CAN SPARE THE TIME AT AVENGERS MANSION...
FOR MORE ON SPIDEY'S TRAINING, SEE THE FREE COMIC BOOK DAY ISSUE OF AMAZING SPIDER-MAN AVAILABLE NOW!--SW
I LIKE THE WHITE COSTUME, BUG.
MAKES YOU A BETTER TARGET.
PSSSSSSSSSSHHHH
OOF! KOF KOF!
BENJAMIN J. GRIMM. RAD TEBYA VIDET.
WOULD YOU LIKE TO DO THE WRESTLING?
IT HAS BEEN LONG TIME.
I'D LIKE NOTHIN' MORE THAN TO GO THREE ROUNDS WITH YA, RHINO--
--BUT WE GOTTA MULTIVERSE-ON-THE-EDGE-O'-OBLIVION DEAL GOIN' ON HERE--
--SO I'M GONNA HAVE TO GO STRAIGHT TO MY FINISHER!
AW, FOR PETE'S SAKE! THAT WAS TOO EASY.
WASSAMATTER WITH YOU, HORNHEAD? YOU USED TA BE A CHALLENGE!

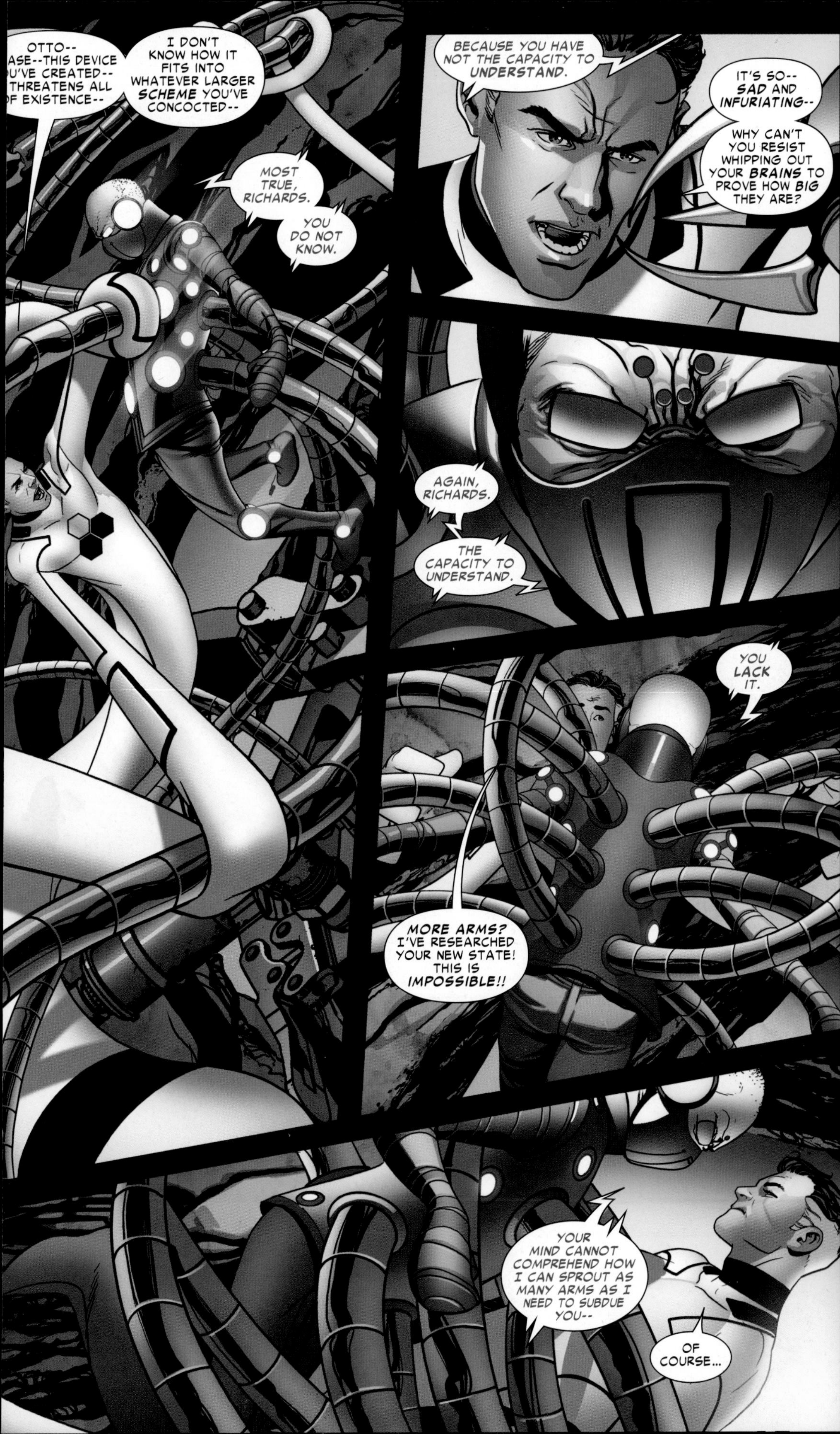
OTTO--
...ASE--THIS DEVICE ...U'VE CREATED-- THREATENS ALL ...OF EXISTENCE--
I DON'T KNOW HOW IT FITS INTO WHATEVER LARGER SCHEME YOU'VE CONCOCTED--
MOST TRUE, RICHARDS.
YOU DO NOT KNOW.
BECAUSE YOU HAVE NOT THE CAPACITY TO UNDERSTAND.
IT'S SO-- SAD AND INFURIATING--
WHY CAN'T YOU RESIST WHIPPING OUT YOUR BRAINS TO PROVE HOW BIG THEY ARE?
AGAIN, RICHARDS.
THE CAPACITY TO UNDERSTAND.
YOU LACK IT.
MORE ARMS? I'VE RESEARCHED YOUR NEW STATE! THIS IS IMPOSSIBLE!!
YOUR MIND CANNOT COMPREHEND HOW I CAN SPROUT AS MANY ARMS AS I NEED TO SUBDUE YOU--
OF COURSE...

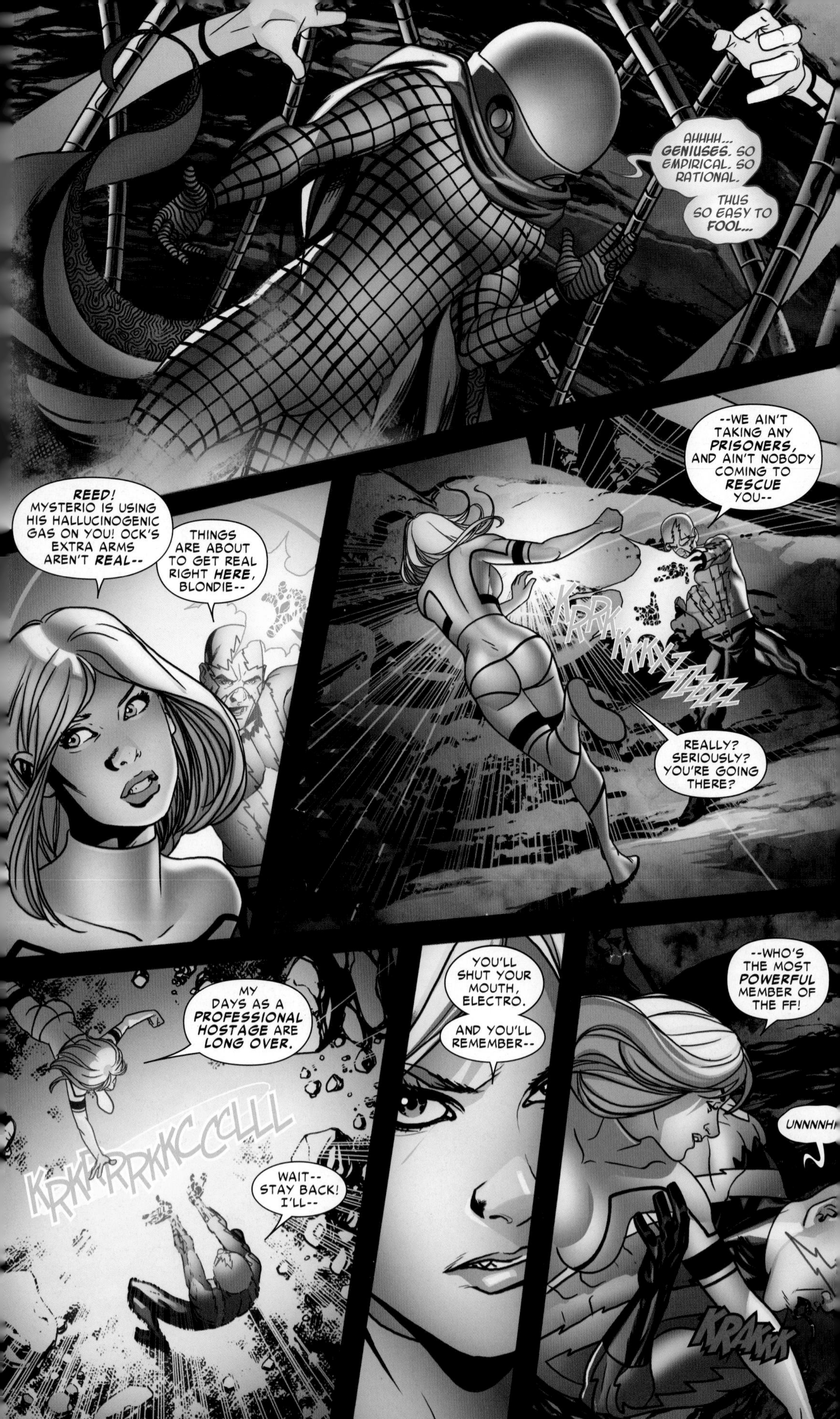
AHHHH... GENIUSES. SO EMPIRICAL. SO RATIONAL.
THUS SO EASY TO FOOL...
REED! MYSTERIO IS USING HIS HALLUCINOGENIC GAS ON YOU! OCK'S EXTRA ARMS AREN'T REAL--
THINGS ARE ABOUT TO GET REAL RIGHT HERE, BLONDIE--
--WE AIN'T TAKING ANY PRISONERS, AND AIN'T NOBODY COMING TO RESCUE YOU--
KRRK KKKXZZZZZZ
REALLY? SERIOUSLY? YOU'RE GOING THERE?
MY DAYS AS A PROFESSIONAL HOSTAGE ARE LONG OVER.
KRKRRRKKCCCLLL
WAIT-- STAY BACK! I'LL--
YOU'LL SHUT YOUR MOUTH, ELECTRO.
AND YOU'LL REMEMBER--
--WHO'S THE MOST POWERFUL MEMBER OF THE FF!
UNNNNH!
KRAKKK

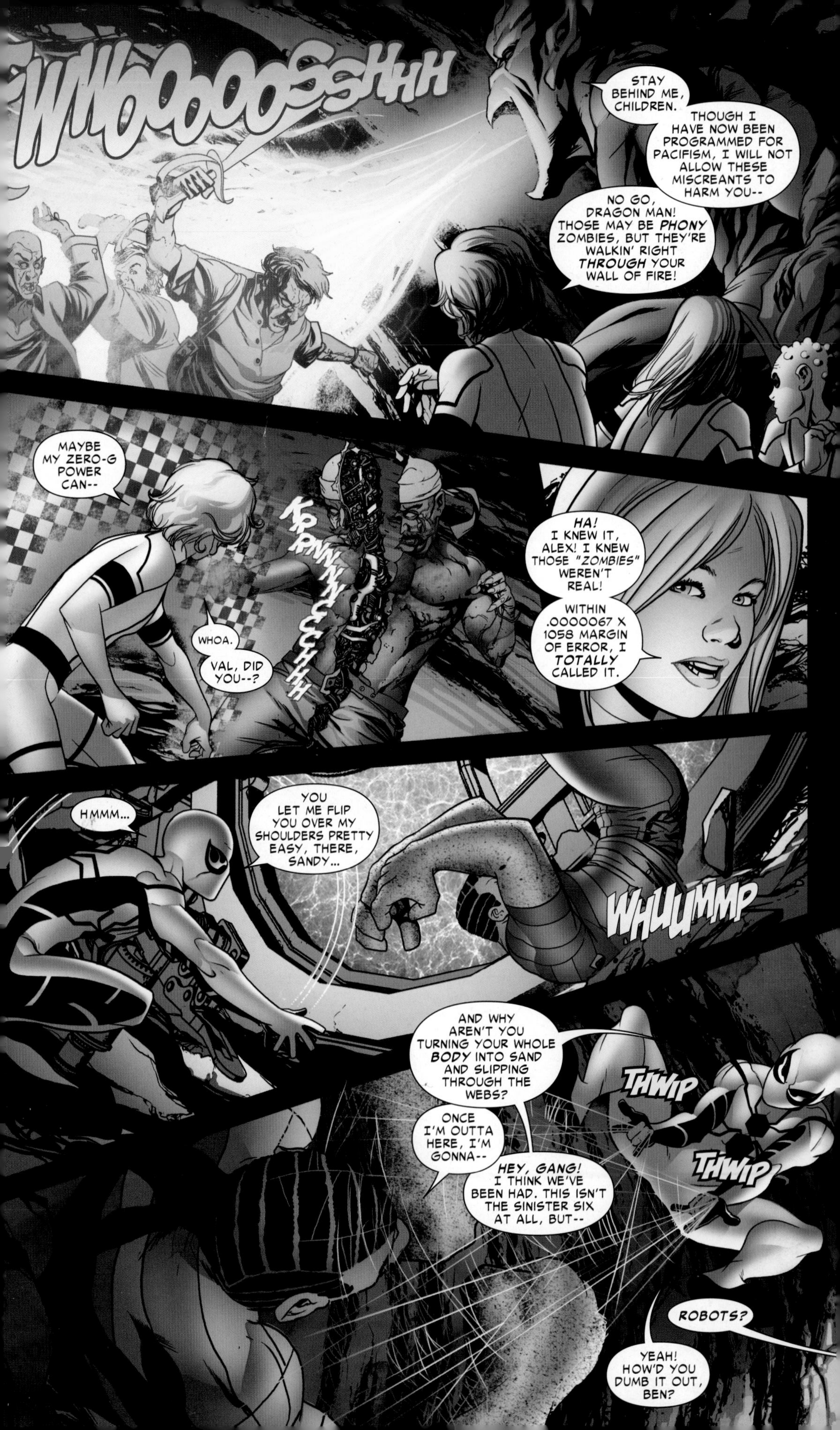
WHOOOOOSSHHH
STAY BEHIND ME, CHILDREN.
THOUGH I HAVE NOW BEEN PROGRAMMED FOR PACIFISM, I WILL NOT ALLOW THESE MISCREANTS TO HARM YOU--
NO GO, DRAGON MAN! THOSE MAY BE PHONY ZOMBIES, BUT THEY'RE WALKIN' RIGHT THROUGH YOUR WALL OF FIRE!
MAYBE MY ZERO-G POWER CAN--
KRRNNNNGGCHHH
WHOA.
VAL, DID YOU--?
HA! I KNEW IT, ALEX! I KNEW THOSE "ZOMBIES" WEREN'T REAL!
WITHIN .0000067 X 1058 MARGIN OF ERROR, I TOTALLY CALLED IT.
HMMM...
YOU LET ME FLIP YOU OVER MY SHOULDERS PRETTY EASY, THERE, SANDY...
WHUUMMP
AND WHY AREN'T YOU TURNING YOUR WHOLE BODY INTO SAND AND SLIPPING THROUGH THE WEBS?
ONCE I'M OUTTA HERE, I'M GONNA--
THWIP
THWIP
HEY, GANG! I THINK WE'VE BEEN HAD. THIS ISN'T THE SINISTER SIX AT ALL, BUT--
ROBOTS?
YEAH! HOW'D YOU DUMB IT OUT, BEN?

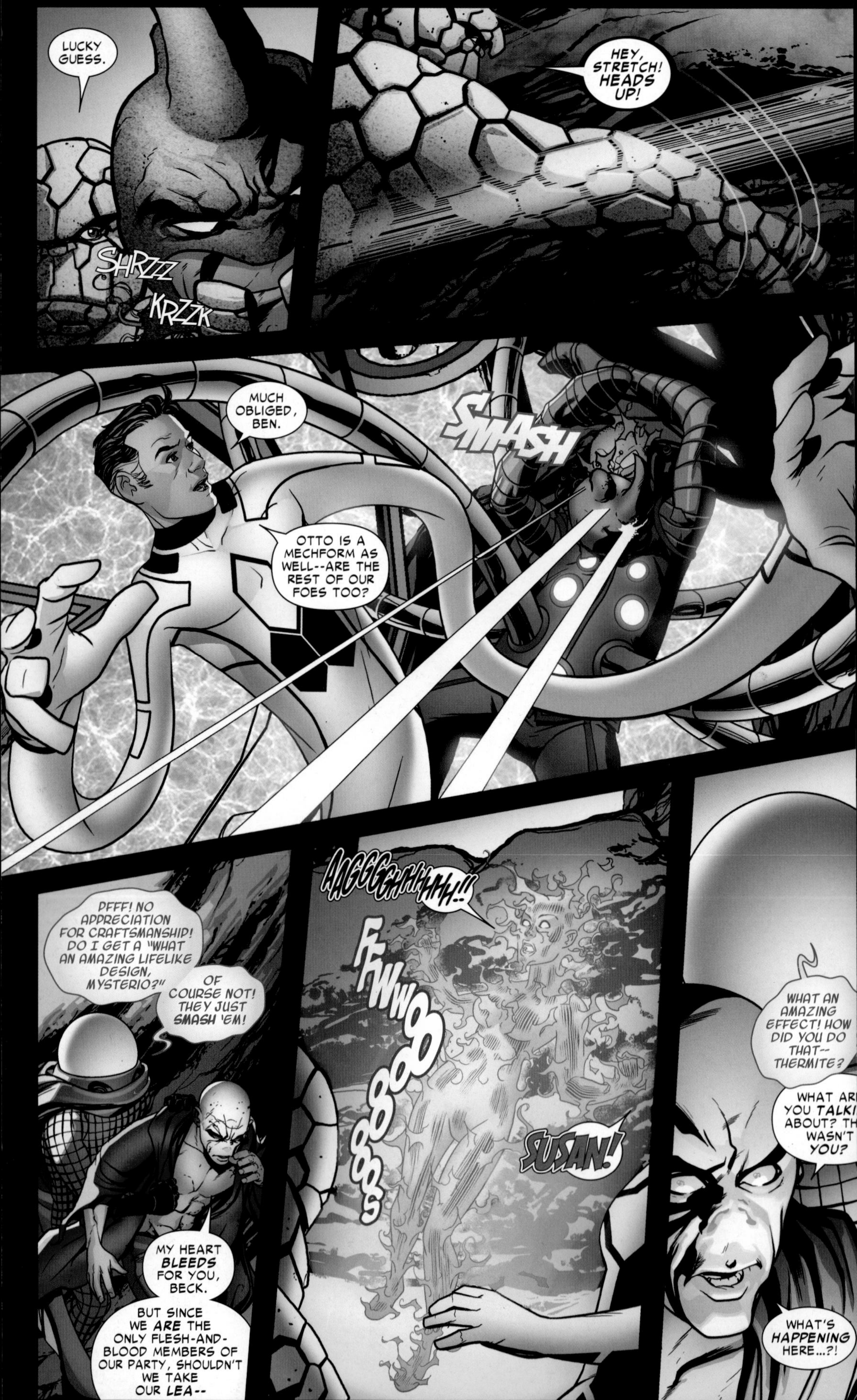
LUCKY GUESS.
HEY, STRETCH! HEADS UP!
SHRZZZ
KRZZK
MUCH OBLIGED, BEN.
SMASH
OTTO IS A MECHFORM AS WELL--ARE THE REST OF OUR FOES TOO?
PFFF! NO APPRECIATION FOR CRAFTSMANSHIP! DO I GET A "WHAT AN AMAZING LIFELIKE DESIGN, MYSTERIO?"
OF COURSE NOT! THEY JUST SMASH 'EM!
MY HEART BLEEDS FOR YOU, BECK.
BUT SINCE WE ARE THE ONLY FLESH-AND-BLOOD MEMBERS OF OUR PARTY, SHOULDN'T WE TAKE OUR LEA--
AAGGGGHHHHHH!!
FFWWOOOOOOOOOS
SUSAN!
WHAT AN AMAZING EFFECT! HOW DID YOU DO THAT--THERMITE?
WHAT'S HAPPENING HERE...?!

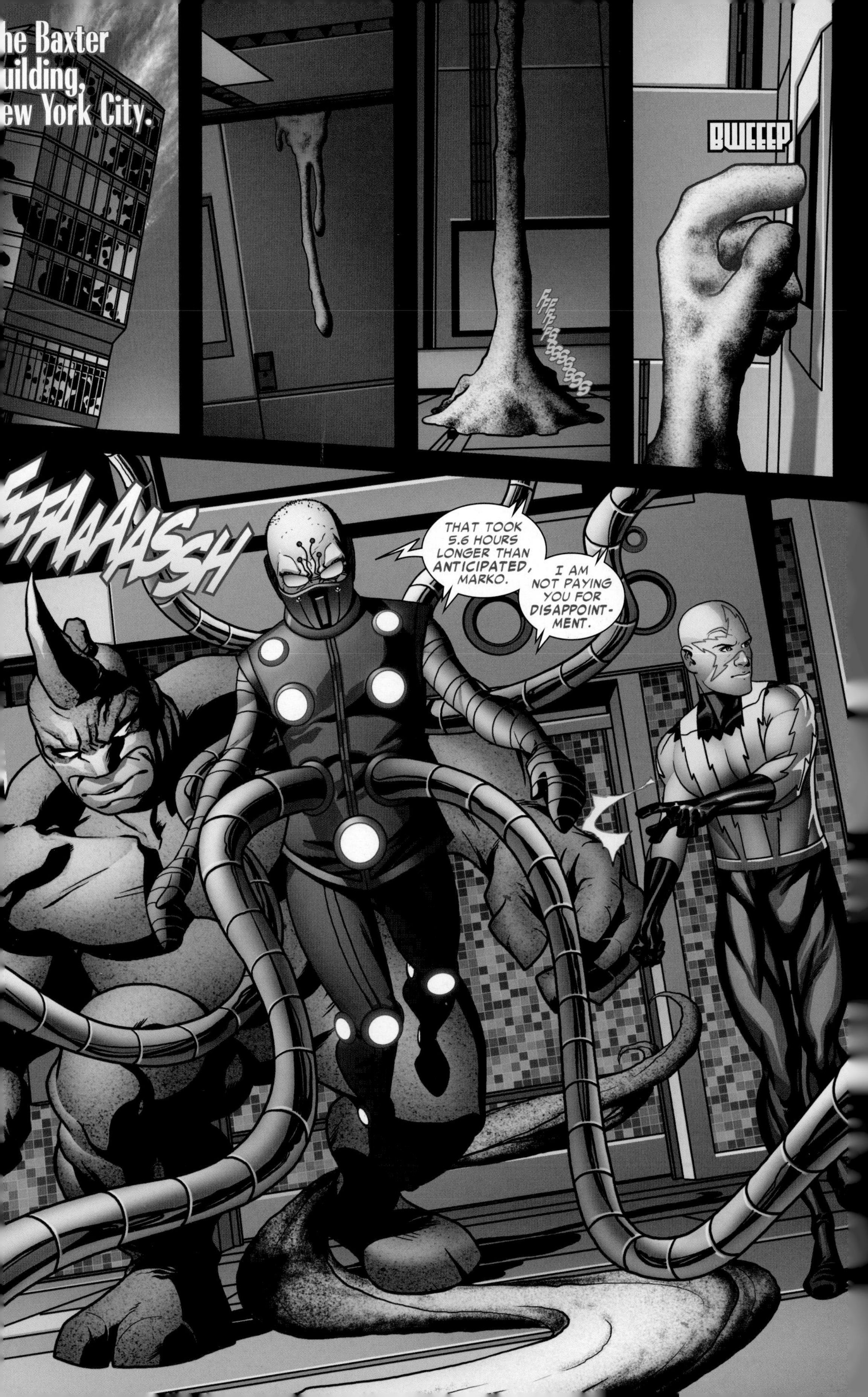
he Baxter
uilding,
ew York City.
BWEEEP
EFAAAASSH
THAT TOOK 5.6 HOURS LONGER THAN ANTICIPATED, MARKO.
I AM NOT PAYING YOU FOR DISAPPOINT-MENT.

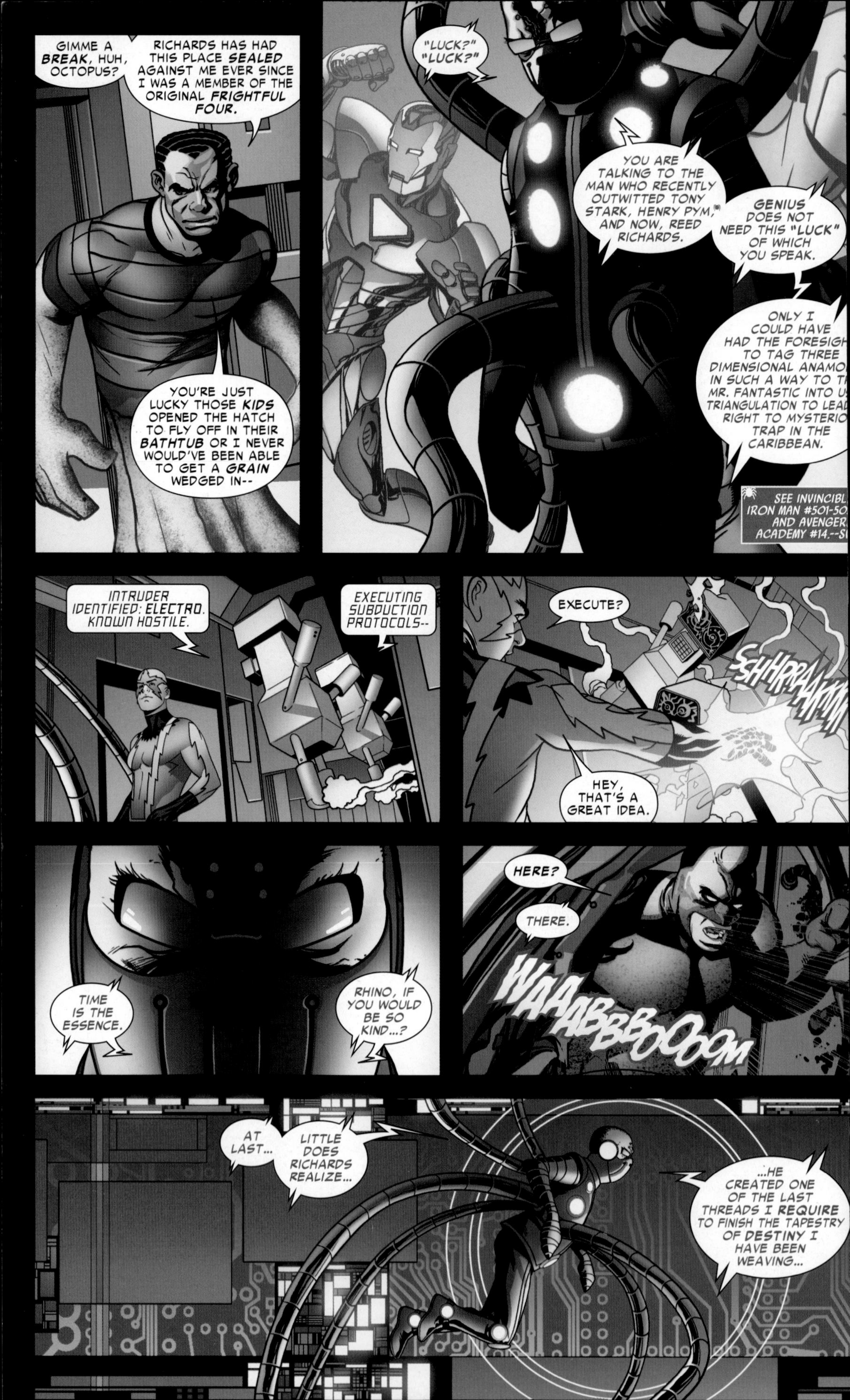

GIMME A BREAK, HUH, OCTOPUS?
RICHARDS HAS HAD THIS PLACE SEALED AGAINST ME EVER SINCE I WAS A MEMBER OF THE ORIGINAL FRIGHTFUL FOUR.
YOU'RE JUST LUCKY THOSE KIDS OPENED THE HATCH TO FLY OFF IN THEIR BATHTUB OR I NEVER WOULD'VE BEEN ABLE TO GET A GRAIN WEDGED IN--
"LUCK?" "LUCK?"
YOU ARE TALKING TO THE MAN WHO RECENTLY OUTWITTED TONY STARK, HENRY PYM,* AND NOW, REED RICHARDS.
GENIUS DOES NOT NEED THIS "LUCK" OF WHICH YOU SPEAK.
ONLY I COULD HAVE HAD THE FORESIGH TO TAG THREE DIMENSIONAL ANAMO IN SUCH A WAY TO T MR. FANTASTIC INTO U TRIANGULATION TO LEAD RIGHT TO MYSTERIO TRAP IN THE CARIBBEAN.
SEE INVINCIBL IRON MAN #501-50 AND AVENGER ACADEMY #14.--S
INTRUDER IDENTIFIED: ELECTRO. KNOWN HOSTILE.
EXECUTING SUBDUCTION PROTOCOLS--
EXECUTE?
SHHRRAKK
HEY, THAT'S A GREAT IDEA.
TIME IS THE ESSENCE.
RHINO, IF YOU WOULD BE SO KIND...?
HERE?
THERE.
WAAABBBOOOOM
AT LAST...
LITTLE DOES RICHARDS REALIZE...
...HE CREATED ONE OF THE LAST THREADS I REQUIRE TO FINISH THE TAPESTRY OF DESTINY I HAVE BEEN WEAVING...

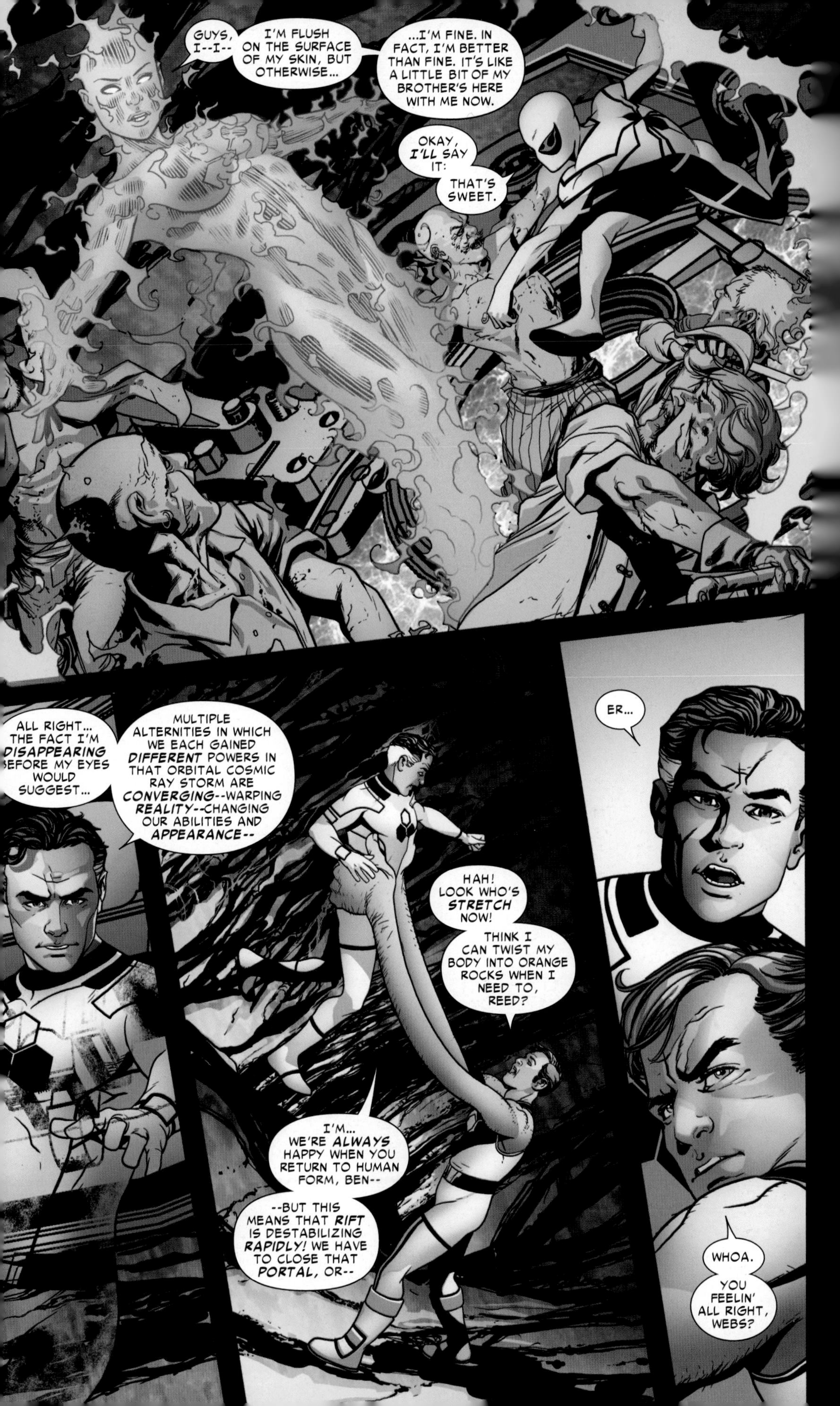
GUYS, I--I--
I'M FLUSH ON THE SURFACE OF MY SKIN, BUT OTHERWISE...
...I'M FINE. IN FACT, I'M BETTER THAN FINE. IT'S LIKE A LITTLE BIT OF MY BROTHER'S HERE WITH ME NOW.
OKAY, I'LL SAY IT:
THAT'S SWEET.
ALL RIGHT... THE FACT I'M DISAPPEARING BEFORE MY EYES WOULD SUGGEST...
MULTIPLE ALTERNITIES IN WHICH WE EACH GAINED DIFFERENT POWERS IN THAT ORBITAL COSMIC RAY STORM ARE CONVERGING--WARPING REALITY--CHANGING OUR ABILITIES AND APPEARANCE--
HAH! LOOK WHO'S STRETCH NOW!
THINK I CAN TWIST MY BODY INTO ORANGE ROCKS WHEN I NEED TO, REED?
I'M... WE'RE ALWAYS HAPPY WHEN YOU RETURN TO HUMAN FORM, BEN--
--BUT THIS MEANS THAT RIFT IS DESTABILIZING RAPIDLY! WE HAVE TO CLOSE THAT PORTAL, OR--
ER...
WHOA.
YOU FEELIN' ALL RIGHT, WEBS?

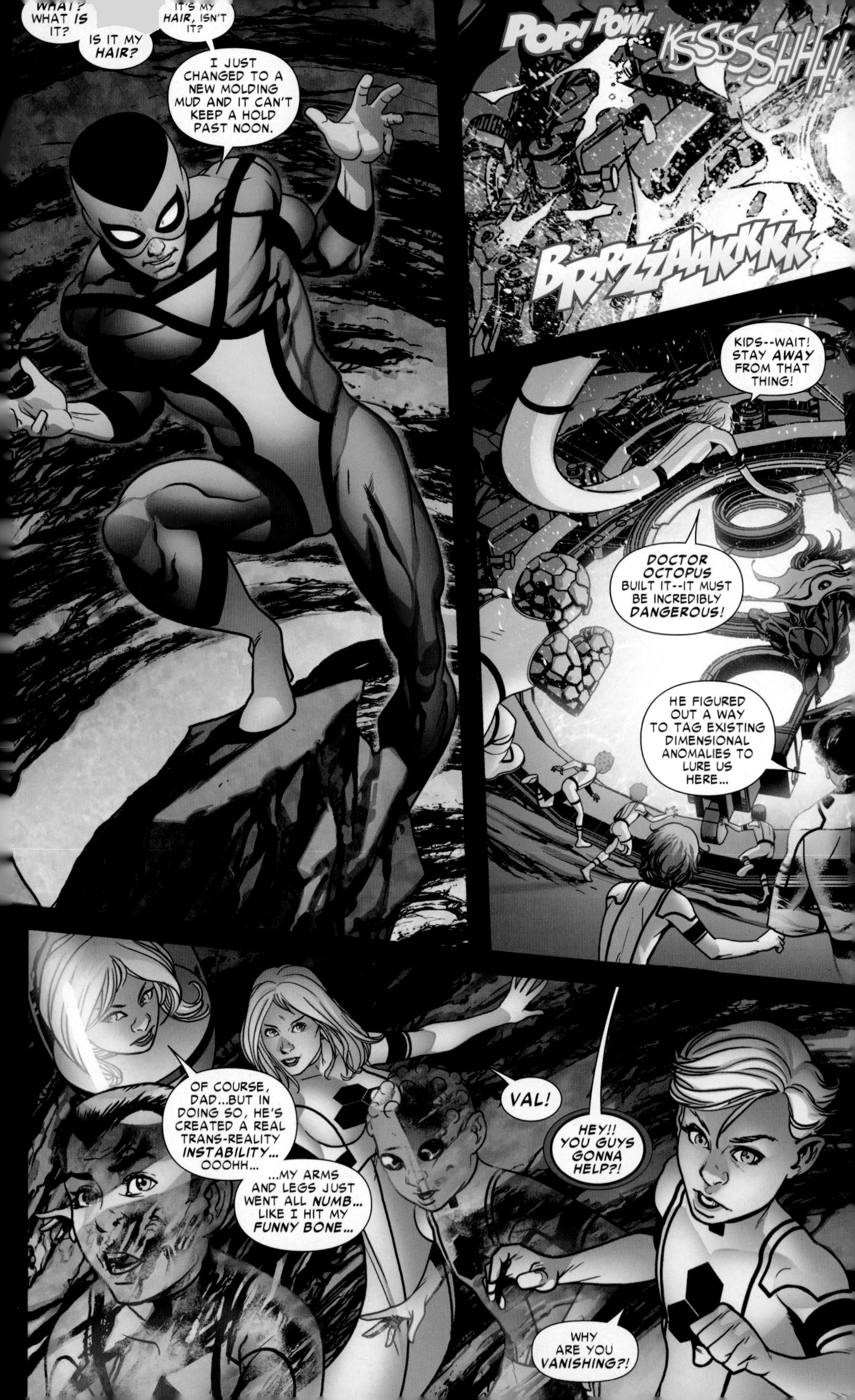
WHAT? WHAT IS IT?
IS IT MY HAIR?
IT'S MY HAIR, ISN'T IT?
I JUST CHANGED TO A NEW MOLDING MUD AND IT CAN'T KEEP A HOLD PAST NOON.
POP! POW!
KSSSSHHH!
BRRZZAAKKKK
KIDS--WAIT! STAY AWAY FROM THAT THING!
DOCTOR OCTOPUS BUILT IT--IT MUST BE INCREDIBLY DANGEROUS!
HE FIGURED OUT A WAY TO TAG EXISTING DIMENSIONAL ANOMALIES TO LURE US HERE...
OF COURSE, DAD...BUT IN DOING SO, HE'S CREATED A REAL TRANS-REALITY INSTABILITY... OOOHH...
...MY ARMS AND LEGS JUST WENT ALL NUMB... LIKE I HIT MY FUNNY BONE...
VAL!
HEY!! YOU GUYS GONNA HELP?!
WHY ARE YOU VANISHING?!

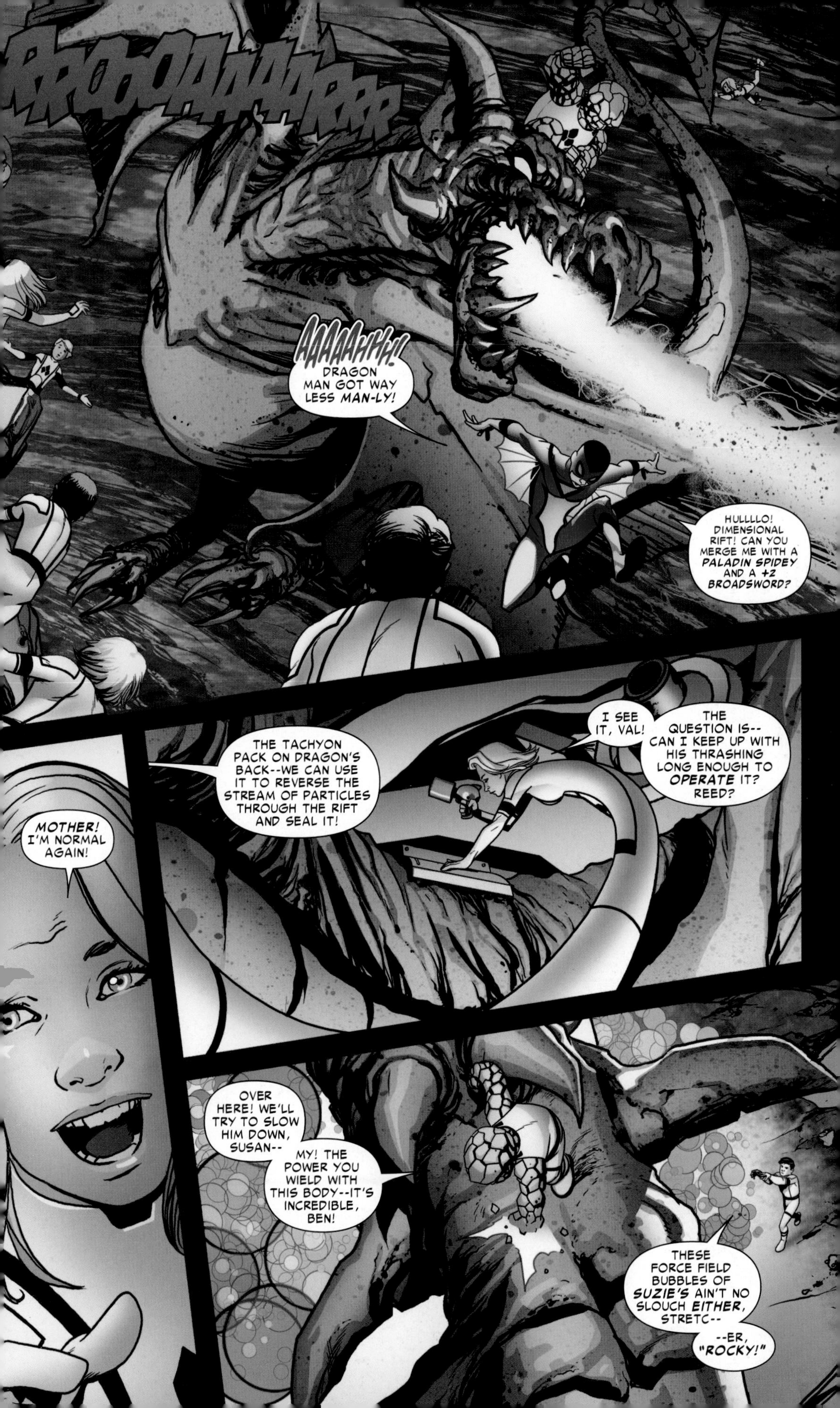
RROOAAAAARRR
AAAAAHHH! DRAGON MAN GOT WAY LESS MAN-LY!
HULLLLO! DIMENSIONAL RIFT! CAN YOU MERGE ME WITH A PALADIN SPIDEY AND A +2 BROADSWORD?
MOTHER! I'M NORMAL AGAIN!
THE TACHYON PACK ON DRAGON'S BACK--WE CAN USE IT TO REVERSE THE STREAM OF PARTICLES THROUGH THE RIFT AND SEAL IT!
I SEE IT, VAL!
THE QUESTION IS-- CAN I KEEP UP WITH HIS THRASHING LONG ENOUGH TO OPERATE IT? REED?
OVER HERE! WE'LL TRY TO SLOW HIM DOWN, SUSAN--
MY! THE POWER YOU WIELD WITH THIS BODY--IT'S INCREDIBLE, BEN!
THESE FORCE FIELD BUBBLES OF SUZIE'S AIN'T NO SLOUCH EITHER, STRETC--
--ER, "ROCKY!"

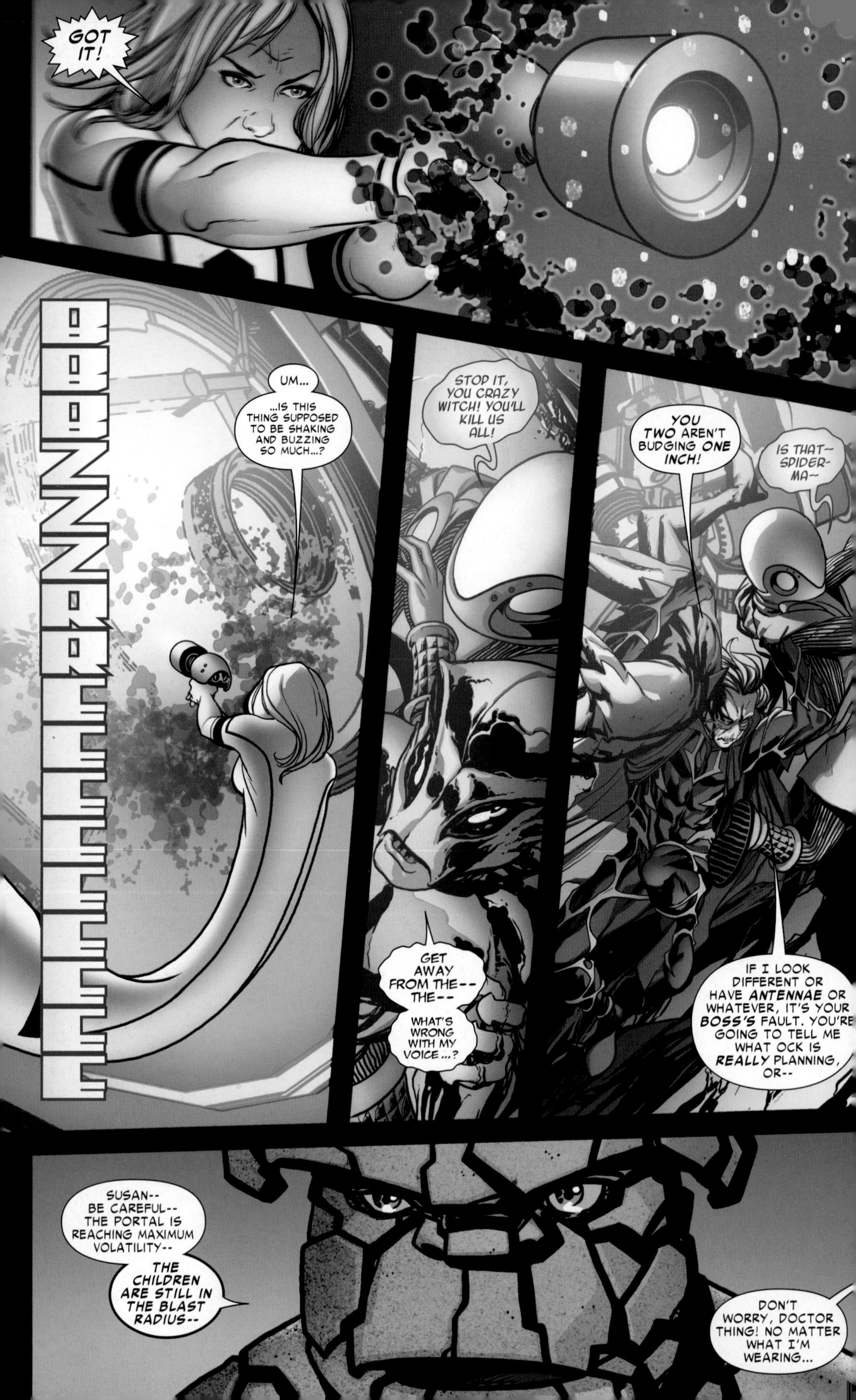

GOT IT!
BBZZZZZZTTTTT!!!
UM...
...IS THIS THING SUPPOSED TO BE SHAKING AND BUZZING SO MUCH...?
STOP IT, YOU CRAZY WITCH! YOU'LL KILL US ALL!
GET AWAY FROM THE-- THE--
WHAT'S WRONG WITH MY VOICE...?
YOU TWO AREN'T BUDGING ONE INCH!
IS THAT-- SPIDER-MA--
IF I LOOK DIFFERENT OR HAVE ANTENNAE OR WHATEVER, IT'S YOUR BOSS'S FAULT. YOU'RE GOING TO TELL ME WHAT OCK IS REALLY PLANNING, OR--
SUSAN-- BE CAREFUL-- THE PORTAL IS REACHING MAXIMUM VOLATILITY--
THE CHILDREN ARE STILL IN THE BLAST RADIUS--
DON'T WORRY, DOCTOR THING! NO MATTER WHAT I'M WEARING...

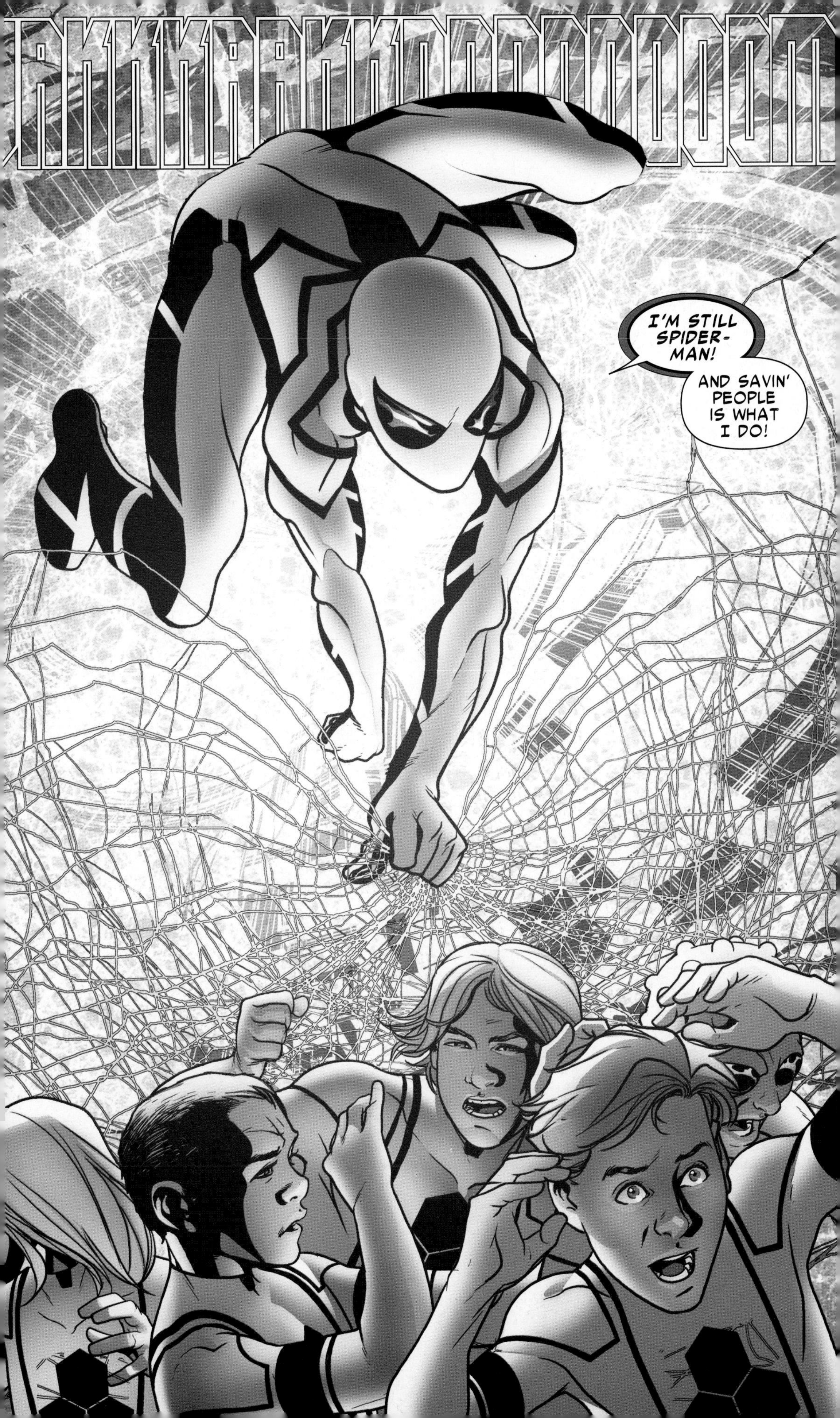
I'M STILL SPIDER-MAN!
AND SAVIN' PEOPLE IS WHAT I DO!

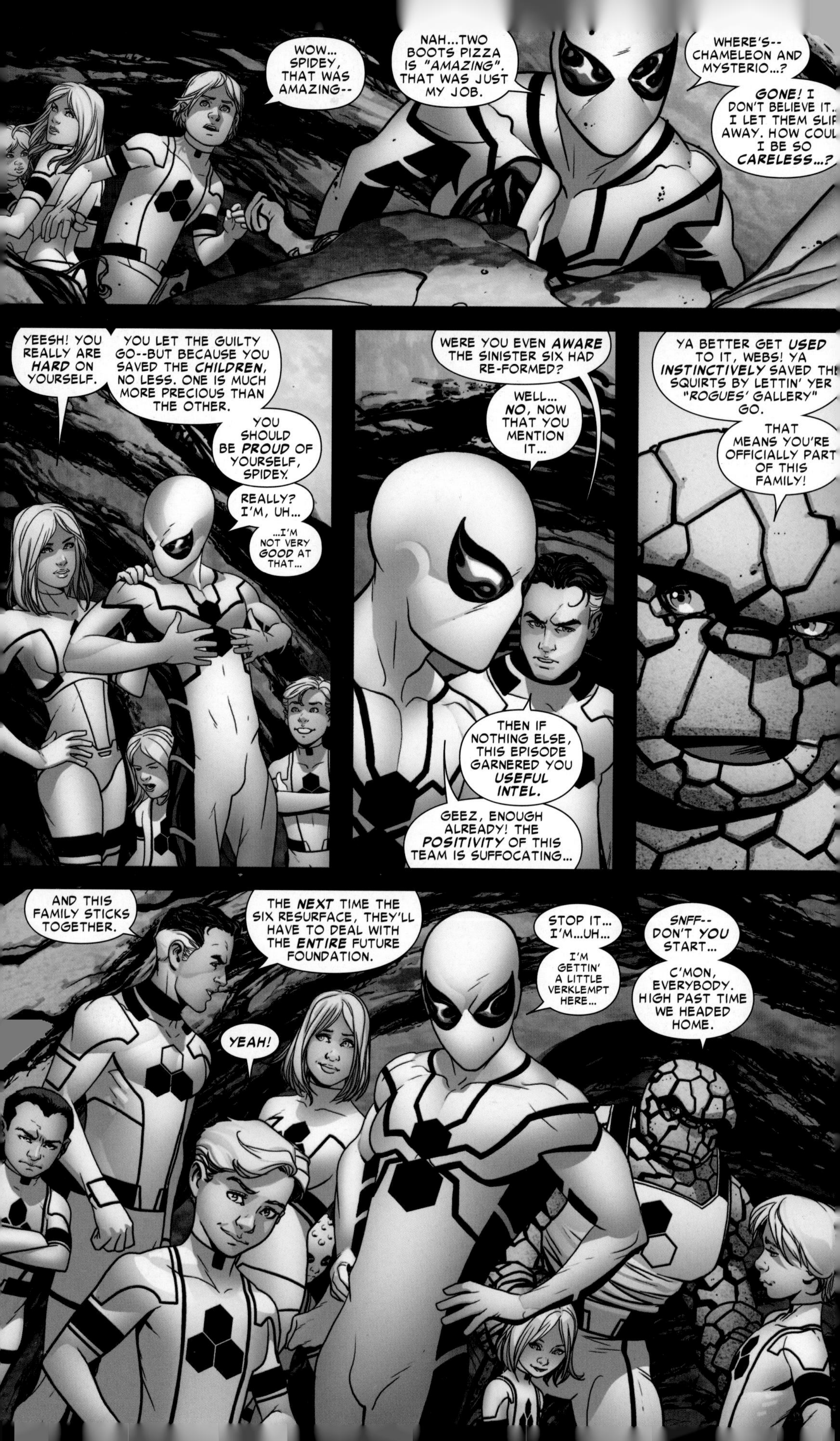
WOW... SPIDEY, THAT WAS AMAZING--
NAH...TWO BOOTS PIZZA IS "AMAZING". THAT WAS JUST MY JOB.
WHERE'S-- CHAMELEON AND MYSTERIO...?
GONE! I DON'T BELIEVE IT... I LET THEM SLIP AWAY. HOW COULD I BE SO CARELESS...?
YEESH! YOU REALLY ARE HARD ON YOURSELF.
YOU LET THE GUILTY GO--BUT BECAUSE YOU SAVED THE CHILDREN, NO LESS. ONE IS MUCH MORE PRECIOUS THAN THE OTHER.
YOU SHOULD BE PROUD OF YOURSELF, SPIDEY.
REALLY? I'M, UH...
...I'M NOT VERY GOOD AT THAT...
WERE YOU EVEN AWARE THE SINISTER SIX HAD RE-FORMED?
WELL... NO, NOW THAT YOU MENTION IT...
THEN IF NOTHING ELSE, THIS EPISODE GARNERED YOU USEFUL INTEL.
GEEZ, ENOUGH ALREADY! THE POSITIVITY OF THIS TEAM IS SUFFOCATING...
YA BETTER GET USED TO IT, WEBS! YA INSTINCTIVELY SAVED THE SQUIRTS BY LETTIN' YER "ROGUES' GALLERY" GO.
THAT MEANS YOU'RE OFFICIALLY PART OF THIS FAMILY!
AND THIS FAMILY STICKS TOGETHER.
THE NEXT TIME THE SIX RESURFACE, THEY'LL HAVE TO DEAL WITH THE ENTIRE FUTURE FOUNDATION.
YEAH!
STOP IT... I'M...UH...
I'M GETTIN' A LITTLE VERKLEMPT HERE...
SNFF-- DON'T YOU START...
C'MON, EVERYBODY. HIGH PAST TIME WE HEADED HOME.

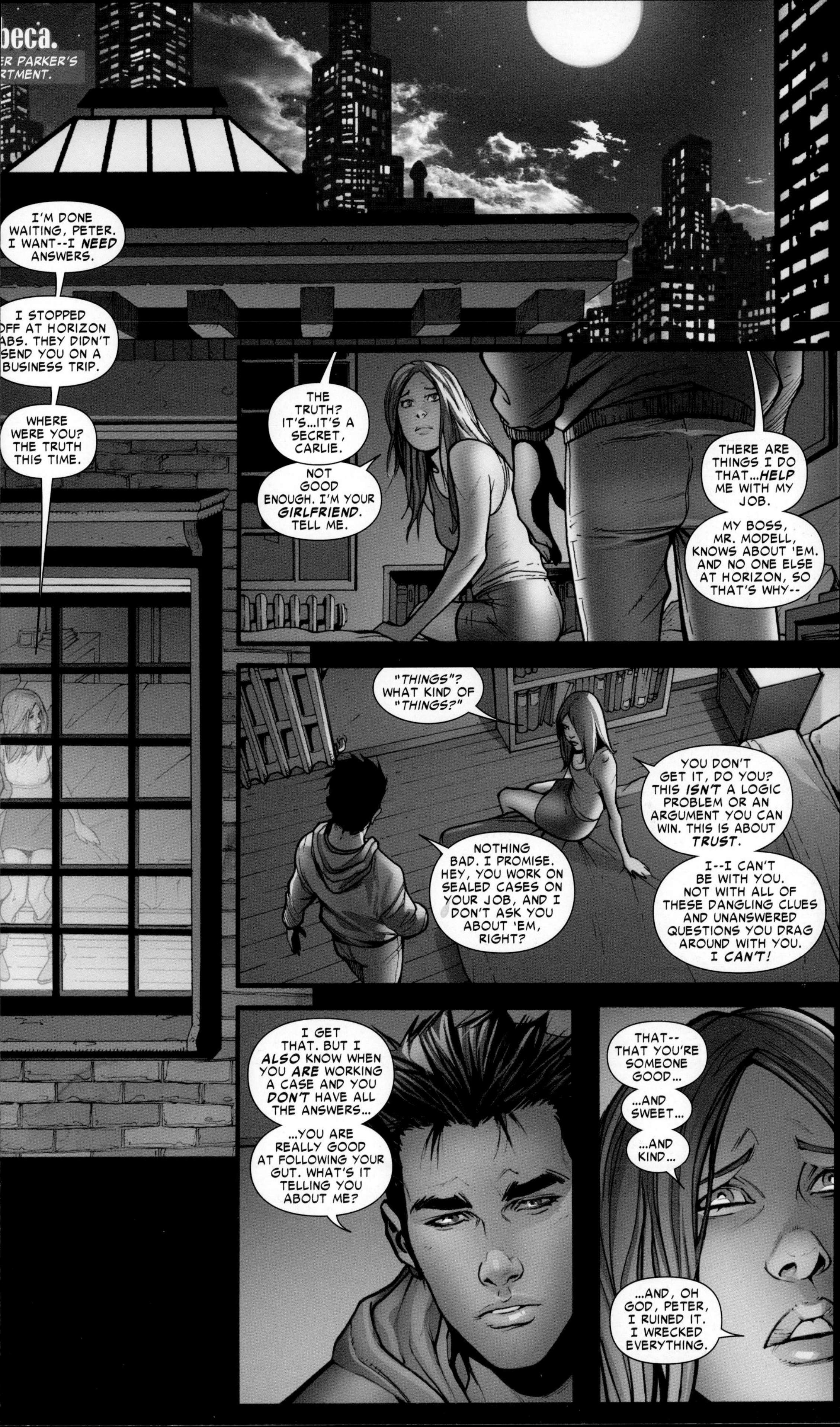

...beca.
...ER PARKER'S ...RTMENT.
I'M DONE WAITING, PETER. I WANT--I NEED ANSWERS.
I STOPPED ...FF AT HORIZON ...ABS. THEY DIDN'T SEND YOU ON A BUSINESS TRIP.
WHERE WERE YOU? THE TRUTH THIS TIME.
THE TRUTH? IT'S...IT'S A SECRET, CARLIE.
NOT GOOD ENOUGH. I'M YOUR GIRLFRIEND. TELL ME.
THERE ARE THINGS I DO THAT...HELP ME WITH MY JOB.
MY BOSS, MR. MODELL, KNOWS ABOUT 'EM. AND NO ONE ELSE AT HORIZON, SO THAT'S WHY--
"THINGS"? WHAT KIND OF "THINGS?"
NOTHING BAD. I PROMISE. HEY, YOU WORK ON SEALED CASES ON YOUR JOB, AND I DON'T ASK YOU ABOUT 'EM, RIGHT?
YOU DON'T GET IT, DO YOU? THIS ISN'T A LOGIC PROBLEM OR AN ARGUMENT YOU CAN WIN. THIS IS ABOUT TRUST.
I--I CAN'T BE WITH YOU. NOT WITH ALL OF THESE DANGLING CLUES AND UNANSWERED QUESTIONS YOU DRAG AROUND WITH YOU. I CAN'T!
I GET THAT. BUT I ALSO KNOW WHEN YOU ARE WORKING A CASE AND YOU DON'T HAVE ALL THE ANSWERS...
...YOU ARE REALLY GOOD AT FOLLOWING YOUR GUT. WHAT'S IT TELLING YOU ABOUT ME?
THAT-- THAT YOU'RE SOMEONE GOOD...
...AND SWEET...
...AND KIND...
...AND, OH GOD, PETER, I RUINED IT. I WRECKED EVERYTHING.

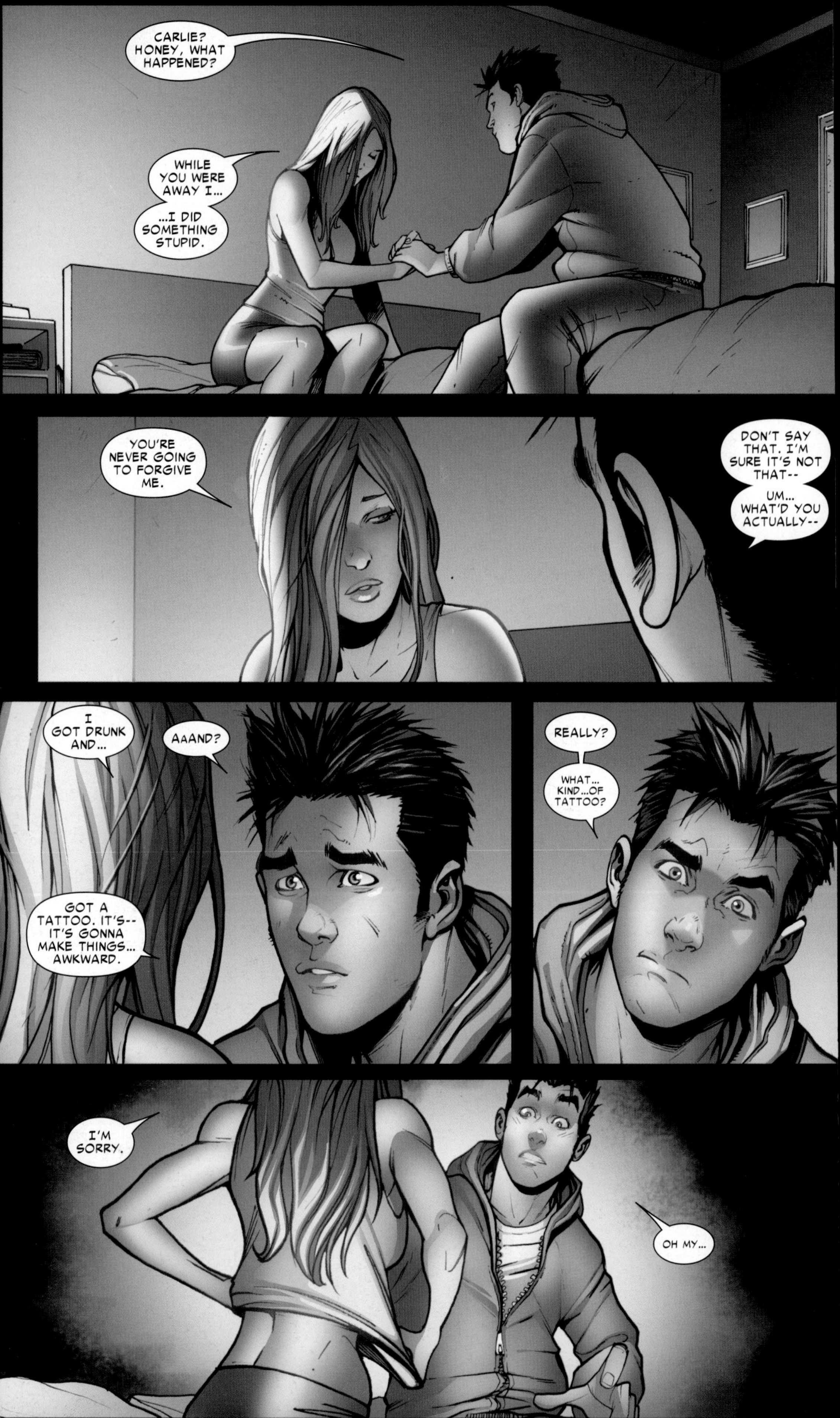
CARLIE? HONEY, WHAT HAPPENED?
WHILE YOU WERE AWAY I...
...I DID SOMETHING STUPID.
YOU'RE NEVER GOING TO FORGIVE ME.
DON'T SAY THAT. I'M SURE IT'S NOT THAT--
UM... WHAT'D YOU ACTUALLY--
I GOT DRUNK AND...
AAAND?
GOT A TATTOO. IT'S-- IT'S GONNA MAKE THINGS... AWKWARD.
REALLY?
WHAT... KIND...OF TATTOO?
I'M SORRY.
OH MY...

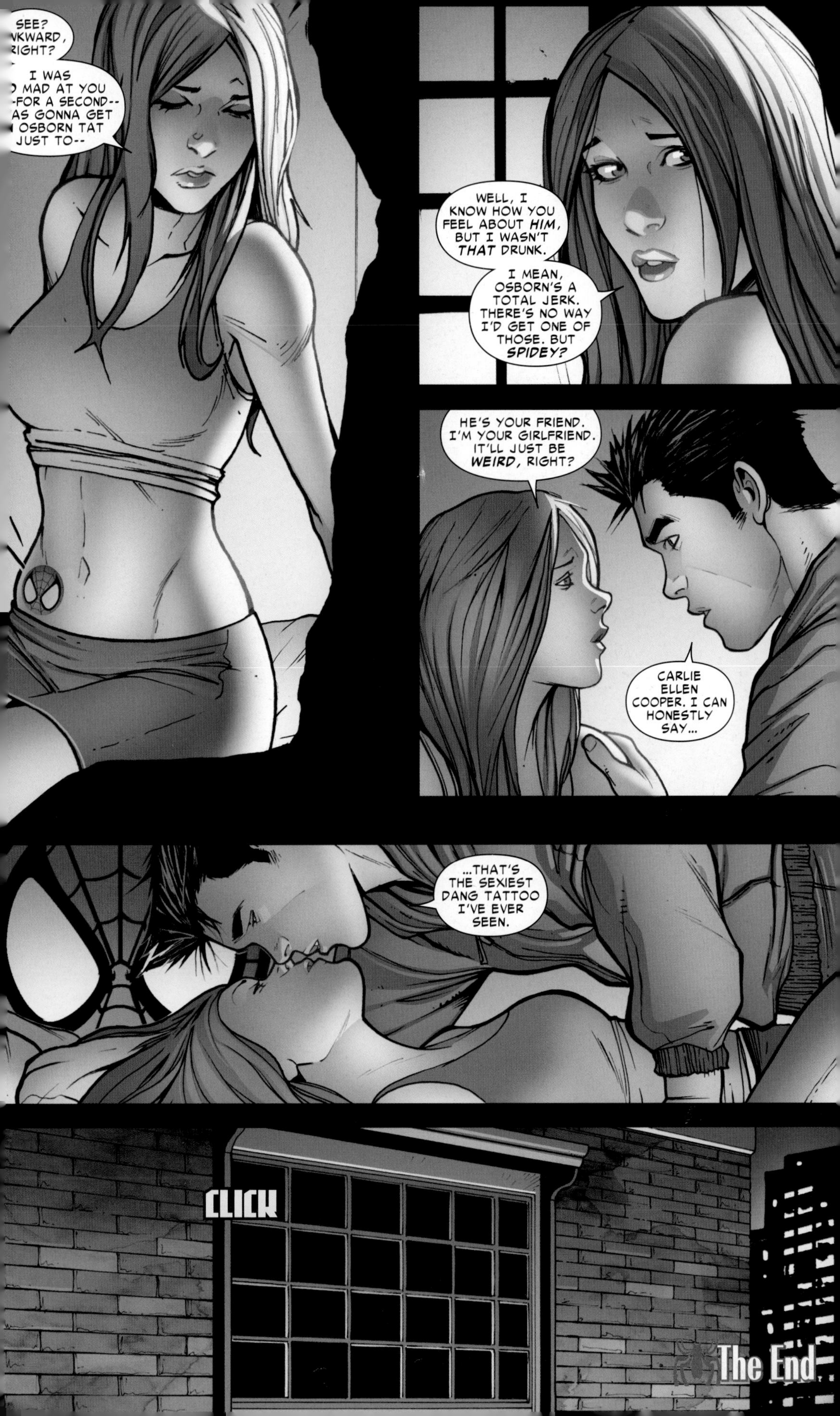
SEE? ...WKWARD, ...RIGHT?
I WAS ...D MAD AT YOU ...-FOR A SECOND-- ...AS GONNA GET ...N OSBORN TAT JUST TO--
WELL, I KNOW HOW YOU FEEL ABOUT *HIM*, BUT I WASN'T *THAT* DRUNK.
I MEAN, OSBORN'S A TOTAL JERK. THERE'S NO WAY I'D GET ONE OF THOSE. BUT *SPIDEY?*
HE'S YOUR FRIEND. I'M YOUR GIRLFRIEND. IT'LL JUST BE *WEIRD*, RIGHT?
CARLIE ELLEN COOPER. I CAN HONESTLY SAY...
...THAT'S THE SEXIEST DANG TATTOO I'VE EVER SEEN.
CLICK
The End

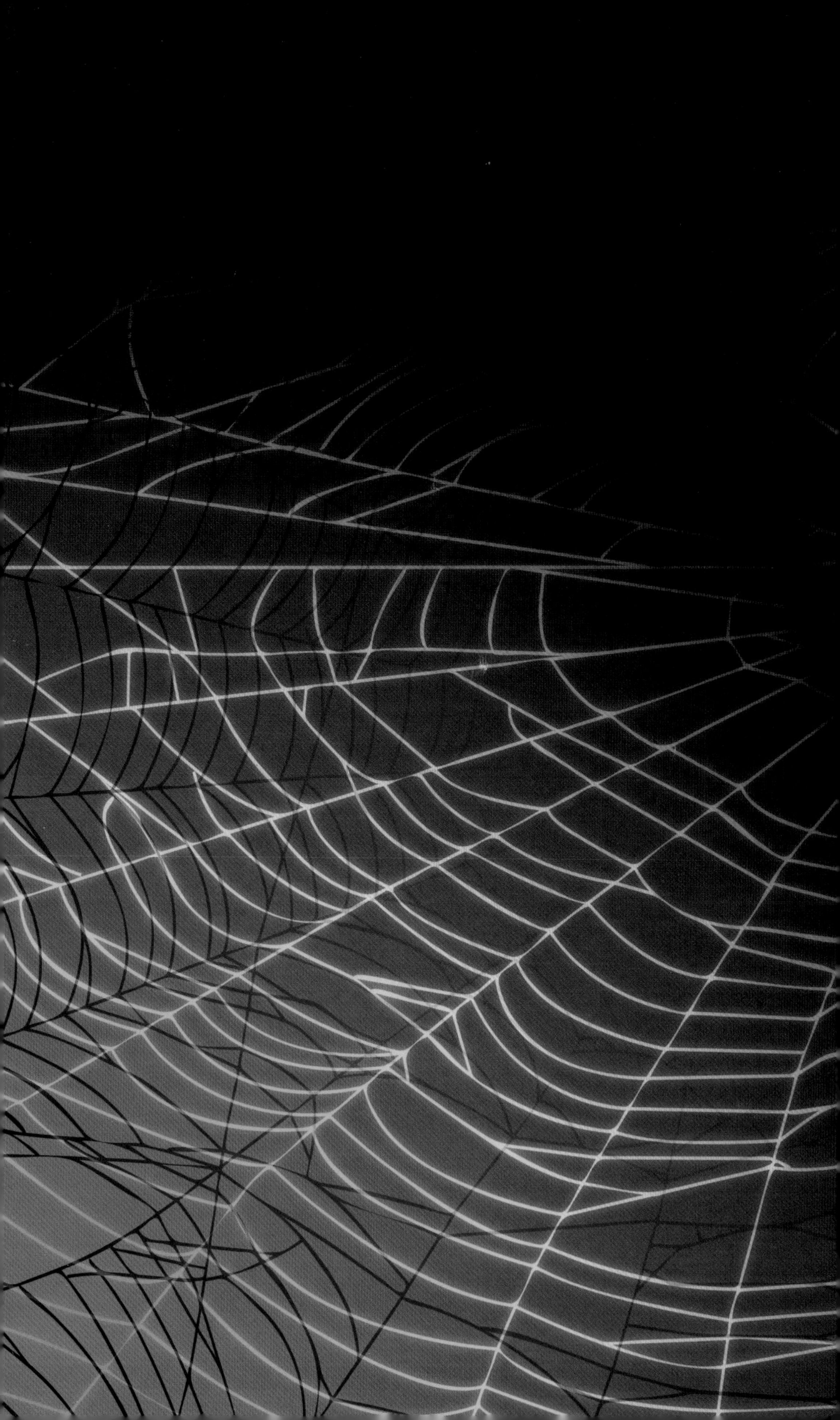

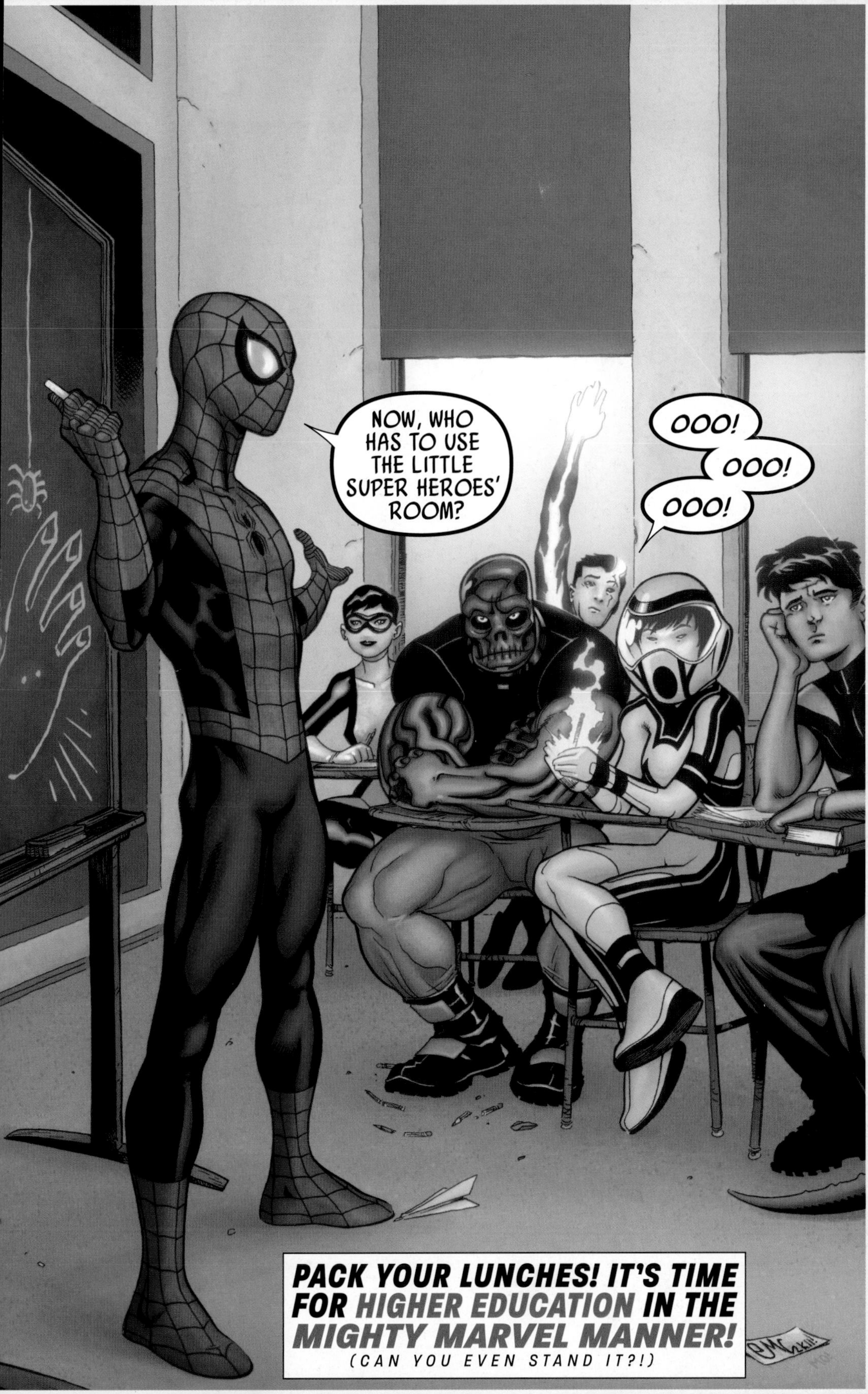
NOW, WHO HAS TO USE THE LITTLE SUPER HEROES' ROOM?
OOO!
OOO!
OOO!
PACK YOUR LUNCHES! IT'S TIME FOR HIGHER EDUCATION IN THE MIGHTY MARVEL MANNER!
(CAN YOU EVEN STAND IT?!)

AMAZING SPIDER-MAN #661
COVER BY ED MCGUINNESS & MORRY HOLLOWELL

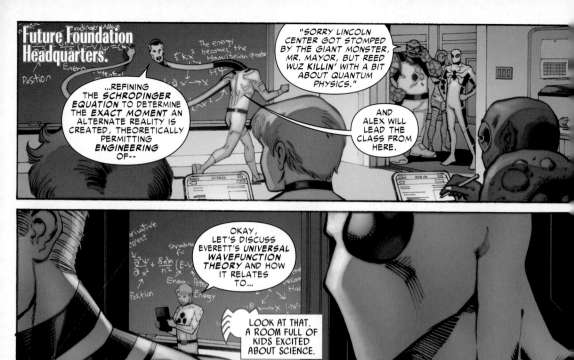

Future Foundation Headquarters.

...REFINING THE *SCHRODINGER* EQUATION TO DETERMINE THE *EXACT MOMENT* AN ALTERNATE REALITY IS CREATED, THEORETICALLY PERMITTING *ENGINEERING* OF--

"SORRY LINCOLN CENTER GOT STOMPED BY THE GIANT MONSTER, MR. MAYOR, BUT REED WUZ KILLIN' WITH A BIT ABOUT QUANTUM PHYSICS."

AND ALEX WILL LEAD THE CLASS FROM HERE.

OKAY, LET'S DISCUSS EVERETT'S *UNIVERSAL WAVEFUNCTION THEORY* AND HOW IT RELATES TO...

LOOK AT THAT. A ROOM FULL OF KIDS EXCITED ABOUT SCIENCE.

MISTER PARKER

BEEN A WHILE SINCE I SAW ONE OF THOSE.

HADN'T REALIZED HOW MUCH I MISS IT.

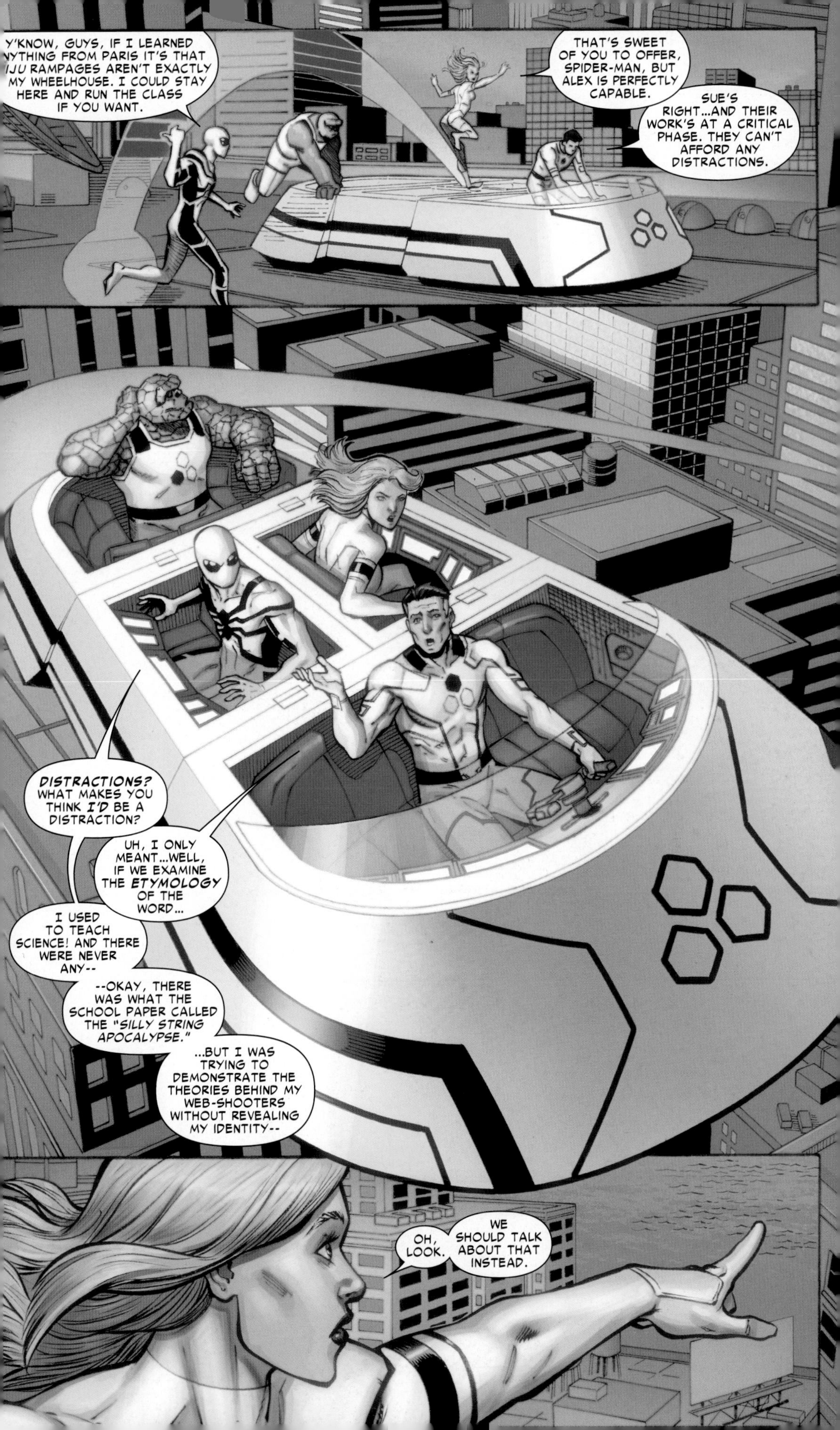

Y'KNOW, GUYS, IF I LEARNED NYTHING FROM PARIS IT'S THAT IJU RAMPAGES AREN'T EXACTLY MY WHEELHOUSE. I COULD STAY HERE AND RUN THE CLASS IF YOU WANT.
THAT'S SWEET OF YOU TO OFFER, SPIDER-MAN, BUT ALEX IS PERFECTLY CAPABLE.
SUE'S RIGHT...AND THEIR WORK'S AT A CRITICAL PHASE. THEY CAN'T AFFORD ANY DISTRACTIONS.
DISTRACTIONS? WHAT MAKES YOU THINK I'D BE A DISTRACTION?
UH, I ONLY MEANT...WELL, IF WE EXAMINE THE ETYMOLOGY OF THE WORD...
I USED TO TEACH SCIENCE! AND THERE WERE NEVER ANY--
--OKAY, THERE WAS WHAT THE SCHOOL PAPER CALLED THE "SILLY STRING APOCALYPSE."
...BUT I WAS TRYING TO DEMONSTRATE THE THEORIES BEHIND MY WEB-SHOOTERS WITHOUT REVEALING MY IDENTITY--
OH, LOOK.
WE SHOULD TALK ABOUT THAT INSTEAD.

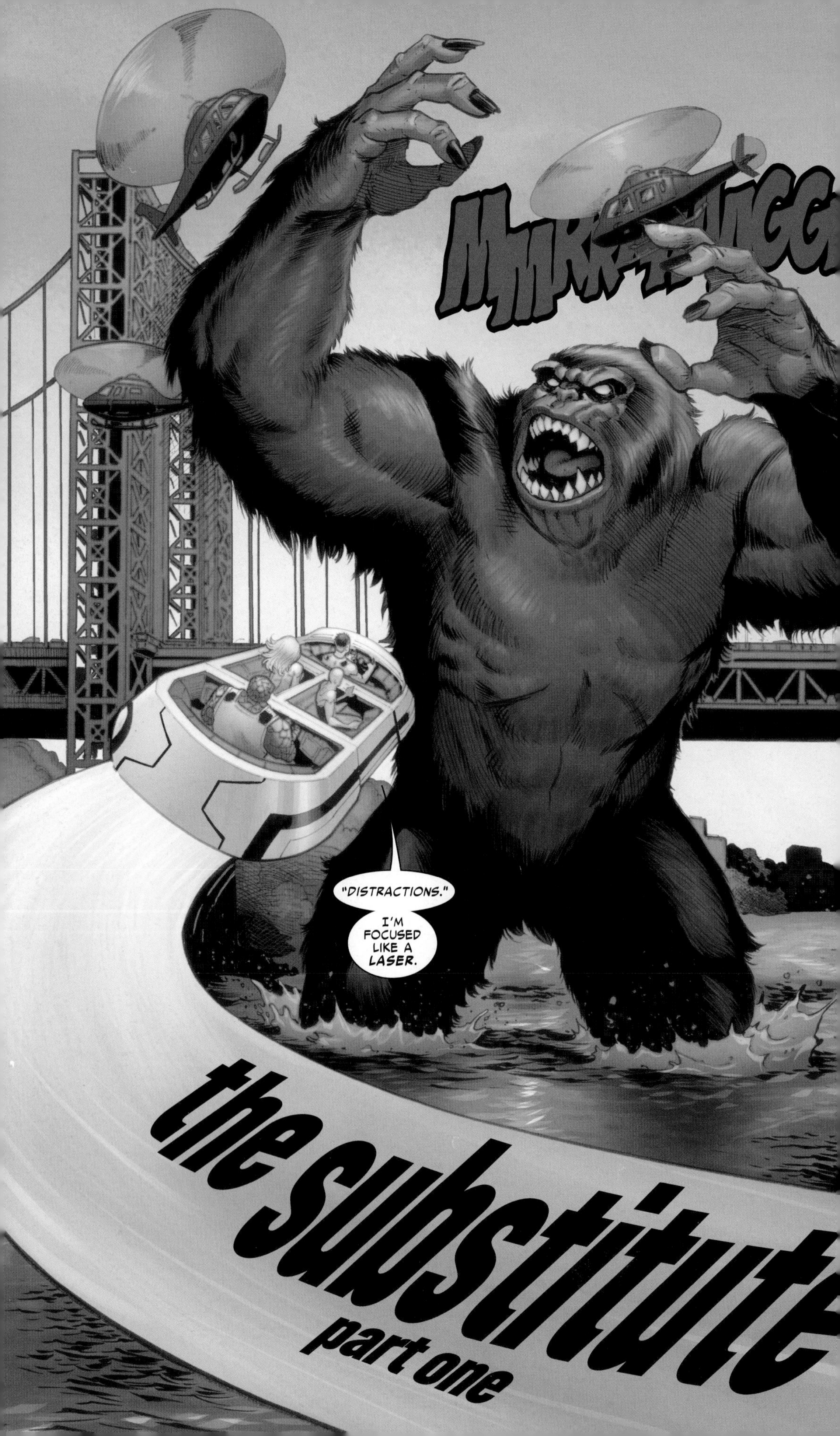
"DISTRACTIONS."
I'M FOCUSED LIKE A LASER.
the substitute
part one

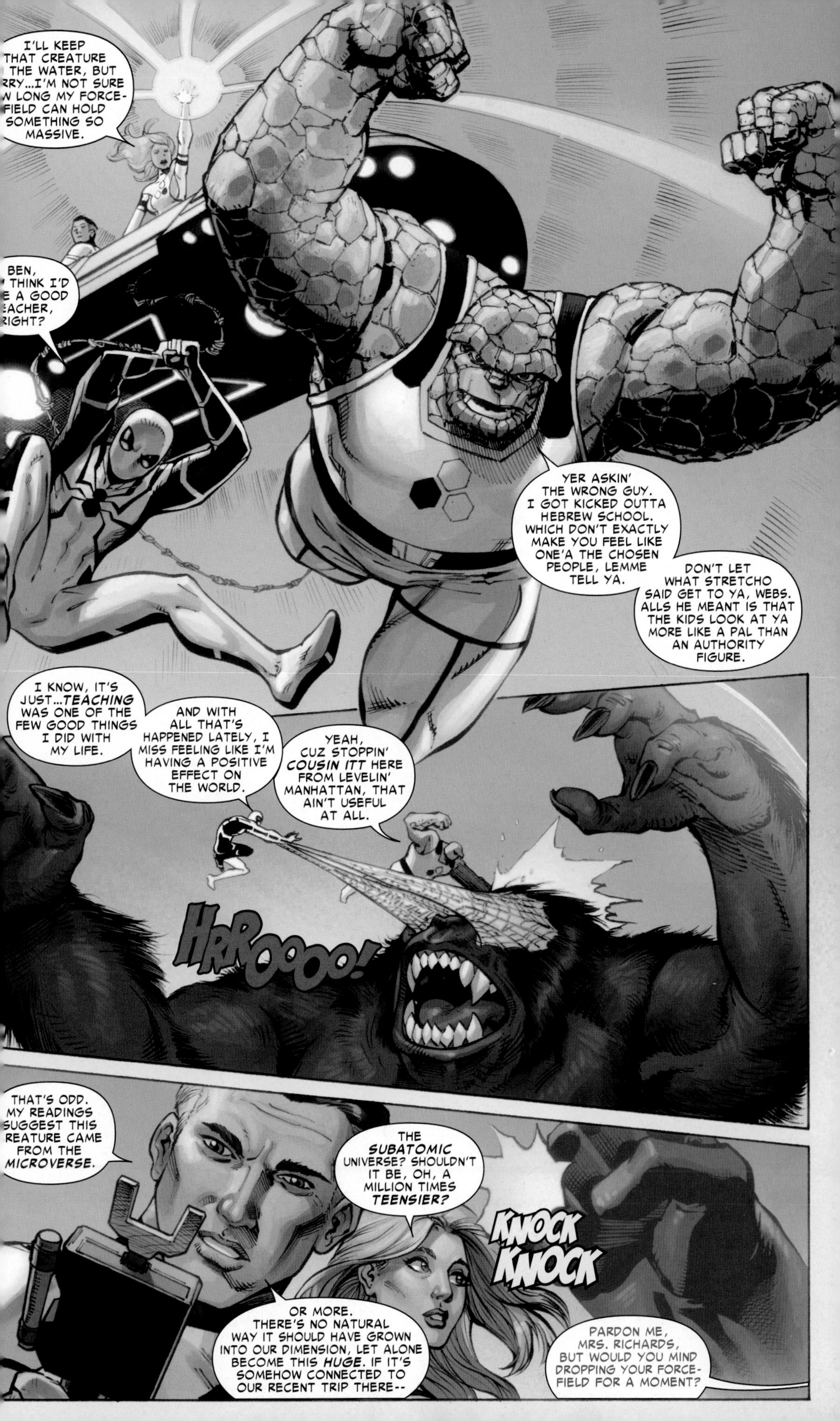
I'LL KEEP THAT CREATURE THE WATER, BUT RRY...I'M NOT SURE W LONG MY FORCE-FIELD CAN HOLD SOMETHING SO MASSIVE.
BEN, THINK I'D E A GOOD EACHER, RIGHT?
YER ASKIN' THE WRONG GUY. I GOT KICKED OUTTA HEBREW SCHOOL. WHICH DON'T EXACTLY MAKE YOU FEEL LIKE ONE'A THE CHOSEN PEOPLE, LEMME TELL YA.
DON'T LET WHAT STRETCHO SAID GET TO YA, WEBS. ALLS HE MEANT IS THAT THE KIDS LOOK AT YA MORE LIKE A PAL THAN AN AUTHORITY FIGURE.
I KNOW, IT'S JUST...*TEACHING* WAS ONE OF THE FEW GOOD THINGS I DID WITH MY LIFE.
AND WITH ALL THAT'S HAPPENED LATELY, I MISS FEELING LIKE I'M HAVING A POSITIVE EFFECT ON THE WORLD.
YEAH, CUZ STOPPIN' *COUSIN ITT* HERE FROM LEVELIN' MANHATTAN, THAT AIN'T USEFUL AT ALL.
HRROOOO!
THAT'S ODD. MY READINGS SUGGEST THIS REATURE CAME FROM THE *MICROVERSE*.
THE *SUBATOMIC* UNIVERSE? SHOULDN'T IT BE, OH, A MILLION TIMES *TEENSIER?*
KNOCK KNOCK
OR MORE. THERE'S NO NATURAL WAY IT SHOULD HAVE GROWN INTO OUR DIMENSION, LET ALONE BECOME THIS *HUGE*. IF IT'S SOMEHOW CONNECTED TO OUR RECENT TRIP THERE--
PARDON ME, MRS. RICHARDS, BUT WOULD YOU MIND DROPPING YOUR FORCE-FIELD FOR A MOMENT?

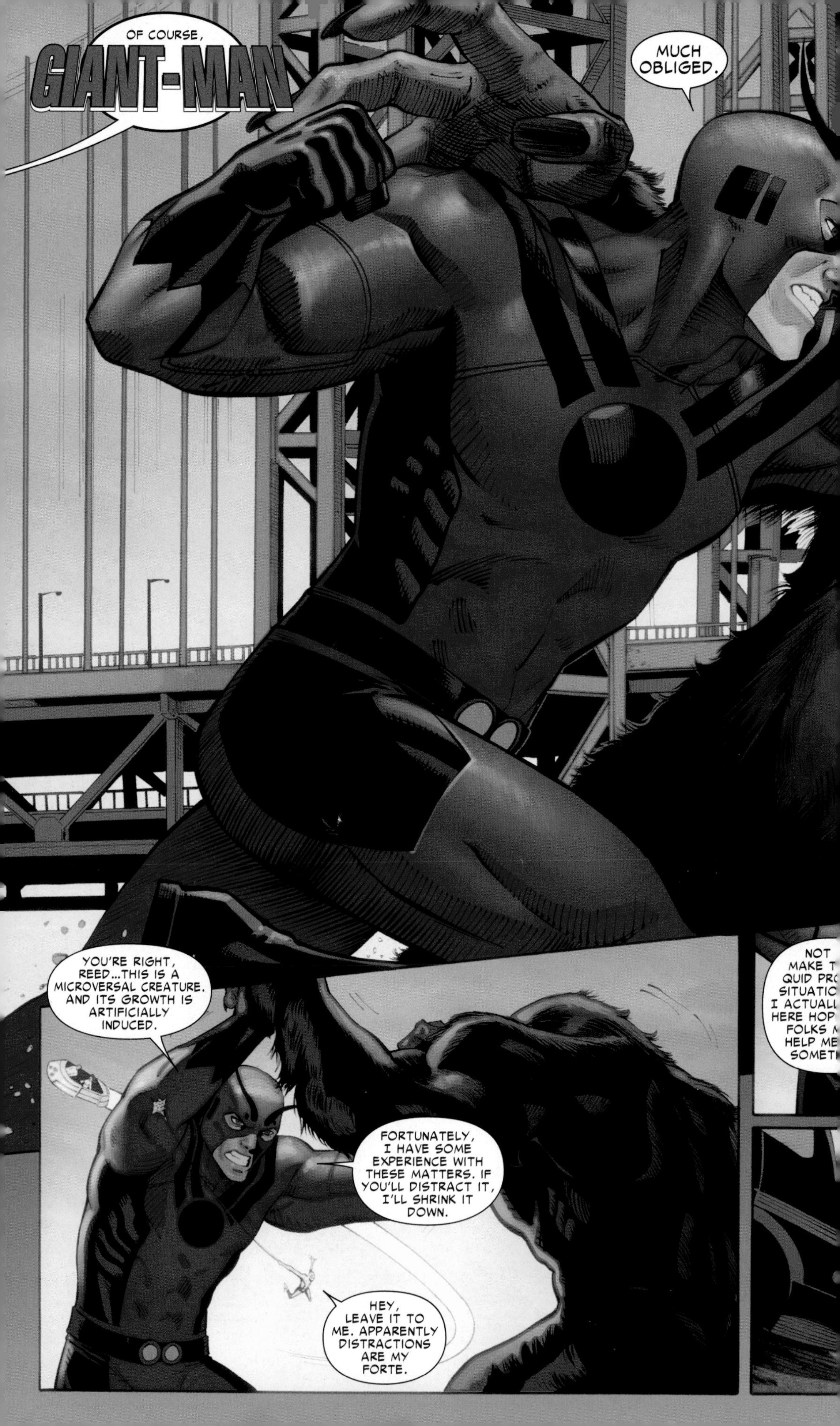
OF COURSE, GIANT-MAN
MUCH OBLIGED.
YOU'RE RIGHT, REED...THIS IS A MICROVERSAL CREATURE. AND ITS GROWTH IS ARTIFICIALLY INDUCED.
FORTUNATELY, I HAVE SOME EXPERIENCE WITH THESE MATTERS. IF YOU'LL DISTRACT IT, I'LL SHRINK IT DOWN.
HEY, LEAVE IT TO ME. APPARENTLY DISTRACTIONS ARE MY FORTE.

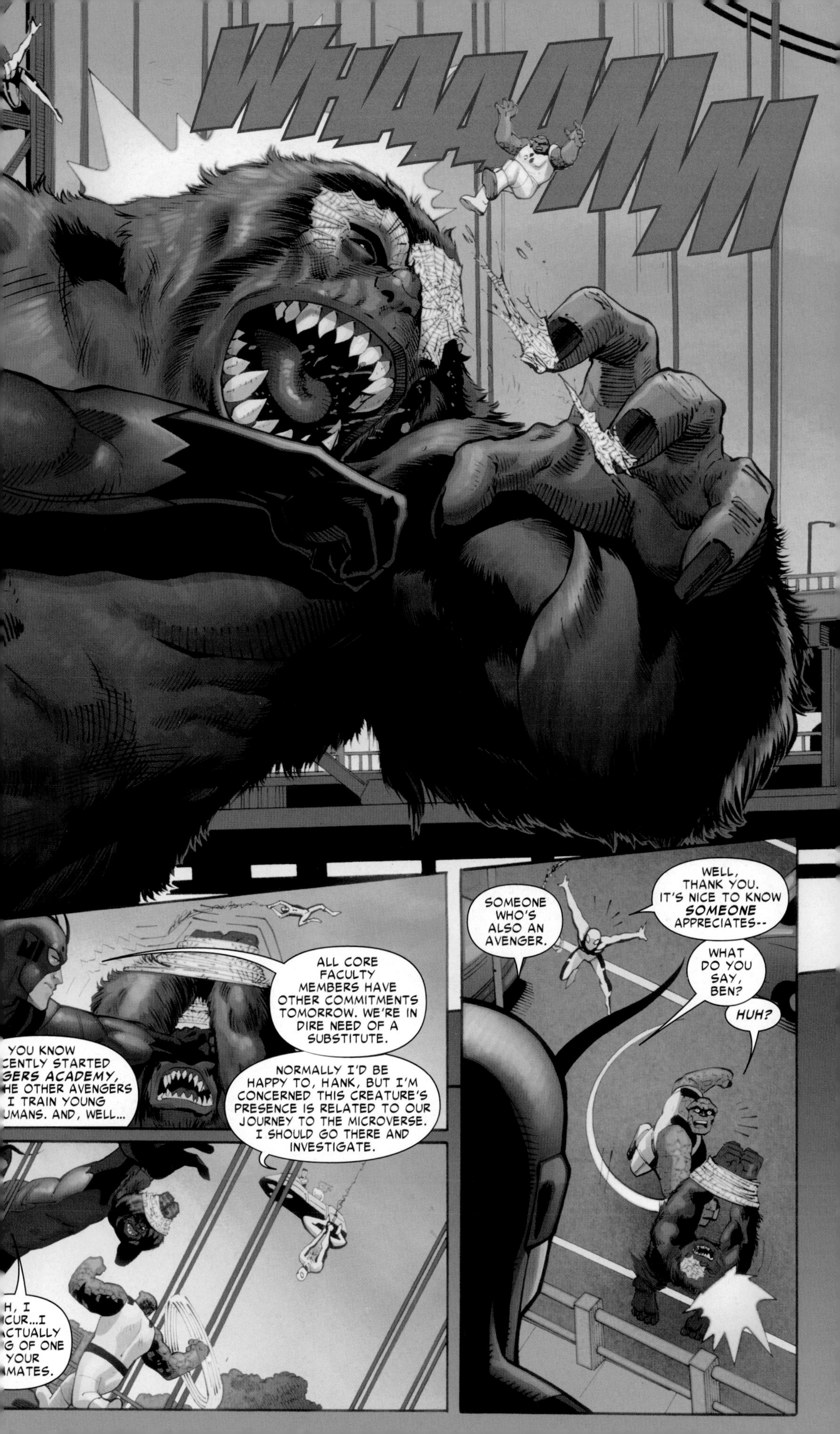
WHAAAMM
ALL CORE FACULTY MEMBERS HAVE OTHER COMMITMENTS TOMORROW. WE'RE IN DIRE NEED OF A SUBSTITUTE.
YOU KNOW CENTLY STARTED GERS ACADEMY, HE OTHER AVENGERS I TRAIN YOUNG UMANS. AND, WELL...
NORMALLY I'D BE HAPPY TO, HANK, BUT I'M CONCERNED THIS CREATURE'S PRESENCE IS RELATED TO OUR JOURNEY TO THE MICROVERSE. I SHOULD GO THERE AND INVESTIGATE.
H, I CUR...I ACTUALLY G OF ONE YOUR MATES.
SOMEONE WHO'S ALSO AN AVENGER.
WELL, THANK YOU. IT'S NICE TO KNOW SOMEONE APPRECIATES--
WHAT DO YOU SAY, BEN?
HUH?

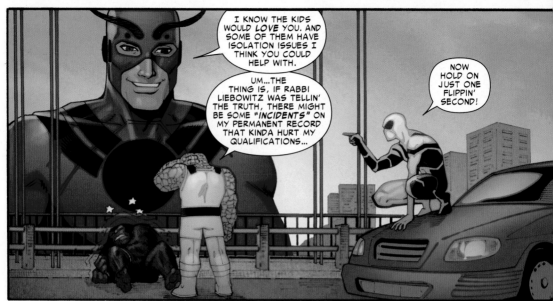

I KNOW THE KIDS WOULD *LOVE* YOU. AND SOME OF THEM HAVE ISOLATION ISSUES I THINK YOU COULD HELP WITH.

UM...THE THING IS, IF RABBI LIEBOWITZ WAS TELLIN' THE TRUTH, THERE MIGHT BE SOME *"INCIDENTS"* ON MY PERMANENT RECORD THAT KINDA HURT MY QUALIFICATIONS...

NOW HOLD ON JUST ONE FLIPPIN' SECOND!

I'M IN THE AVENGERS TOO! I'M ON *BOTH FREAKIN'* TEAMS!

YOU'RE TRAINING TEEN SUPER HEROES? I WAS THE *ORIGINAL* TEENAGE SUPER HERO!

AND I HAVE A *TEACHER'S LICENSE!* I TAUGHT KIDS FOR A *LIVING!*

YOU DID?

THIS CHANGES EVERYTHING. YOU'RE THE *IDEAL* CHOICE! THESE ARE *AT-RISK* KIDS, AND YOU'VE ALREADY MADE VIRTUALLY *EVERY* MISTAKE A YOUNG HERO POSSIBLY COULD.

HUH? LIKE WHAT?

WELL, YOUR ILL-ADVISED PROFESSIONAL WRESTLING CAREER... ALLOWING YOURSELF TO BE BRANDED A *MENACE,* WHICH SEEMS TO HAVE STUCK...THE *SPIDER-MOBILE*...WE USE YOU AS AN EXAMPLE OF WHAT NOT--

OKAY! LET'S LEAVE IT AT *"IDEAL CHOICE"* AND MOVE ON.

HOW ARE THESE KIDS AT RISK? FROM DRUGS AND GANGS?

NOT EXACTLY. YOUR OLD ENEMY *NORMAN OSBORN* TRIED TO MOLD THEM IN HIS IMAGE...OFTEN THROUGH TORTURE AND *BRAINWASHING.*

IF WE DON'T LEAD THEM DOWN THE RIGHT PATH, WE'RE *ALL* AT RISK OF THEIR BECOMING *CRIMINALS.*

VERY *POWERFUL* ONES.

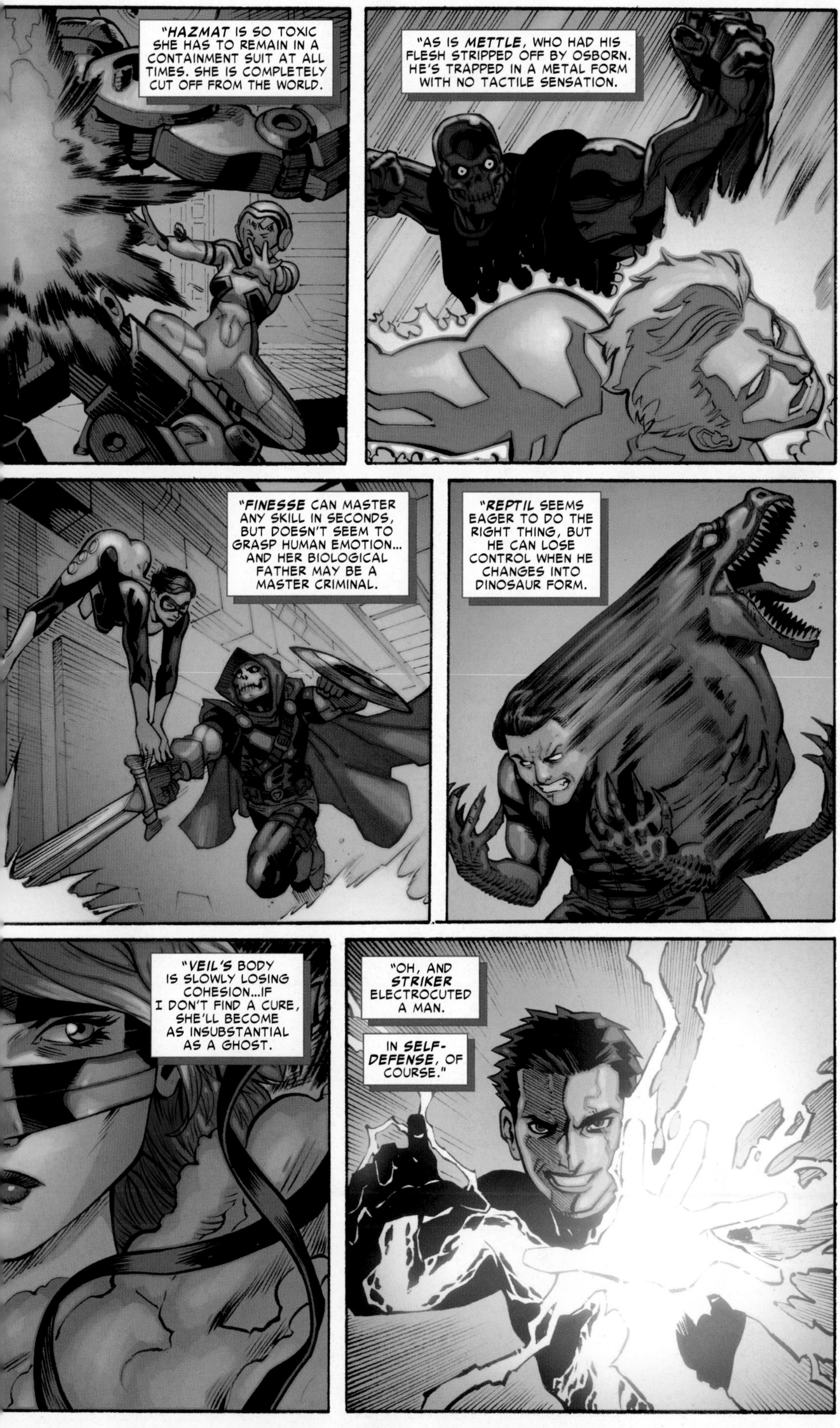
"HAZMAT IS SO TOXIC SHE HAS TO REMAIN IN A CONTAINMENT SUIT AT ALL TIMES. SHE IS COMPLETELY CUT OFF FROM THE WORLD.
"AS IS METTLE, WHO HAD HIS FLESH STRIPPED OFF BY OSBORN. HE'S TRAPPED IN A METAL FORM WITH NO TACTILE SENSATION.
"FINESSE CAN MASTER ANY SKILL IN SECONDS, BUT DOESN'T SEEM TO GRASP HUMAN EMOTION... AND HER BIOLOGICAL FATHER MAY BE A MASTER CRIMINAL.
"REPTIL SEEMS EAGER TO DO THE RIGHT THING, BUT HE CAN LOSE CONTROL WHEN HE CHANGES INTO DINOSAUR FORM.
"VEIL'S BODY IS SLOWLY LOSING COHESION...IF I DON'T FIND A CURE, SHE'LL BECOME AS INSUBSTANTIAL AS A GHOST.
"OH, AND STRIKER ELECTROCUTED A MAN.
IN SELF-DEFENSE, OF COURSE."

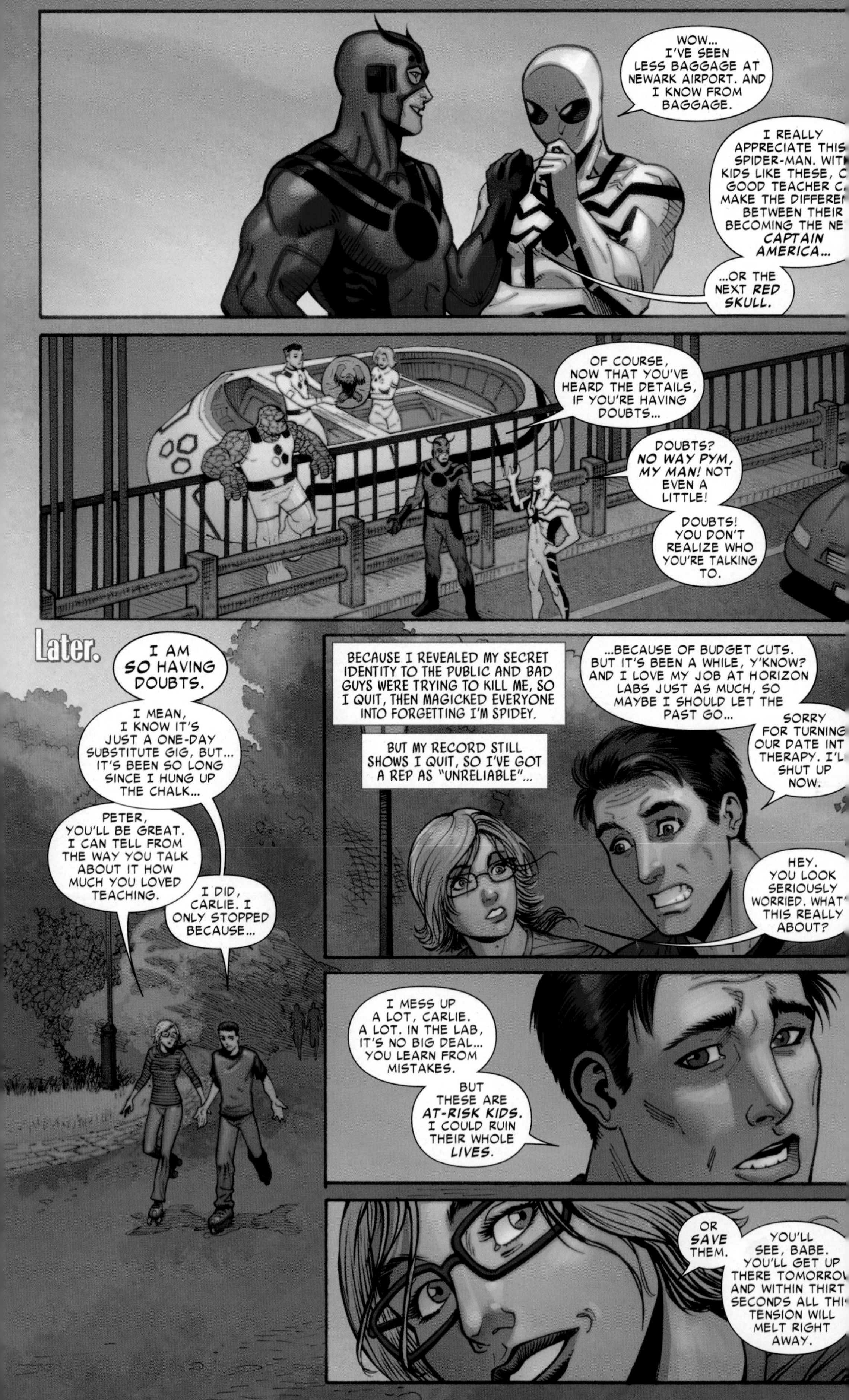
WOW... I'VE SEEN LESS BAGGAGE AT NEWARK AIRPORT. AND I KNOW FROM BAGGAGE.
I REALLY APPRECIATE THIS SPIDER-MAN. WIT KIDS LIKE THESE, C GOOD TEACHER C MAKE THE DIFFERE BETWEEN THEIR BECOMING THE NE CAPTAIN AMERICA...
...OR THE NEXT RED SKULL.
OF COURSE, NOW THAT YOU'VE HEARD THE DETAILS, IF YOU'RE HAVING DOUBTS...
DOUBTS? NO WAY PYM, MY MAN! NOT EVEN A LITTLE!
DOUBTS! YOU DON'T REALIZE WHO YOU'RE TALKING TO.
Later.
I AM SO HAVING DOUBTS.
I MEAN, I KNOW IT'S JUST A ONE-DAY SUBSTITUTE GIG, BUT... IT'S BEEN SO LONG SINCE I HUNG UP THE CHALK...
PETER, YOU'LL BE GREAT. I CAN TELL FROM THE WAY YOU TALK ABOUT IT HOW MUCH YOU LOVED TEACHING.
I DID, CARLIE. I ONLY STOPPED BECAUSE...
BECAUSE I REVEALED MY SECRET IDENTITY TO THE PUBLIC AND BAD GUYS WERE TRYING TO KILL ME, SO I QUIT, THEN MAGICKED EVERYONE INTO FORGETTING I'M SPIDEY.
BUT MY RECORD STILL SHOWS I QUIT, SO I'VE GOT A REP AS "UNRELIABLE"...
...BECAUSE OF BUDGET CUTS. BUT IT'S BEEN A WHILE, Y'KNOW? AND I LOVE MY JOB AT HORIZON LABS JUST AS MUCH, SO MAYBE I SHOULD LET THE PAST GO...
SORRY FOR TURNING OUR DATE INT THERAPY. I'L SHUT UP NOW.
HEY. YOU LOOK SERIOUSLY WORRIED. WHAT' THIS REALLY ABOUT?
I MESS UP A LOT, CARLIE. A LOT. IN THE LAB, IT'S NO BIG DEAL... YOU LEARN FROM MISTAKES.
BUT THESE ARE AT-RISK KIDS. I COULD RUIN THEIR WHOLE LIVES.
OR SAVE THEM.
YOU'LL SEE, BABE. YOU'LL GET UP THERE TOMORROW AND WITHIN THIRT SECONDS ALL THI TENSION WILL MELT RIGHT AWAY.

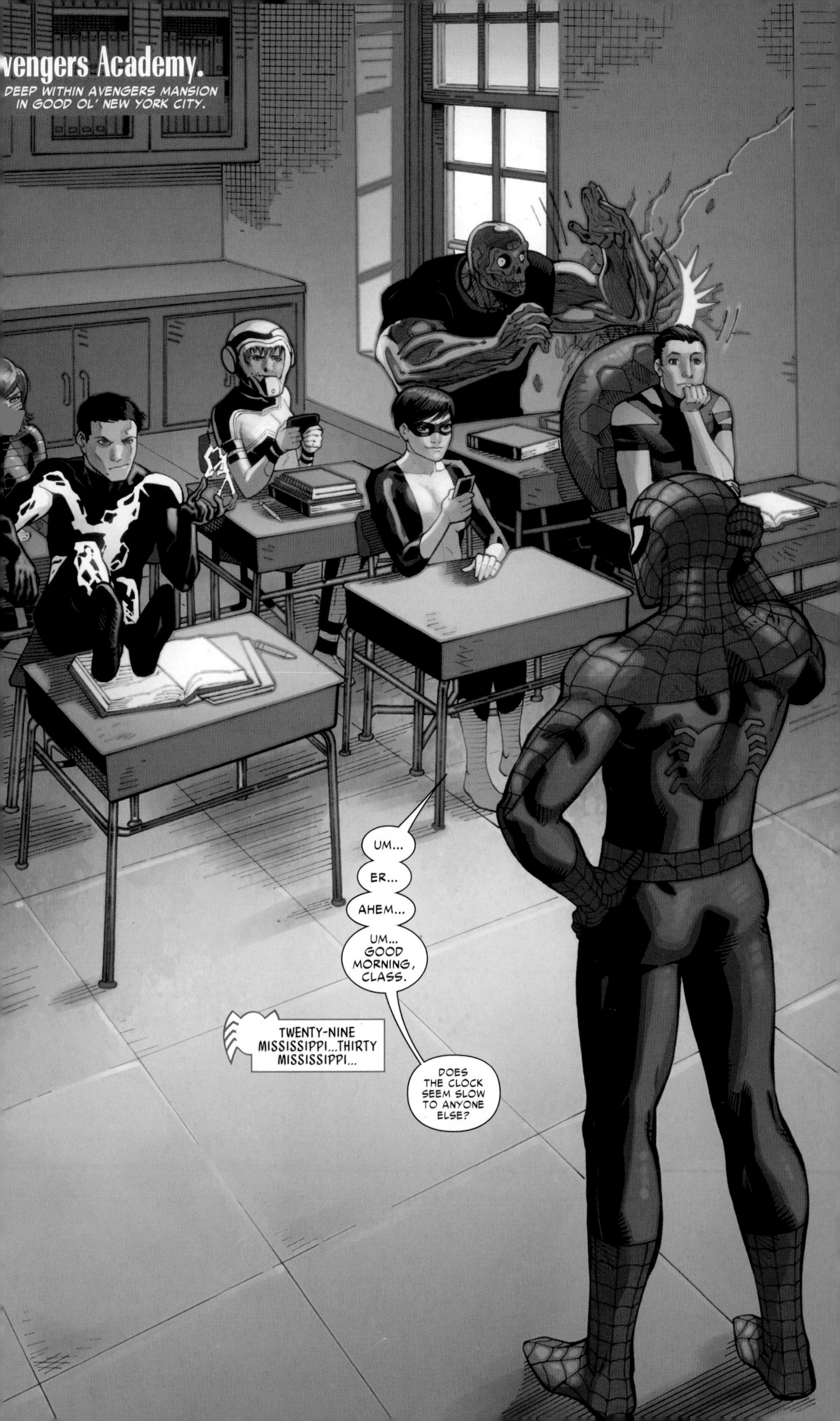
Avengers Academy.
DEEP WITHIN AVENGERS MANSION IN GOOD OL' NEW YORK CITY.
UM...
ER...
AHEM...
UM... GOOD MORNING, CLASS.
TWENTY-NINE MISSISSIPPI...THIRTY MISSISSIPPI...
DOES THE CLOCK SEEM SLOW TO ANYONE ELSE?

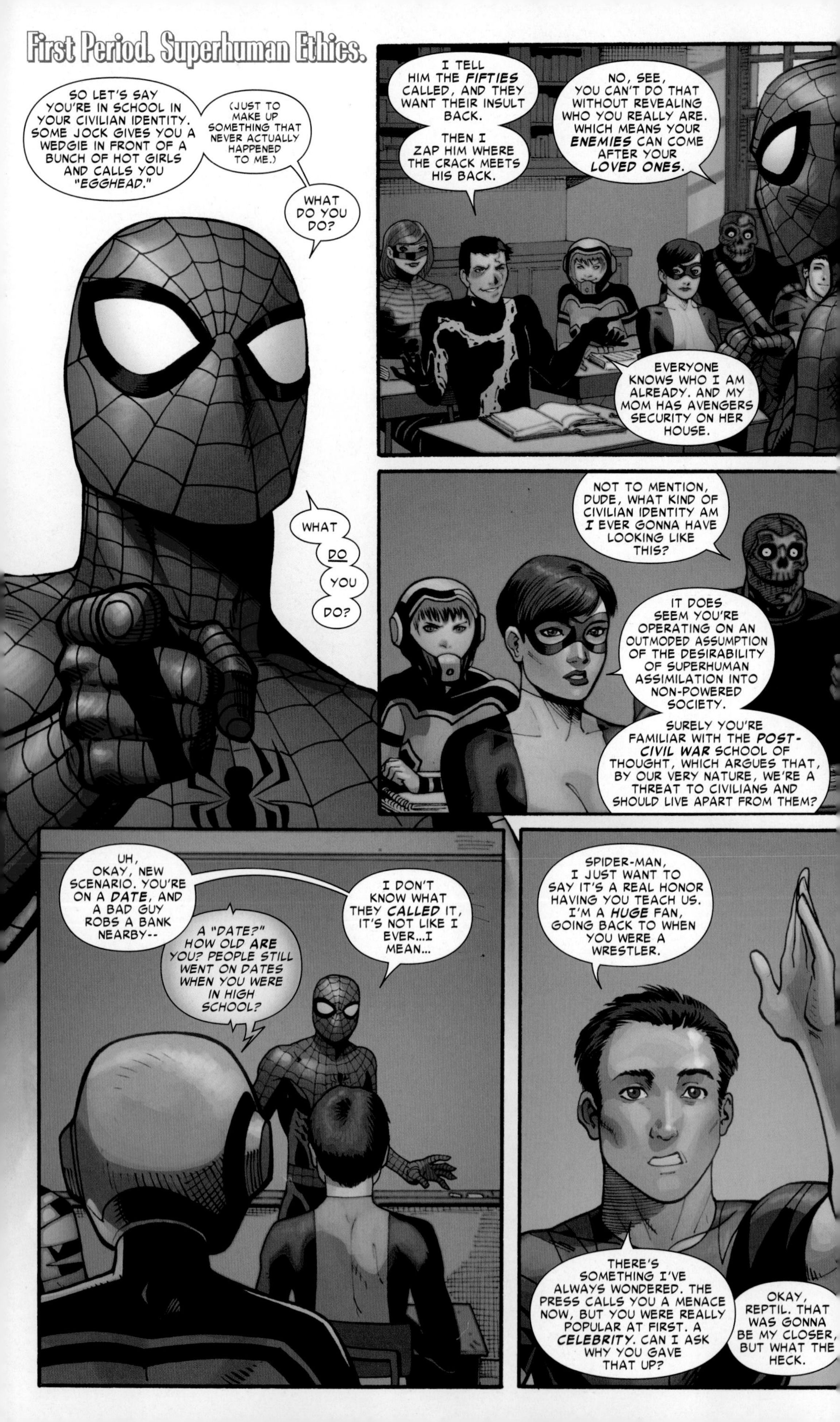
First Period. Superhuman Ethics.
SO LET'S SAY YOU'RE IN SCHOOL IN YOUR CIVILIAN IDENTITY. SOME JOCK GIVES YOU A WEDGIE IN FRONT OF A BUNCH OF HOT GIRLS AND CALLS YOU "EGGHEAD."
(JUST TO MAKE UP SOMETHING THAT NEVER ACTUALLY HAPPENED TO ME.)
WHAT DO YOU DO?
I TELL HIM THE FIFTIES CALLED, AND THEY WANT THEIR INSULT BACK.
THEN I ZAP HIM WHERE THE CRACK MEETS HIS BACK.
NO, SEE, YOU CAN'T DO THAT WITHOUT REVEALING WHO YOU REALLY ARE. WHICH MEANS YOUR ENEMIES CAN COME AFTER YOUR LOVED ONES.
EVERYONE KNOWS WHO I AM ALREADY. AND MY MOM HAS AVENGERS SECURITY ON HER HOUSE.
WHAT
DO
YOU
DO?
NOT TO MENTION, DUDE, WHAT KIND OF CIVILIAN IDENTITY AM I EVER GONNA HAVE LOOKING LIKE THIS?
IT DOES SEEM YOU'RE OPERATING ON AN OUTMODED ASSUMPTION OF THE DESIRABILITY OF SUPERHUMAN ASSIMILATION INTO NON-POWERED SOCIETY.
SURELY YOU'RE FAMILIAR WITH THE POST-CIVIL WAR SCHOOL OF THOUGHT, WHICH ARGUES THAT, BY OUR VERY NATURE, WE'RE A THREAT TO CIVILIANS AND SHOULD LIVE APART FROM THEM?
UH, OKAY, NEW SCENARIO. YOU'RE ON A DATE, AND A BAD GUY ROBS A BANK NEARBY--
A "DATE?" HOW OLD ARE YOU? PEOPLE STILL WENT ON DATES WHEN YOU WERE IN HIGH SCHOOL?
I DON'T KNOW WHAT THEY CALLED IT, IT'S NOT LIKE I EVER...I MEAN...
SPIDER-MAN, I JUST WANT TO SAY IT'S A REAL HONOR HAVING YOU TEACH US. I'M A HUGE FAN, GOING BACK TO WHEN YOU WERE A WRESTLER.
THERE'S SOMETHING I'VE ALWAYS WONDERED. THE PRESS CALLS YOU A MENACE NOW, BUT YOU WERE REALLY POPULAR AT FIRST. A CELEBRITY. CAN I ASK WHY YOU GAVE THAT UP?
OKAY, REPTIL. THAT WAS GONNA BE MY CLOSER, BUT WHAT THE HECK.

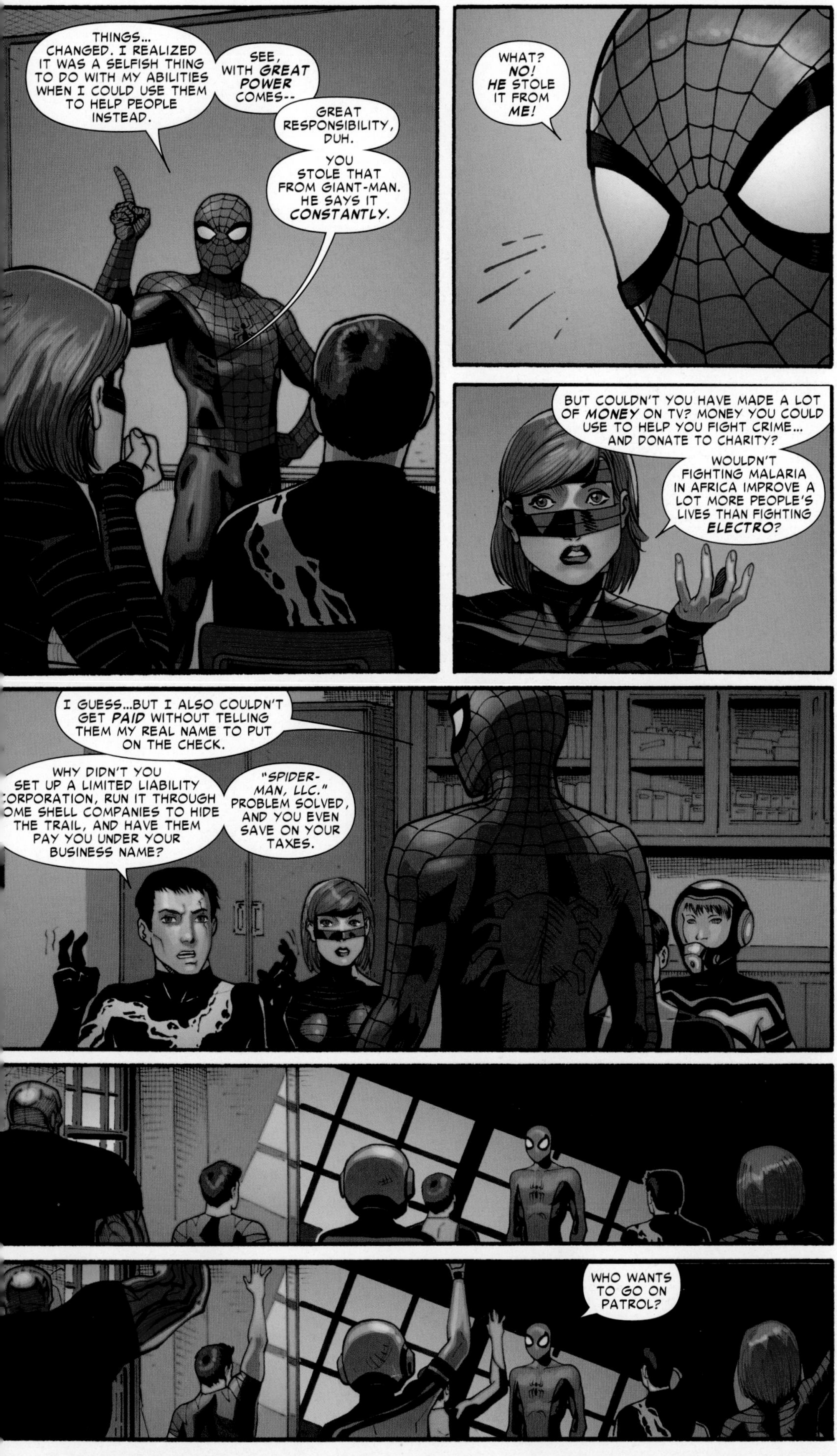
THINGS... CHANGED. I REALIZED IT WAS A SELFISH THING TO DO WITH MY ABILITIES WHEN I COULD USE THEM TO HELP PEOPLE INSTEAD.
SEE, WITH GREAT POWER COMES--
GREAT RESPONSIBILITY, DUH.
YOU STOLE THAT FROM GIANT-MAN. HE SAYS IT CONSTANTLY.
WHAT? NO! HE STOLE IT FROM ME!
BUT COULDN'T YOU HAVE MADE A LOT OF MONEY ON TV? MONEY YOU COULD USE TO HELP YOU FIGHT CRIME... AND DONATE TO CHARITY?
WOULDN'T FIGHTING MALARIA IN AFRICA IMPROVE A LOT MORE PEOPLE'S LIVES THAN FIGHTING ELECTRO?
I GUESS...BUT I ALSO COULDN'T GET PAID WITHOUT TELLING THEM MY REAL NAME TO PUT ON THE CHECK.
WHY DIDN'T YOU SET UP A LIMITED LIABILITY CORPORATION, RUN IT THROUGH OME SHELL COMPANIES TO HIDE THE TRAIL, AND HAVE THEM PAY YOU UNDER YOUR BUSINESS NAME?
"SPIDER-MAN, LLC." PROBLEM SOLVED, AND YOU EVEN SAVE ON YOUR TAXES.
WHO WANTS TO GO ON PATROL?

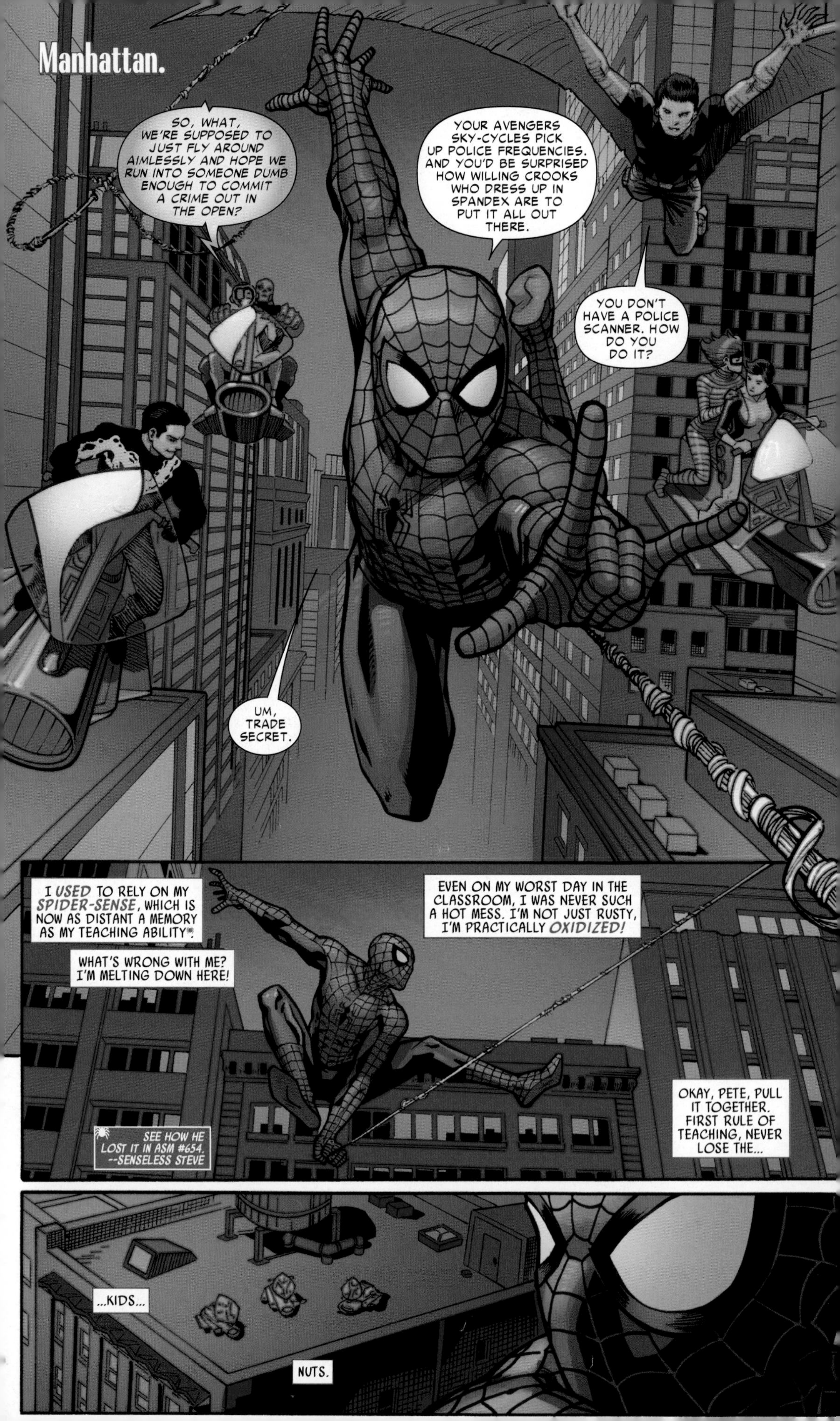
Manhattan.
SO, WHAT, WE'RE SUPPOSED TO JUST FLY AROUND AIMLESSLY AND HOPE WE RUN INTO SOMEONE DUMB ENOUGH TO COMMIT A CRIME OUT IN THE OPEN?
YOUR AVENGERS SKY-CYCLES PICK UP POLICE FREQUENCIES. AND YOU'D BE SURPRISED HOW WILLING CROOKS WHO DRESS UP IN SPANDEX ARE TO PUT IT ALL OUT THERE.
YOU DON'T HAVE A POLICE SCANNER. HOW DO YOU DO IT?
UM, TRADE SECRET.
I USED TO RELY ON MY SPIDER-SENSE, WHICH IS NOW AS DISTANT A MEMORY AS MY TEACHING ABILITY*.
WHAT'S WRONG WITH ME? I'M MELTING DOWN HERE!
EVEN ON MY WORST DAY IN THE CLASSROOM, I WAS NEVER SUCH A HOT MESS. I'M NOT JUST RUSTY, I'M PRACTICALLY OXIDIZED!
*SEE HOW HE LOST IT IN ASM #654. --SENSELESS STEVE
OKAY, PETE, PULL IT TOGETHER. FIRST RULE OF TEACHING, NEVER LOSE THE...
...KIDS...
NUTS.

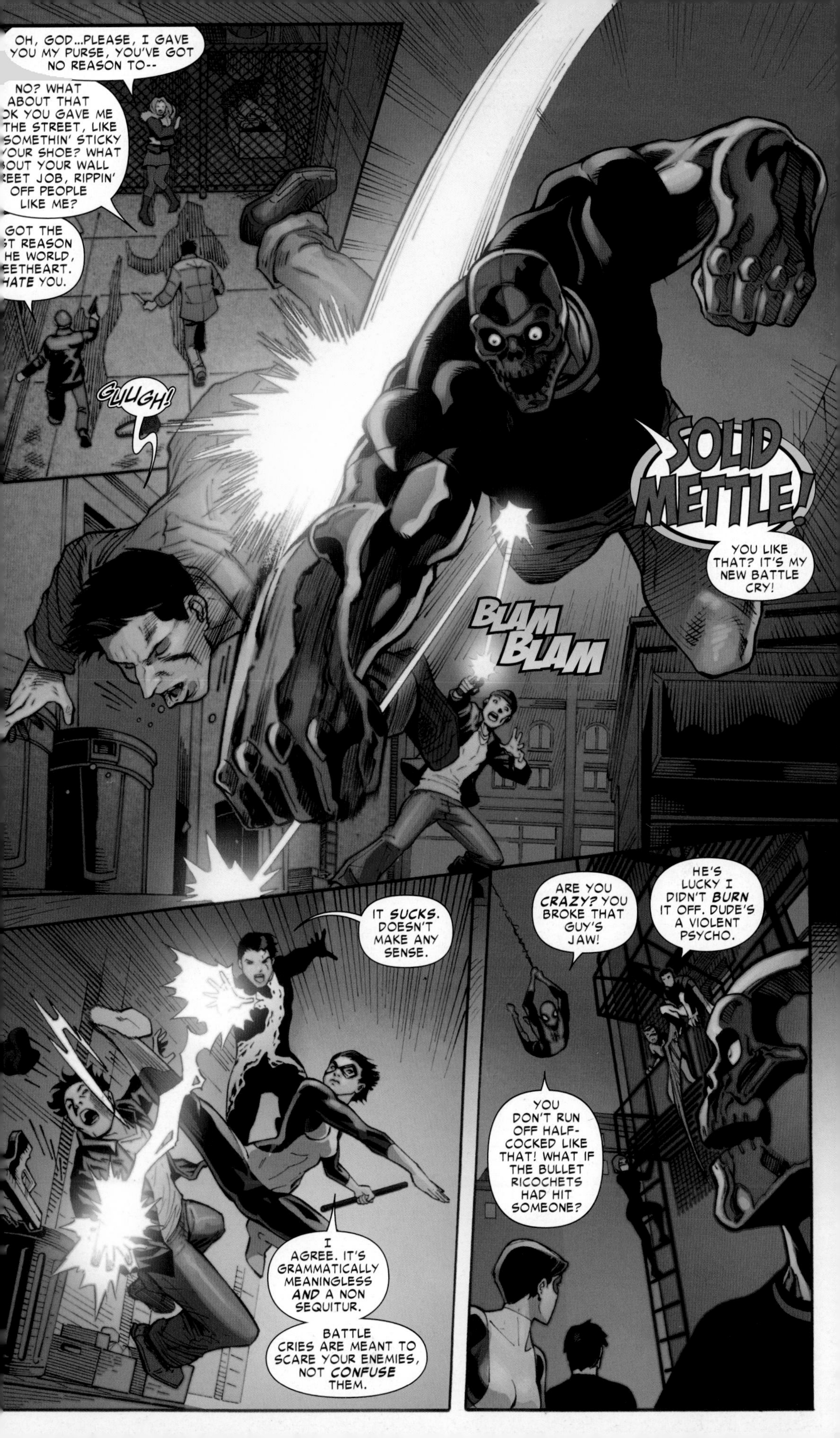
OH, GOD...PLEASE, I GAVE YOU MY PURSE, YOU'VE GOT NO REASON TO--
NO? WHAT ABOUT THAT OK YOU GAVE ME THE STREET, LIKE SOMETHIN' STICKY YOUR SHOE? WHAT BOUT YOUR WALL REET JOB, RIPPIN' OFF PEOPLE LIKE ME?
GOT THE T REASON HE WORLD, EETHEART. HATE YOU.
GULUGH!
SOLID METTLE!
YOU LIKE THAT? IT'S MY NEW BATTLE CRY!
BLAM BLAM
IT SUCKS. DOESN'T MAKE ANY SENSE.
I AGREE. IT'S GRAMMATICALLY MEANINGLESS AND A NON SEQUITUR.
BATTLE CRIES ARE MEANT TO SCARE YOUR ENEMIES, NOT CONFUSE THEM.
ARE YOU CRAZY? YOU BROKE THAT GUY'S JAW!
HE'S LUCKY I DIDN'T BURN IT OFF. DUDE'S A VIOLENT PSYCHO.
YOU DON'T RUN OFF HALF-COCKED LIKE THAT! WHAT IF THE BULLET RICOCHETS HAD HIT SOMEONE?

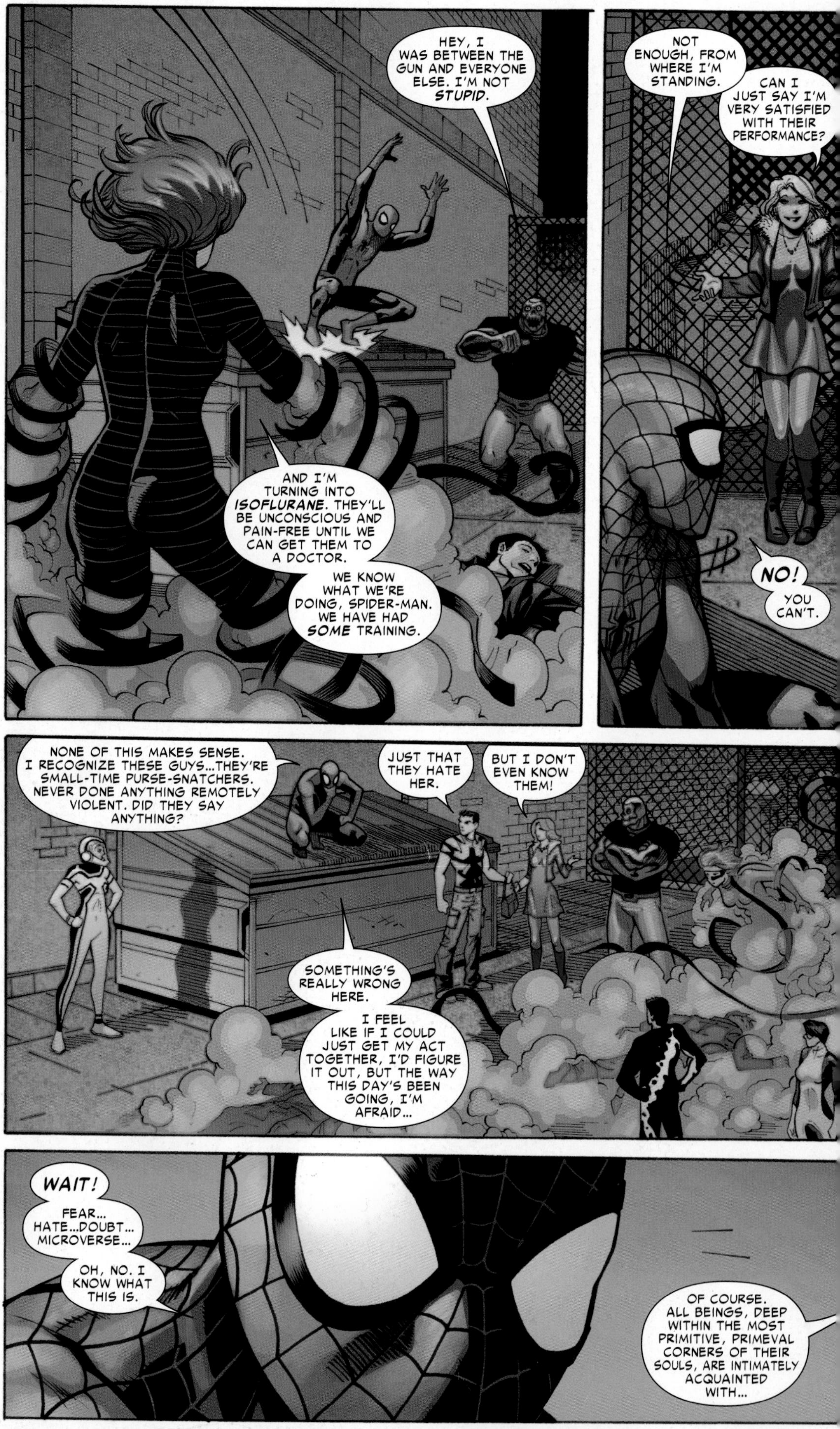
HEY, I WAS BETWEEN THE GUN AND EVERYONE ELSE. I'M NOT STUPID.
AND I'M TURNING INTO ISOFLURANE. THEY'LL BE UNCONSCIOUS AND PAIN-FREE UNTIL WE CAN GET THEM TO A DOCTOR.
WE KNOW WHAT WE'RE DOING, SPIDER-MAN. WE HAVE HAD SOME TRAINING.
NOT ENOUGH, FROM WHERE I'M STANDING.
CAN I JUST SAY I'M VERY SATISFIED WITH THEIR PERFORMANCE?
NO! YOU CAN'T.
NONE OF THIS MAKES SENSE. I RECOGNIZE THESE GUYS...THEY'RE SMALL-TIME PURSE-SNATCHERS. NEVER DONE ANYTHING REMOTELY VIOLENT. DID THEY SAY ANYTHING?
JUST THAT THEY HATE HER.
BUT I DON'T EVEN KNOW THEM!
SOMETHING'S REALLY WRONG HERE.
I FEEL LIKE IF I COULD JUST GET MY ACT TOGETHER, I'D FIGURE IT OUT, BUT THE WAY THIS DAY'S BEEN GOING, I'M AFRAID...
WAIT!
FEAR... HATE...DOUBT... MICROVERSE...
OH, NO. I KNOW WHAT THIS IS.
OF COURSE. ALL BEINGS, DEEP WITHIN THE MOST PRIMITIVE, PRIMEVAL CORNERS OF THEIR SOULS, ARE INTIMATELY ACQUAINTED WITH...

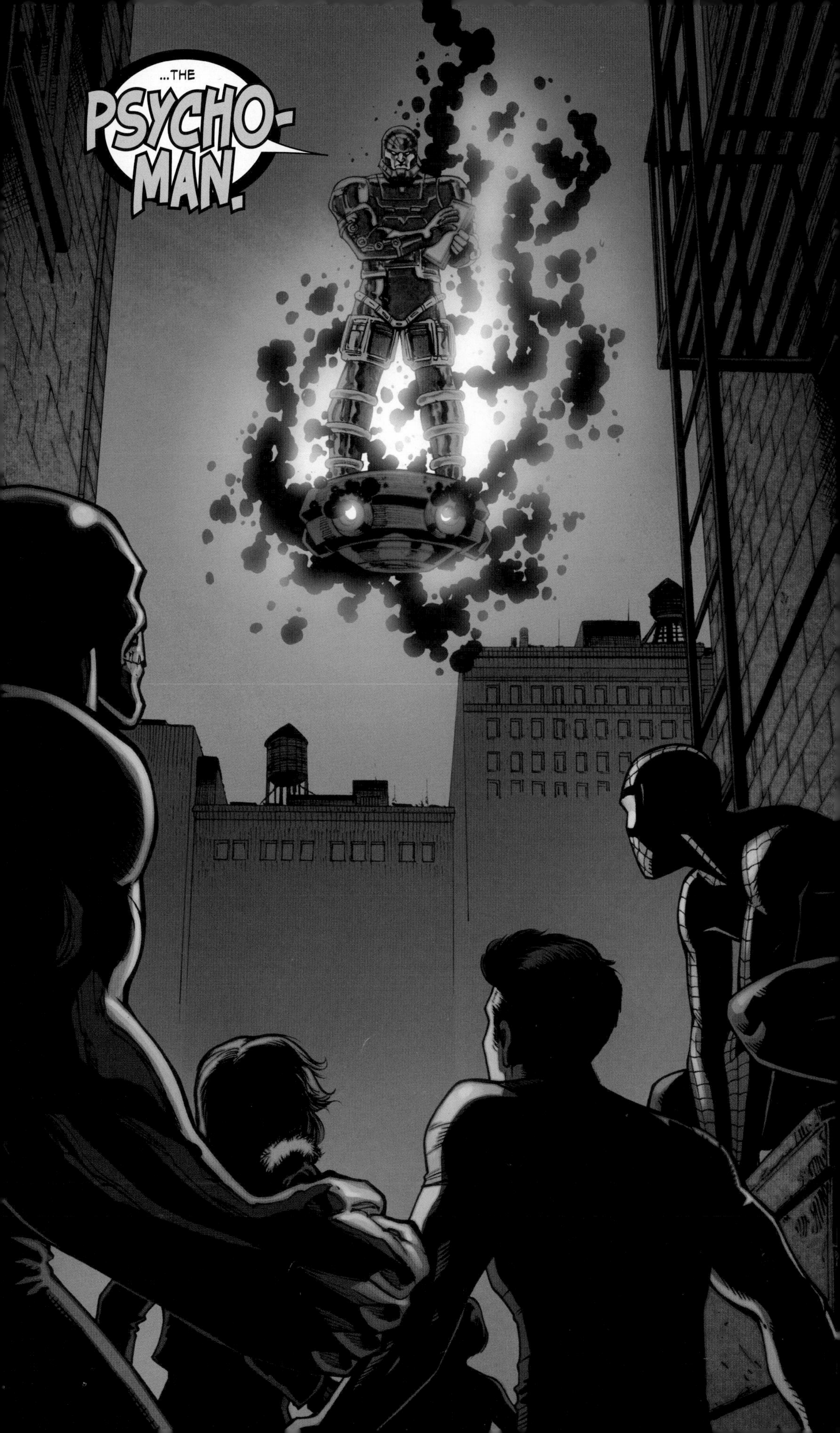
...THE PSYCHO-MAN.

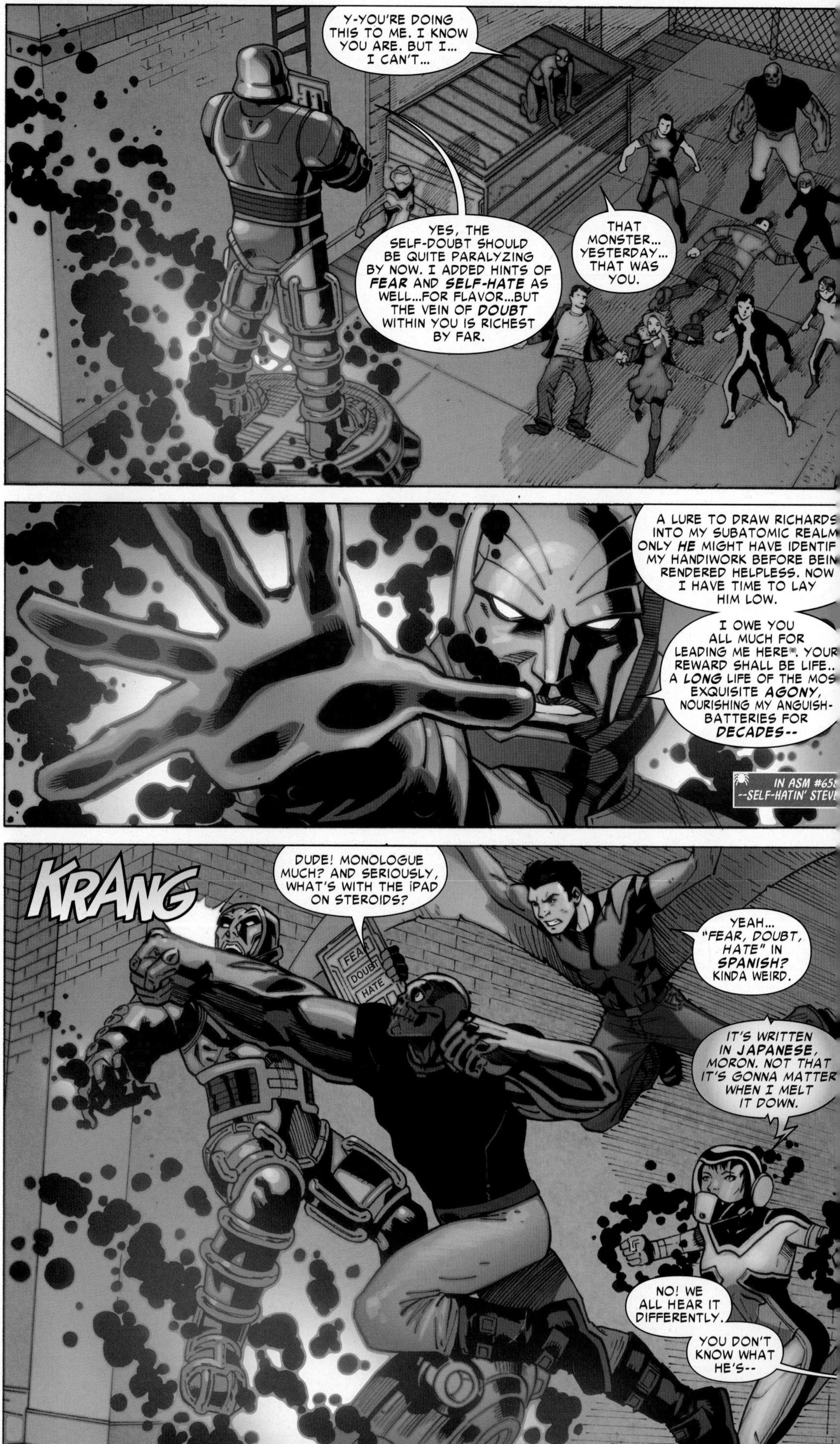
Y-YOU'RE DOING THIS TO ME. I KNOW YOU ARE. BUT I... I CAN'T...
YES, THE SELF-DOUBT SHOULD BE QUITE PARALYZING BY NOW. I ADDED HINTS OF FEAR AND SELF-HATE AS WELL...FOR FLAVOR...BUT THE VEIN OF DOUBT WITHIN YOU IS RICHEST BY FAR.
THAT MONSTER... YESTERDAY... THAT WAS YOU.
A LURE TO DRAW RICHARDS INTO MY SUBATOMIC REALM ONLY HE MIGHT HAVE IDENTIF MY HANDIWORK BEFORE BEIN RENDERED HELPLESS. NOW I HAVE TIME TO LAY HIM LOW.
I OWE YOU ALL MUCH FOR LEADING HERE*. YOUR REWARD SHALL BE LIFE.. A LONG LIFE OF THE MOS EXQUISITE AGONY, NOURISHING MY ANGUISH-BATTERIES FOR DECADES--
IN ASM #65
--SELF-HATIN' STEV
KRANG
DUDE! MONOLOGUE MUCH? AND SERIOUSLY, WHAT'S WITH THE iPAD ON STEROIDS?
FEAR
DOUBT
HATE
YEAH... "FEAR, DOUBT, HATE" IN SPANISH? KINDA WEIRD.
IT'S WRITTEN IN JAPANESE, MORON. NOT THAT IT'S GONNA MATTER WHEN I MELT IT DOWN.
NO! WE ALL HEAR IT DIFFERENTLY.
YOU DON'T KNOW WHAT HE'S--

WSHAMM!

--CAPABLE OF.

WRETCHED URCHINS!

THEY DON'T KNOW. THEY'VE NEVER FELT IT.

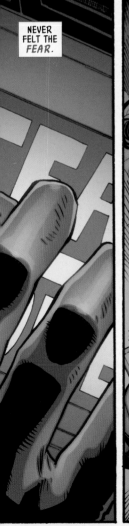

NEVER FELT THE *FEAR*.

STRIKER, SEE IF YOU CAN SHORT OUT HIS SYSTEMS!

I'LL TRY TO PENETRATE THAT ARMOR AND--AND--

NO!

GOT TO STAY SOLID OR I'LL DRIFT AWAY...LIKE SMOKE...

HE'LL KILL ME... OH, GOD, I DON'T WANT TO DIE...

THEY'VE NEVER GONE UP AGAINST *MR. FEAR* OR THE *LIZARD* OR THE *PURPLE MAN*. THEY DON'T KNOW HOW TO FIGHT IT.

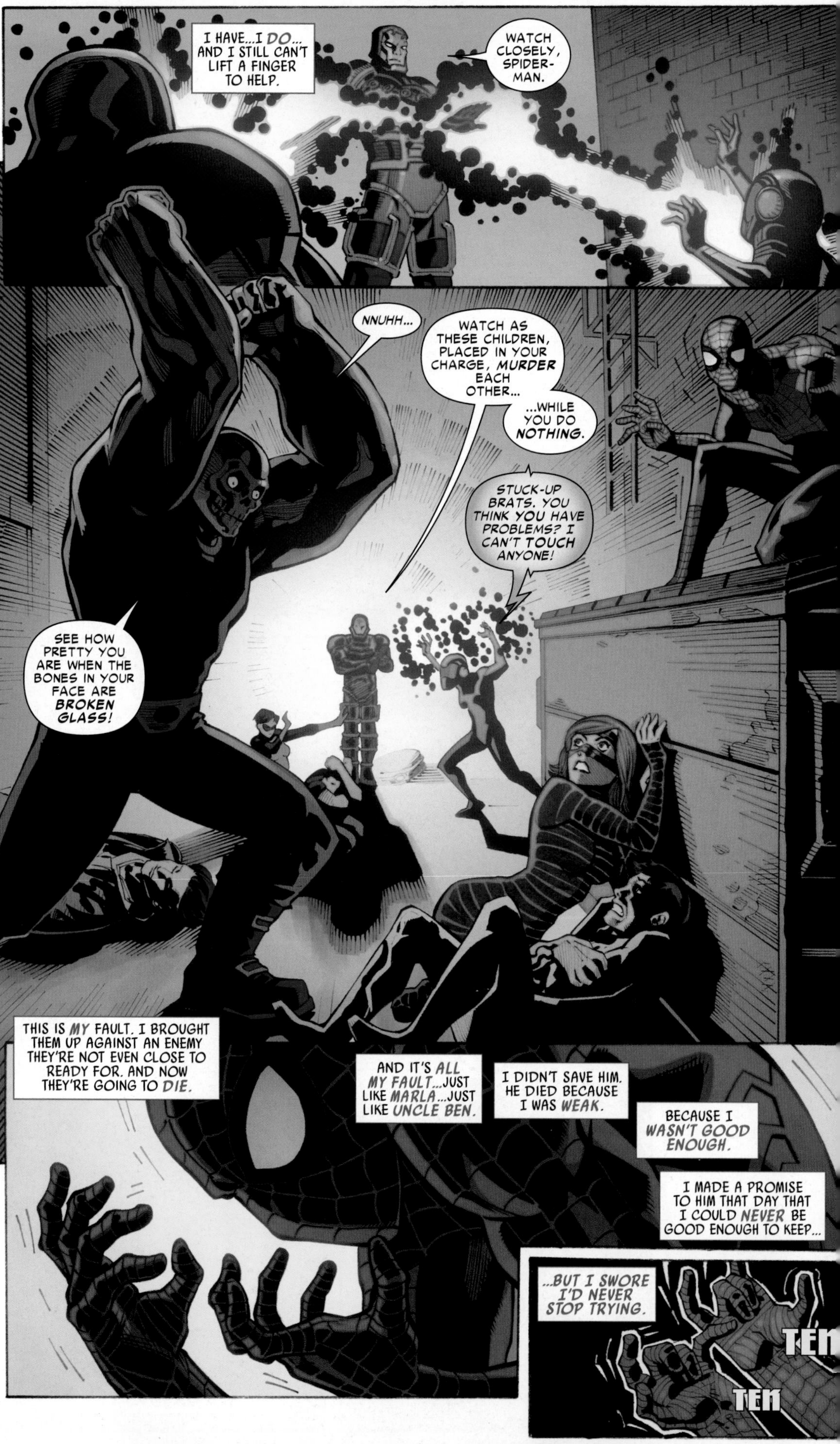
I HAVE...I DO... AND I STILL CAN'T LIFT A FINGER TO HELP.
WATCH CLOSELY, SPIDER-MAN.
NNUHH...
WATCH AS THESE CHILDREN, PLACED IN YOUR CHARGE, MURDER EACH OTHER...
...WHILE YOU DO NOTHING.
STUCK-UP BRATS. YOU THINK YOU HAVE PROBLEMS? I CAN'T TOUCH ANYONE!
SEE HOW PRETTY YOU ARE WHEN THE BONES IN YOUR FACE ARE BROKEN GLASS!
THIS IS MY FAULT. I BROUGHT THEM UP AGAINST AN ENEMY THEY'RE NOT EVEN CLOSE TO READY FOR. AND NOW THEY'RE GOING TO DIE.
AND IT'S ALL MY FAULT...JUST LIKE MARLA...JUST LIKE UNCLE BEN.
I DIDN'T SAVE HIM. HE DIED BECAUSE I WAS WEAK.
BECAUSE I WASN'T GOOD ENOUGH.
I MADE A PROMISE TO HIM THAT DAY THAT I COULD NEVER BE GOOD ENOUGH TO KEEP...
...BUT I SWORE I'D NEVER STOP TRYING.
TEN
TEN

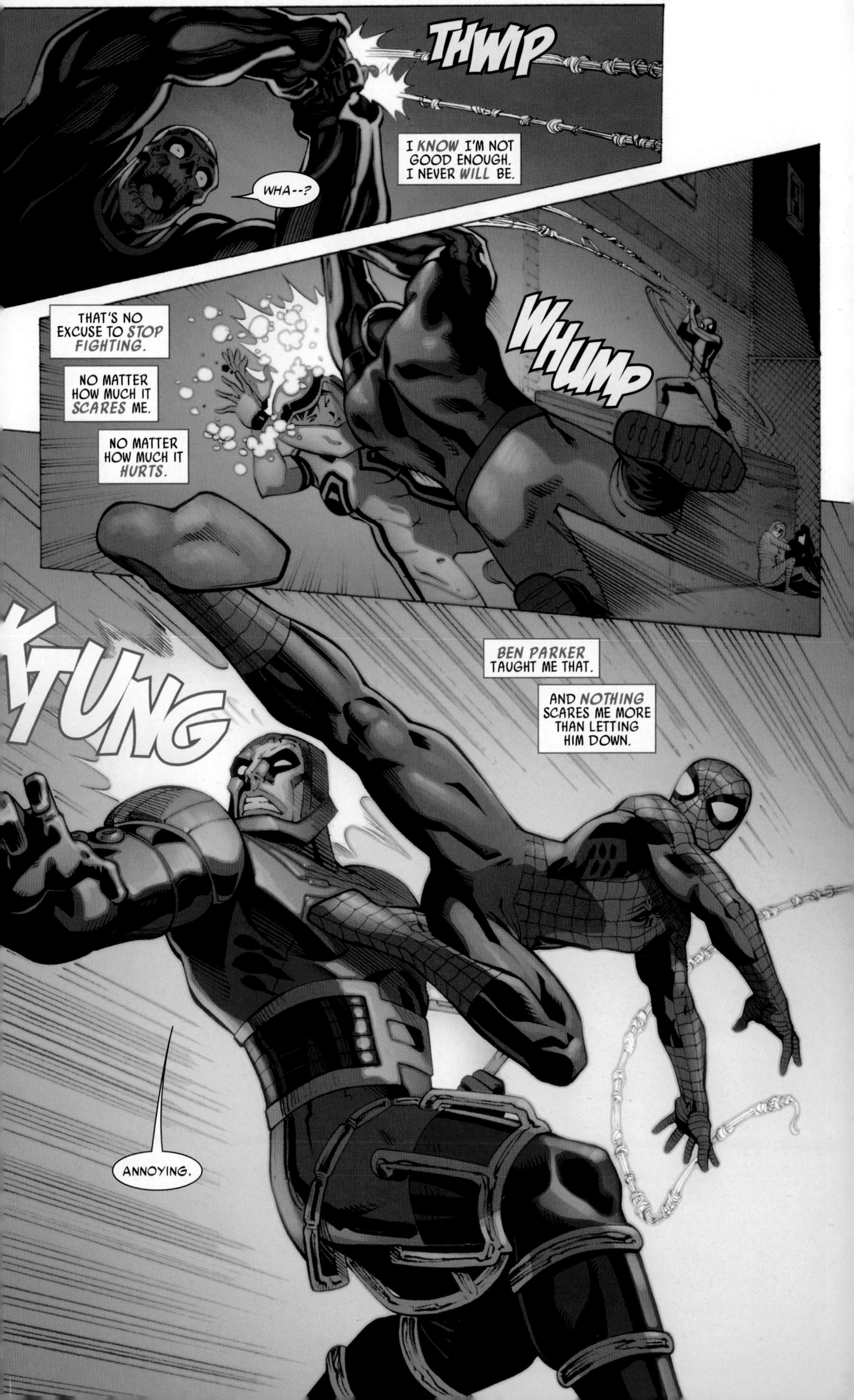
THWIP
I KNOW I'M NOT GOOD ENOUGH. I NEVER WILL BE.
WHA--?
THAT'S NO EXCUSE TO STOP FIGHTING.
NO MATTER HOW MUCH IT SCARES ME.
NO MATTER HOW MUCH IT HURTS.
WHUMP
BEN PARKER TAUGHT ME THAT.
AND NOTHING SCARES ME MORE THAN LETTING HIM DOWN.
ANNOYING.

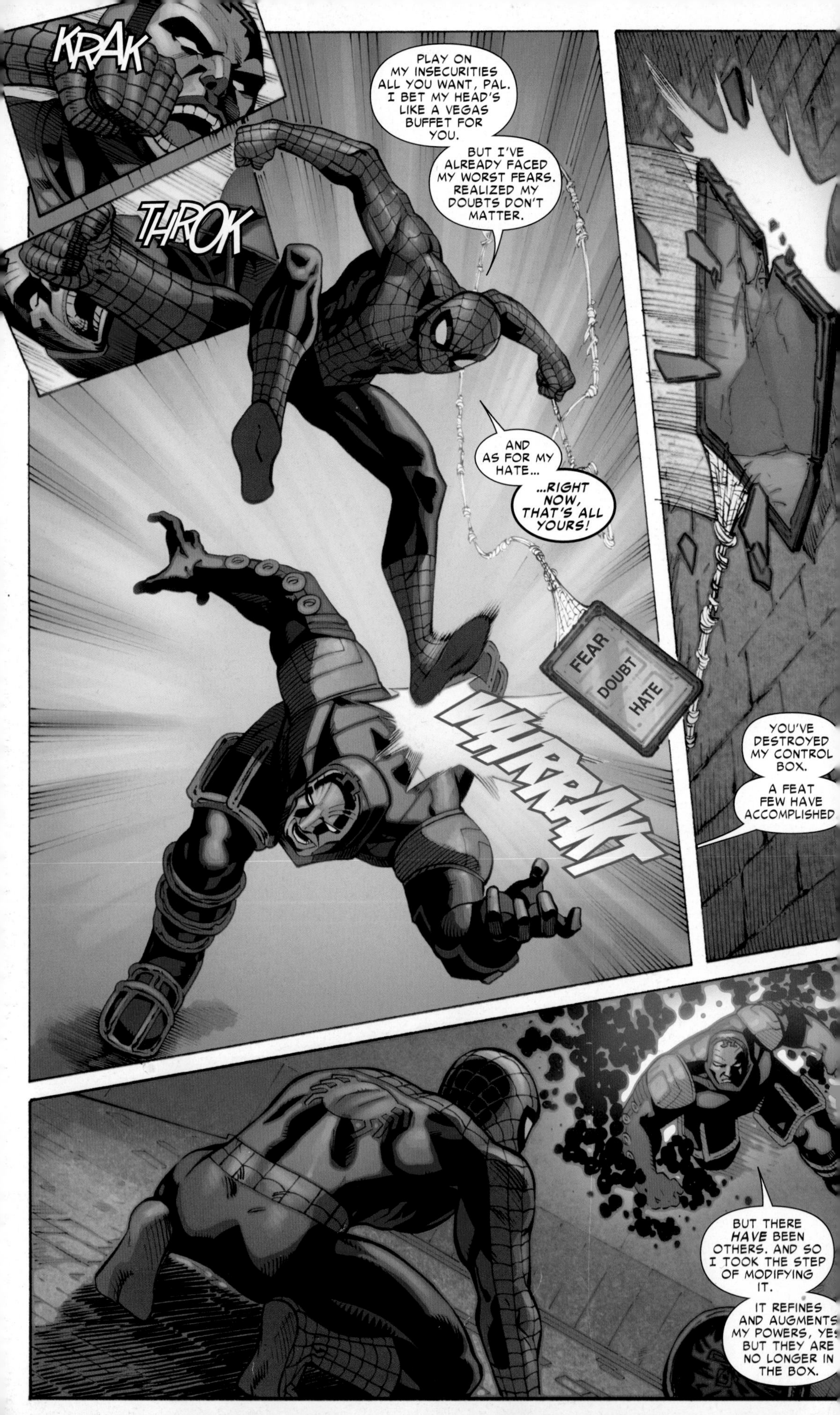

KRAK
THROK
PLAY ON MY INSECURITIES ALL YOU WANT, PAL. I BET MY HEAD'S LIKE A VEGAS BUFFET FOR YOU.
BUT I'VE ALREADY FACED MY WORST FEARS. REALIZED MY DOUBTS DON'T MATTER.
AND AS FOR MY HATE...
...RIGHT NOW, THAT'S ALL YOURS!
FEAR
DOUBT
HATE
WHRRAKT
YOU'VE DESTROYED MY CONTROL BOX.
A FEAT FEW HAVE ACCOMPLISHED
BUT THERE *HAVE* BEEN OTHERS. AND SO I TOOK THE STEP OF MODIFYING IT.
IT REFINES AND AUGMENTS MY POWERS, YES BUT THEY ARE NO LONGER IN THE BOX.

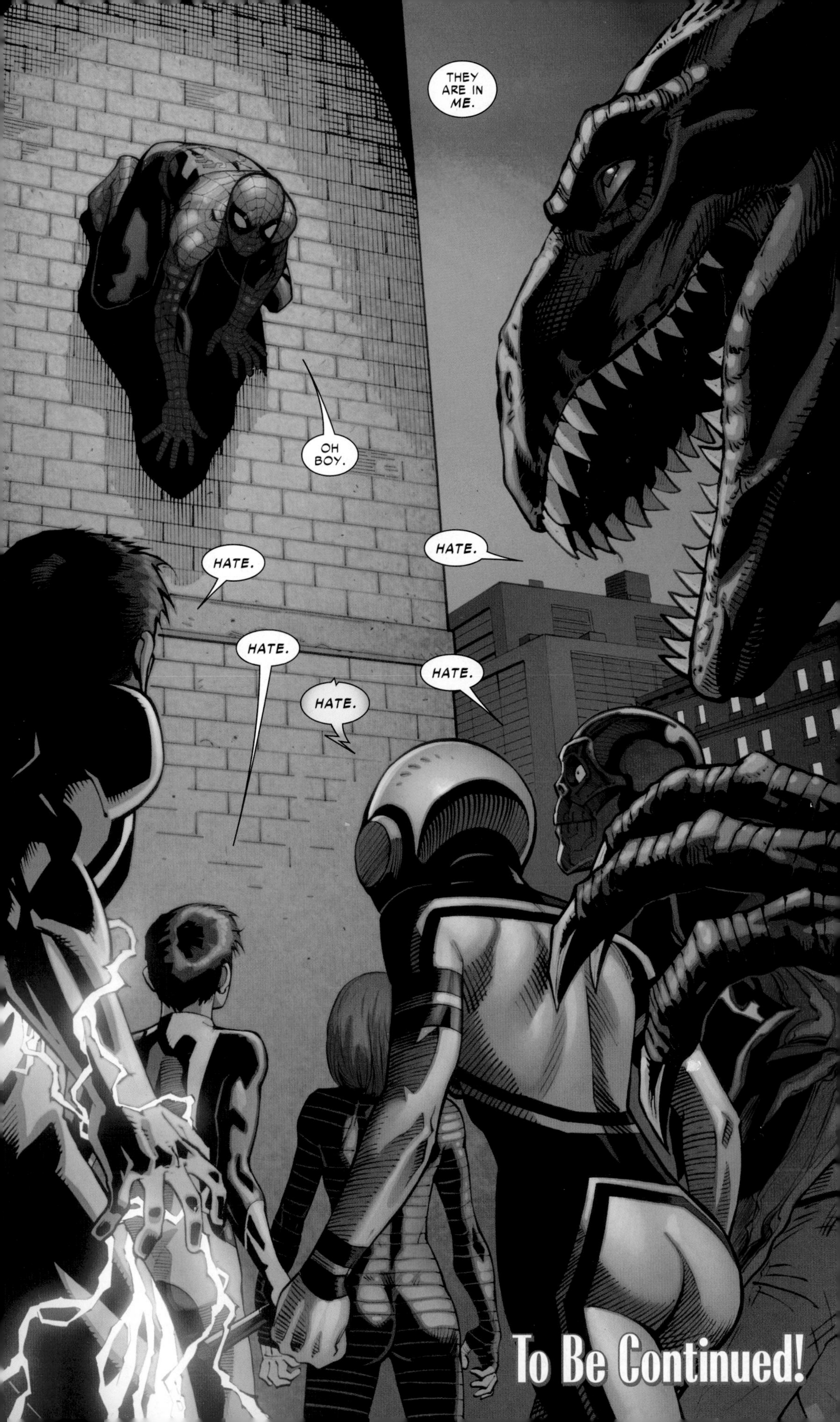
THEY ARE IN ME.
OH BOY.
HATE.
HATE.
HATE.
HATE.
HATE.
To Be Continued!

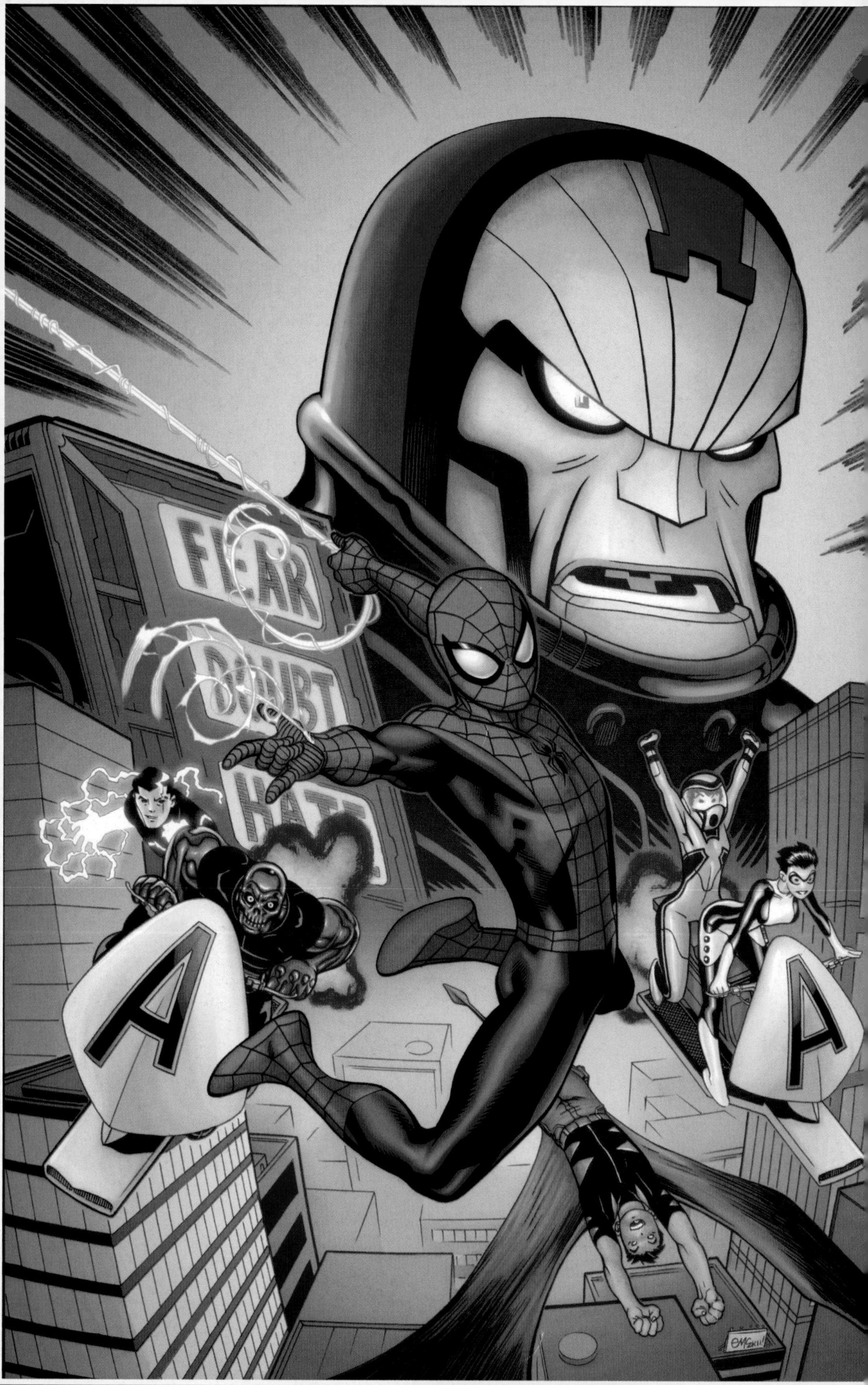
FEAR
DOUBT

he Substitute PART TWO

CHRISTOS GAGE WRITER
REILLY BROWN PENCILER
VICTOR OLAZABA INKER
JOHN RAUCH COLORIST
VC's JOE CARAMAGNA LETTERER
McGUINNESS & HOLLOWELL COVER

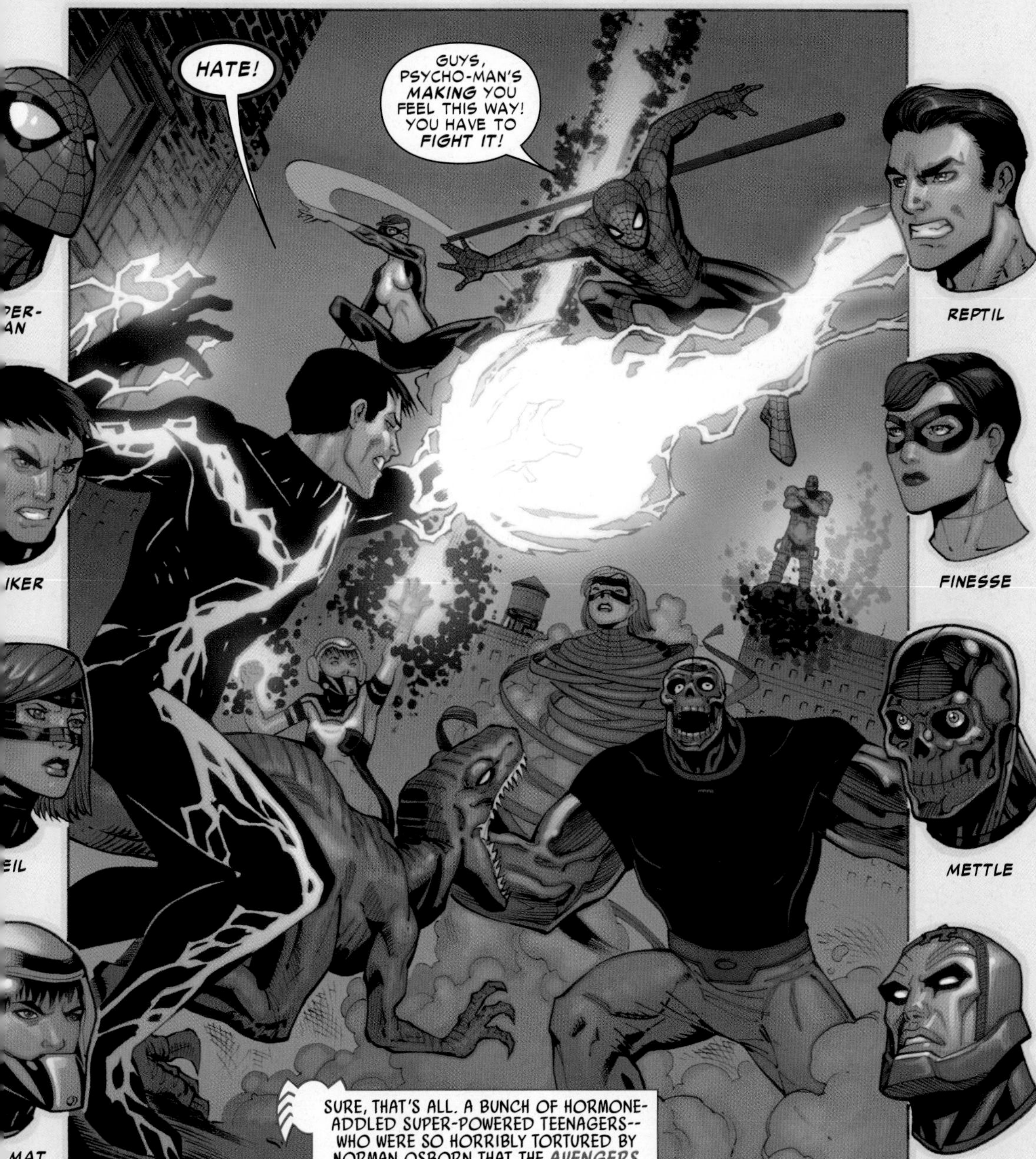

HATE!
GUYS, PSYCHO-MAN'S MAKING YOU FEEL THIS WAY! YOU HAVE TO FIGHT IT!
SURE, THAT'S ALL. A BUNCH OF HORMONE-ADDLED SUPER-POWERED TEENAGERS--WHO WERE SO HORRIBLY TORTURED BY NORMAN OSBORN THAT THE AVENGERS ARE DESPERATELY TRYING TO KEEP THEM FROM TURNING INTO VILLAINS--JUST HAVE TO CONTROL THEIR EMOTIONS.
I AM SO DEAD.
REPTIL
FINESSE
METTLE
PSYCHO-MAN

ELLIE PYLE ASSISTANT EDITOR
STEPHEN WACKER SENIOR EDITOR
AXEL ALONSO EDITOR IN CHIEF
JOE QUESADA CHIEF CREATIVE OFFICER
DAN BUCKLEY PUBLISHER
ALAN FINE EXECUTIVE PRODUCER

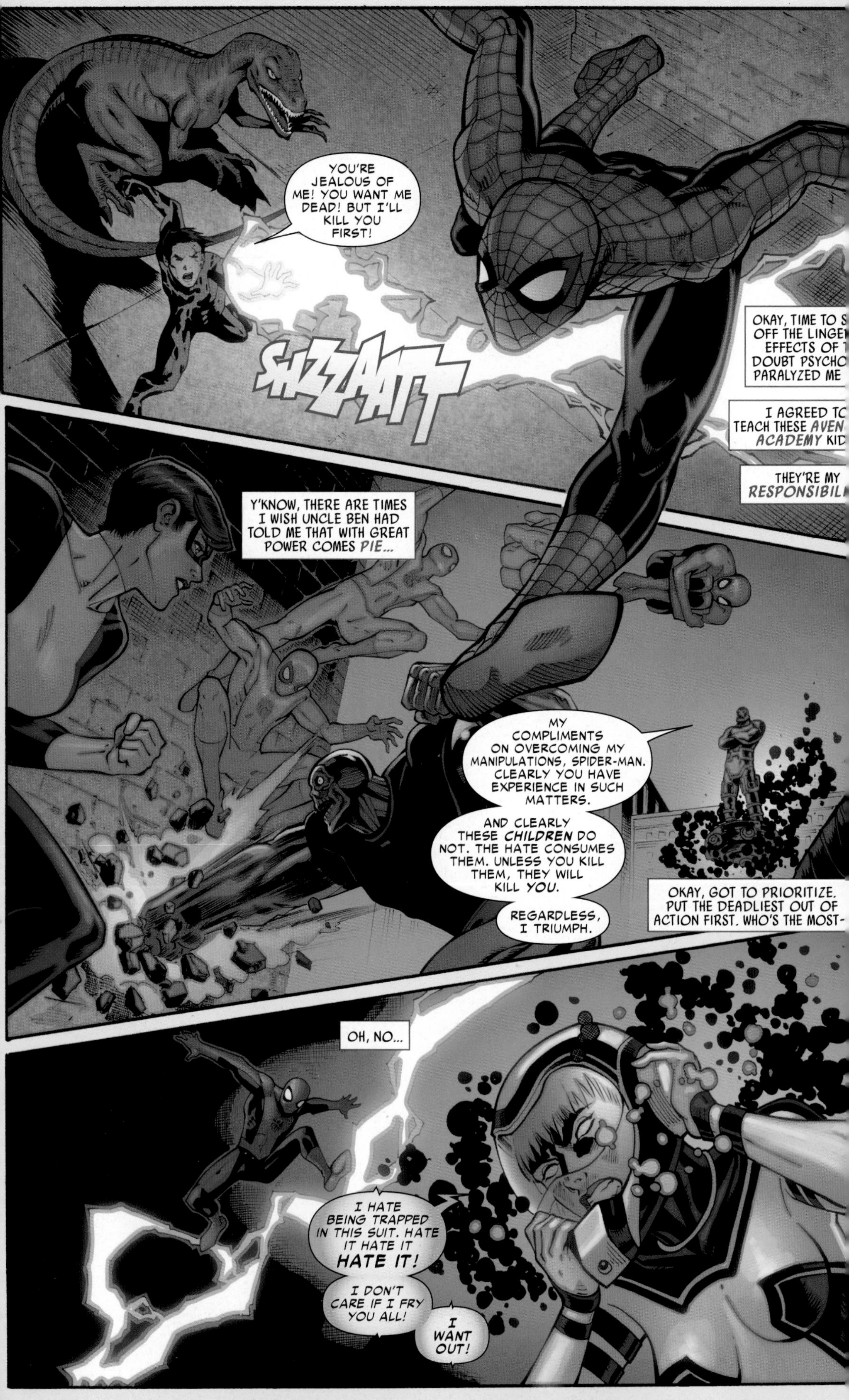
YOU'RE JEALOUS OF ME! YOU WANT ME DEAD! BUT I'LL KILL YOU FIRST!
SHZZAATT
OKAY, TIME TO S OFF THE LINGE EFFECTS OF T DOUBT PSYCHO PARALYZED ME
I AGREED TO TEACH THESE AVEN ACADEMY KID
THEY'RE MY RESPONSIBIL
Y'KNOW, THERE ARE TIMES I WISH UNCLE BEN HAD TOLD ME THAT WITH GREAT POWER COMES PIE...
MY COMPLIMENTS ON OVERCOMING MY MANIPULATIONS, SPIDER-MAN. CLEARLY YOU HAVE EXPERIENCE IN SUCH MATTERS.
AND CLEARLY THESE CHILDREN DO NOT. THE HATE CONSUMES THEM. UNLESS YOU KILL THEM, THEY WILL KILL YOU.
REGARDLESS, I TRIUMPH.
OKAY, GOT TO PRIORITIZE. PUT THE DEADLIEST OUT OF ACTION FIRST. WHO'S THE MOST-
OH, NO...
I HATE BEING TRAPPED IN THIS SUIT. HATE IT HATE IT HATE IT!
I DON'T CARE IF I FRY YOU ALL!
I WANT OUT!

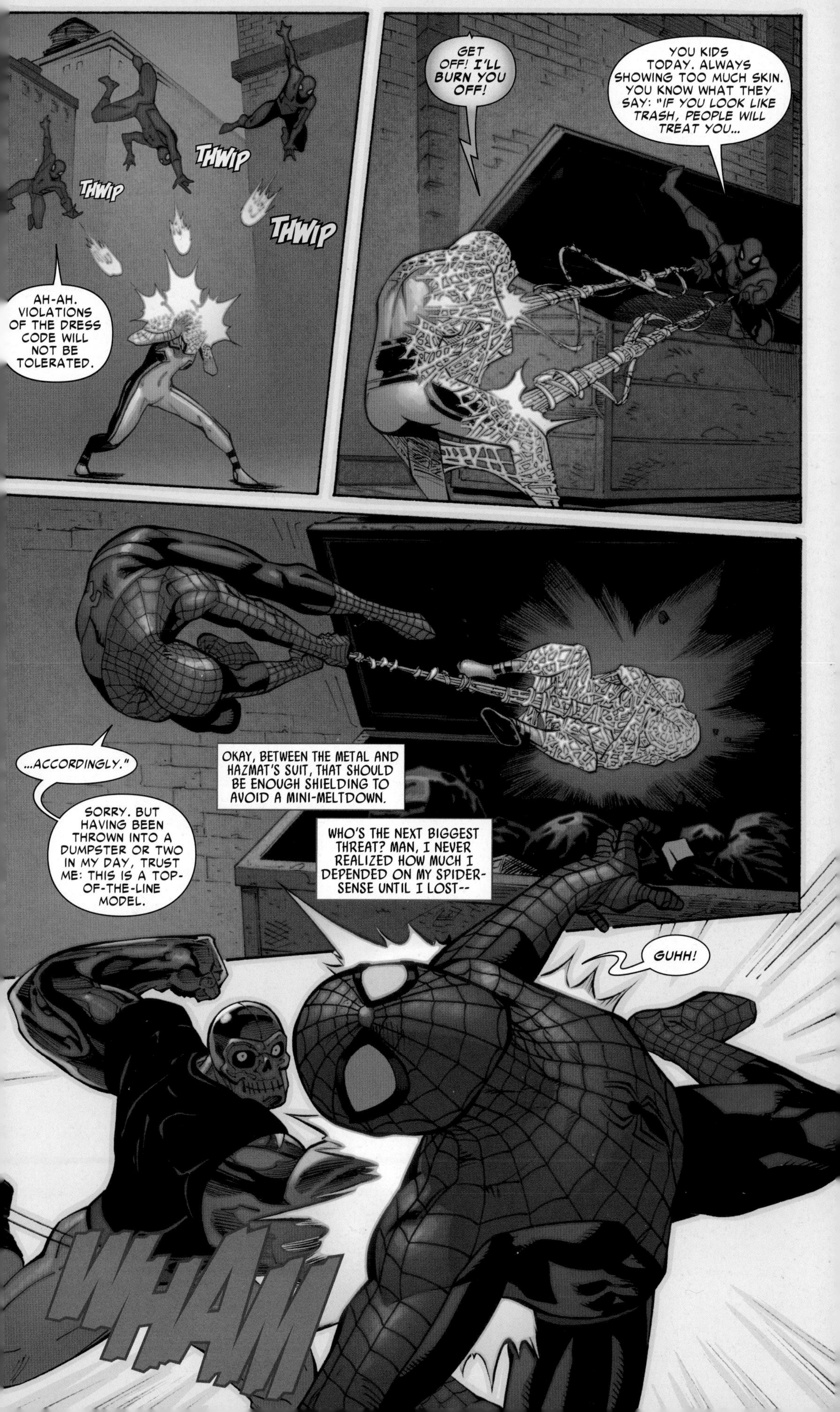
THWIP
THWIP
THWIP
AH-AH. VIOLATIONS OF THE DRESS CODE WILL NOT BE TOLERATED.
GET OFF! I'LL BURN YOU OFF!
YOU KIDS TODAY. ALWAYS SHOWING TOO MUCH SKIN. YOU KNOW WHAT THEY SAY: "IF YOU LOOK LIKE TRASH, PEOPLE WILL TREAT YOU...
...ACCORDINGLY."
SORRY. BUT HAVING BEEN THROWN INTO A DUMPSTER OR TWO IN MY DAY, TRUST ME: THIS IS A TOP-OF-THE-LINE MODEL.
OKAY, BETWEEN THE METAL AND HAZMAT'S SUIT, THAT SHOULD BE ENOUGH SHIELDING TO AVOID A MINI-MELTDOWN.
WHO'S THE NEXT BIGGEST THREAT? MAN, I NEVER REALIZED HOW MUCH I DEPENDED ON MY SPIDER-SENSE UNTIL I LOST--
GUHH!
WHAM

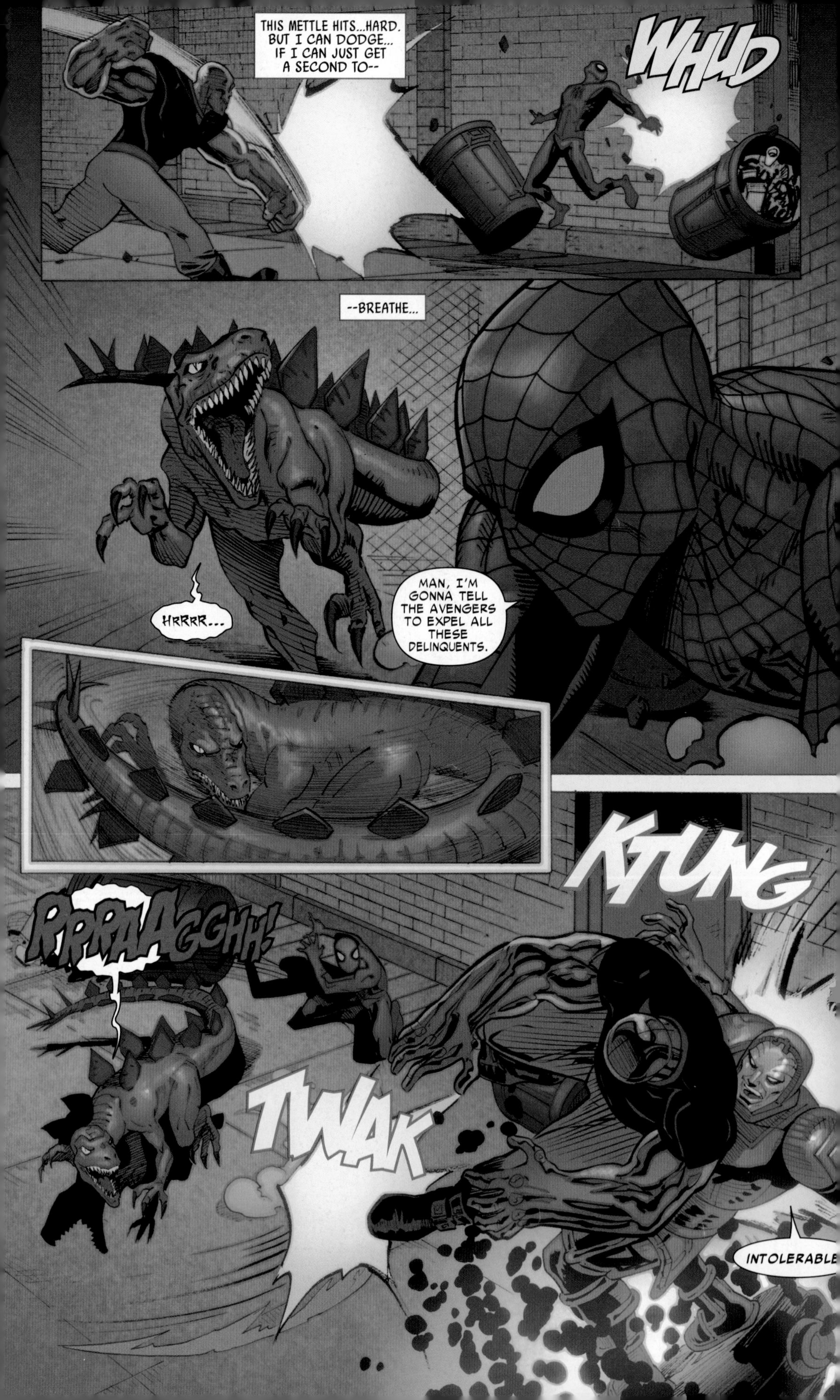
THIS METTLE HITS...HARD. BUT I CAN DODGE... IF I CAN JUST GET A SECOND TO--
WHUD
--BREATHE...
HRRRR...
MAN, I'M GONNA TELL THE AVENGERS TO EXPEL ALL THESE DELINQUENTS.
KTUNG
RPRRAAGGHH!
TWAK
INTOLERABLE

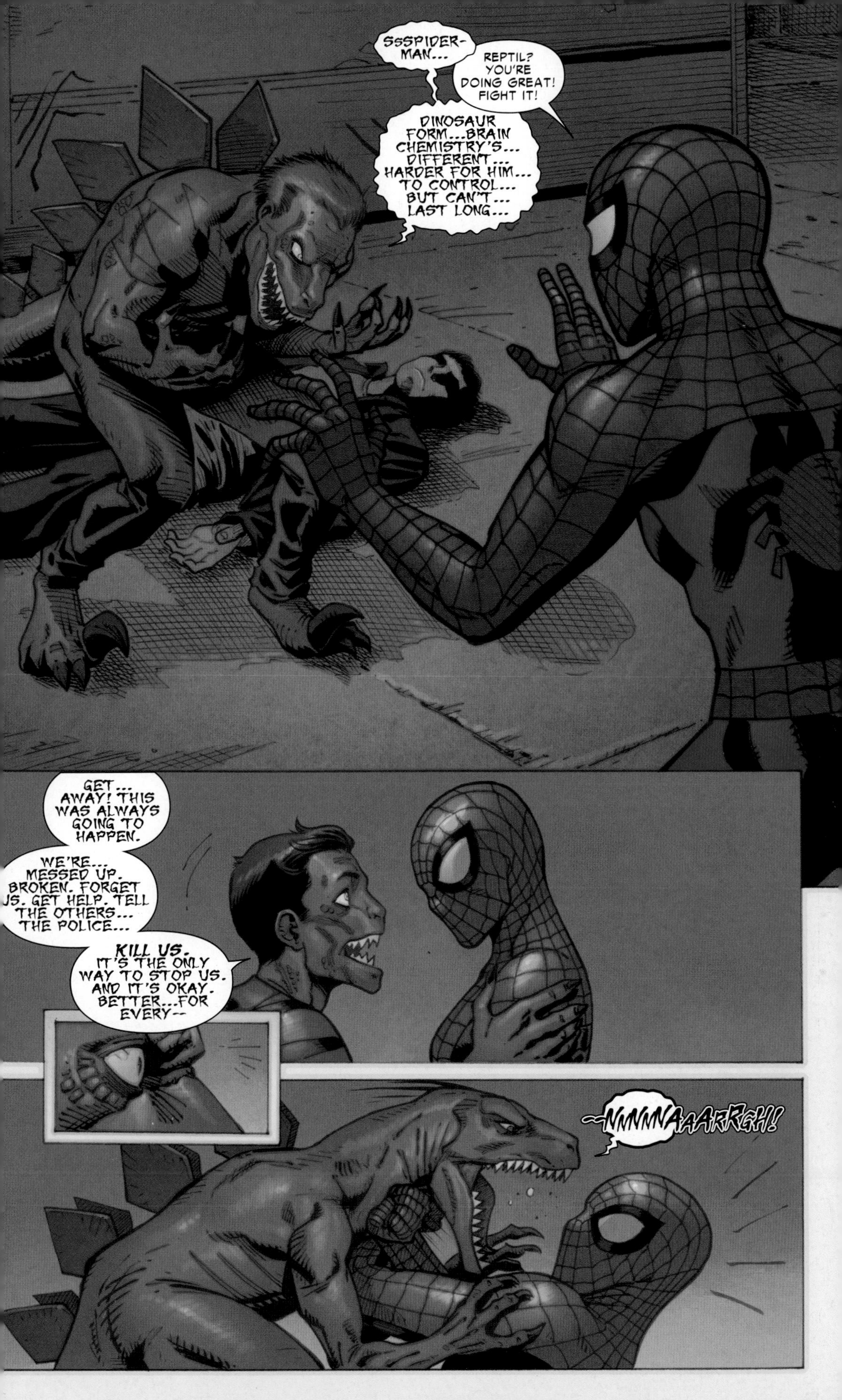

SsSPIDER-MAN...
REPTIL? YOU'RE DOING GREAT! FIGHT IT!
DINOSAUR FORM...BRAIN CHEMISTRY'S... DIFFERENT... HARDER FOR HIM... TO CONTROL... BUT CAN'T... LAST LONG...
GET... AWAY! THIS WAS ALWAYS GOING TO HAPPEN.
WE'RE... MESSED UP. BROKEN. FORGET US. GET HELP. TELL THE OTHERS... THE POLICE...
KILL US. IT'S THE ONLY WAY TO STOP US. AND IT'S OKAY. BETTER...FOR EVERY--
--NNNNNAAARRGH!

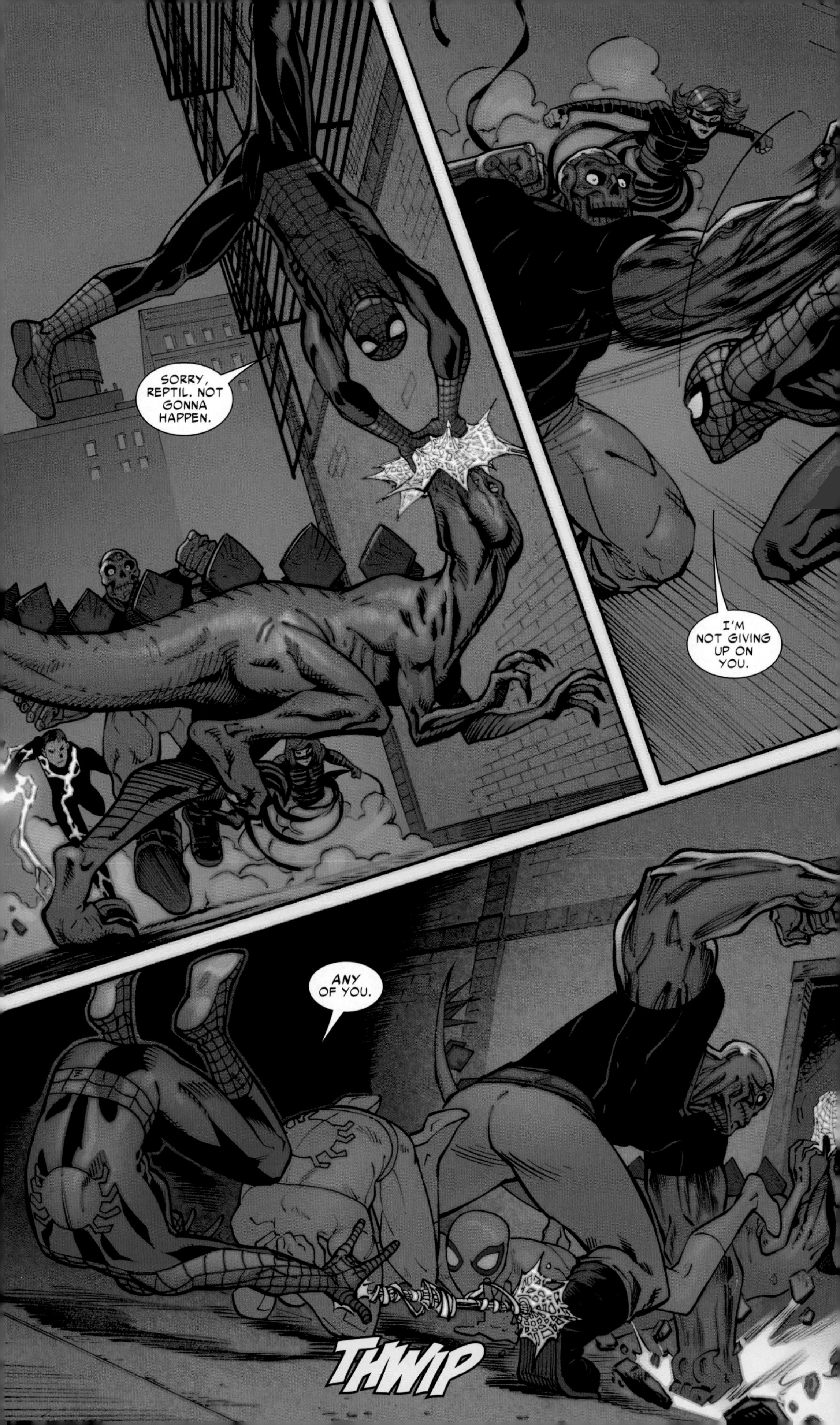
SORRY, REPTIL. NOT GONNA HAPPEN.
I'M NOT GIVING UP ON YOU.
ANY OF YOU.
THWIP

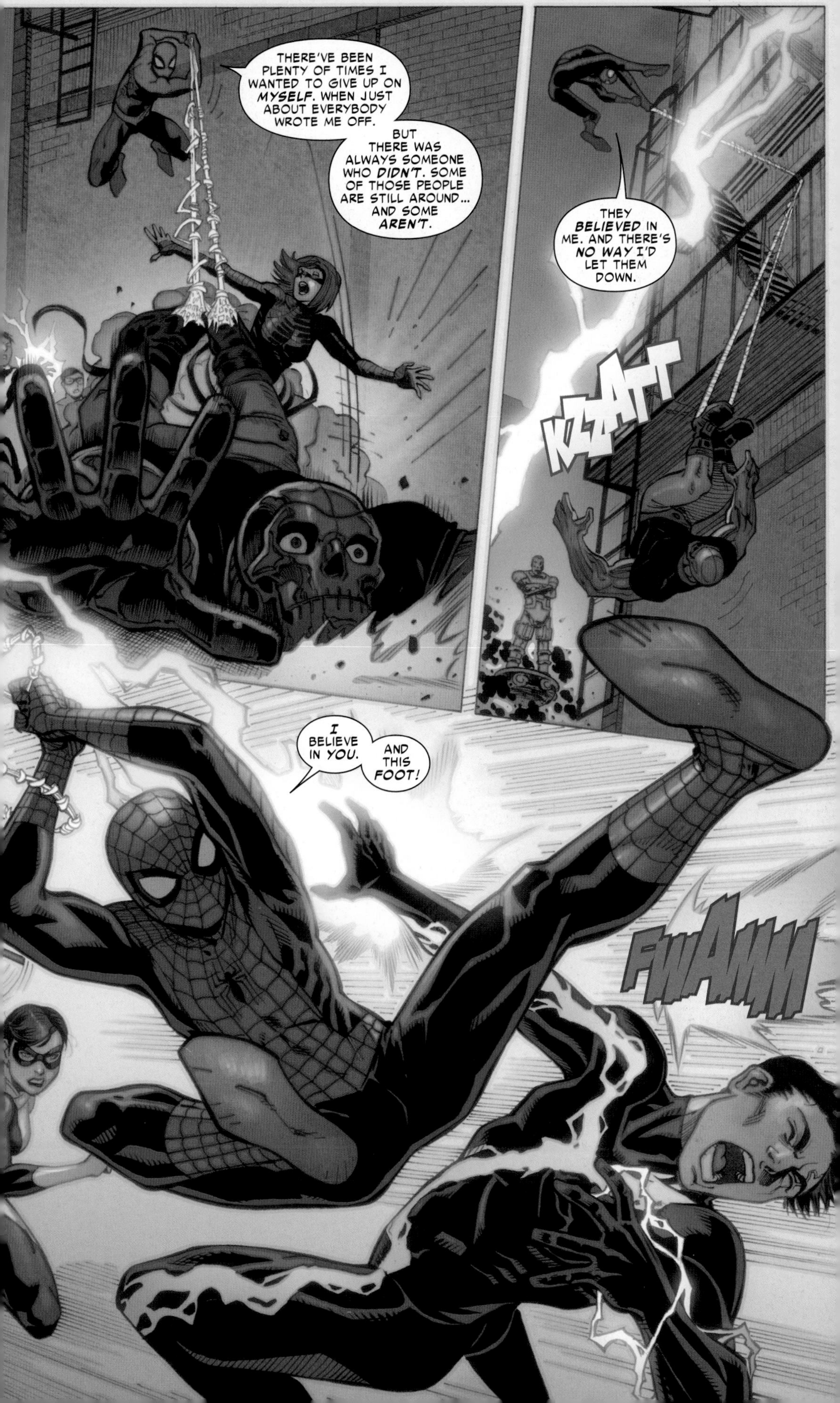
THERE'VE BEEN PLENTY OF TIMES I WANTED TO GIVE UP ON MYSELF. WHEN JUST ABOUT EVERYBODY WROTE ME OFF.
BUT THERE WAS ALWAYS SOMEONE WHO DIDN'T. SOME OF THOSE PEOPLE ARE STILL AROUND... AND SOME AREN'T.
THEY BELIEVED IN ME. AND THERE'S NO WAY I'D LET THEM DOWN.
KZZAATT
I BELIEVE IN YOU.
AND THIS FOOT!
FWAMM

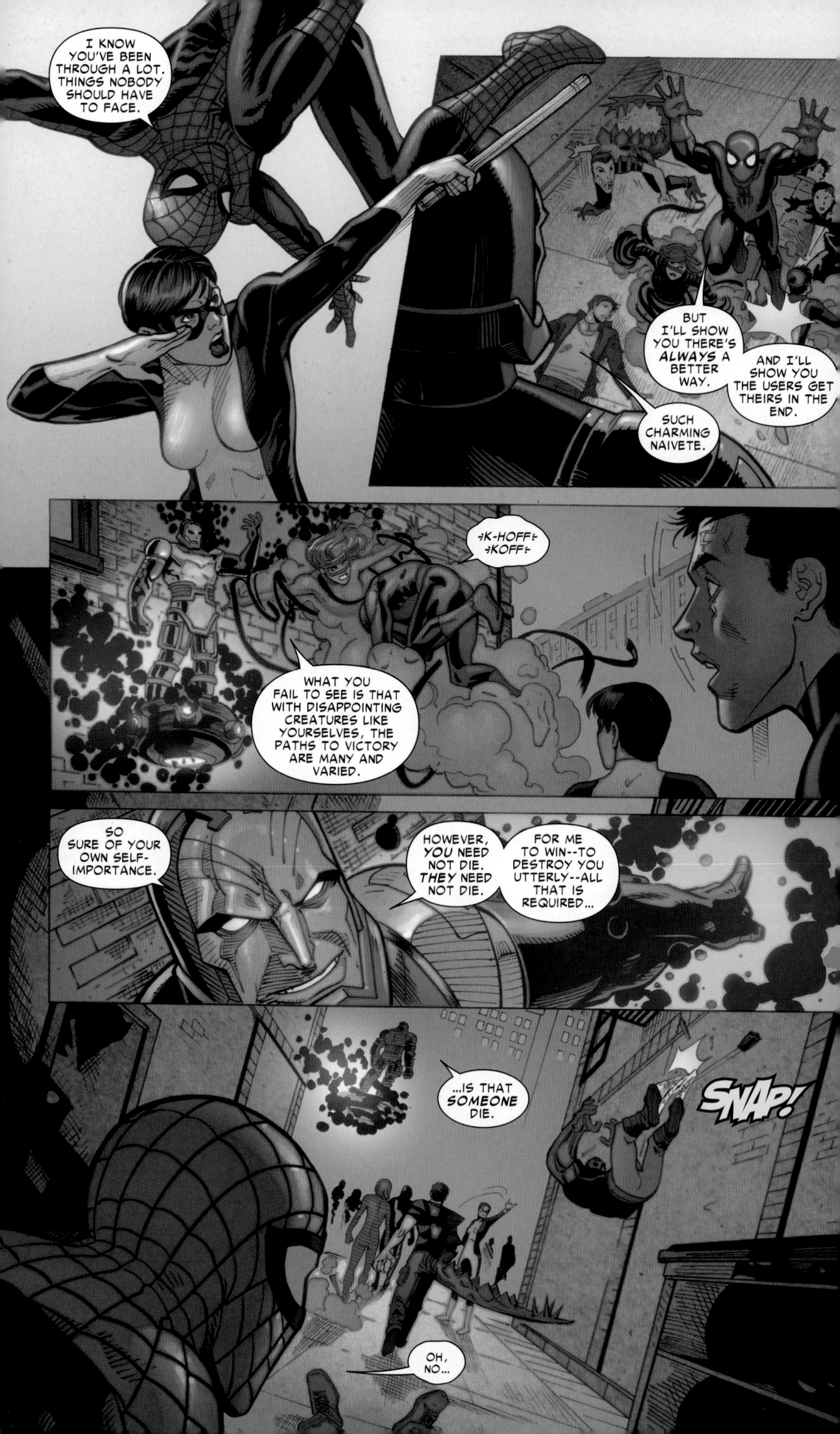
I KNOW YOU'VE BEEN THROUGH A LOT. THINGS NOBODY SHOULD HAVE TO FACE.
BUT I'LL SHOW YOU THERE'S ALWAYS A BETTER WAY.
AND I'LL SHOW YOU THE USERS GET THEIRS IN THE END.
SUCH CHARMING NAIVETE.
K-HOFF KOFF
WHAT YOU FAIL TO SEE IS THAT WITH DISAPPOINTING CREATURES LIKE YOURSELVES, THE PATHS TO VICTORY ARE MANY AND VARIED.
SO SURE OF YOUR OWN SELF-IMPORTANCE.
HOWEVER, YOU NEED NOT DIE. THEY NEED NOT DIE.
FOR ME TO WIN--TO DESTROY YOU UTTERLY--ALL THAT IS REQUIRED...
...IS THAT SOMEONE DIE.
SNAP!
OH, NO...

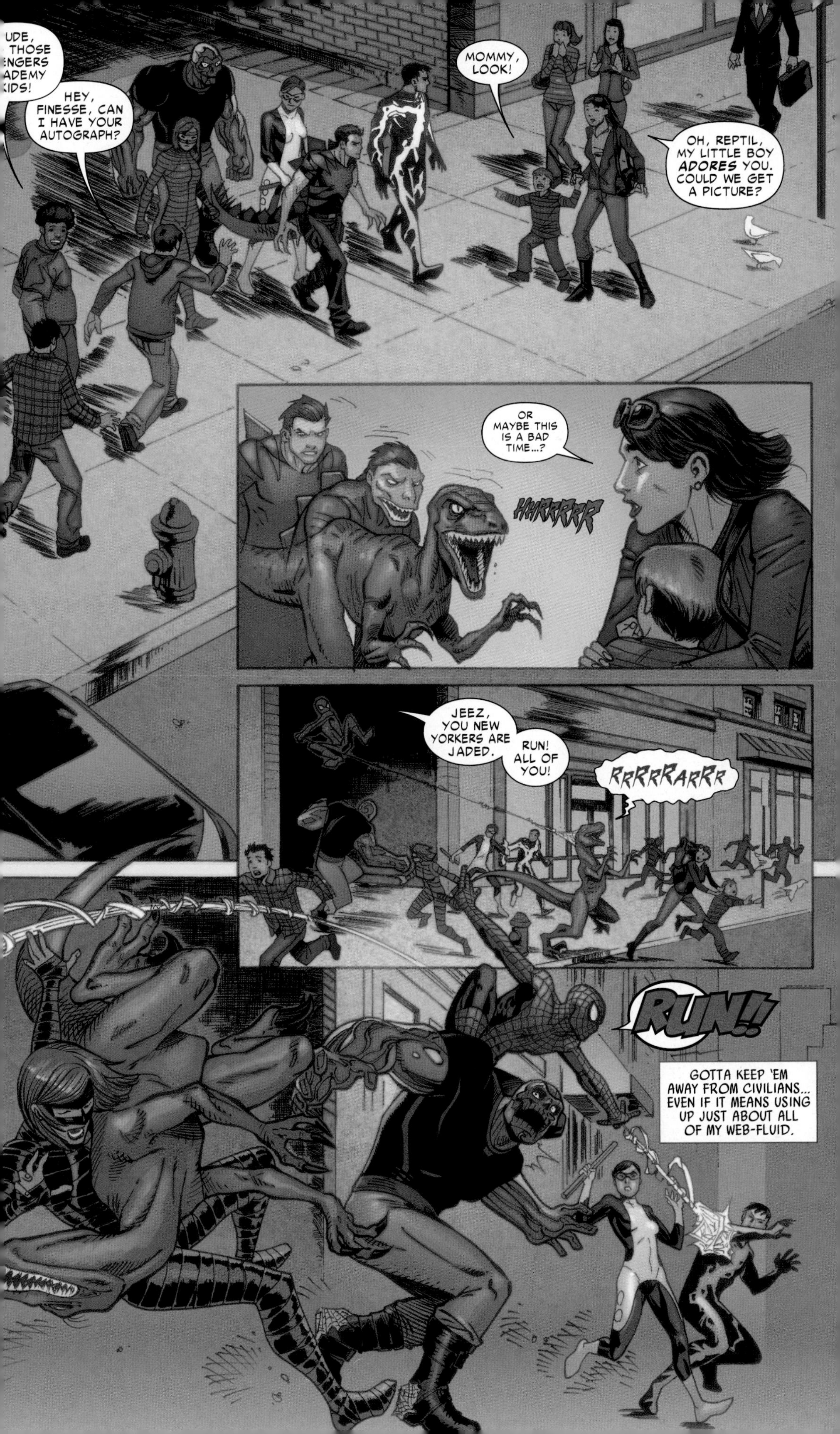
UDE, THOSE ENGERS ADEMY KIDS!
HEY, FINESSE, CAN I HAVE YOUR AUTOGRAPH?
MOMMY, LOOK!
OH, REPTIL, MY LITTLE BOY ADORES YOU. COULD WE GET A PICTURE?
OR MAYBE THIS IS A BAD TIME...?
HHRRRRR
JEEZ, YOU NEW YORKERS ARE JADED.
RUN! ALL OF YOU!
RRRRRARRR
RUN!!
GOTTA KEEP 'EM AWAY FROM CIVILIANS... EVEN IF IT MEANS USING UP JUST ABOUT ALL OF MY WEB-FLUID.

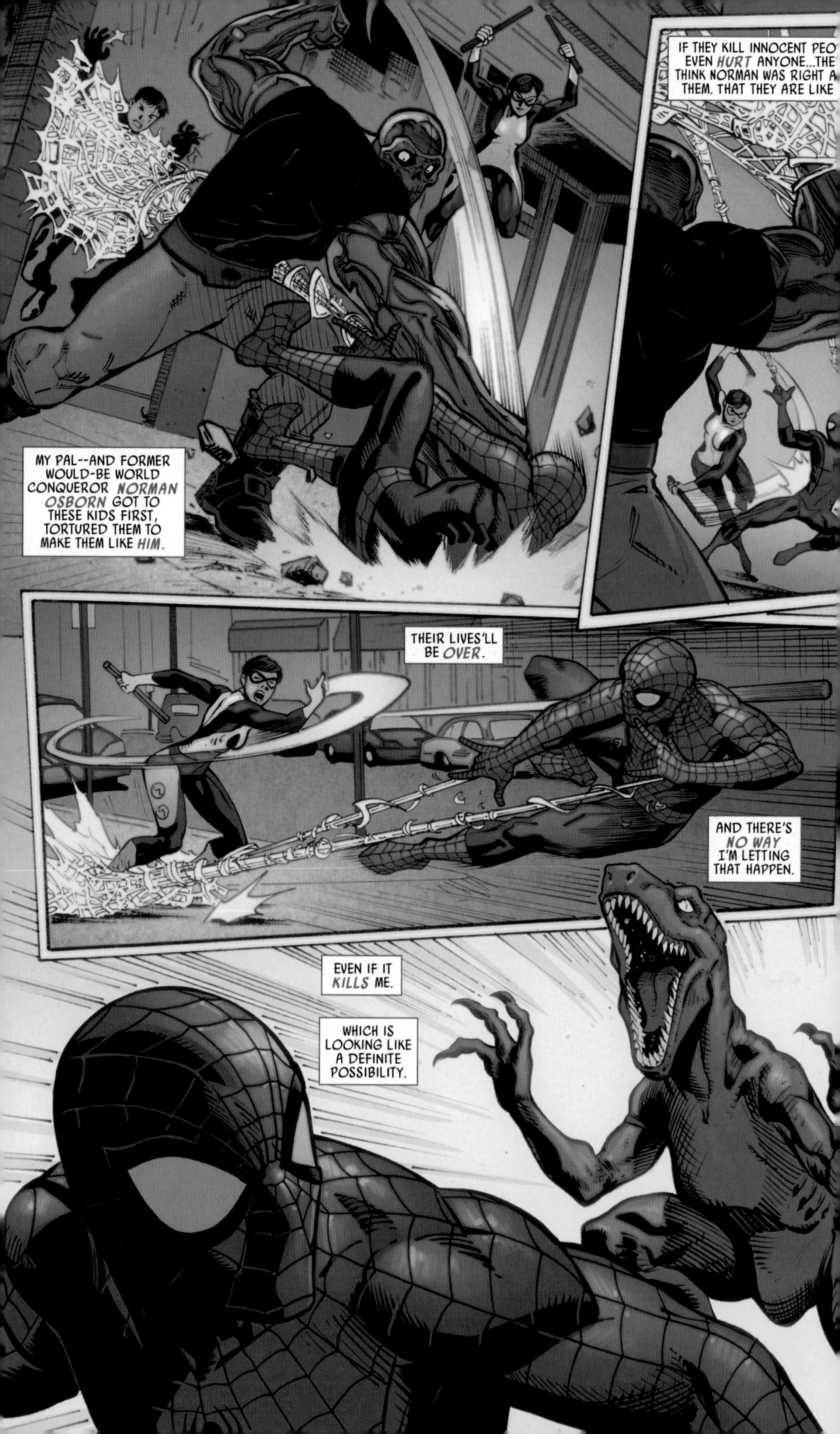
MY PAL--AND FORMER WOULD-BE WORLD CONQUEROR NORMAN OSBORN GOT TO THESE KIDS FIRST, TORTURED THEM TO MAKE THEM LIKE HIM.
IF THEY KILL INNOCENT PEO EVEN HURT ANYONE...THE THINK NORMAN WAS RIGHT A THEM. THAT THEY ARE LIKE
THEIR LIVES'LL BE OVER.
AND THERE'S NO WAY I'M LETTING THAT HAPPEN.
EVEN IF IT KILLS ME.
WHICH IS LOOKING LIKE A DEFINITE POSSIBILITY.

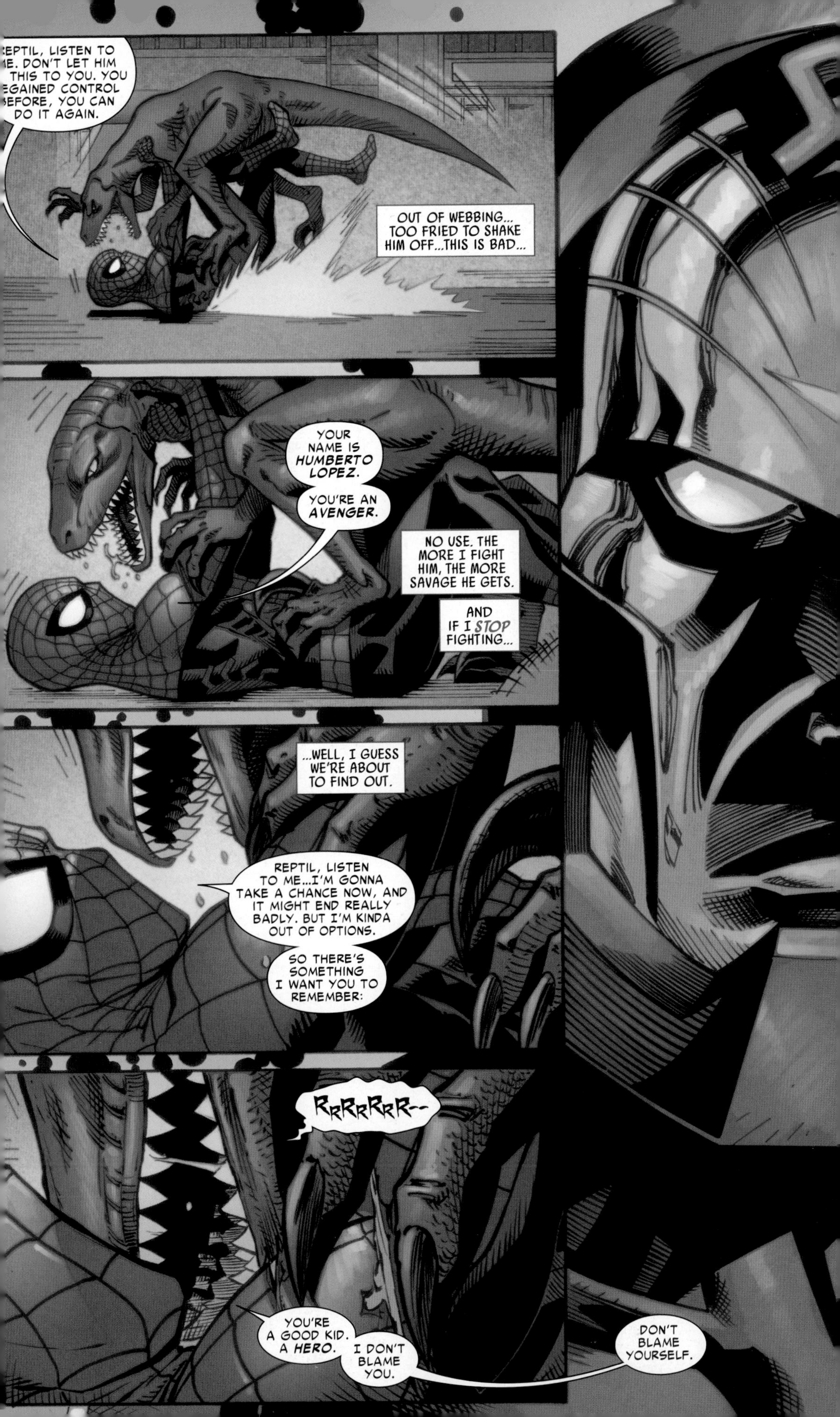

REPTIL, LISTEN TO ME. DON'T LET HIM THIS TO YOU. YOU REGAINED CONTROL BEFORE, YOU CAN DO IT AGAIN.
OUT OF WEBBING... TOO FRIED TO SHAKE HIM OFF...THIS IS BAD...
YOUR NAME IS HUMBERTO LOPEZ.
YOU'RE AN AVENGER.
NO USE. THE MORE I FIGHT HIM, THE MORE SAVAGE HE GETS.
AND IF I STOP FIGHTING...
...WELL, I GUESS WE'RE ABOUT TO FIND OUT.
REPTIL, LISTEN TO ME...I'M GONNA TAKE A CHANCE NOW, AND IT MIGHT END REALLY BADLY. BUT I'M KINDA OUT OF OPTIONS.
SO THERE'S SOMETHING I WANT YOU TO REMEMBER:
RRRRRRR--
YOU'RE A GOOD KID. A HERO.
I DON'T BLAME YOU.
DON'T BLAME YOURSELF.

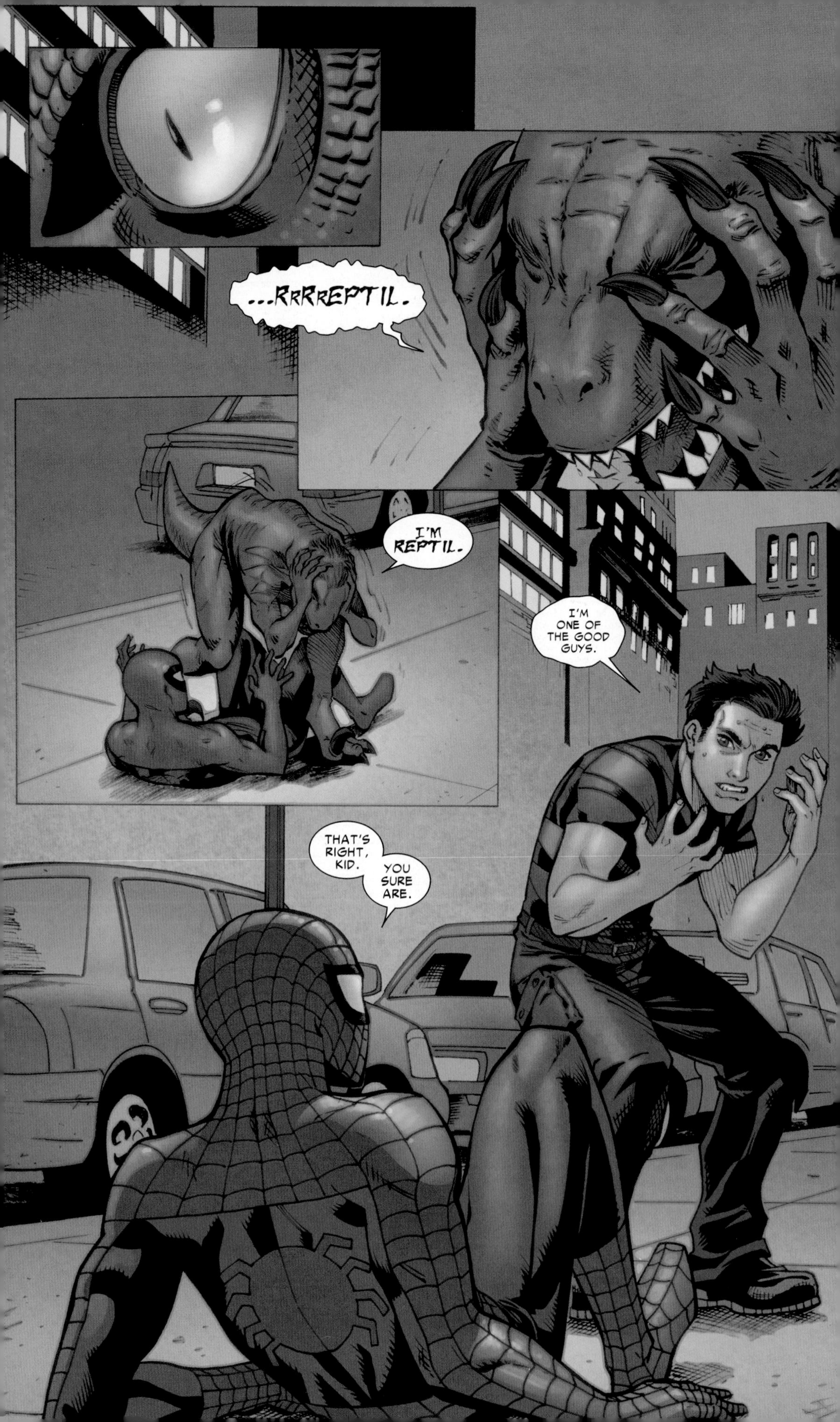
...RRRREPTIL.
I'M REPTIL.
I'M ONE OF THE GOOD GUYS.
THAT'S RIGHT, KID.
YOU SURE ARE.

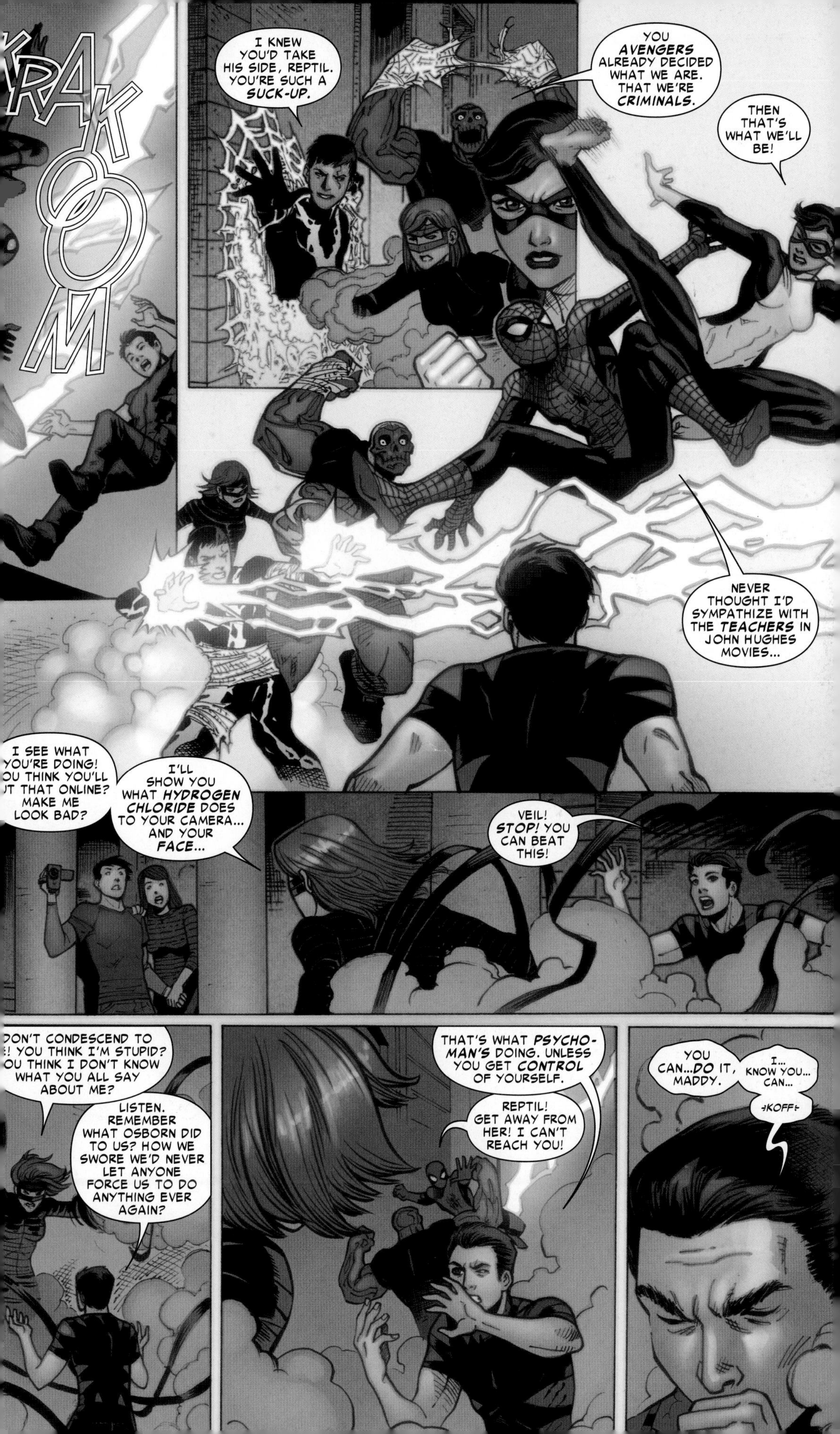
KRAKOOM
I KNEW YOU'D TAKE HIS SIDE, REPTIL. YOU'RE SUCH A SUCK-UP.
YOU AVENGERS ALREADY DECIDED WHAT WE ARE. THAT WE'RE CRIMINALS.
THEN THAT'S WHAT WE'LL BE!
NEVER THOUGHT I'D SYMPATHIZE WITH THE TEACHERS IN JOHN HUGHES MOVIES...
I SEE WHAT YOU'RE DOING! OU THINK YOU'LL T THAT ONLINE? MAKE ME LOOK BAD?
I'LL SHOW YOU WHAT HYDROGEN CHLORIDE DOES TO YOUR CAMERA... AND YOUR FACE...
VEIL! STOP! YOU CAN BEAT THIS!
DON'T CONDESCEND TO E! YOU THINK I'M STUPID? OU THINK I DON'T KNOW WHAT YOU ALL SAY ABOUT ME?
LISTEN. REMEMBER WHAT OSBORN DID TO US? HOW WE SWORE WE'D NEVER LET ANYONE FORCE US TO DO ANYTHING EVER AGAIN?
THAT'S WHAT PSYCHO-MAN'S DOING. UNLESS YOU GET CONTROL OF YOURSELF.
REPTIL! GET AWAY FROM HER! I CAN'T REACH YOU!
YOU CAN...DO IT, MADDY.
I... KNOW YOU... CAN...
KOFF

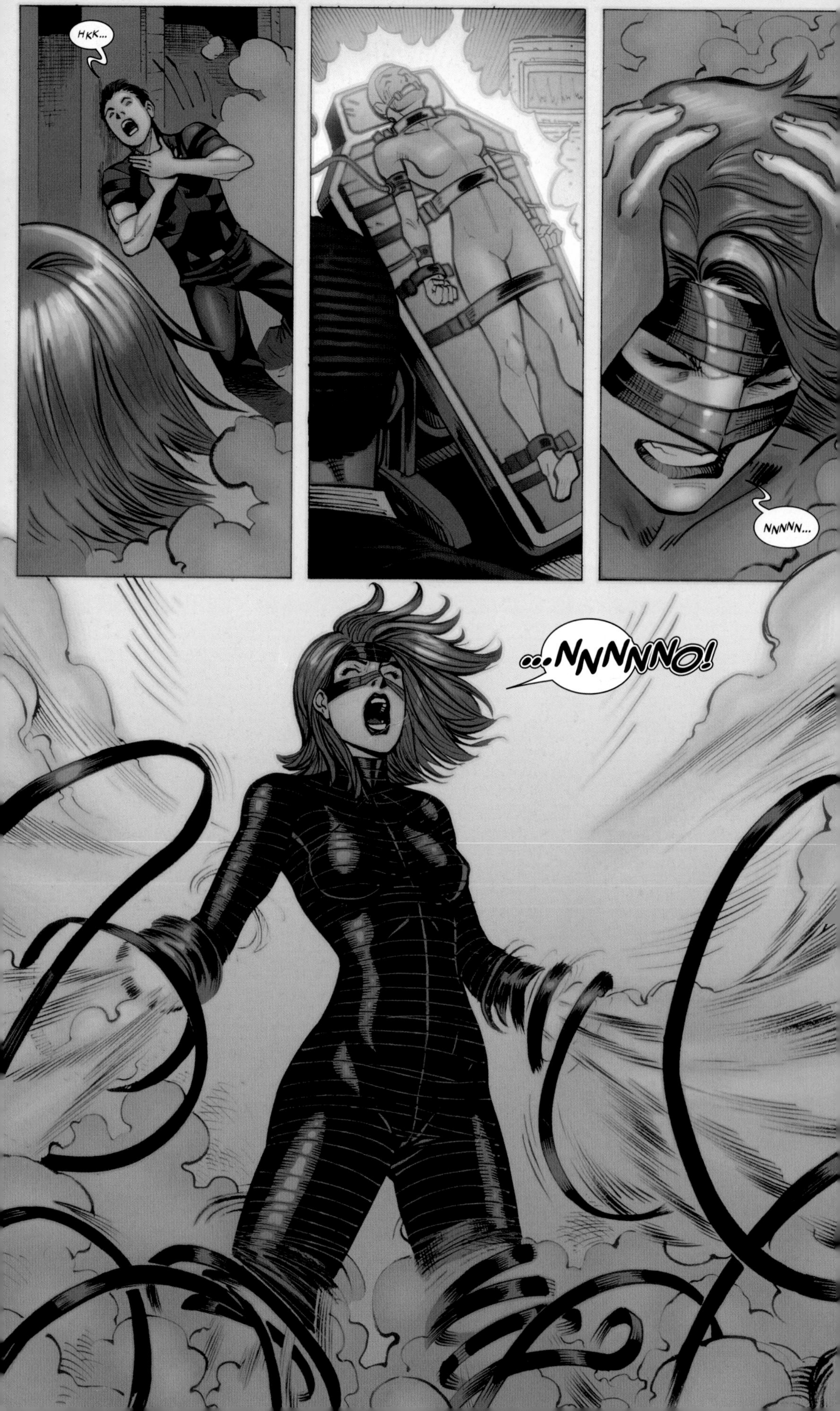
HKK...
NNNNN...
...NNNNNO!

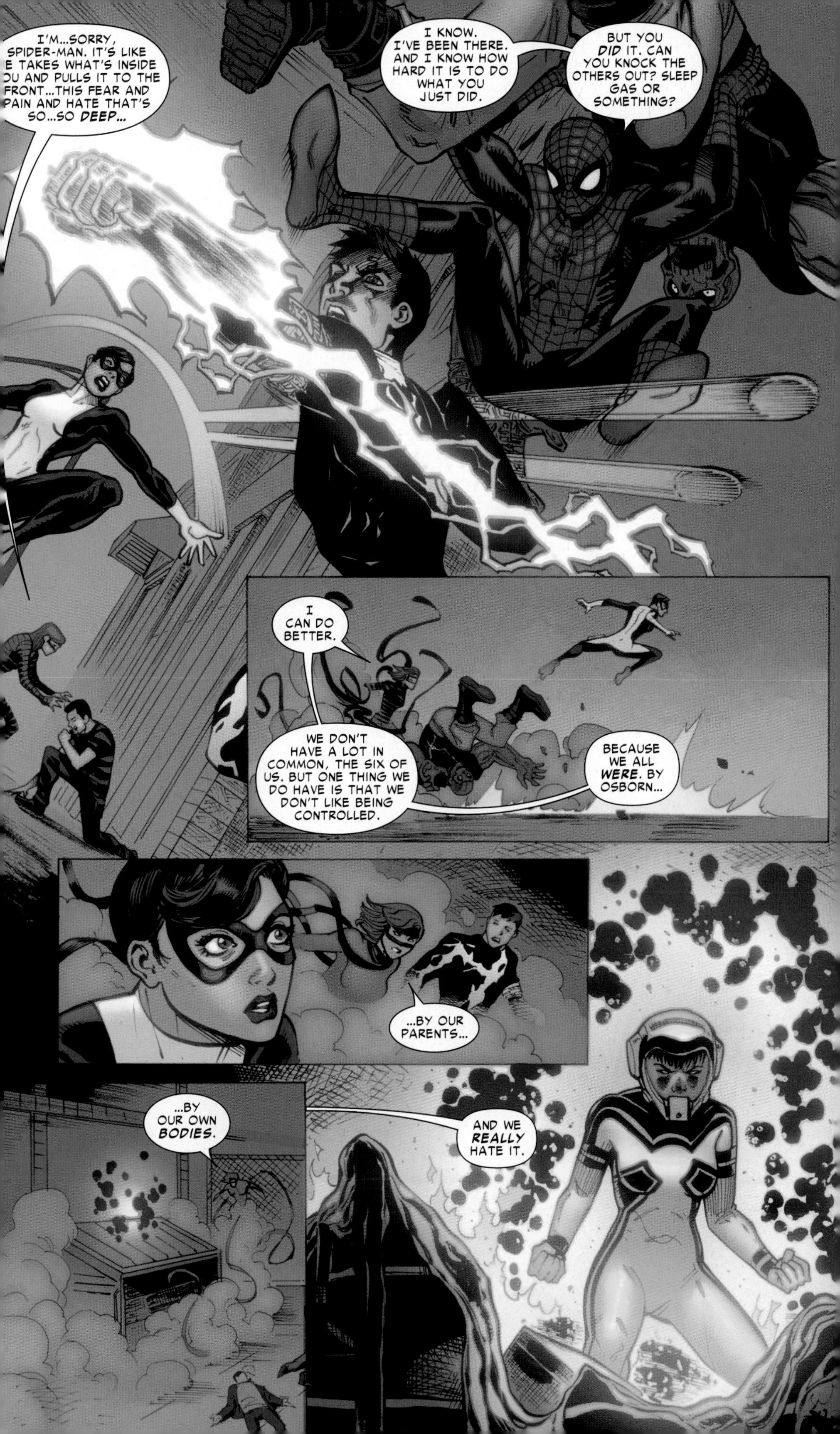
I'M...SORRY, SPIDER-MAN. IT'S LIKE E TAKES WHAT'S INSIDE OU AND PULLS IT TO THE FRONT...THIS FEAR AND PAIN AND HATE THAT'S SO...SO DEEP...
I KNOW. I'VE BEEN THERE. AND I KNOW HOW HARD IT IS TO DO WHAT YOU JUST DID.
BUT YOU DID IT. CAN YOU KNOCK THE OTHERS OUT? SLEEP GAS OR SOMETHING?
I CAN DO BETTER.
WE DON'T HAVE A LOT IN COMMON, THE SIX OF US. BUT ONE THING WE DO HAVE IS THAT WE DON'T LIKE BEING CONTROLLED.
BECAUSE WE ALL WERE. BY OSBORN...
...BY OUR PARENTS...
...BY OUR OWN BODIES.
AND WE REALLY HATE IT.

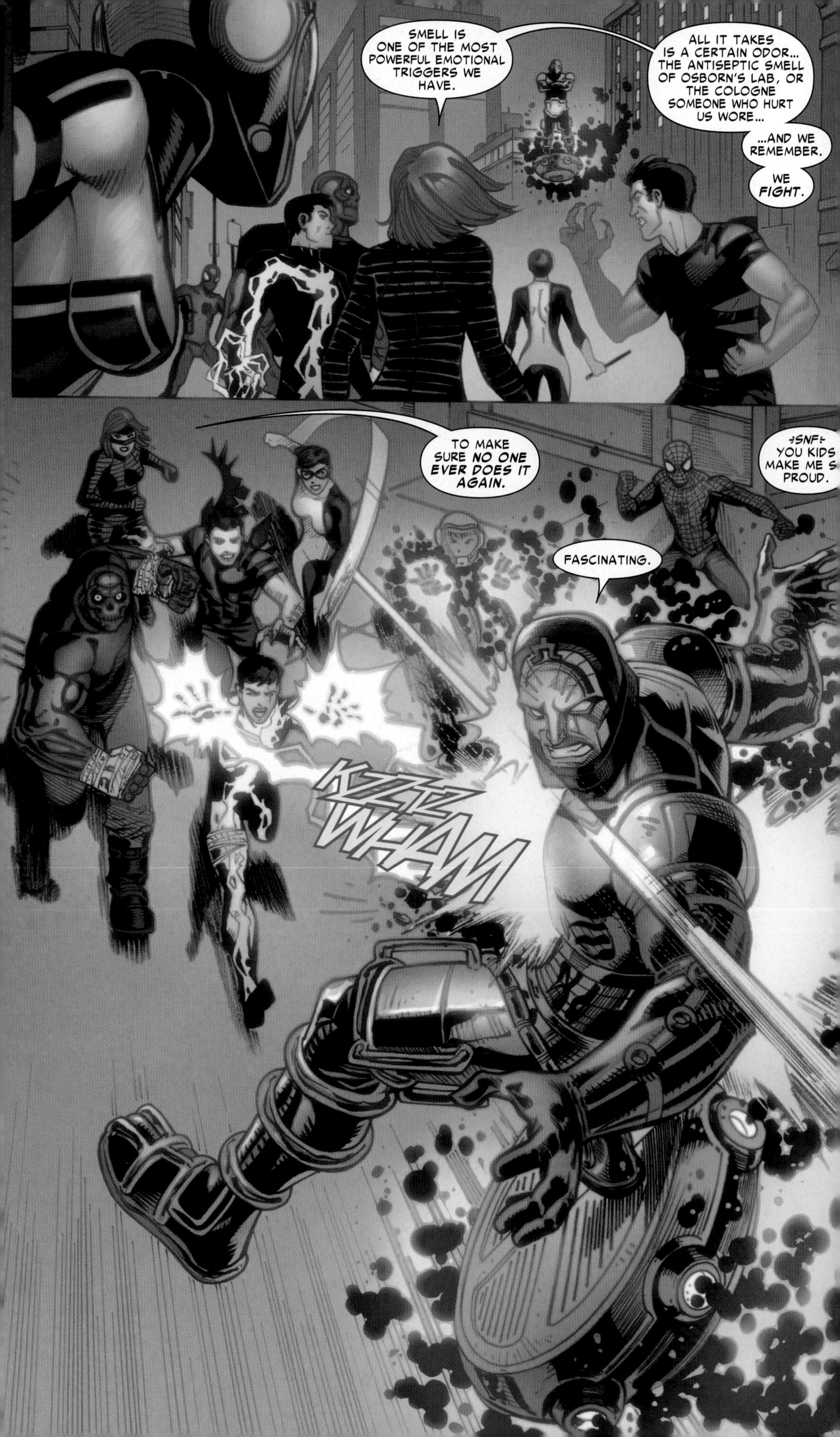
SMELL IS ONE OF THE MOST POWERFUL EMOTIONAL TRIGGERS WE HAVE.
ALL IT TAKES IS A CERTAIN ODOR... THE ANTISEPTIC SMELL OF OSBORN'S LAB, OR THE COLOGNE SOMEONE WHO HURT US WORE...
...AND WE REMEMBER.
WE *FIGHT*.
TO MAKE SURE *NO ONE EVER DOES* IT AGAIN.
SNF YOU KIDS MAKE ME S PROUD.
FASCINATING.
KZZZ WHAM

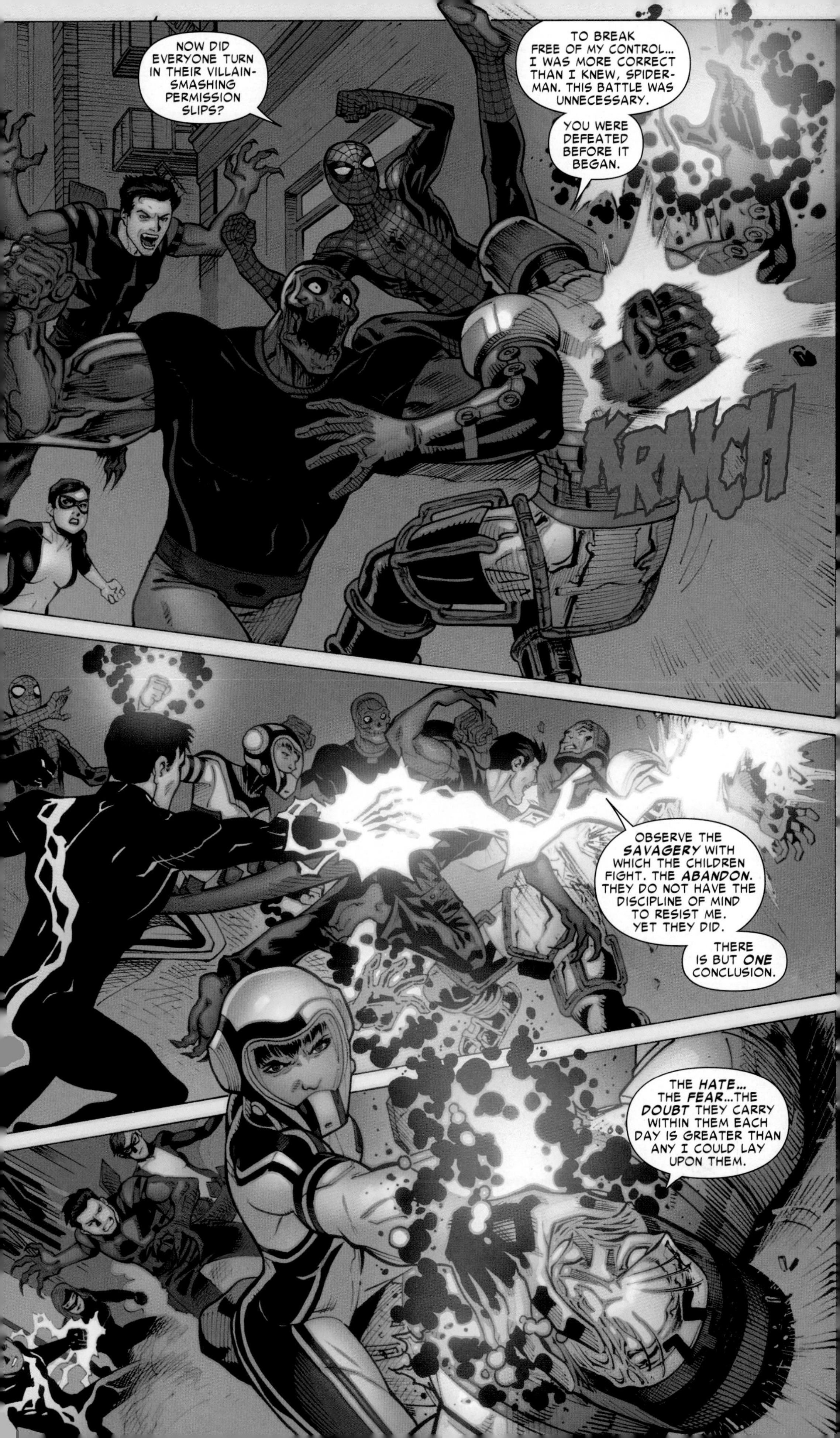
NOW DID EVERYONE TURN IN THEIR VILLAIN-SMASHING PERMISSION SLIPS?
TO BREAK FREE OF MY CONTROL... I WAS MORE CORRECT THAN I KNEW, SPIDER-MAN. THIS BATTLE WAS UNNECESSARY.
YOU WERE DEFEATED BEFORE IT BEGAN.
KRNCH
OBSERVE THE SAVAGERY WITH WHICH THE CHILDREN FIGHT. THE ABANDON. THEY DO NOT HAVE THE DISCIPLINE OF MIND TO RESIST ME. YET THEY DID.
THERE IS BUT ONE CONCLUSION.
THE HATE... THE FEAR...THE DOUBT THEY CARRY WITHIN THEM EACH DAY IS GREATER THAN ANY I COULD LAY UPON THEM.

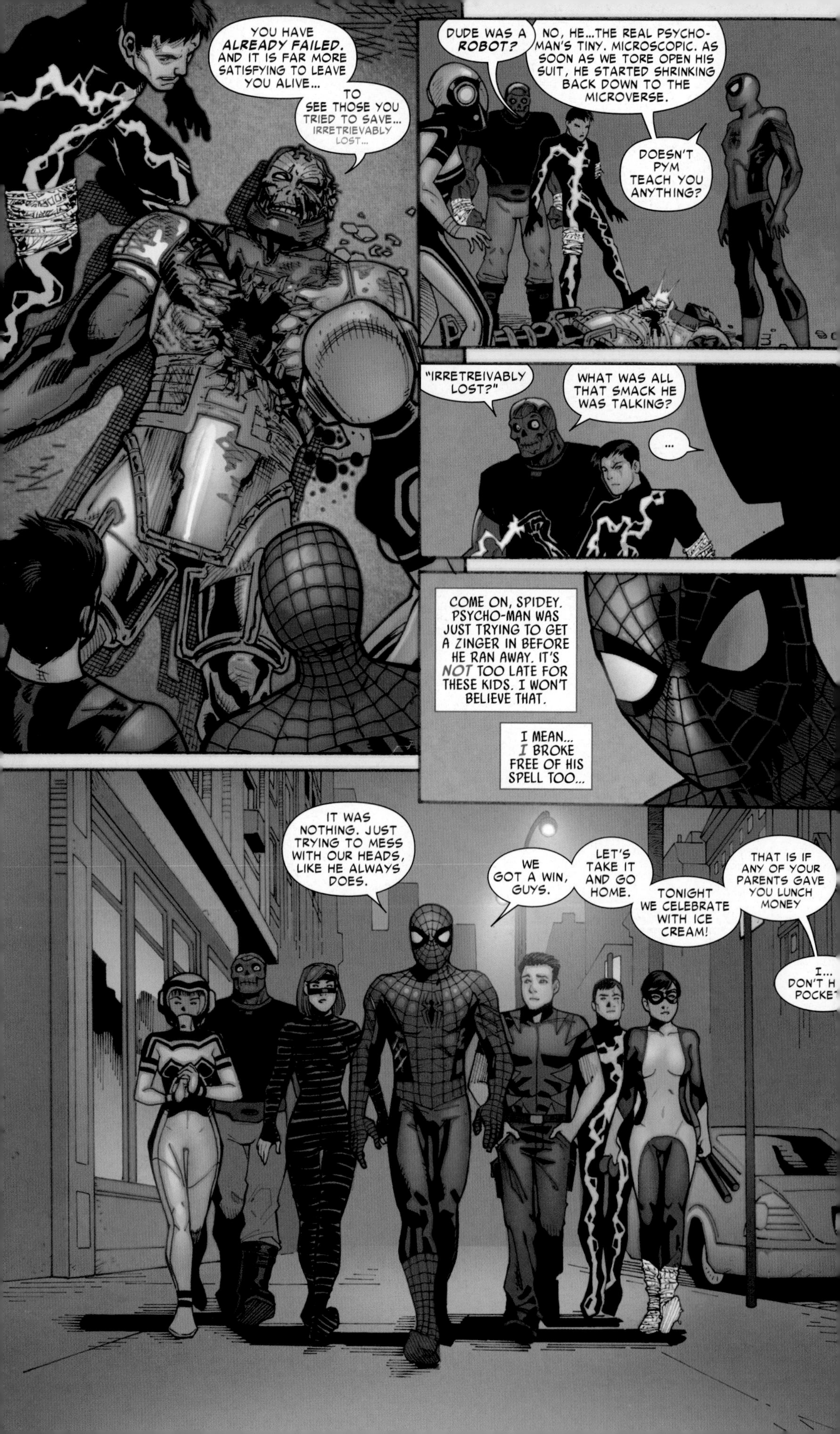
YOU HAVE ALREADY FAILED. AND IT IS FAR MORE SATISFYING TO LEAVE YOU ALIVE...
TO SEE THOSE YOU TRIED TO SAVE... IRRETRIEVABLY LOST...
DUDE WAS A ROBOT?
NO, HE...THE REAL PSYCHO-MAN'S TINY. MICROSCOPIC. AS SOON AS WE TORE OPEN HIS SUIT, HE STARTED SHRINKING BACK DOWN TO THE MICROVERSE.
DOESN'T PYM TEACH YOU ANYTHING?
"IRRETREIVABLY LOST?"
WHAT WAS ALL THAT SMACK HE WAS TALKING?
...
COME ON, SPIDEY. PSYCHO-MAN WAS JUST TRYING TO GET A ZINGER IN BEFORE HE RAN AWAY. IT'S NOT TOO LATE FOR THESE KIDS. I WON'T BELIEVE THAT.
I MEAN... I BROKE FREE OF HIS SPELL TOO...
IT WAS NOTHING. JUST TRYING TO MESS WITH OUR HEADS, LIKE HE ALWAYS DOES.
WE GOT A WIN, GUYS.
LET'S TAKE IT AND GO HOME.
TONIGHT WE CELEBRATE WITH ICE CREAM!
THAT IS IF ANY OF YOUR PARENTS GAVE YOU LUNCH MONEY

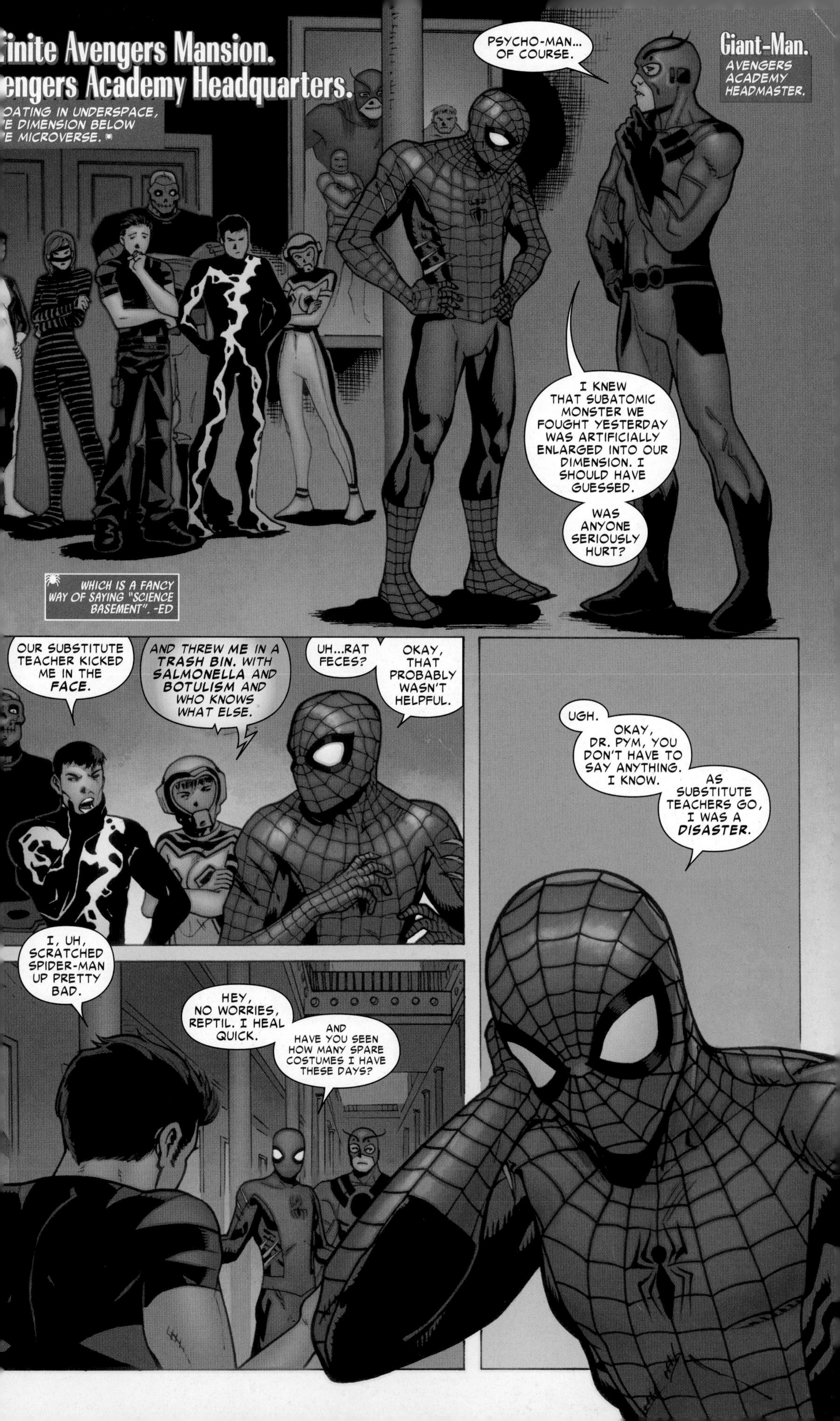

inite Avengers Mansion.
engers Academy Headquarters.
OATING IN UNDERSPACE, E DIMENSION BELOW E MICROVERSE.
PSYCHO-MAN... OF COURSE.
Giant-Man.
AVENGERS ACADEMY HEADMASTER.
I KNEW THAT SUBATOMIC MONSTER WE FOUGHT YESTERDAY WAS ARTIFICIALLY ENLARGED INTO OUR DIMENSION. I SHOULD HAVE GUESSED.
WAS ANYONE SERIOUSLY HURT?
WHICH IS A FANCY WAY OF SAYING "SCIENCE BASEMENT". -ED
OUR SUBSTITUTE TEACHER KICKED ME IN THE FACE.
AND THREW ME IN A TRASH BIN. WITH SALMONELLA AND BOTULISM AND WHO KNOWS WHAT ELSE.
UH...RAT FECES?
OKAY, THAT PROBABLY WASN'T HELPFUL.
UGH.
OKAY, DR. PYM, YOU DON'T HAVE TO SAY ANYTHING. I KNOW.
AS SUBSTITUTE TEACHERS GO, I WAS A DISASTER.
I, UH, SCRATCHED SPIDER-MAN UP PRETTY BAD.
HEY, NO WORRIES, REPTIL. I HEAL QUICK.
AND HAVE YOU SEEN HOW MANY SPARE COSTUMES I HAVE THESE DAYS?

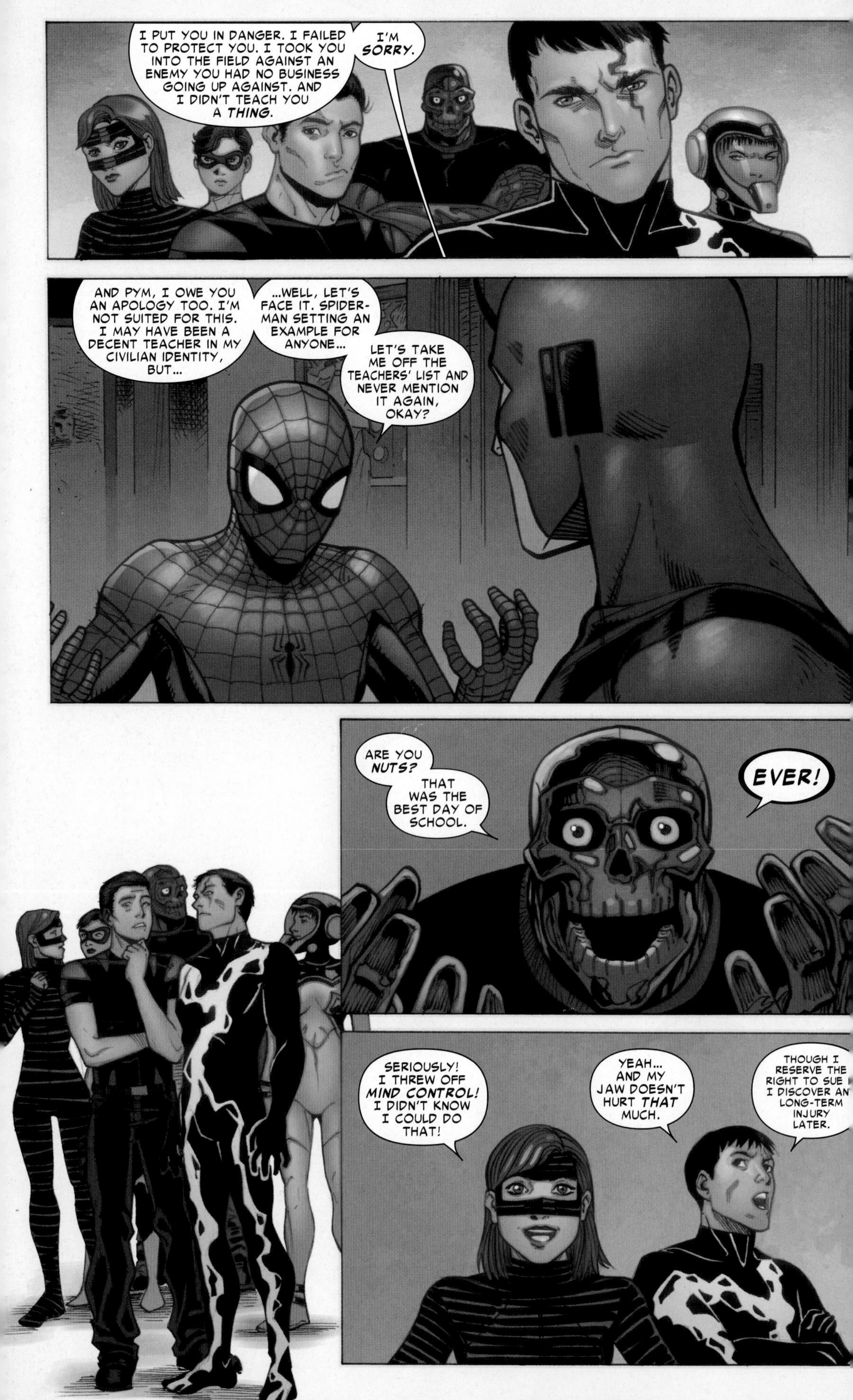

I PUT YOU IN DANGER. I FAILED TO PROTECT YOU. I TOOK YOU INTO THE FIELD AGAINST AN ENEMY YOU HAD NO BUSINESS GOING UP AGAINST. AND I DIDN'T TEACH YOU A *THING*.
I'M *SORRY*.
AND PYM, I OWE YOU AN APOLOGY TOO. I'M NOT SUITED FOR THIS. I MAY HAVE BEEN A DECENT TEACHER IN MY CIVILIAN IDENTITY, BUT...
...WELL, LET'S FACE IT. SPIDER-MAN SETTING AN EXAMPLE FOR ANYONE...
LET'S TAKE ME OFF THE TEACHERS' LIST AND NEVER MENTION IT AGAIN, OKAY?
ARE YOU *NUTS?*
THAT WAS THE BEST DAY OF SCHOOL.
EVER!
SERIOUSLY! I THREW OFF *MIND CONTROL!* I DIDN'T KNOW I COULD DO THAT!
YEAH... AND MY JAW DOESN'T HURT *THAT* MUCH.
THOUGH I RESERVE THE RIGHT TO SUE I DISCOVER AN LONG-TERM INJURY LATER.

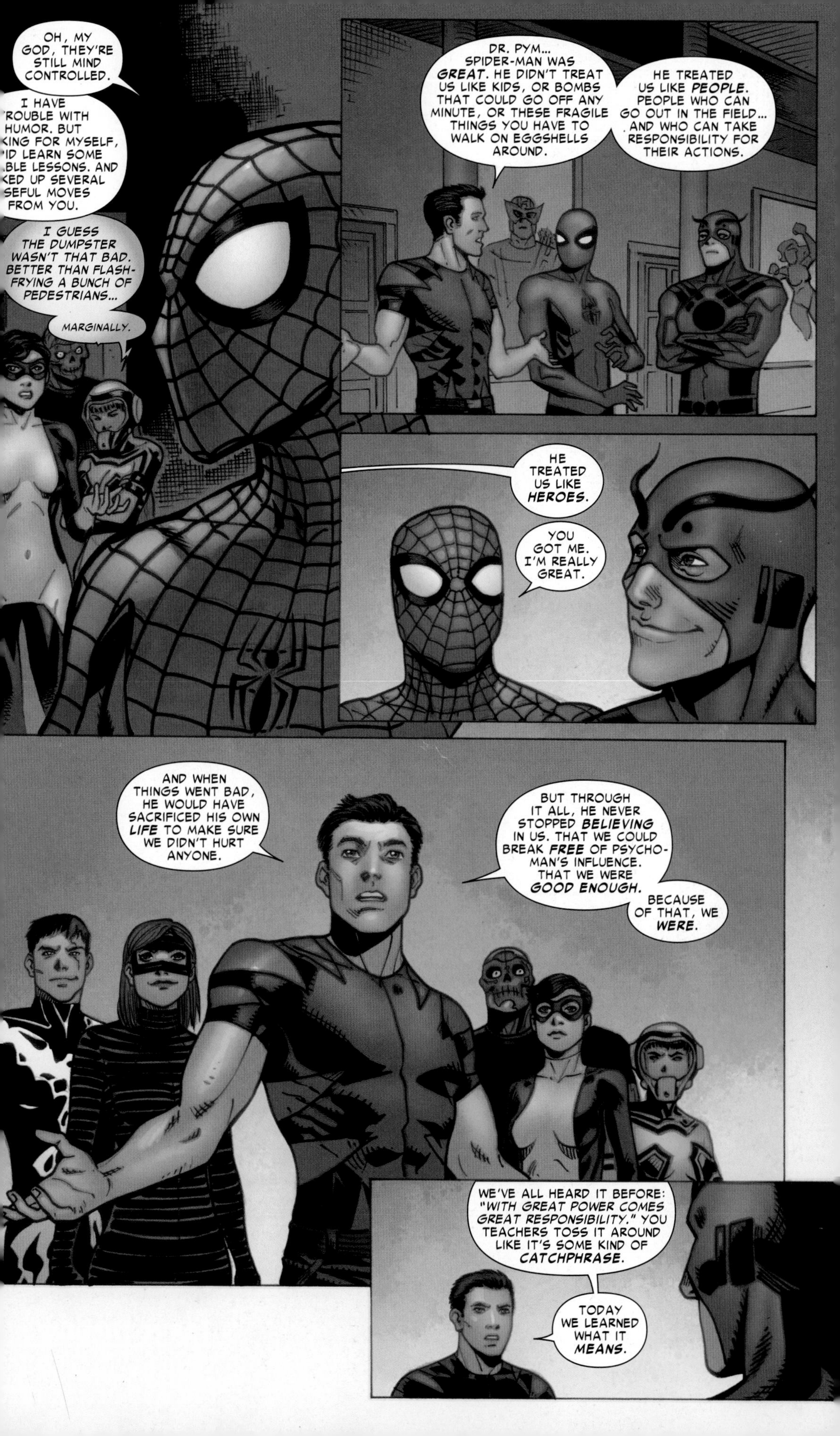

OH, MY GOD, THEY'RE STILL MIND CONTROLLED.
I HAVE 'ROUBLE WITH HUMOR. BUT KING FOR MYSELF, 'ID LEARN SOME BLE LESSONS. AND KED UP SEVERAL SEFUL MOVES FROM YOU.
I GUESS THE DUMPSTER WASN'T THAT BAD. BETTER THAN FLASH-FRYING A BUNCH OF PEDESTRIANS...
MARGINALLY.
DR. PYM... SPIDER-MAN WAS GREAT. HE DIDN'T TREAT US LIKE KIDS, OR BOMBS THAT COULD GO OFF ANY MINUTE, OR THESE FRAGILE THINGS YOU HAVE TO WALK ON EGGSHELLS AROUND.
HE TREATED US LIKE PEOPLE. PEOPLE WHO CAN GO OUT IN THE FIELD... AND WHO CAN TAKE RESPONSIBILITY FOR THEIR ACTIONS.
HE TREATED US LIKE HEROES.
YOU GOT ME. I'M REALLY GREAT.
AND WHEN THINGS WENT BAD, HE WOULD HAVE SACRIFICED HIS OWN LIFE TO MAKE SURE WE DIDN'T HURT ANYONE.
BUT THROUGH IT ALL, HE NEVER STOPPED BELIEVING IN US. THAT WE COULD BREAK FREE OF PSYCHO-MAN'S INFLUENCE. THAT WE WERE GOOD ENOUGH.
BECAUSE OF THAT, WE WERE.
WE'VE ALL HEARD IT BEFORE: "WITH GREAT POWER COMES GREAT RESPONSIBILITY." YOU TEACHERS TOSS IT AROUND LIKE IT'S SOME KIND OF CATCHPHRASE.
TODAY WE LEARNED WHAT IT MEANS.

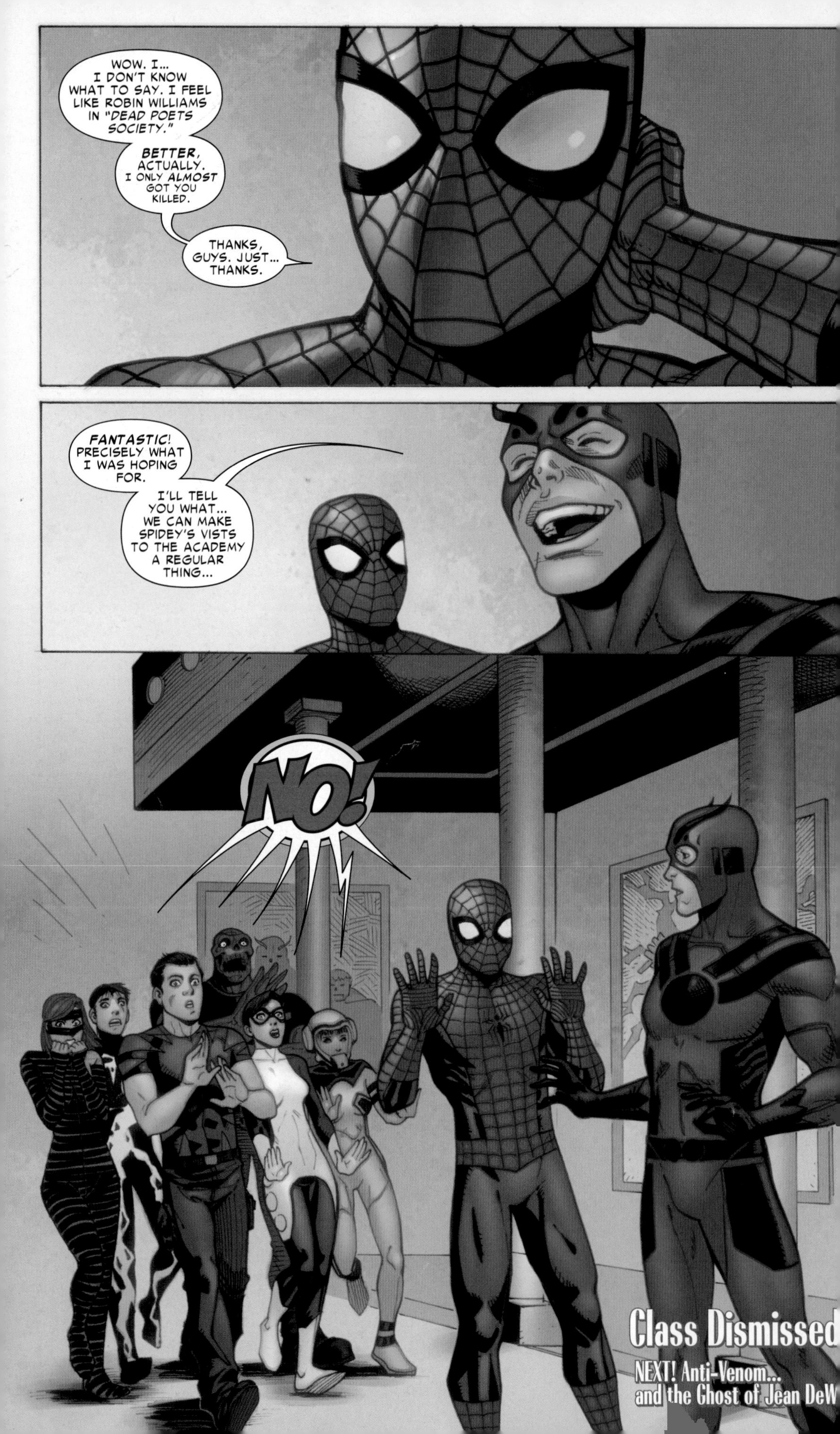
WOW. I... I DON'T KNOW WHAT TO SAY. I FEEL LIKE ROBIN WILLIAMS IN "DEAD POETS SOCIETY."
BETTER, ACTUALLY. I ONLY ALMOST GOT YOU KILLED.
THANKS, GUYS. JUST... THANKS.
FANTASTIC! PRECISELY WHAT I WAS HOPING FOR.
I'LL TELL YOU WHAT... WE CAN MAKE SPIDEY'S VISTS TO THE ACADEMY A REGULAR THING...
NO!
Class Dismissed
NEXT! Anti-Venom... and the Ghost of Jean DeW

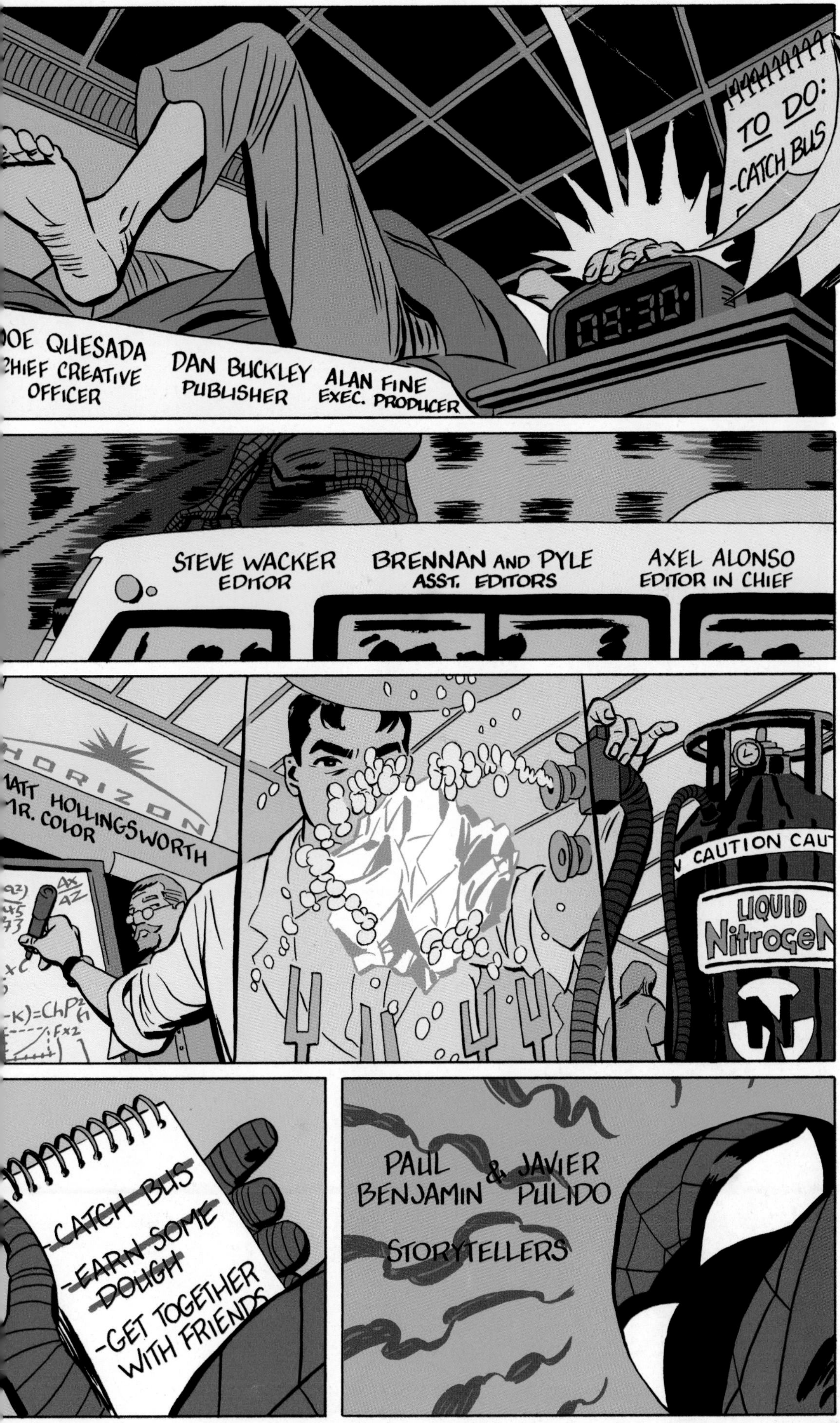

TO DO:
-CATCH BUS
09:30
JOE QUESADA CHIEF CREATIVE OFFICER
DAN BUCKLEY PUBLISHER
ALAN FINE EXEC. PRODUCER
STEVE WACKER EDITOR
BRENNAN AND PYLE ASST. EDITORS
AXEL ALONSO EDITOR IN CHIEF
HORIZON
MATT HOLLINGSWORTH MR. COLOR
CAUTION CAUT
LIQUID NitrogeN
-CATCH BUS
-EARN SOME DOUGH
-GET TOGETHER WITH FRIENDS
PAUL BENJAMIN & JAVIER PULIDO
STORYTELLERS

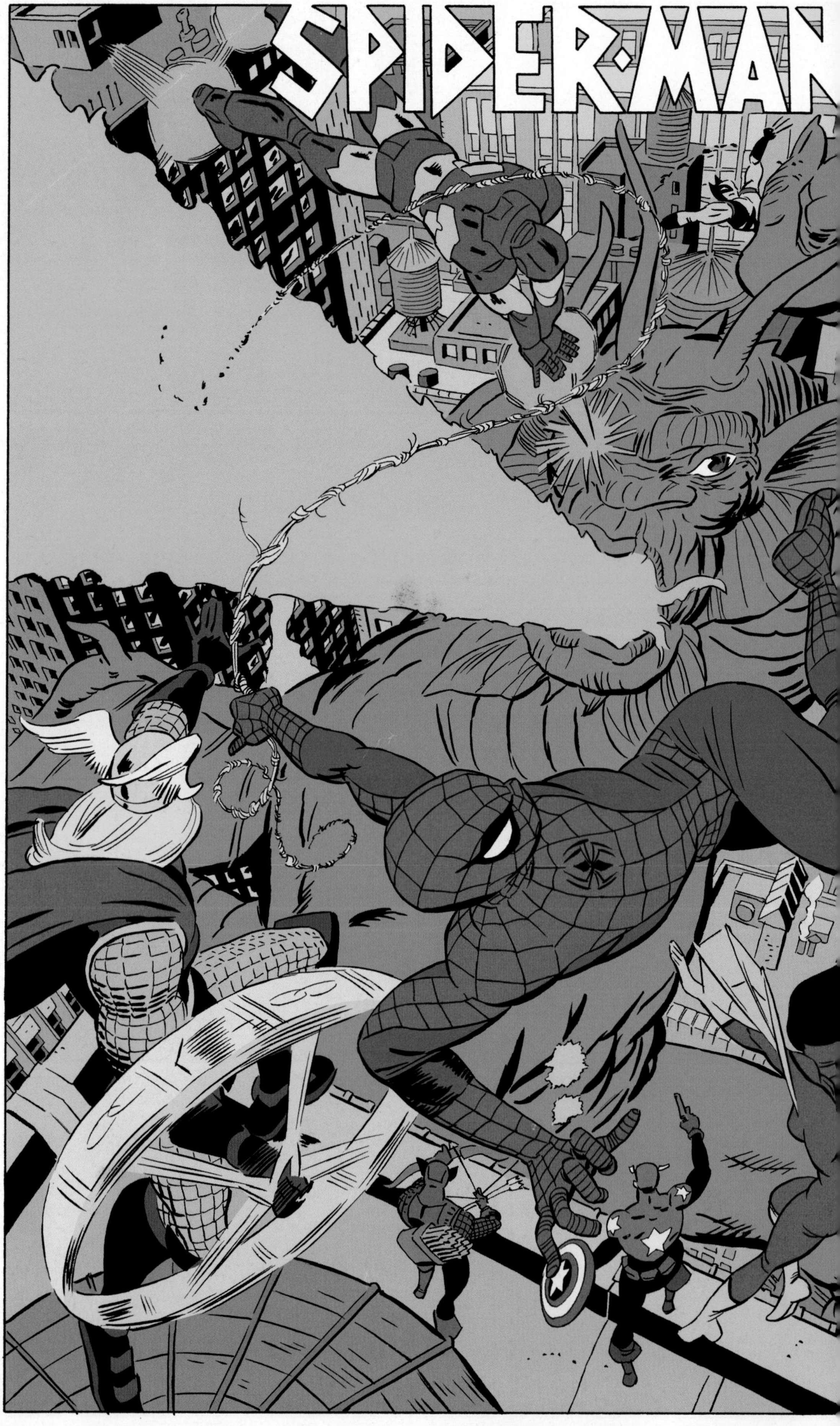
SPIDER-MAN

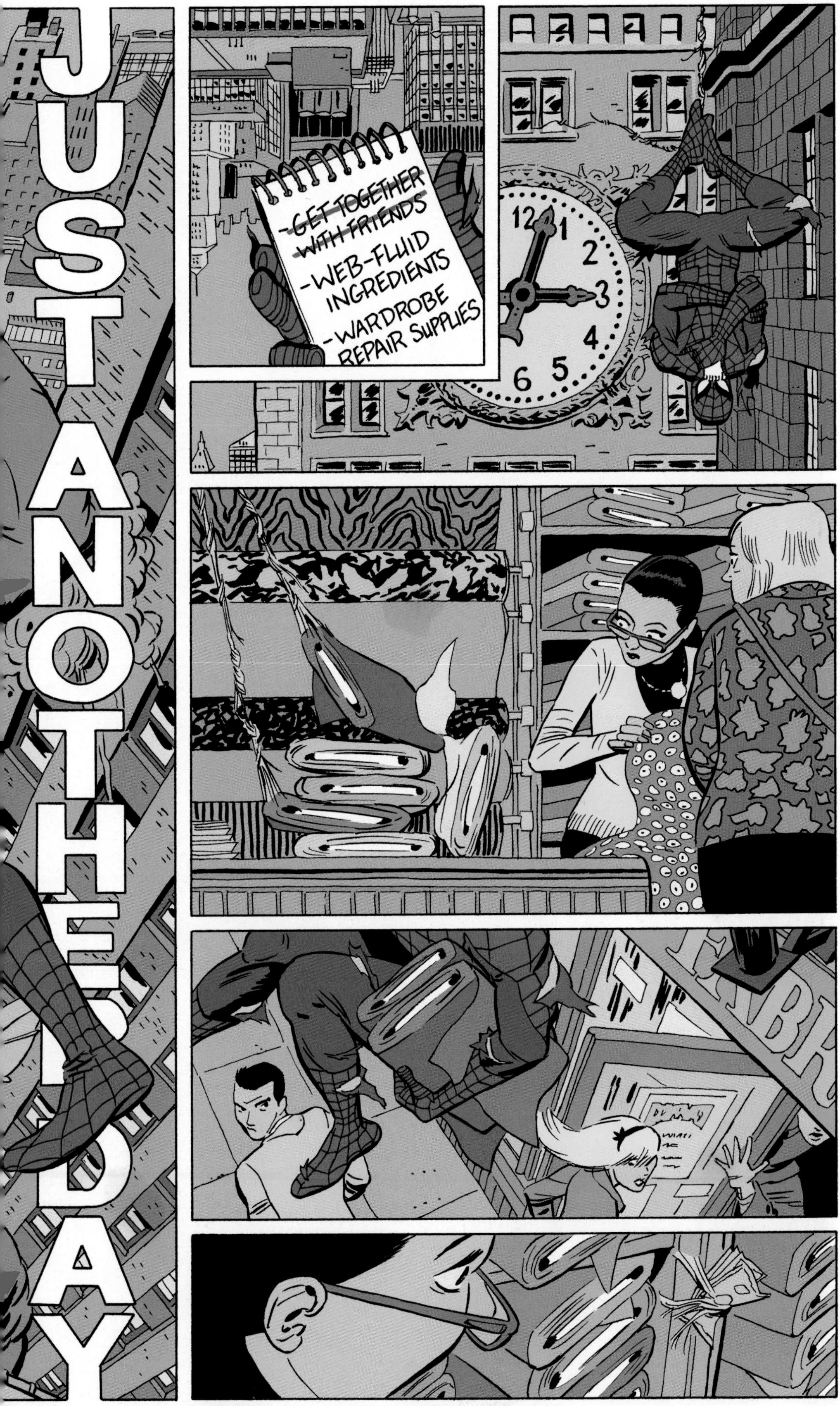
JUST ANOTHER DAY
-GET TOGETHER WITH FRIENDS
-WEB-FLUID INGREDIENTS
-WARDROBE REPAIR SUPPLIES

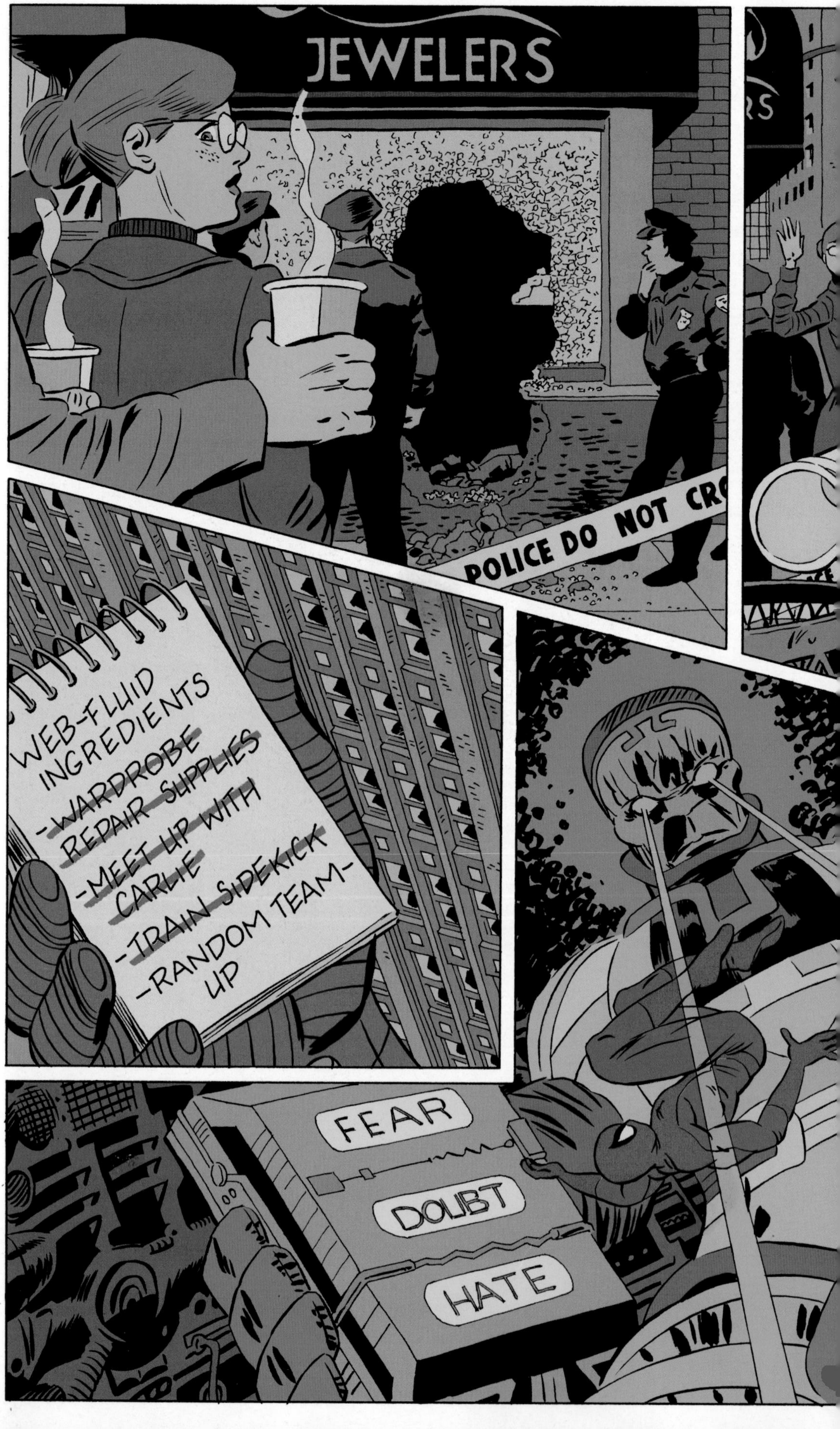
JEWELERS
POLICE DO NOT CRO
WEB-FLUID INGREDIENTS
-WARDROBE REPAIR SUPPLIES
-MEET UP WITH CARLIE
-TRAIN SIDEKICK
-RANDOM TEAM-UP
FEAR
DOUBT
HATE

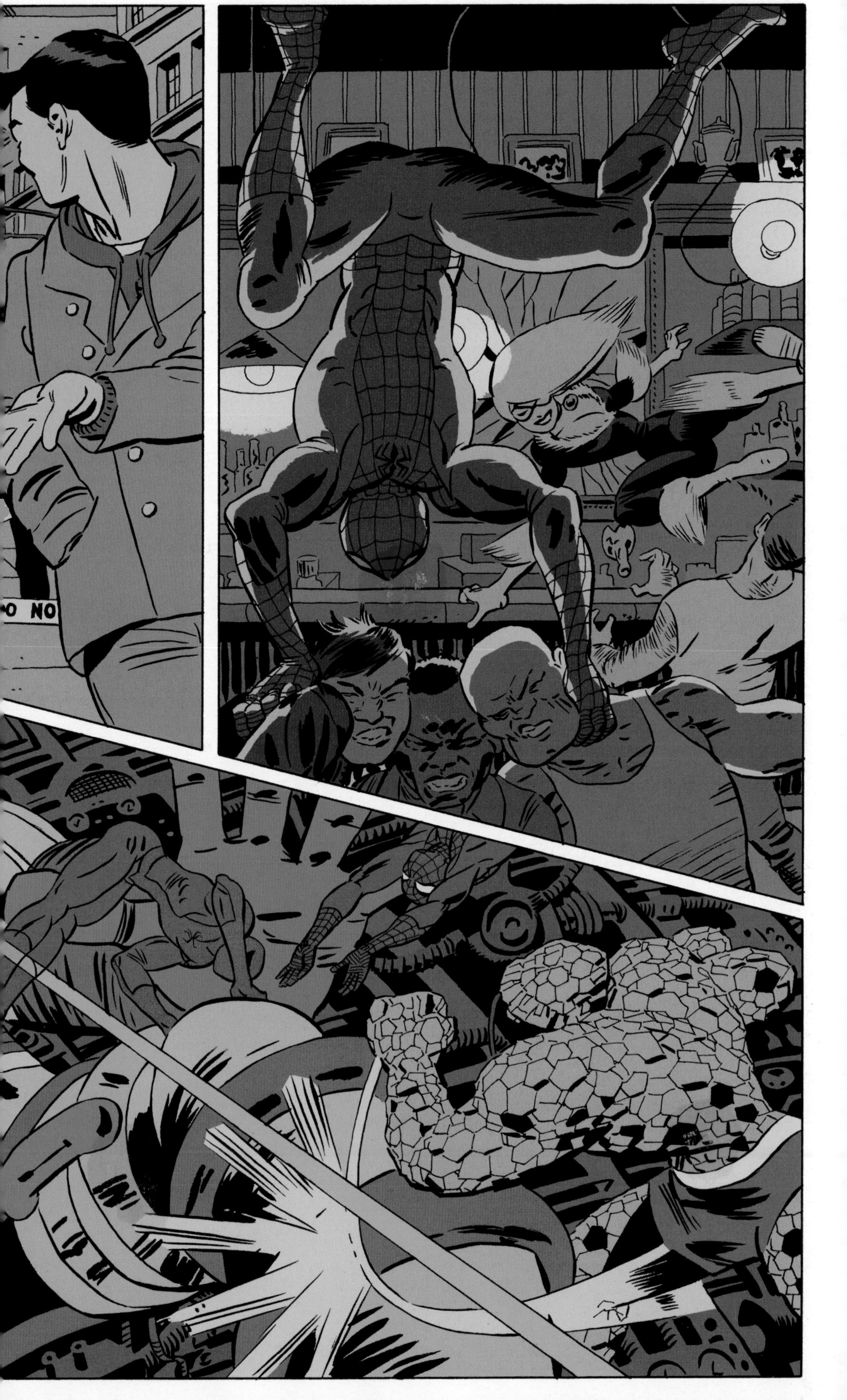
O NO

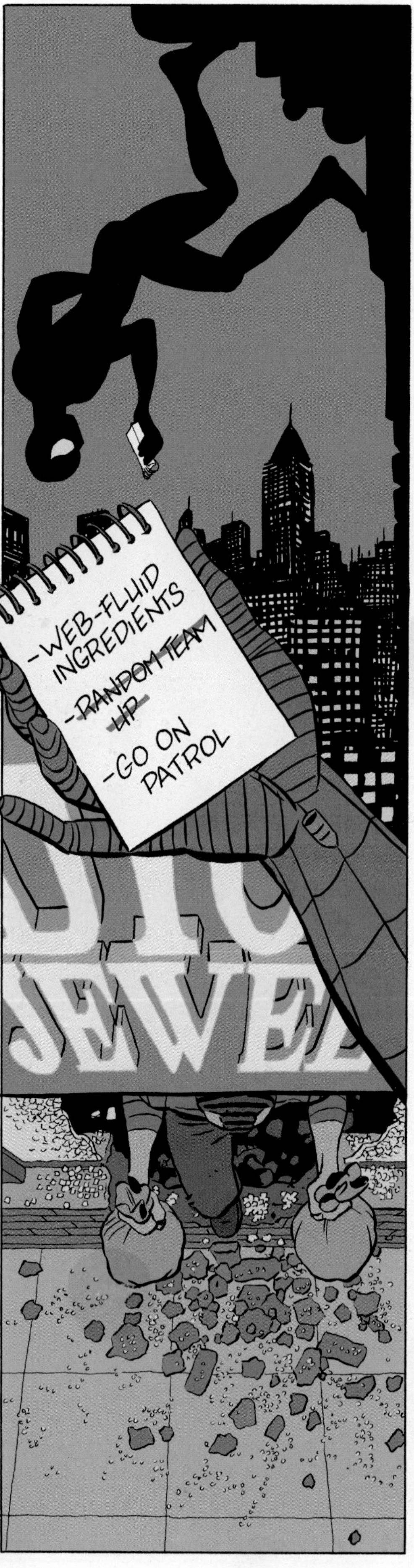
-WEB-FLUID INGREDIENTS
-RANDOM TEAM UP
-GO ON PATROL

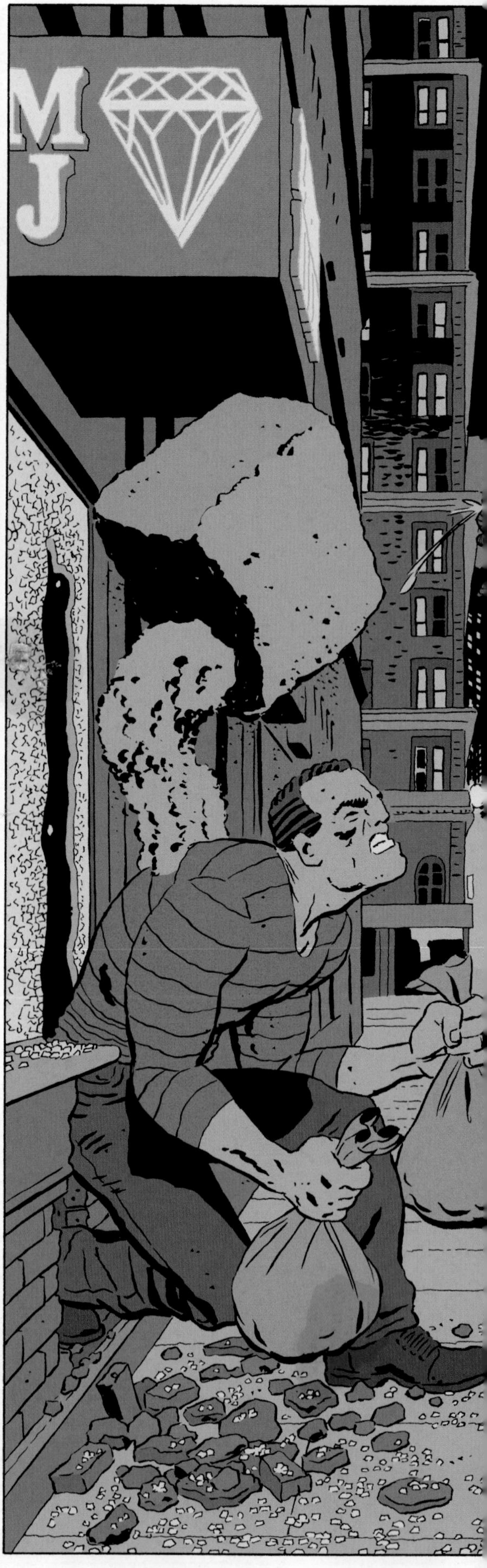
M J

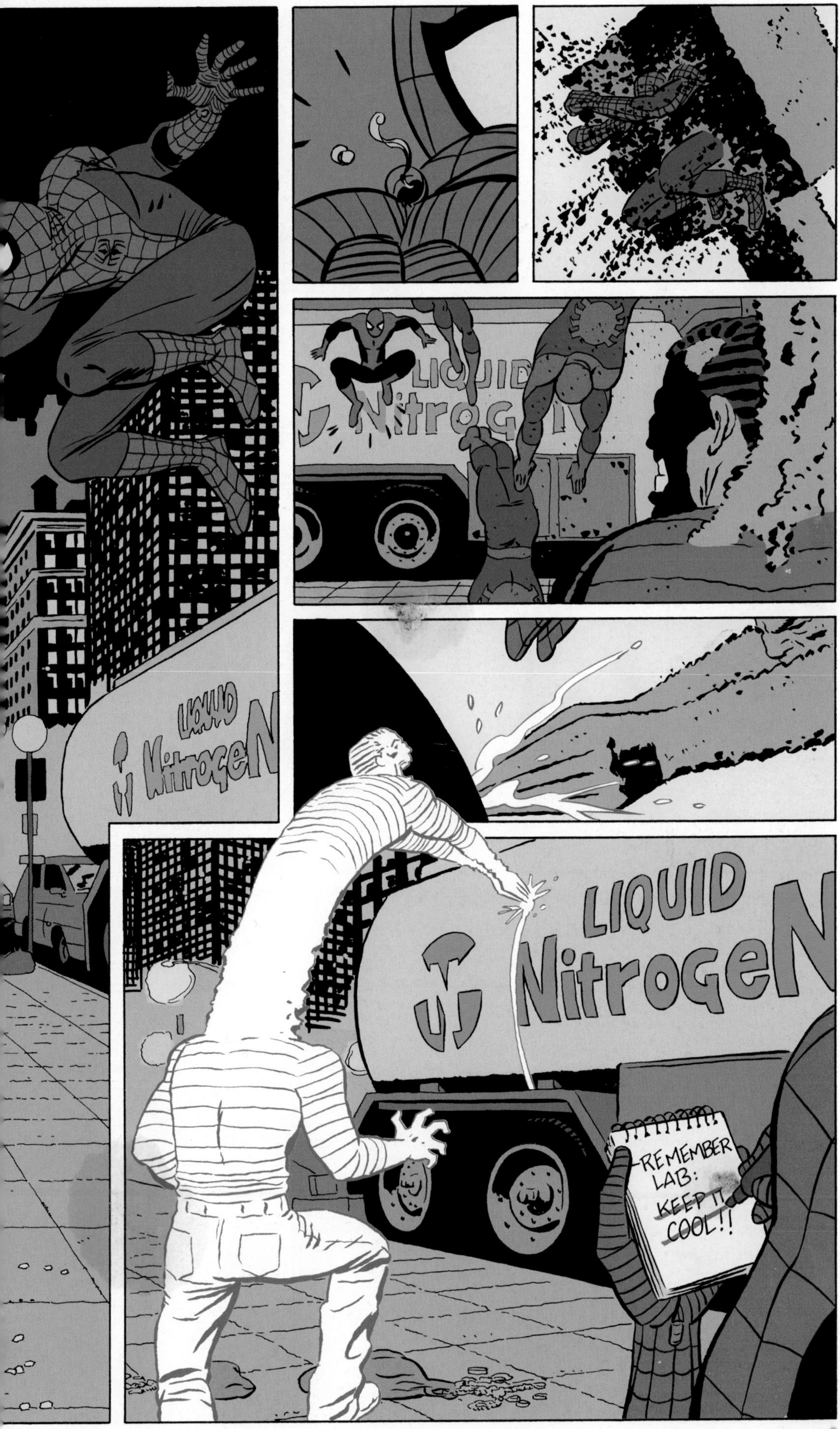
LIQUID
Nitrogen
LIQUID
NitrogeN
LIQUID
NitrogeN
REMEMBER
LAB:
KEEP IT
COOL!!

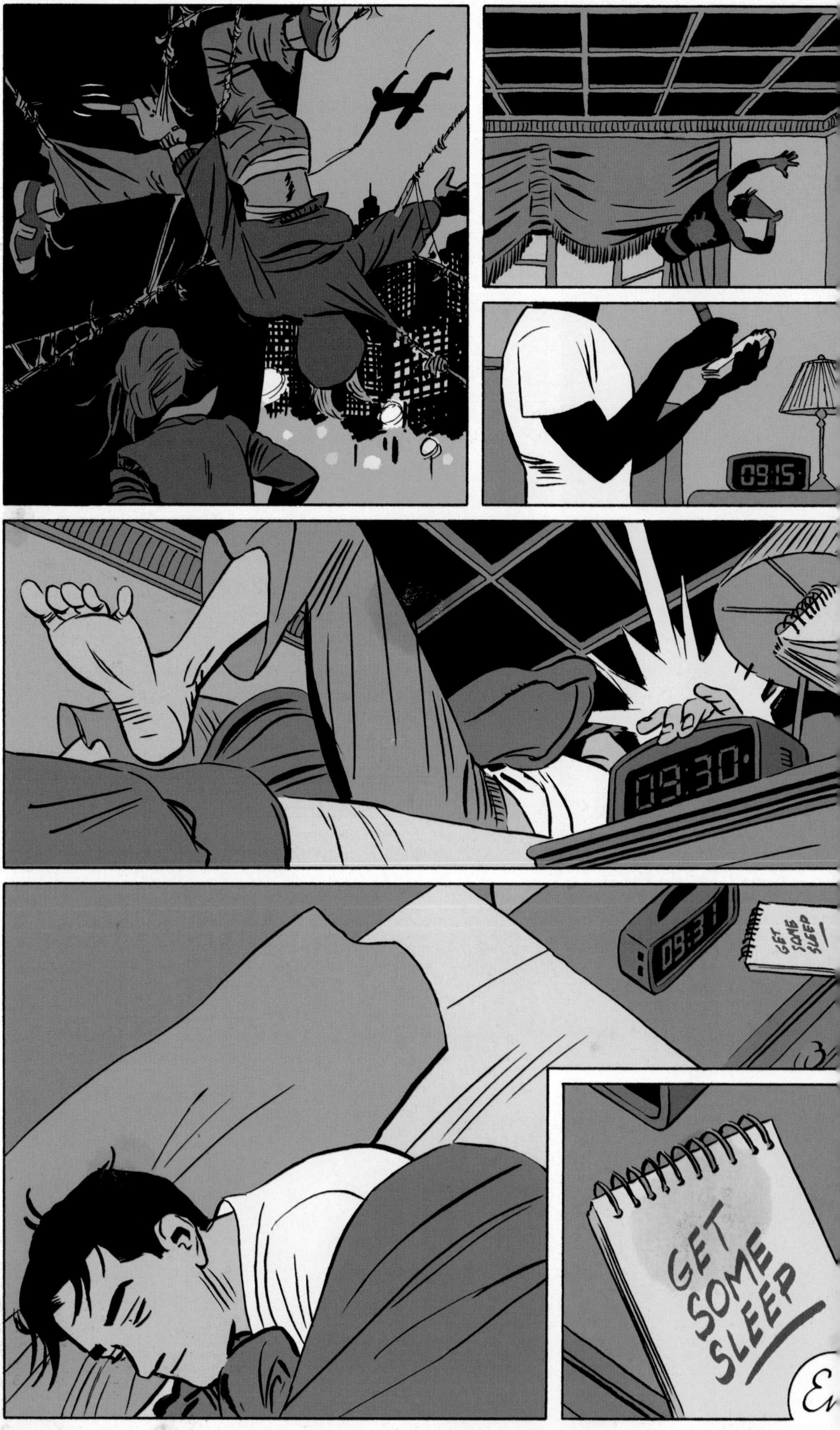
09:15
09:30
09:31
GET SOME SLEEP
GET SOME SLEEP

INTRODUCING:
MAGNETIC MAN
IN
THE CHOICE

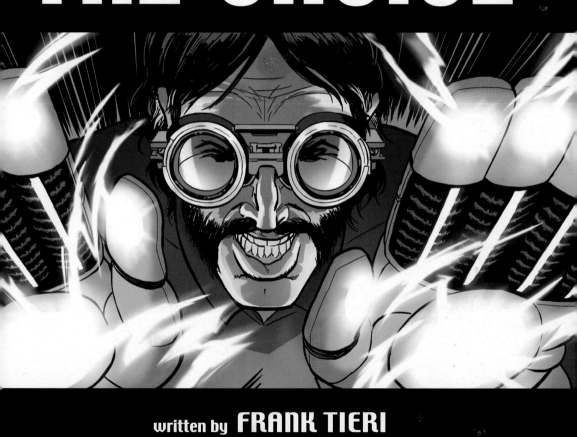

written by **FRANK TIERI**
art by **JAVIER RODRIGUEZ**
lettered by **VC's JOE CARAMAGNA**

assistant editor **ELLIE PYLE**   senior editor **STEPHEN WACKER**
editor in chief **AXEL ALONSO**   chief creative officer **JOE QUESADA**
publisher **DAN BUCKLEY**   executive producer **ALAN FINE**

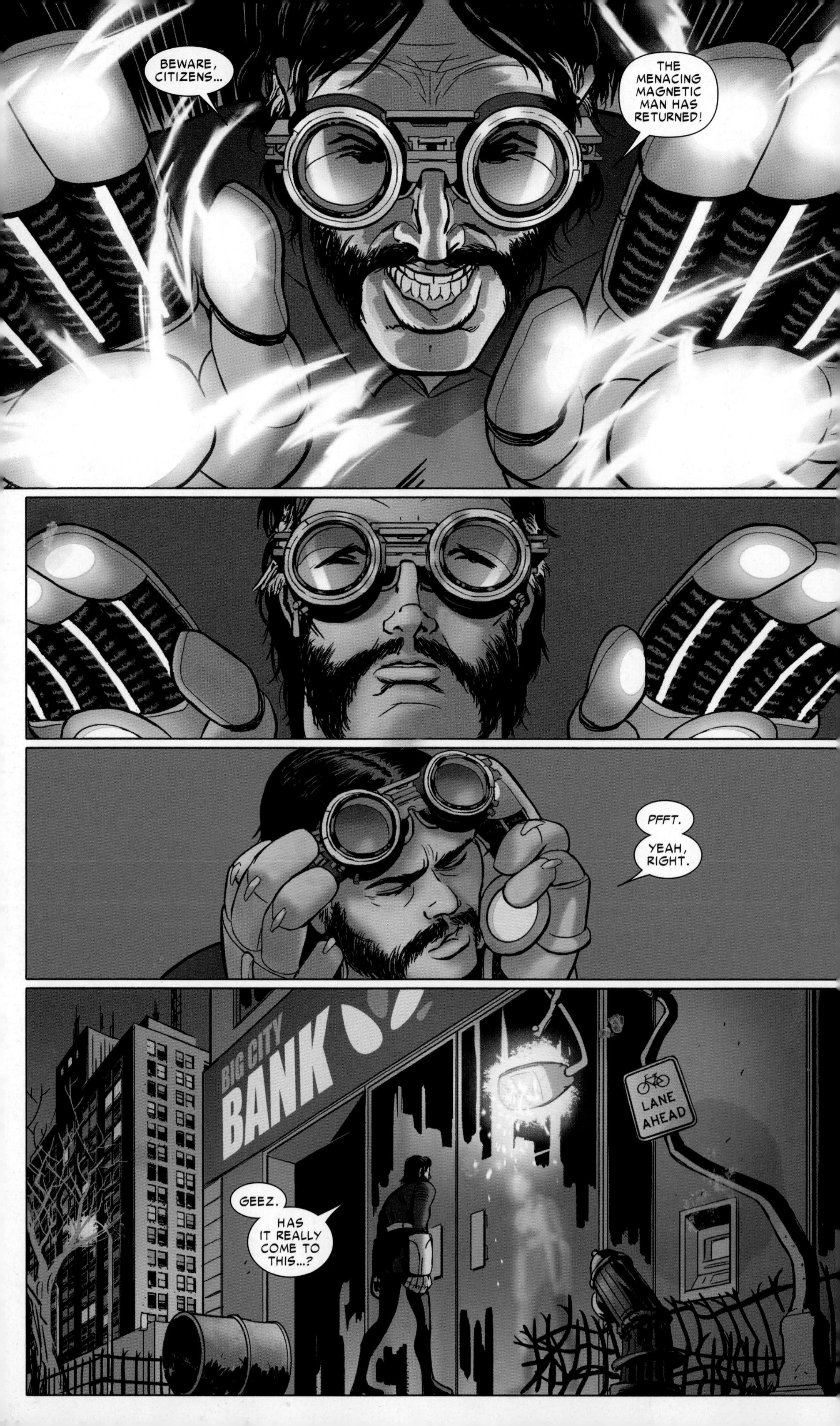
BEWARE, CITIZENS...
THE MENACING MAGNETIC MAN HAS RETURNED!
PFFT.
YEAH, RIGHT.
BIG CITY BANK
LANE AHEAD
GEEZ.
HAS IT REALLY COME TO THIS...?

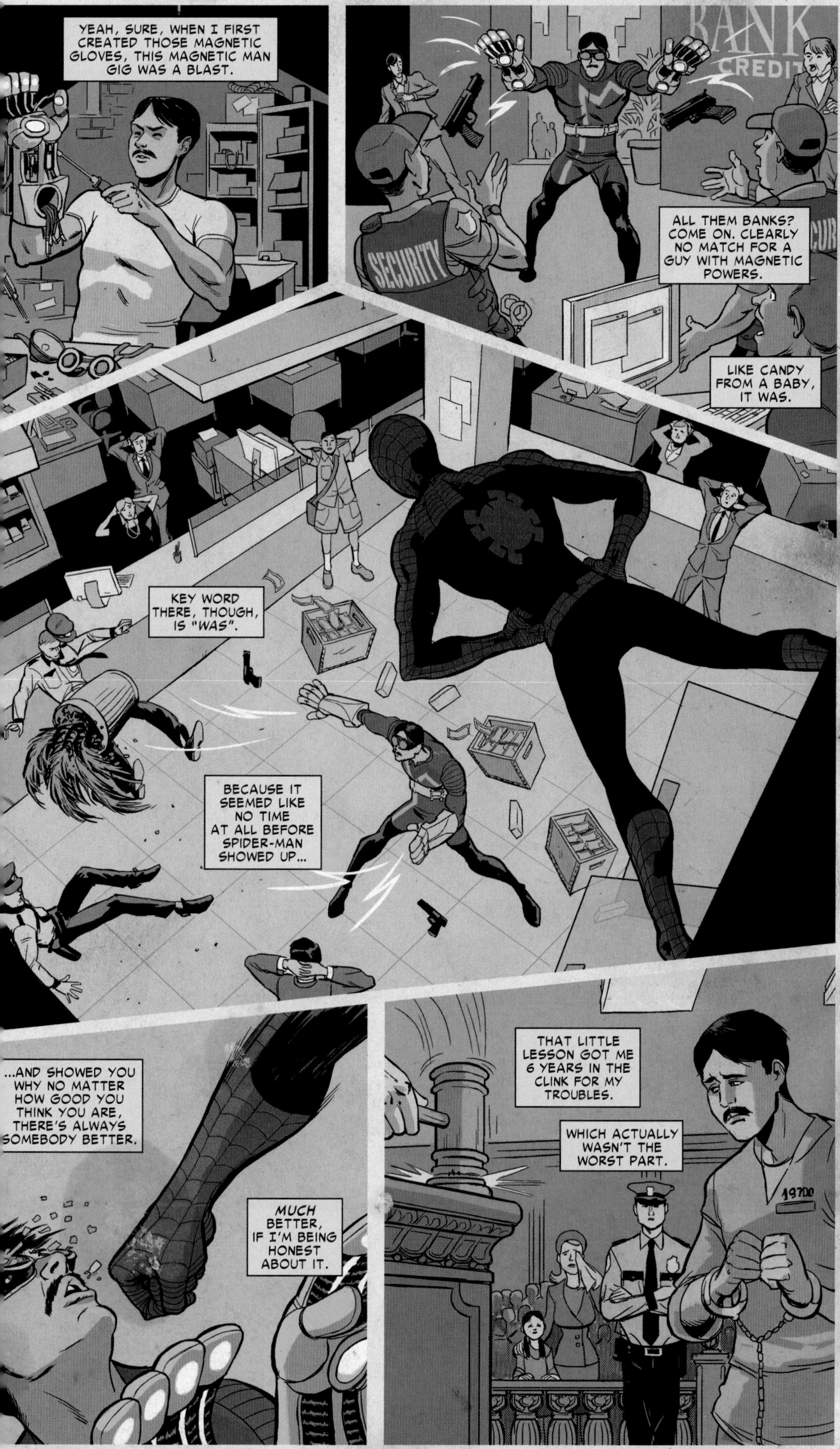

YEAH, SURE, WHEN I FIRST CREATED THOSE MAGNETIC GLOVES, THIS MAGNETIC MAN GIG WAS A BLAST.
BANK
CREDIT
SECURITY
ALL THEM BANKS? COME ON. CLEARLY NO MATCH FOR A GUY WITH MAGNETIC POWERS.
LIKE CANDY FROM A BABY, IT WAS.
KEY WORD THERE, THOUGH, IS "WAS".
BECAUSE IT SEEMED LIKE NO TIME AT ALL BEFORE SPIDER-MAN SHOWED UP...
...AND SHOWED YOU WHY NO MATTER HOW GOOD YOU THINK YOU ARE, THERE'S ALWAYS SOMEBODY BETTER.
MUCH BETTER, IF I'M BEING HONEST ABOUT IT.
THAT LITTLE LESSON GOT ME 6 YEARS IN THE CLINK FOR MY TROUBLES.
WHICH ACTUALLY WASN'T THE WORST PART.
19700

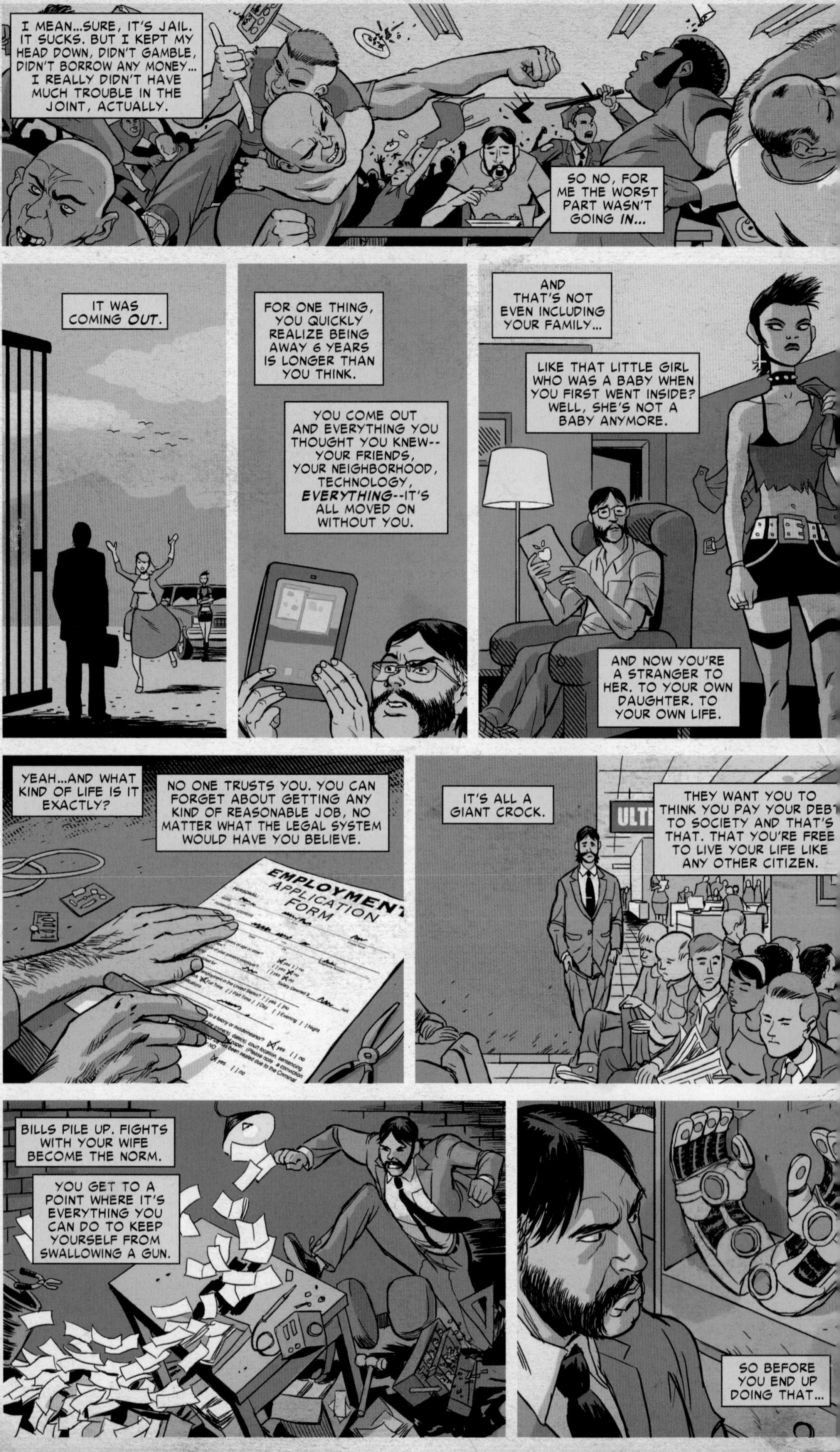
I MEAN...SURE, IT'S JAIL. IT SUCKS. BUT I KEPT MY HEAD DOWN, DIDN'T GAMBLE, DIDN'T BORROW ANY MONEY... I REALLY DIDN'T HAVE MUCH TROUBLE IN THE JOINT, ACTUALLY.
SO NO, FOR ME THE WORST PART WASN'T GOING *IN*...
IT WAS COMING *OUT*.
FOR ONE THING, YOU QUICKLY REALIZE BEING AWAY 6 YEARS IS LONGER THAN YOU THINK.
YOU COME OUT AND EVERYTHING YOU THOUGHT YOU KNEW-- YOUR FRIENDS, YOUR NEIGHBORHOOD, TECHNOLOGY, ***EVERYTHING***--IT'S ALL MOVED ON WITHOUT YOU.
AND THAT'S NOT EVEN INCLUDING YOUR FAMILY...
LIKE THAT LITTLE GIRL WHO WAS A BABY WHEN YOU FIRST WENT INSIDE? WELL, SHE'S NOT A BABY ANYMORE.
AND NOW YOU'RE A STRANGER TO HER. TO YOUR OWN DAUGHTER. TO YOUR OWN LIFE.
YEAH...AND WHAT KIND OF LIFE IS IT EXACTLY?
NO ONE TRUSTS YOU. YOU CAN FORGET ABOUT GETTING ANY KIND OF REASONABLE JOB, NO MATTER WHAT THE LEGAL SYSTEM WOULD HAVE YOU BELIEVE.
EMPLOYMENT APPLICATION FORM
IT'S ALL A GIANT CROCK.
THEY WANT YOU TO THINK YOU PAY YOUR DEBT TO SOCIETY AND THAT'S THAT. THAT YOU'RE FREE TO LIVE YOUR LIFE LIKE ANY OTHER CITIZEN.
BILLS PILE UP. FIGHTS WITH YOUR WIFE BECOME THE NORM.
YOU GET TO A POINT WHERE IT'S EVERYTHING YOU CAN DO TO KEEP YOURSELF FROM SWALLOWING A GUN.
SO BEFORE YOU END UP DOING THAT...

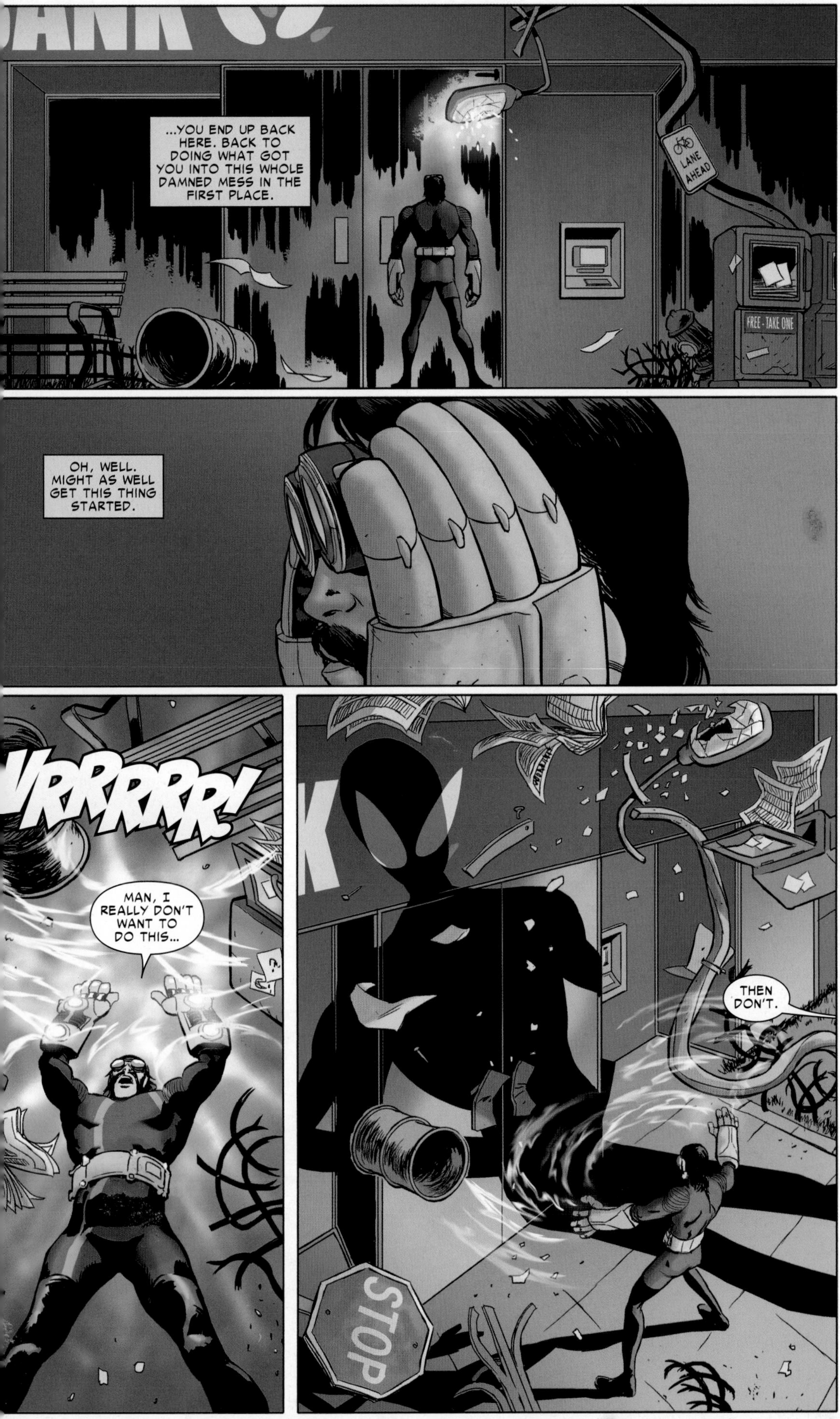
BANK
...YOU END UP BACK HERE. BACK TO DOING WHAT GOT YOU INTO THIS WHOLE DAMNED MESS IN THE FIRST PLACE.
LANE AHEAD
FREE - TAKE ONE
OH, WELL. MIGHT AS WELL GET THIS THING STARTED.
VRRRRR!
MAN, I REALLY DON'T WANT TO DO THIS...
K
THEN DON'T.
STOP

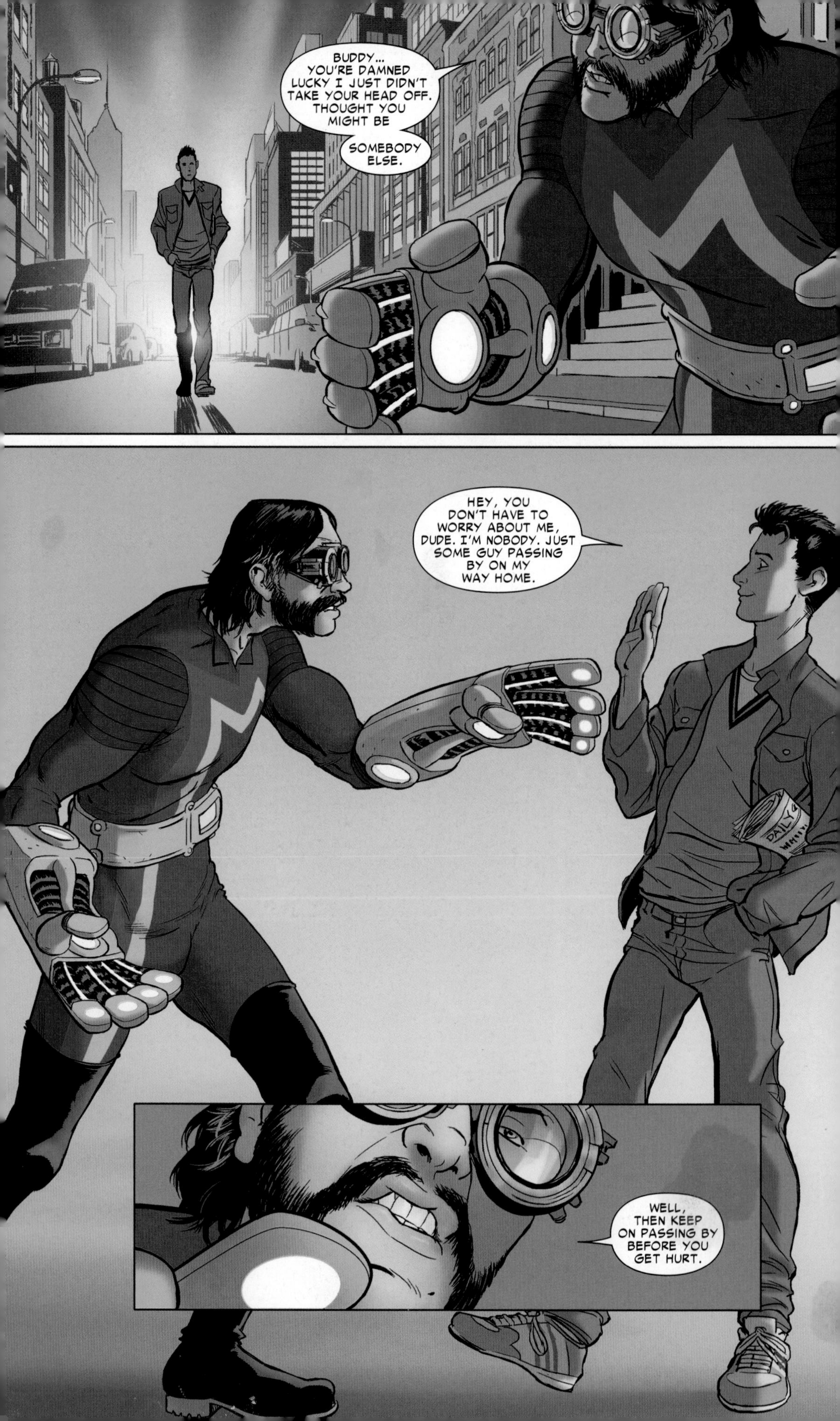
BUDDY... YOU'RE DAMNED LUCKY I JUST DIDN'T TAKE YOUR HEAD OFF. THOUGHT YOU MIGHT BE
SOMEBODY ELSE.
HEY, YOU DON'T HAVE TO WORRY ABOUT ME, DUDE. I'M NOBODY. JUST SOME GUY PASSING BY ON MY WAY HOME.
WELL, THEN KEEP ON PASSING BY BEFORE YOU GET HURT.

SEE, THAT'S THE THING...I GET THE FEELING YOU *DON'T* WANT TO HURT ME ANY MORE THAN YOU WANT TO ROB THAT BANK.

MAYBE SO. BUT THAT DON'T MEAN I WON'T.

I'VE GOT NO *CHOICE,* UNDERSTAND?

BANK ROBBING WAS THE ONLY THING IN MY *LOSER* LIFE THAT I WAS EVER SEMI-GOOD AT. SO IF YOU'LL EXCUSE ME...

WRONG. YOU WERE APPARENTLY PRETTY DARN GOOD AT SOMETHING ELSE...

THOSE GLOVES. YOU BUILT THOSE, RIGHT?

WHAT? YEAH...SO WHAT IF I DID?

HOW MANY PEOPLE DO YOU THINK COULD BUILD THOSE? NOT TOO MANY.

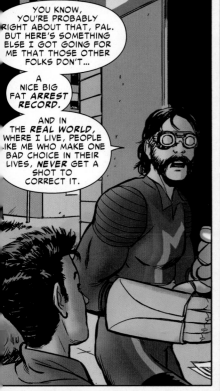

YOU KNOW, YOU'RE PROBABLY *RIGHT* ABOUT THAT, PAL. BUT HERE'S SOMETHING ELSE I GOT GOING FOR ME THAT THOSE OTHER FOLKS DON'T...

A NICE BIG FAT *ARREST* RECORD.

AND IN THE *REAL WORLD,* WHERE I LIVE, PEOPLE LIKE ME WHO MAKE ONE BAD CHOICE IN THEIR LIVES, *NEVER* GET A SHOT TO CORRECT IT.

THAT SO?

I DON'T GET IT. WHAT'S THE GAG?

NO GAG. THIS IS HORIZON LABS, WHERE I WORK. WE COULD SOMETIMES USE AN EXTRA HAND, THAT'S ALL.

PETER PARKER

HORIZON LABS

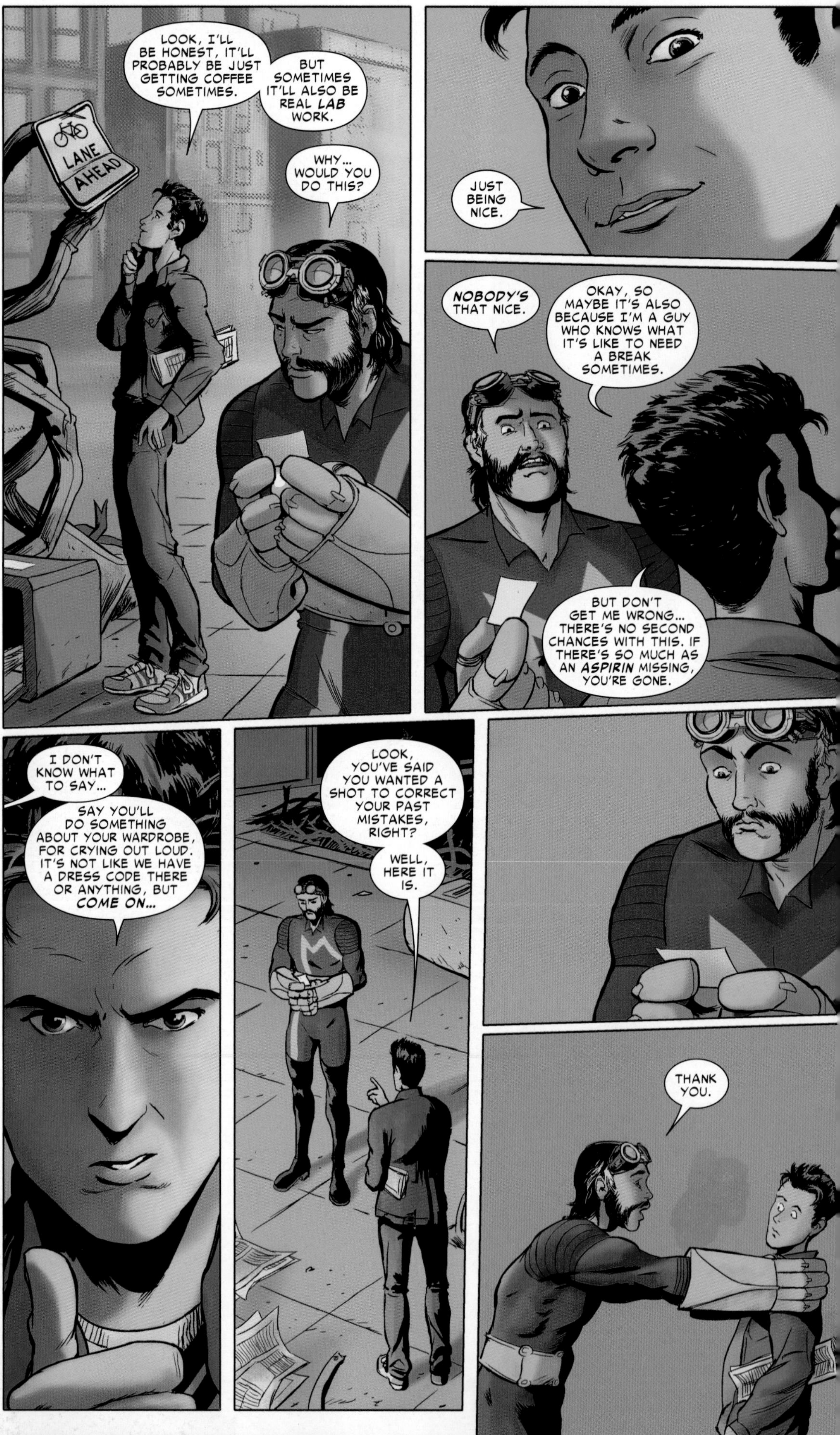
LOOK, I'LL BE HONEST, IT'LL PROBABLY BE JUST GETTING COFFEE SOMETIMES.
BUT SOMETIMES IT'LL ALSO BE REAL LAB WORK.
LANE AHEAD
WHY... WOULD YOU DO THIS?
JUST BEING NICE.
NOBODY'S THAT NICE.
OKAY, SO MAYBE IT'S ALSO BECAUSE I'M A GUY WHO KNOWS WHAT IT'S LIKE TO NEED A BREAK SOMETIMES.
BUT DON'T GET ME WRONG... THERE'S NO SECOND CHANCES WITH THIS. IF THERE'S SO MUCH AS AN ASPIRIN MISSING, YOU'RE GONE.
I DON'T KNOW WHAT TO SAY...
SAY YOU'LL DO SOMETHING ABOUT YOUR WARDROBE, FOR CRYING OUT LOUD. IT'S NOT LIKE WE HAVE A DRESS CODE THERE OR ANYTHING, BUT COME ON...
LOOK, YOU'VE SAID YOU WANTED A SHOT TO CORRECT YOUR PAST MISTAKES, RIGHT?
WELL, HERE IT IS.
THANK YOU.

GIVE ME A CALL NEXT WEEK AND WE'LL LOOK TO GET YOU SET UP.

AND BUY A SUIT!

YOU KNOW... THE GUY I *THOUGHT* YOU WERE, *HE* WOULDN'T HAVE DONE SOMETHING LIKE THIS.

HE PUTS GUYS LIKE ME IN THE JOINT. DON'T CARE MUCH WHAT HAPPENS TO THEM WHEN THEY GET OUT.

ANYWAY, THANKS AGAIN.

HMN.

ACTUALLY, MY FRIEND...

DAILY BUGLE

Magnetic Man Says Goodbye to Iron Bars

Small time crook released on good behavior

HONEY, YOU'RE NOT GOING TO BELIEVE THIS. I GOT A *JOB!*

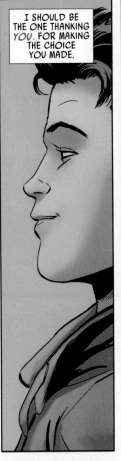

I SHOULD BE THE ONE THANKING *YOU.* FOR MAKING THE CHOICE YOU MADE.

AND NOT FORCING ME TO MAKE ONE I DIDN'T WANT TO.

The End

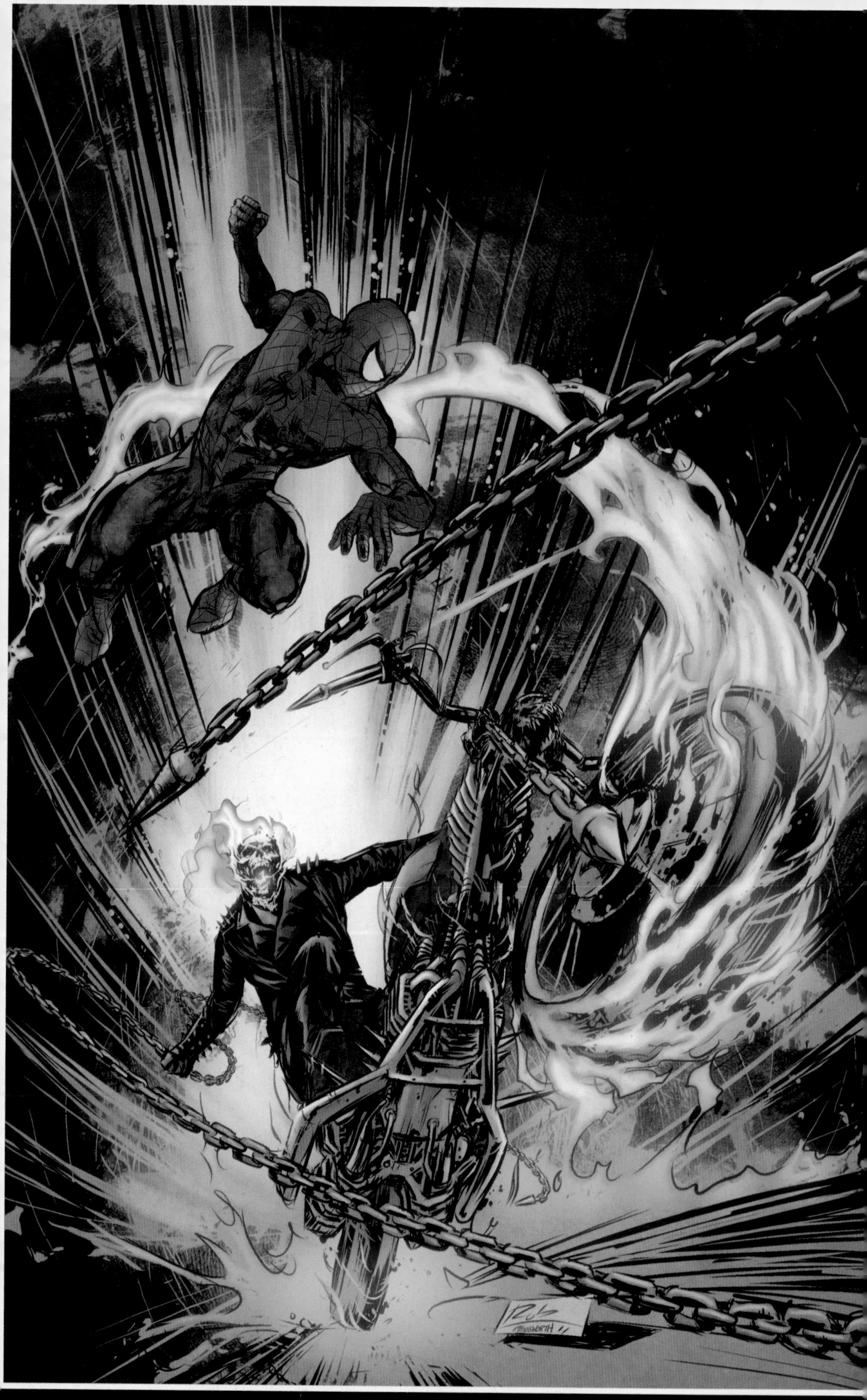

"CAN'T GET THE SERVICE" FROM AMAZING SPIDER-MAN #658-660
COVER BY ROBERTO DE LA TORRE & MATT HOLLINGSWORTH

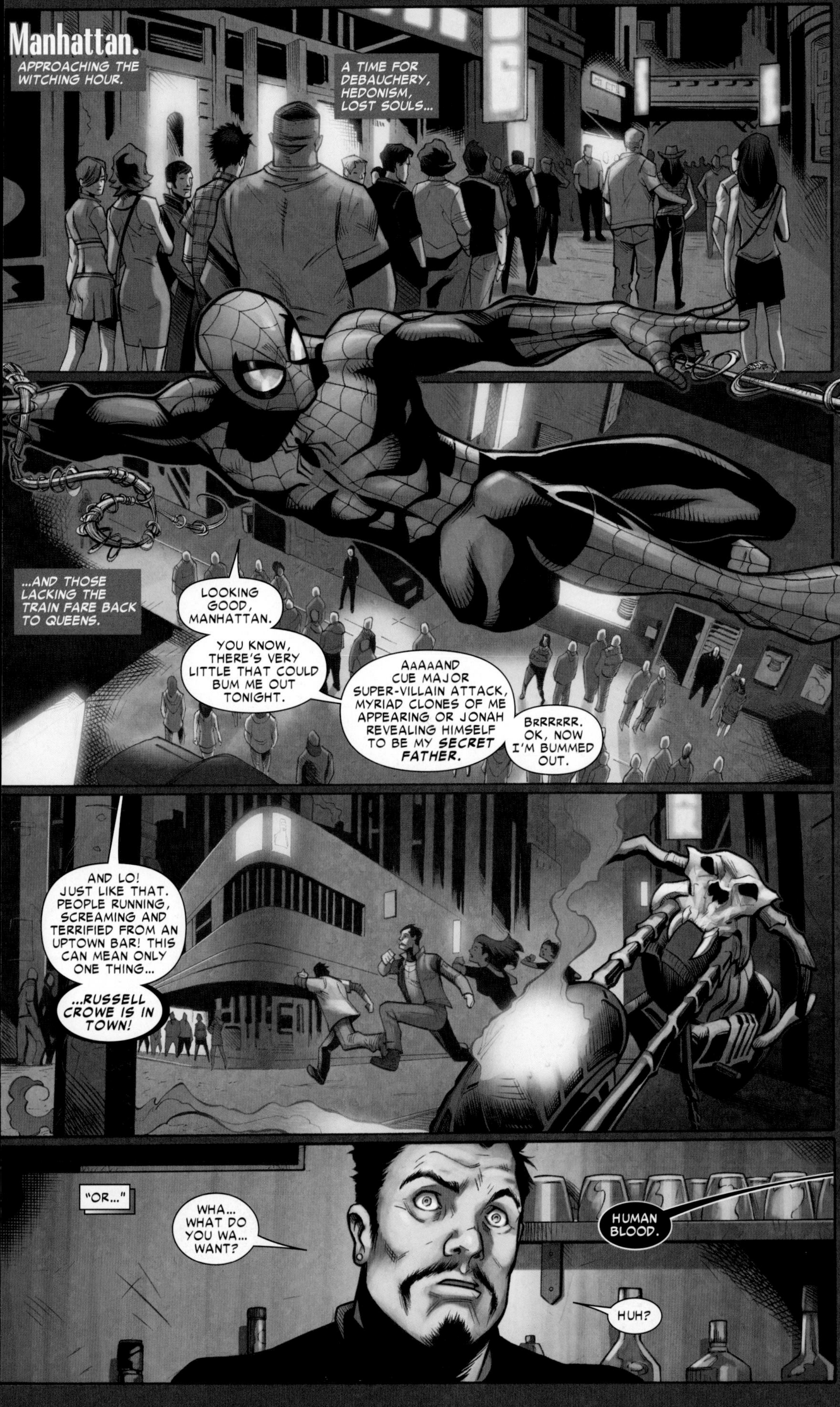

Manhattan.
APPROACHING THE WITCHING HOUR.
A TIME FOR DEBAUCHERY, HEDONISM, LOST SOULS...
...AND THOSE LACKING THE TRAIN FARE BACK TO QUEENS.
LOOKING GOOD, MANHATTAN.
YOU KNOW, THERE'S VERY LITTLE THAT COULD BUM ME OUT TONIGHT.
AAAAAND CUE MAJOR SUPER-VILLAIN ATTACK, MYRIAD CLONES OF ME APPEARING OR JONAH REVEALING HIMSELF TO BE MY SECRET FATHER.
BRRRRRR. OK, NOW I'M BUMMED OUT.
AND LO! JUST LIKE THAT. PEOPLE RUNNING, SCREAMING AND TERRIFIED FROM AN UPTOWN BAR! THIS CAN MEAN ONLY ONE THING...
...RUSSELL CROWE IS IN TOWN!
"OR..."
WHA... WHAT DO YOU WA... WANT?
HUMAN BLOOD.
HUH?

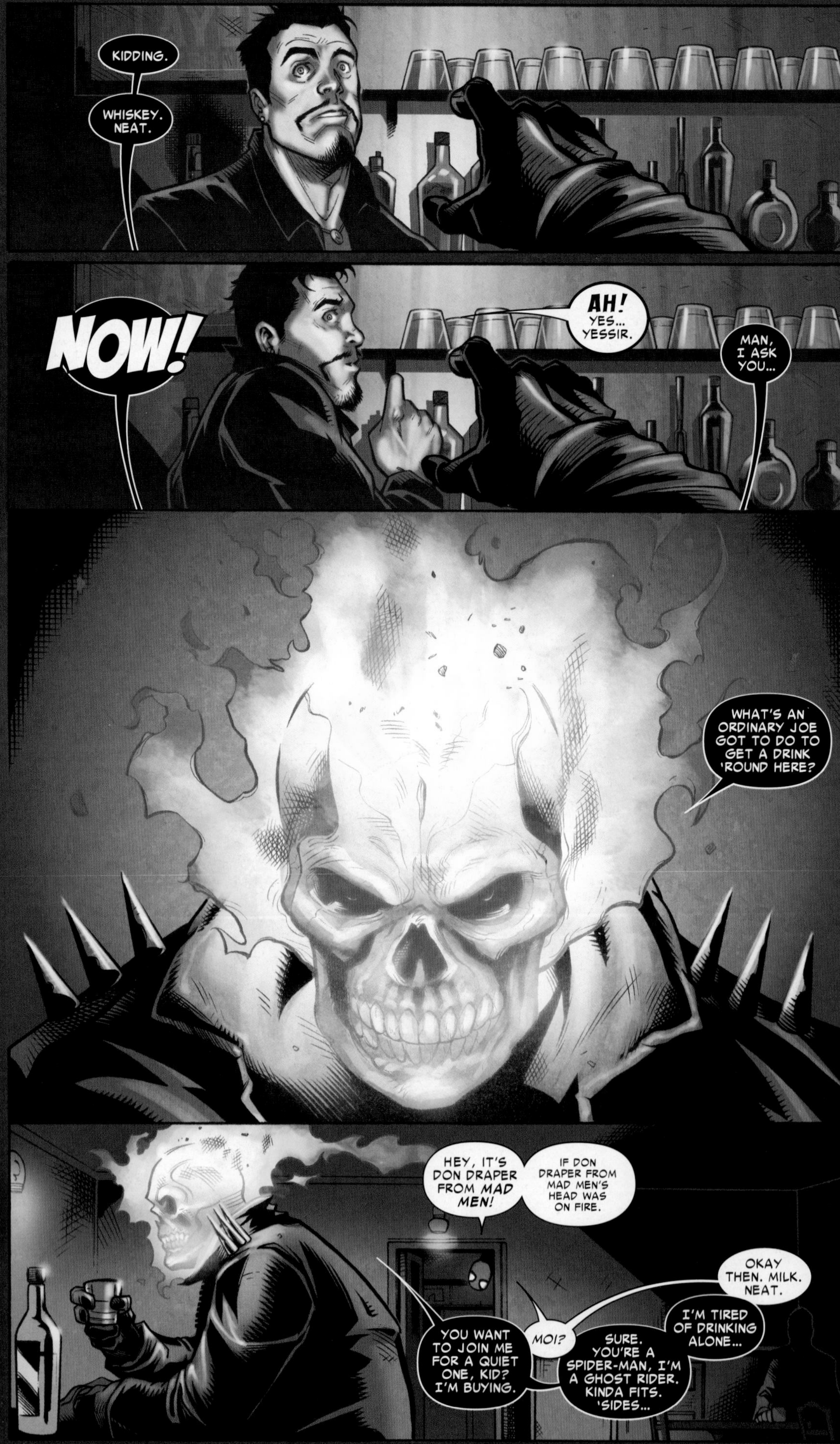
KIDDING.
WHISKEY. NEAT.
NOW!
AH! YES... YESSIR.
MAN, I ASK YOU...
WHAT'S AN ORDINARY JOE GOT TO DO TO GET A DRINK 'ROUND HERE?
HEY, IT'S DON DRAPER FROM MAD MEN!
IF DON DRAPER FROM MAD MEN'S HEAD WAS ON FIRE.
OKAY THEN. MILK. NEAT.
YOU WANT TO JOIN ME FOR A QUIET ONE, KID? I'M BUYING.
MOI?
SURE. YOU'RE A SPIDER-MAN, I'M A GHOST RIDER. KINDA FITS. 'SIDES...
I'M TIRED OF DRINKING ALONE...

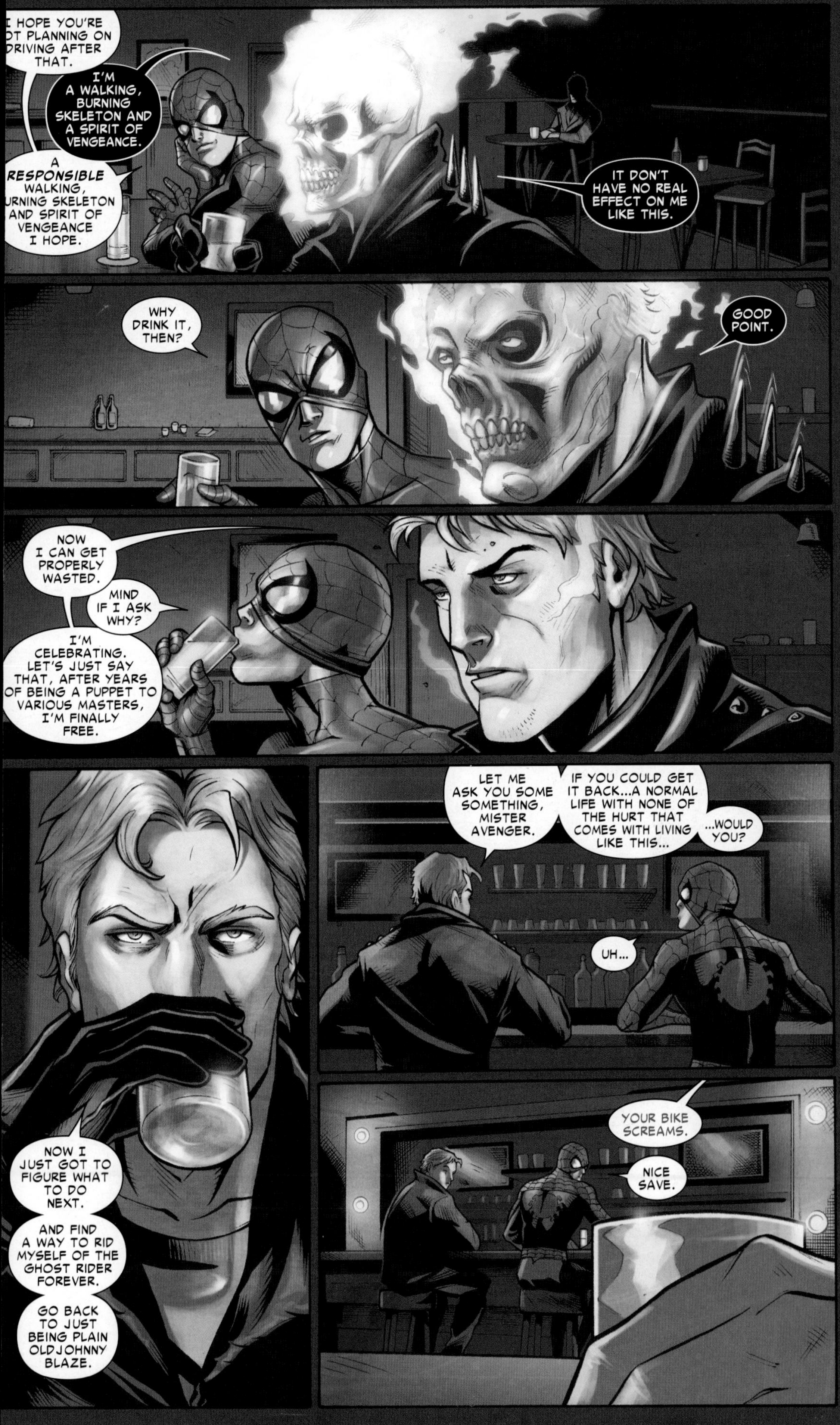
I HOPE YOU'RE NOT PLANNING ON DRIVING AFTER THAT.
I'M A WALKING, BURNING SKELETON AND A SPIRIT OF VENGEANCE.
A *RESPONSIBLE* WALKING, BURNING SKELETON AND SPIRIT OF VENGEANCE I HOPE.
IT DON'T HAVE NO REAL EFFECT ON ME LIKE THIS.
WHY DRINK IT, THEN?
GOOD POINT.
NOW I CAN GET PROPERLY WASTED.
MIND IF I ASK WHY?
I'M CELEBRATING. LET'S JUST SAY THAT, AFTER YEARS OF BEING A PUPPET TO VARIOUS MASTERS, I'M FINALLY FREE.
NOW I JUST GOT TO FIGURE WHAT TO DO NEXT.
AND FIND A WAY TO RID MYSELF OF THE GHOST RIDER FOREVER.
GO BACK TO JUST BEING PLAIN OLD JOHNNY BLAZE.
LET ME ASK YOU SOME SOMETHING, MISTER AVENGER.
IF YOU COULD GET IT BACK...A NORMAL LIFE WITH NONE OF THE HURT THAT COMES WITH LIVING LIKE THIS...
...WOULD YOU?
UH...
YOUR BIKE SCREAMS.
NICE SAVE.

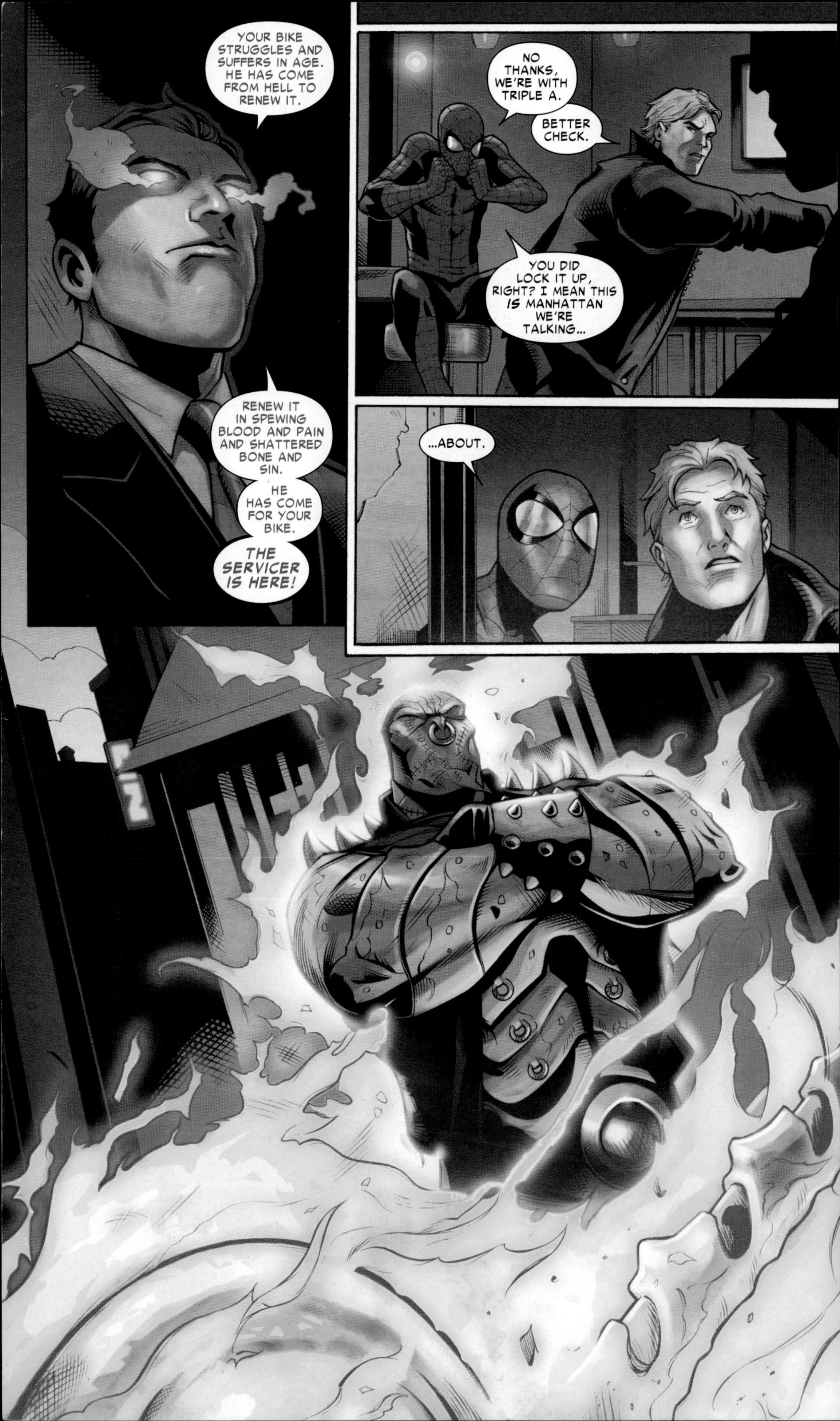
YOUR BIKE STRUGGLES AND SUFFERS IN AGE. HE HAS COME FROM HELL TO RENEW IT.
RENEW IT IN SPEWING BLOOD AND PAIN AND SHATTERED BONE AND SIN.
HE HAS COME FOR YOUR BIKE.
THE SERVICER IS HERE!
NO THANKS, WE'RE WITH TRIPLE A.
BETTER CHECK.
YOU DID LOCK IT UP, RIGHT? I MEAN THIS IS MANHATTAN WE'RE TALKING...
...ABOUT.

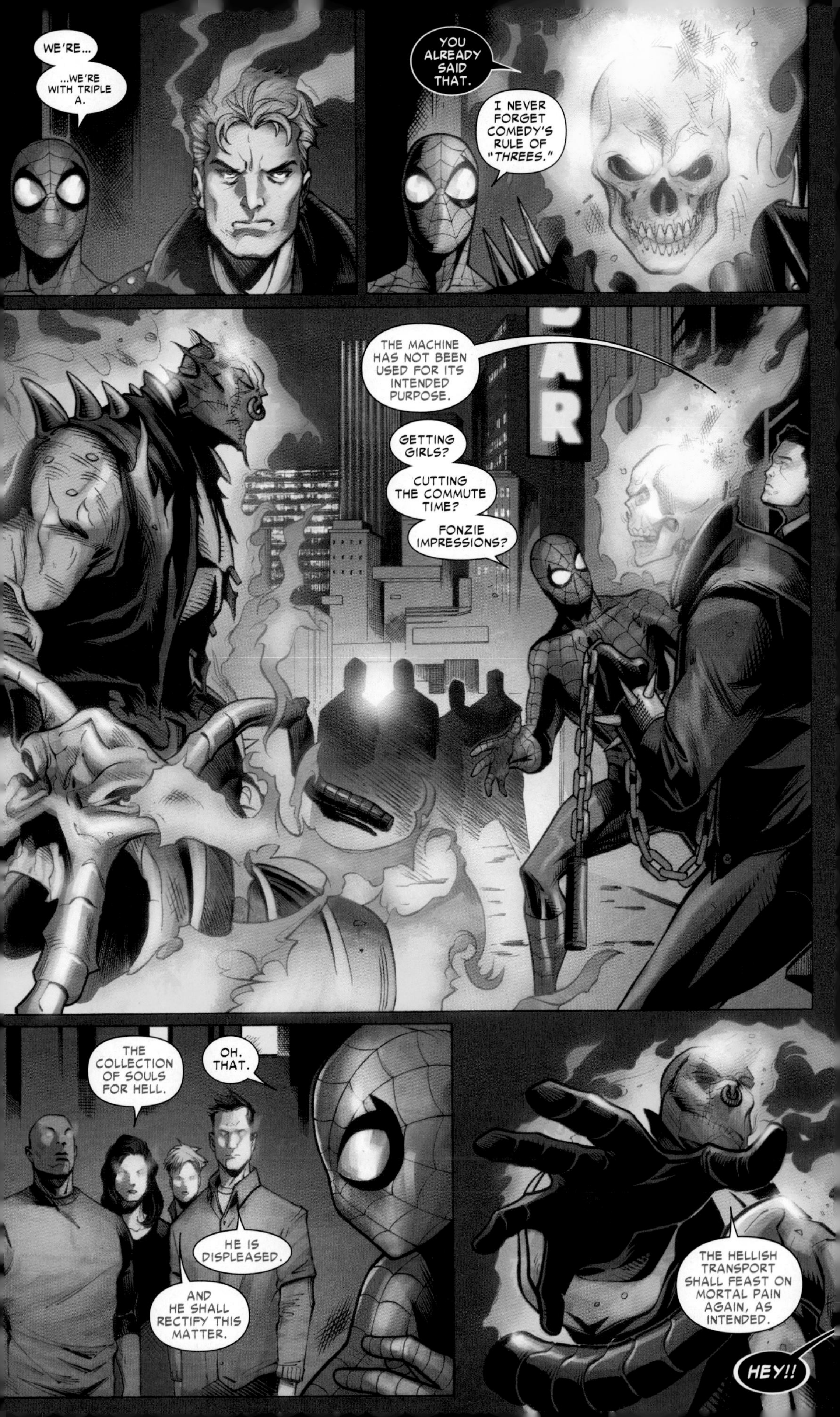
WE'RE...
...WE'RE WITH TRIPLE A.
YOU ALREADY SAID THAT.
I NEVER FORGET COMEDY'S RULE OF "THREES."
BAR
THE MACHINE HAS NOT BEEN USED FOR ITS INTENDED PURPOSE.
GETTING GIRLS?
CUTTING THE COMMUTE TIME?
FONZIE IMPRESSIONS?
THE COLLECTION OF SOULS FOR HELL.
OH. THAT.
HE IS DISPLEASED.
AND HE SHALL RECTIFY THIS MATTER.
THE HELLISH TRANSPORT SHALL FEAST ON MORTAL PAIN AGAIN, AS INTENDED.
HEY!!

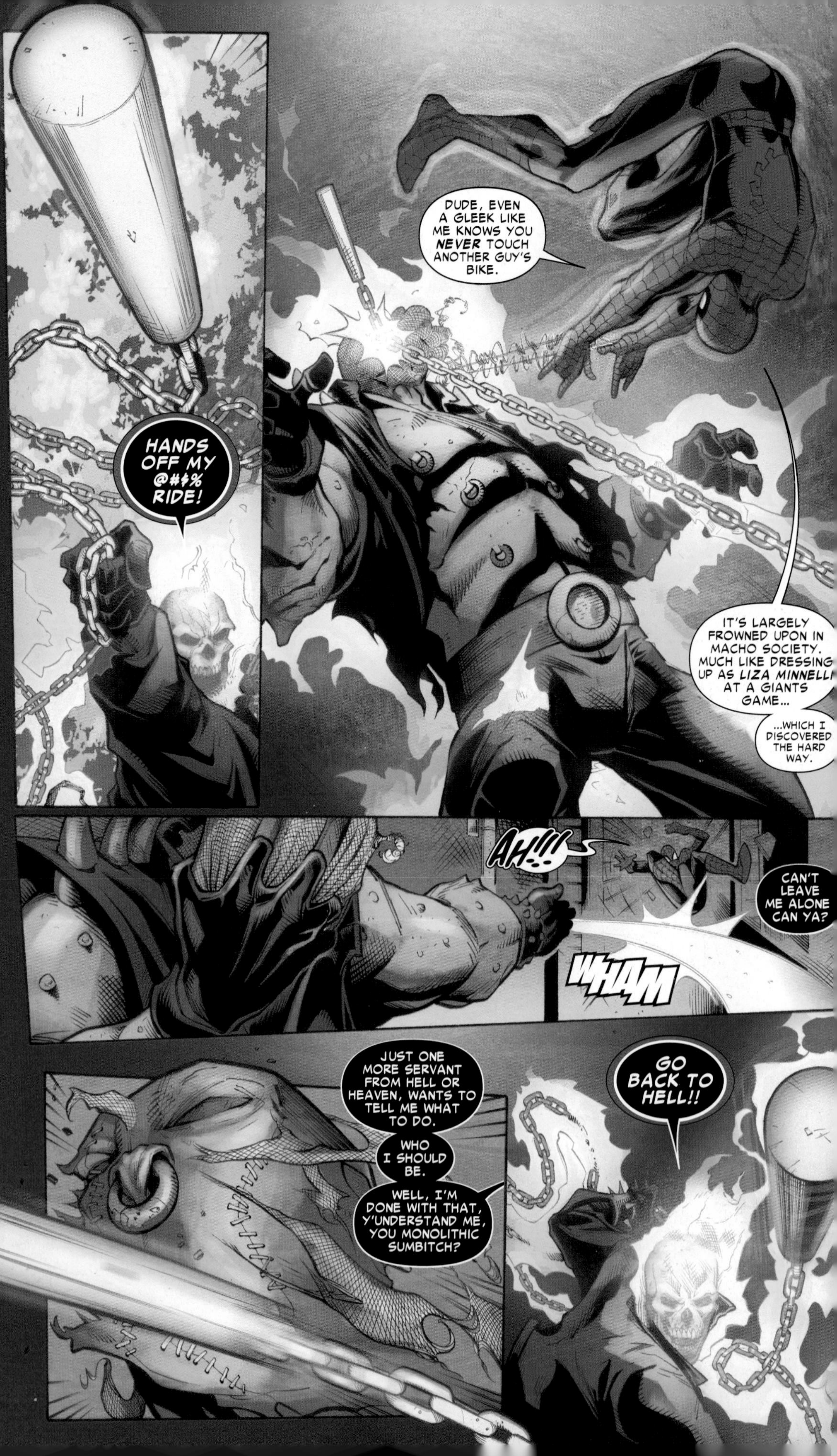
DUDE, EVEN A GLEEK LIKE ME KNOWS YOU NEVER TOUCH ANOTHER GUY'S BIKE.
HANDS OFF MY @#$% RIDE!
IT'S LARGELY FROWNED UPON IN MACHO SOCIETY. MUCH LIKE DRESSING UP AS LIZA MINNELLI AT A GIANTS GAME...
...WHICH I DISCOVERED THE HARD WAY.
AH!!!
CAN'T LEAVE ME ALONE CAN YA?
WHAM
JUST ONE MORE SERVANT FROM HELL OR HEAVEN, WANTS TO TELL ME WHAT TO DO.
WHO I SHOULD BE.
WELL, I'M DONE WITH THAT, Y'UNDERSTAND ME, YOU MONOLITHIC SUMBITCH?
GO BACK TO HELL!!

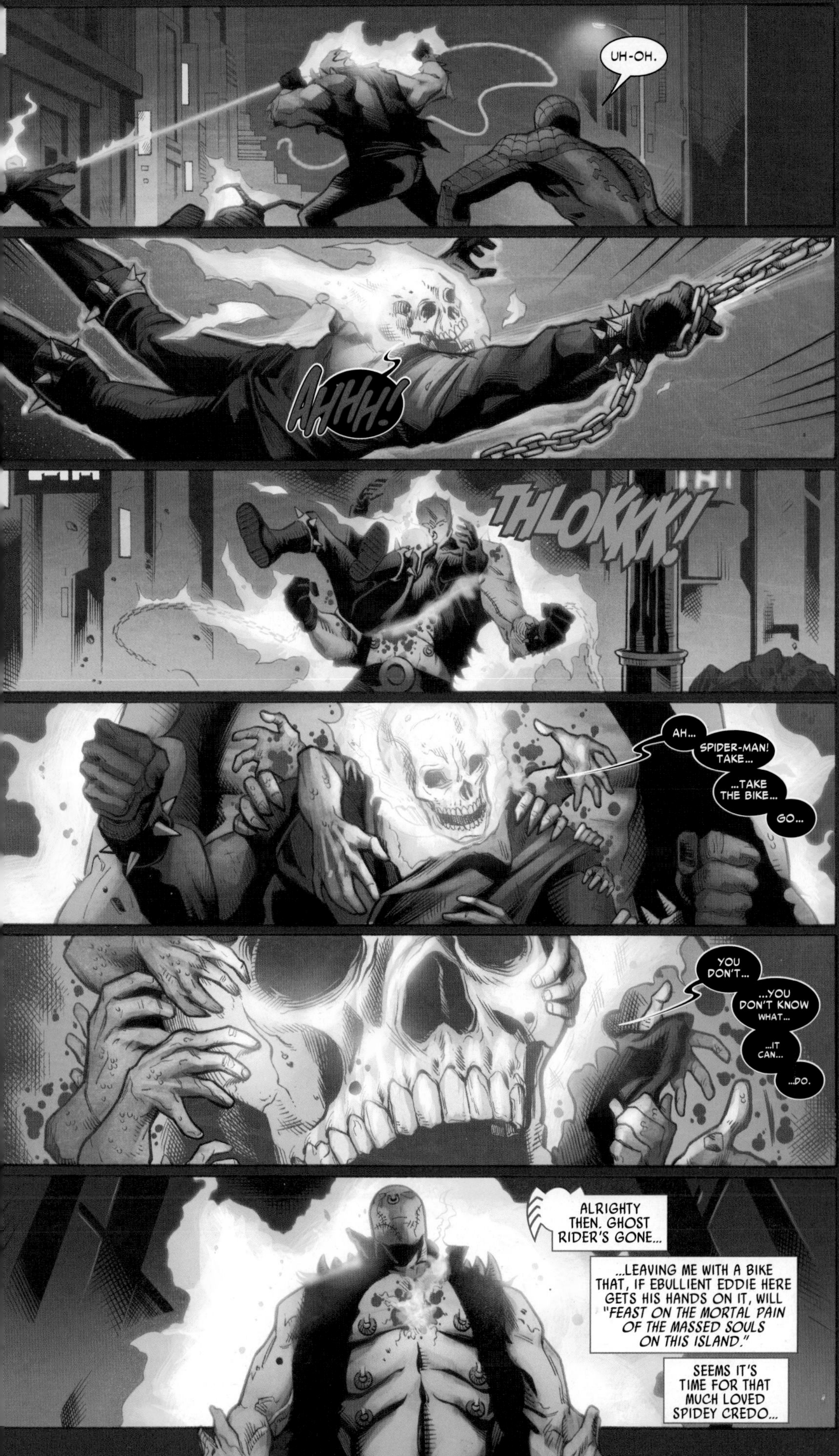
UH-OH.
AHHH!
THLOKKK!
AH...
SPIDER-MAN! TAKE...
...TAKE THE BIKE...
GO...
YOU DON'T...
...YOU DON'T KNOW WHAT...
...IT CAN...
...DO.
ALRIGHTY THEN. GHOST RIDER'S GONE...
...LEAVING ME WITH A BIKE THAT, IF EBULLIENT EDDIE HERE GETS HIS HANDS ON IT, WILL *"FEAST ON THE MORTAL PAIN OF THE MASSED SOULS ON THIS ISLAND."*
SEEMS IT'S TIME FOR THAT MUCH LOVED SPIDEY CREDO...

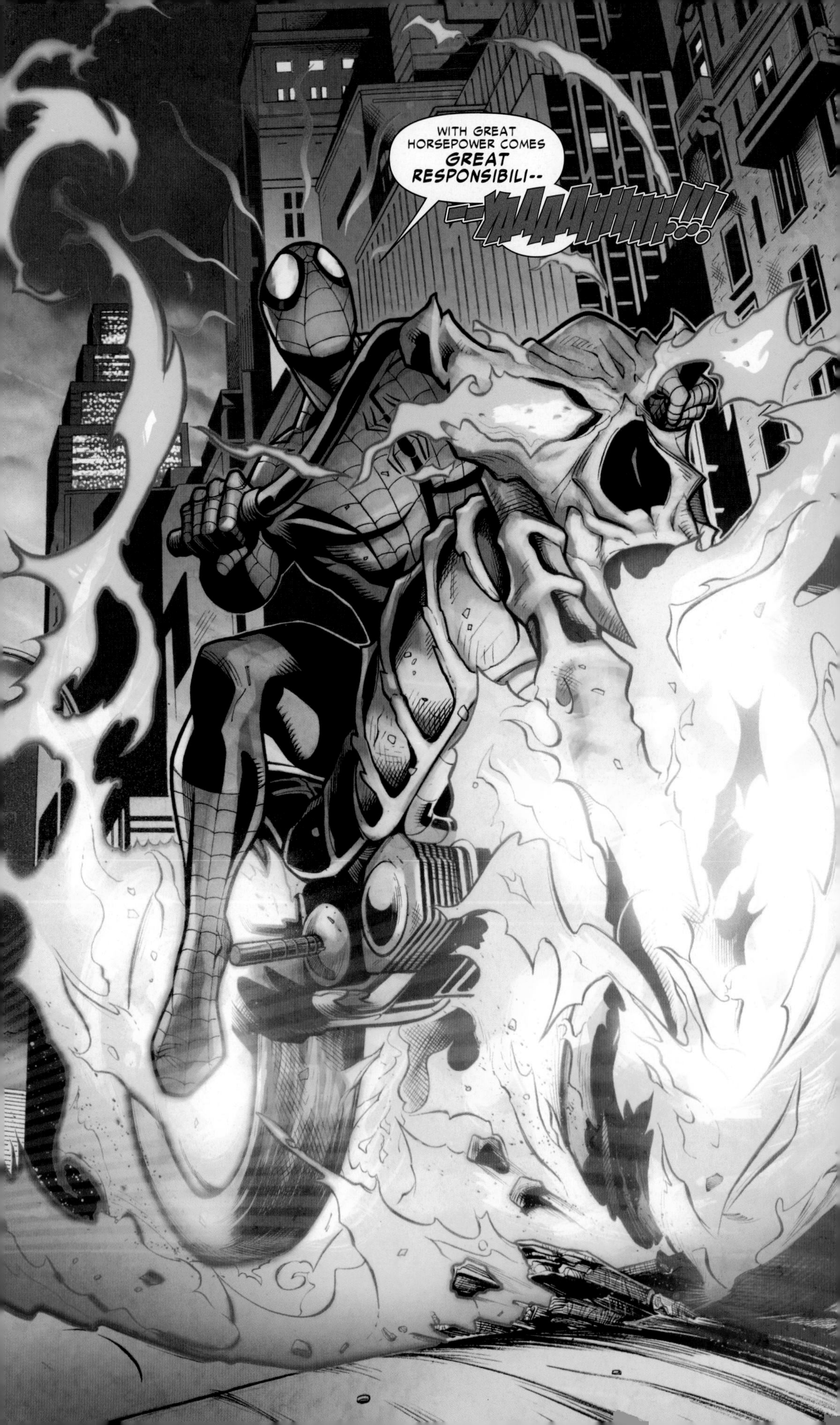
WITH GREAT HORSEPOWER COMES GREAT RESPONSIBILI--
--YAAAAHHHH!!!!

DON'T...
...PLEASE.

THAT'S ALL I HAVE. I SWEAR.

SHOULDN'T BE OUT THIS LATE 'LESS YOU CAN PAY YOUR WAY. AND WHAT YOU HOLDING HERE AIN'T GONNA CUT IT.

STREETS BE DANGEROUS.

LOTTA SIN OUT HERE. LOTTA DEBTS TO PAY.

LOTTA PAIN.

HEY!

RRRRRRRRRRRRRRRRRR!

YOU KNOW WHAT ELSE CAN CAUSE PAIN?

RRRRRRRRRRRRRRRRRRRRRRRR!

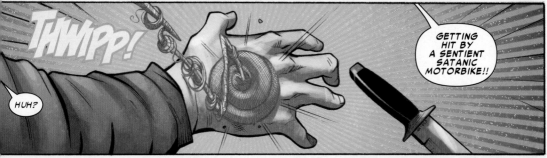

THWIPP!

HUH?

GETTING HIT BY A SENTIENT SATANIC MOTORBIKE!!

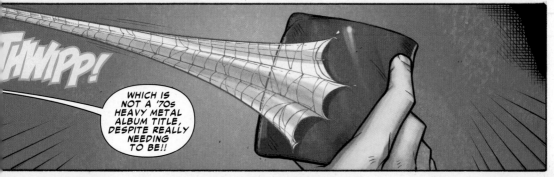

THWIPP!

WHICH IS NOT A '70s HEAVY METAL ALBUM TITLE, DESPITE REALLY NEEDING TO BE!!

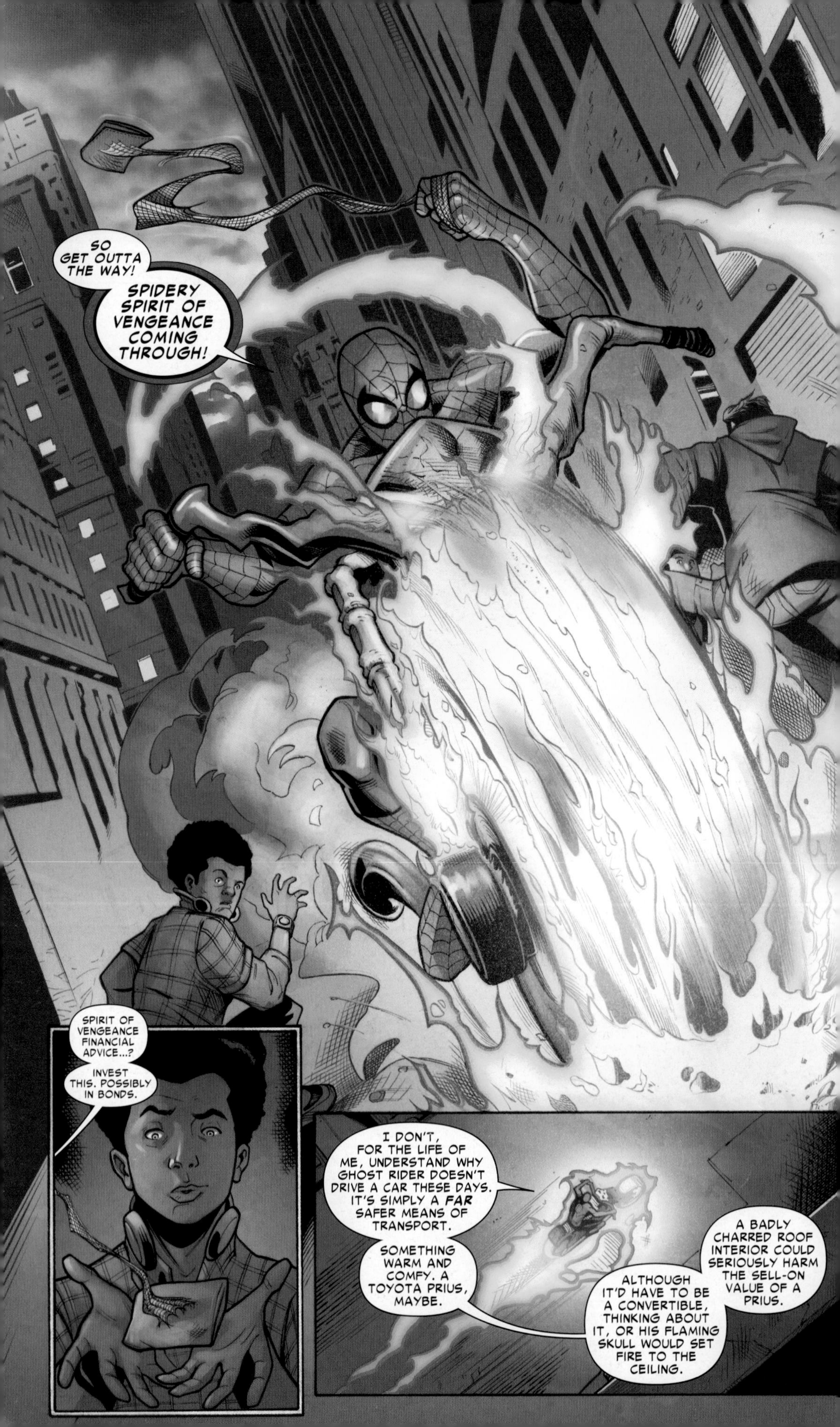
SO GET OUTTA THE WAY!
SPIDERY SPIRIT OF VENGEANCE COMING THROUGH!
SPIRIT OF VENGEANCE FINANCIAL ADVICE...?
INVEST THIS. POSSIBLY IN BONDS.
I DON'T, FOR THE LIFE OF ME, UNDERSTAND WHY GHOST RIDER DOESN'T DRIVE A CAR THESE DAYS. IT'S SIMPLY A FAR SAFER MEANS OF TRANSPORT.
SOMETHING WARM AND COMFY. A TOYOTA PRIUS, MAYBE.
ALTHOUGH IT'D HAVE TO BE A CONVERTIBLE, THINKING ABOUT IT, OR HIS FLAMING SKULL WOULD SET FIRE TO THE CEILING.
A BADLY CHARRED ROOF INTERIOR COULD SERIOUSLY HARM THE SELL-ON VALUE OF A PRIUS.

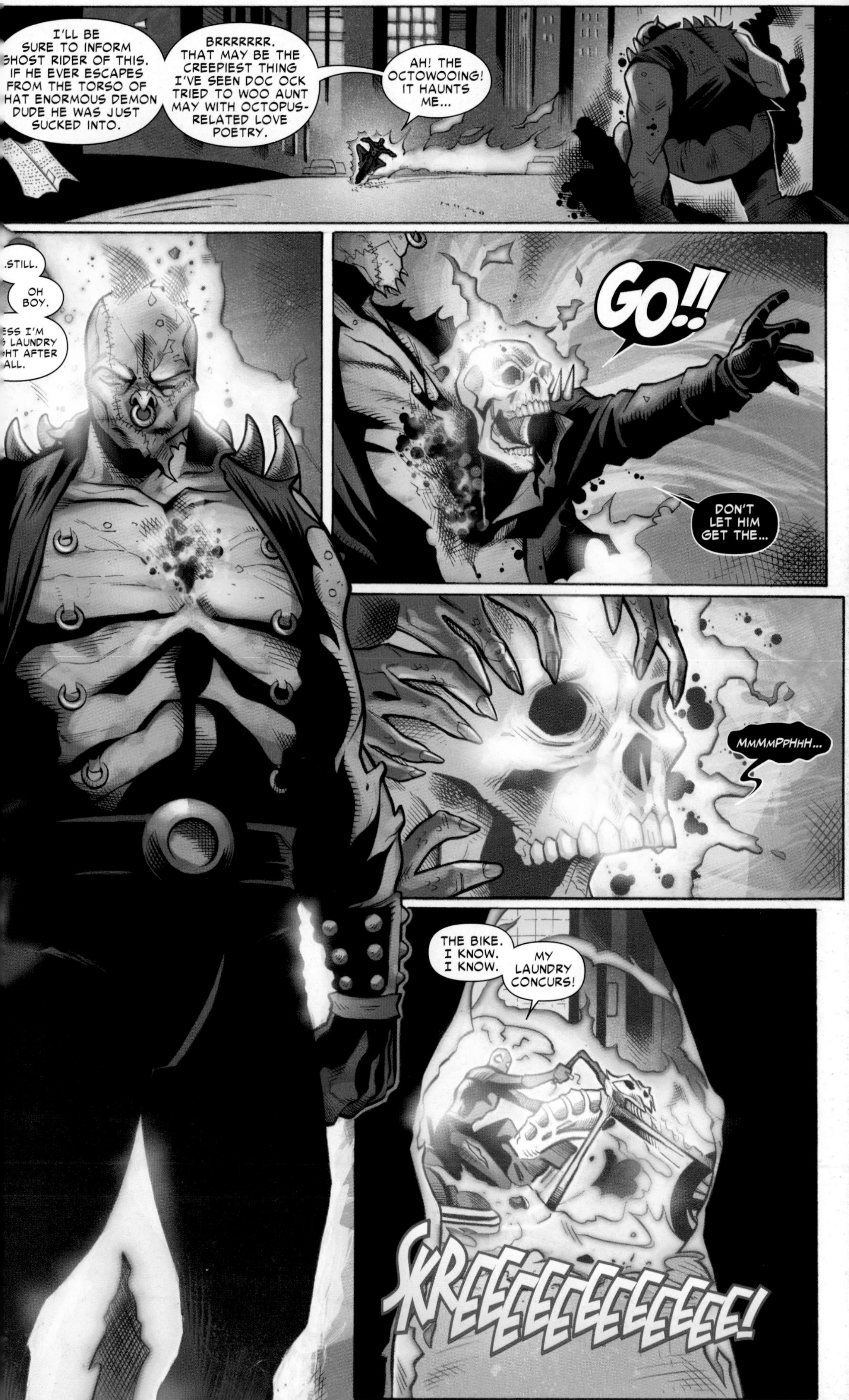
I'LL BE SURE TO INFORM GHOST RIDER OF THIS. IF HE EVER ESCAPES FROM THE TORSO OF THAT ENORMOUS DEMON DUDE HE WAS JUST SUCKED INTO.
BRRRRRRR. THAT MAY BE THE CREEPIEST THING I'VE SEEN DOC OCK TRIED TO WOO AUNT MAY WITH OCTOPUS-RELATED LOVE POETRY.
AH! THE OCTOWOOING! IT HAUNTS ME...
...STILL.
OH BOY.
ESS I'M LAUNDRY HT AFTER ALL.
GO!!
DON'T LET HIM GET THE...
MMMMPPHHH...
THE BIKE. I KNOW. I KNOW.
MY LAUNDRY CONCURS!
SKREEEEEEEEEEEEEE!

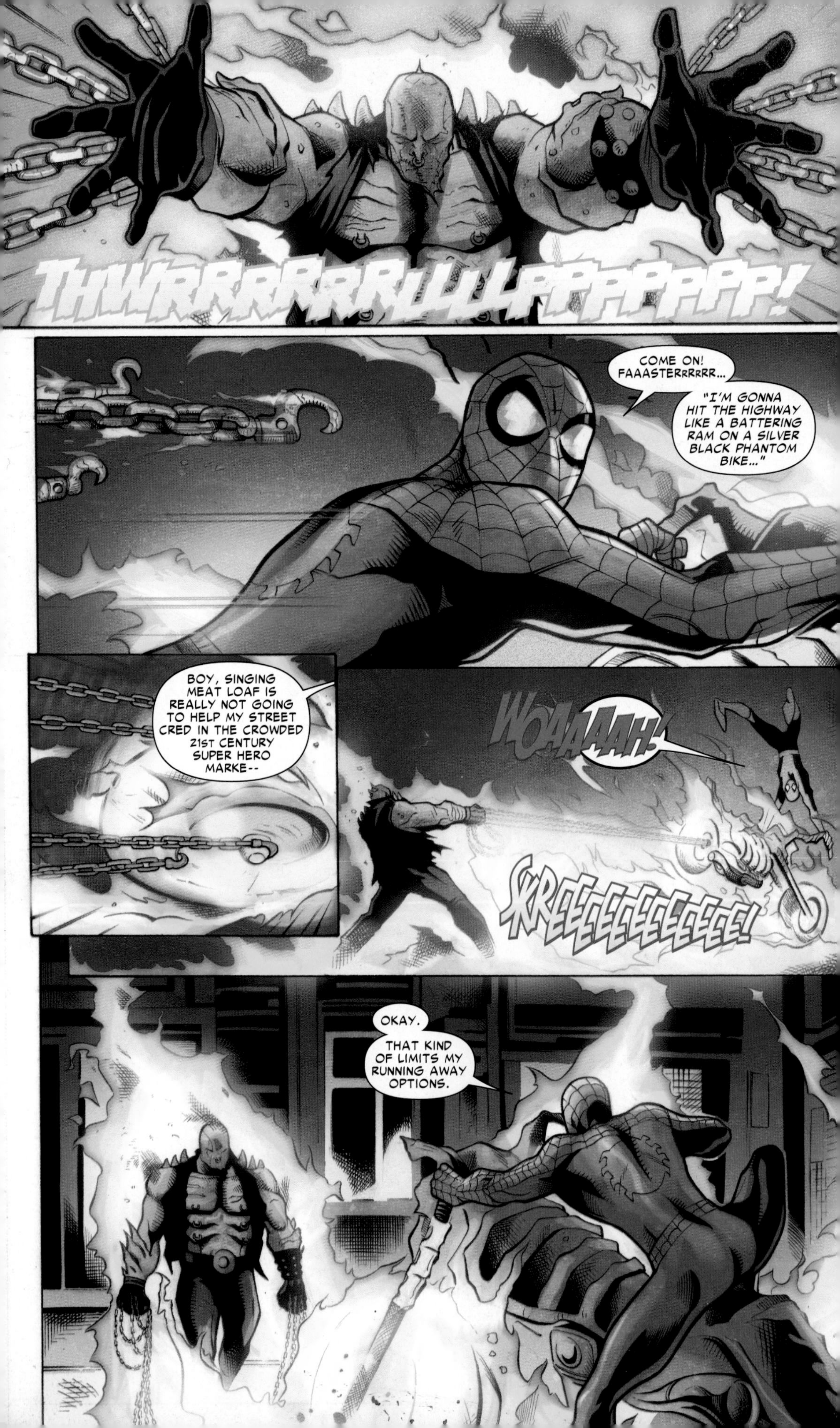
THWRRRRRRRLLLLPPPPPPP!
COME ON! FAAASTERRRRRR...
"I'M GONNA HIT THE HIGHWAY LIKE A BATTERING RAM ON A SILVER BLACK PHANTOM BIKE..."
BOY, SINGING MEAT LOAF IS REALLY NOT GOING TO HELP MY STREET CRED IN THE CROWDED 21ST CENTURY SUPER HERO MARKE--
WOAAAAH!
SKREEEEEEEEEEEEEE!
OKAY.
THAT KIND OF LIMITS MY RUNNING AWAY OPTIONS.

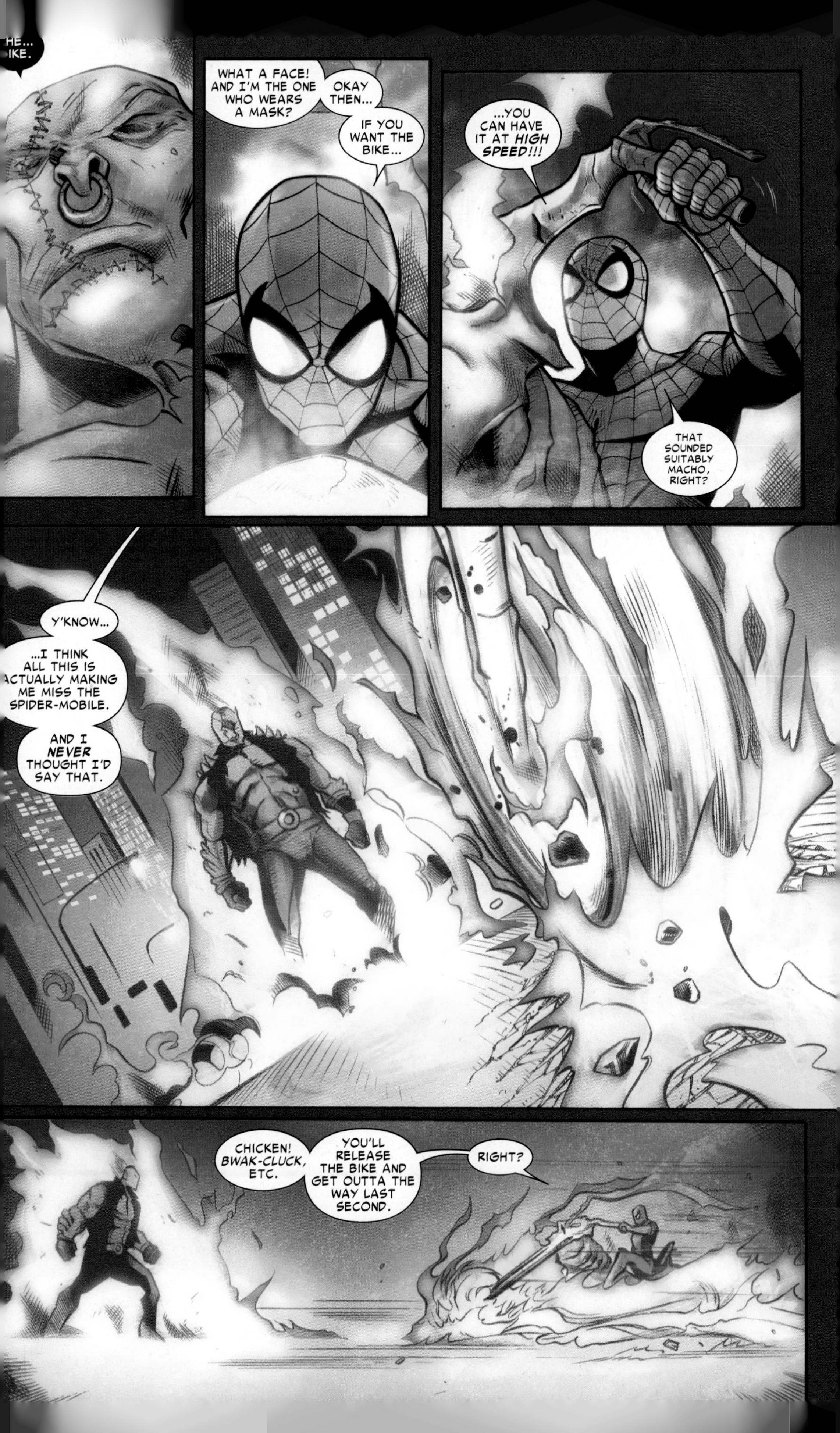
HE...
IKE.
WHAT A FACE! AND I'M THE ONE WHO WEARS A MASK?
OKAY THEN...
IF YOU WANT THE BIKE...
...YOU CAN HAVE IT AT HIGH SPEED!!!
THAT SOUNDED SUITABLY MACHO, RIGHT?
Y'KNOW...
...I THINK ALL THIS IS ACTUALLY MAKING ME MISS THE SPIDER-MOBILE.
AND I NEVER THOUGHT I'D SAY THAT.
CHICKEN! BWAK-CLUCK, ETC.
YOU'LL RELEASE THE BIKE AND GET OUTTA THE WAY LAST SECOND.
RIGHT?

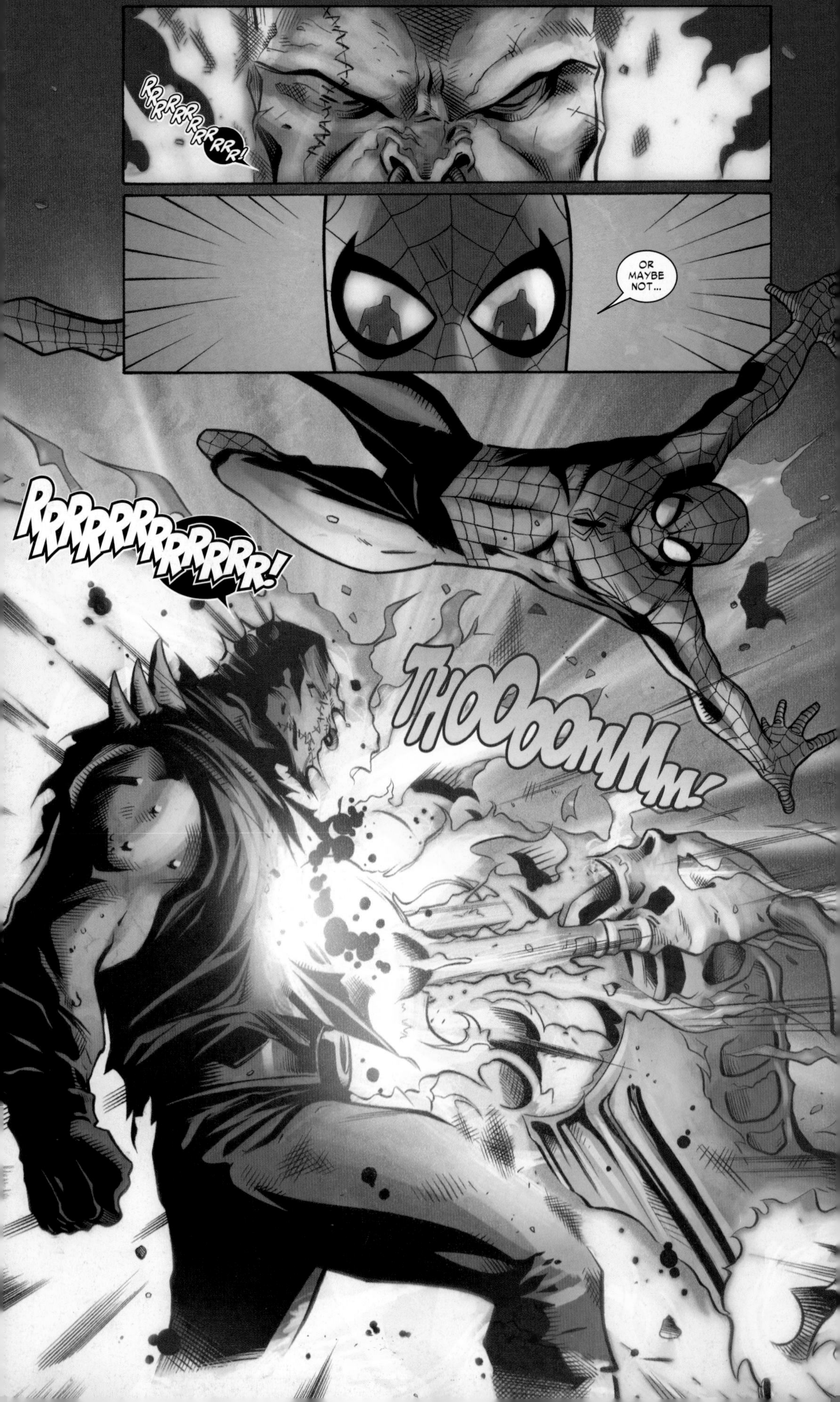
RRRRRRRRRRR!
OR MAYBE NOT...
RRRRRRRRRRRRRR!
THOOOOMMM!

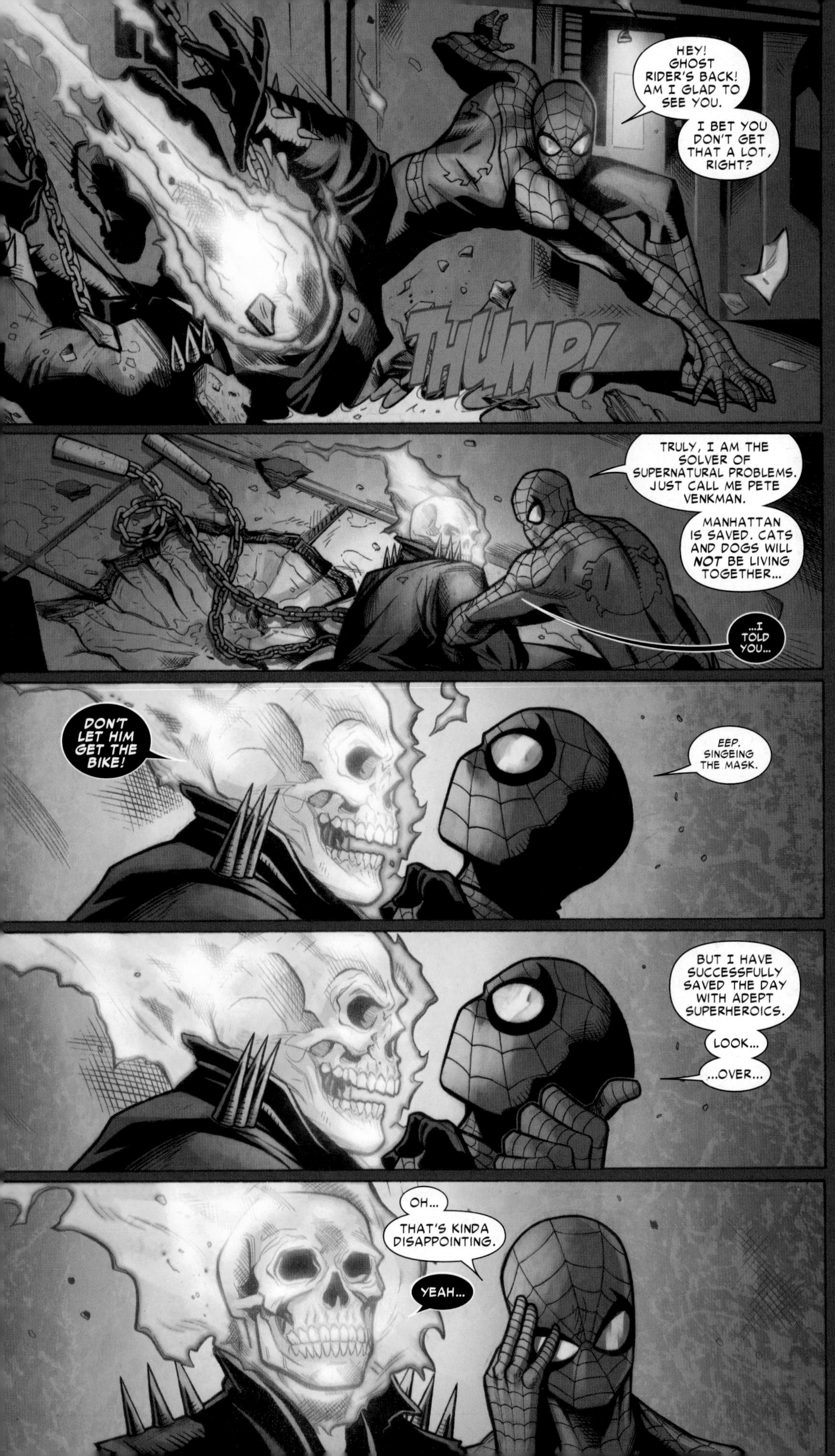
HEY! GHOST RIDER'S BACK! AM I GLAD TO SEE YOU.
I BET YOU DON'T GET THAT A LOT, RIGHT?
THUMP!
TRULY, I AM THE SOLVER OF SUPERNATURAL PROBLEMS. JUST CALL ME PETE VENKMAN.
MANHATTAN IS SAVED. CATS AND DOGS WILL NOT BE LIVING TOGETHER...
...I TOLD YOU...
DON'T LET HIM GET THE BIKE!
EEP. SINGEING THE MASK.
BUT I HAVE SUCCESSFULLY SAVED THE DAY WITH ADEPT SUPERHEROICS.
LOOK...
...OVER...
OH...
THAT'S KINDA DISAPPOINTING.
YEAH...

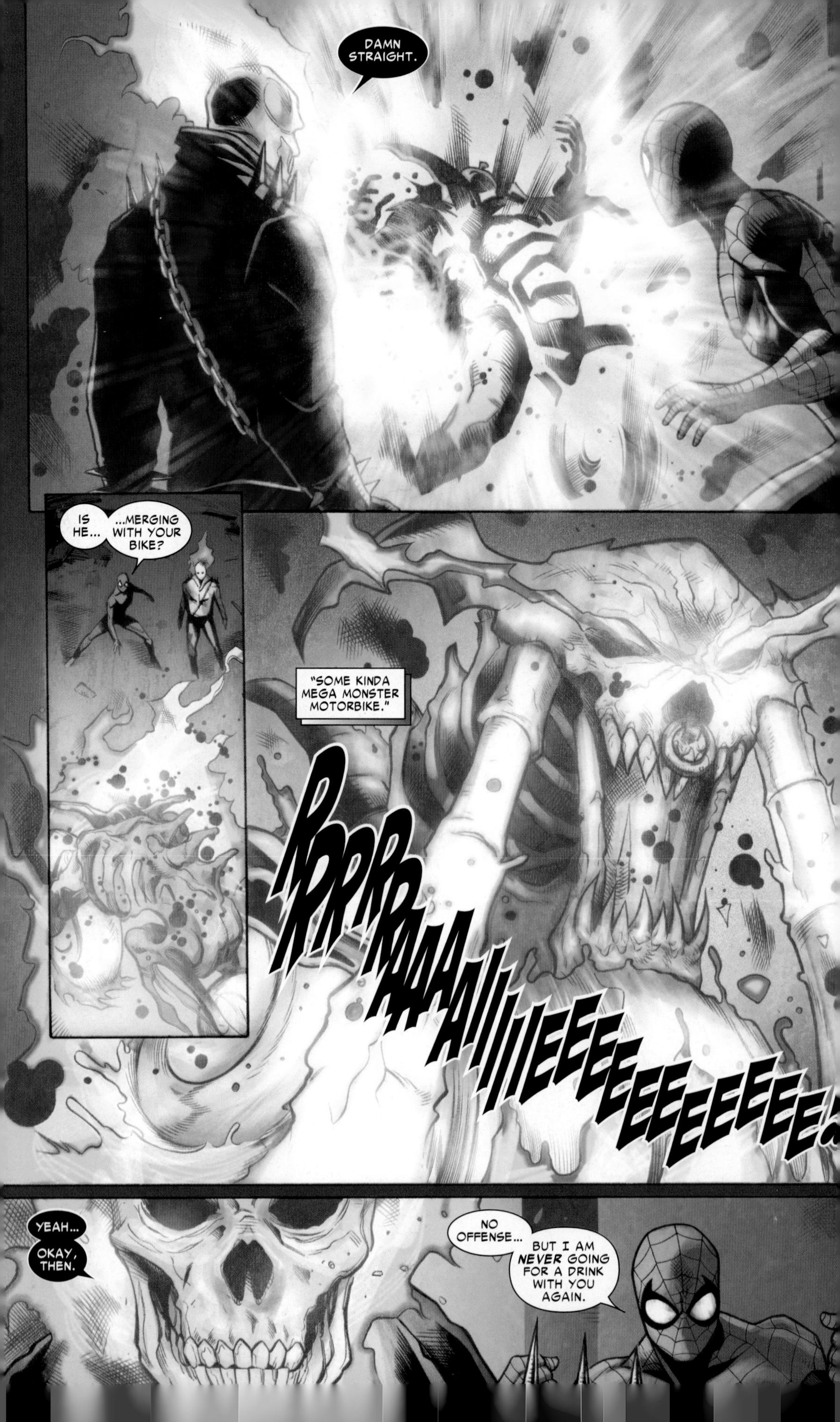
DAMN STRAIGHT.
IS HE...
...MERGING WITH YOUR BIKE?
"SOME KINDA MEGA MONSTER MOTORBIKE."
RRRRRAAAAIIIIIEEEEEEEEEEEE...
YEAH... OKAY, THEN.
NO OFFENSE...
BUT I AM NEVER GOING FOR A DRINK WITH YOU AGAIN.

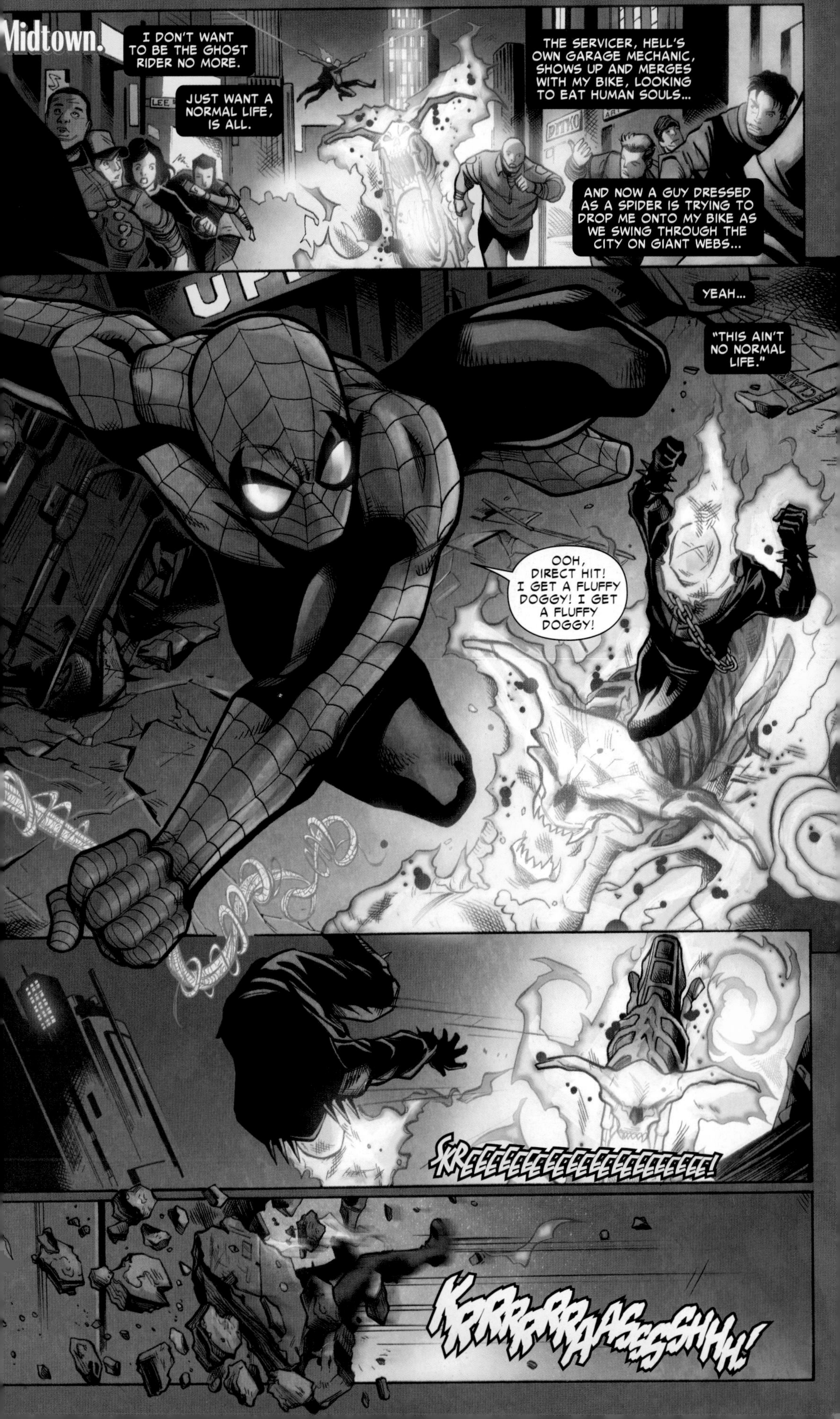
Midtown.
I DON'T WANT TO BE THE GHOST RIDER NO MORE.
JUST WANT A NORMAL LIFE, IS ALL.
THE SERVICER, HELL'S OWN GARAGE MECHANIC, SHOWS UP AND MERGES WITH MY BIKE, LOOKING TO EAT HUMAN SOULS...
AND NOW A GUY DRESSED AS A SPIDER IS TRYING TO DROP ME ONTO MY BIKE AS WE SWING THROUGH THE CITY ON GIANT WEBS...
YEAH...
"THIS AIN'T NO NORMAL LIFE."
OOH, DIRECT HIT! I GET A FLUFFY DOGGY! I GET A FLUFFY DOGGY!
SKREEEEEEEEEEEEEEEEEEEEEE!
KRRRRRAASSSHHH!

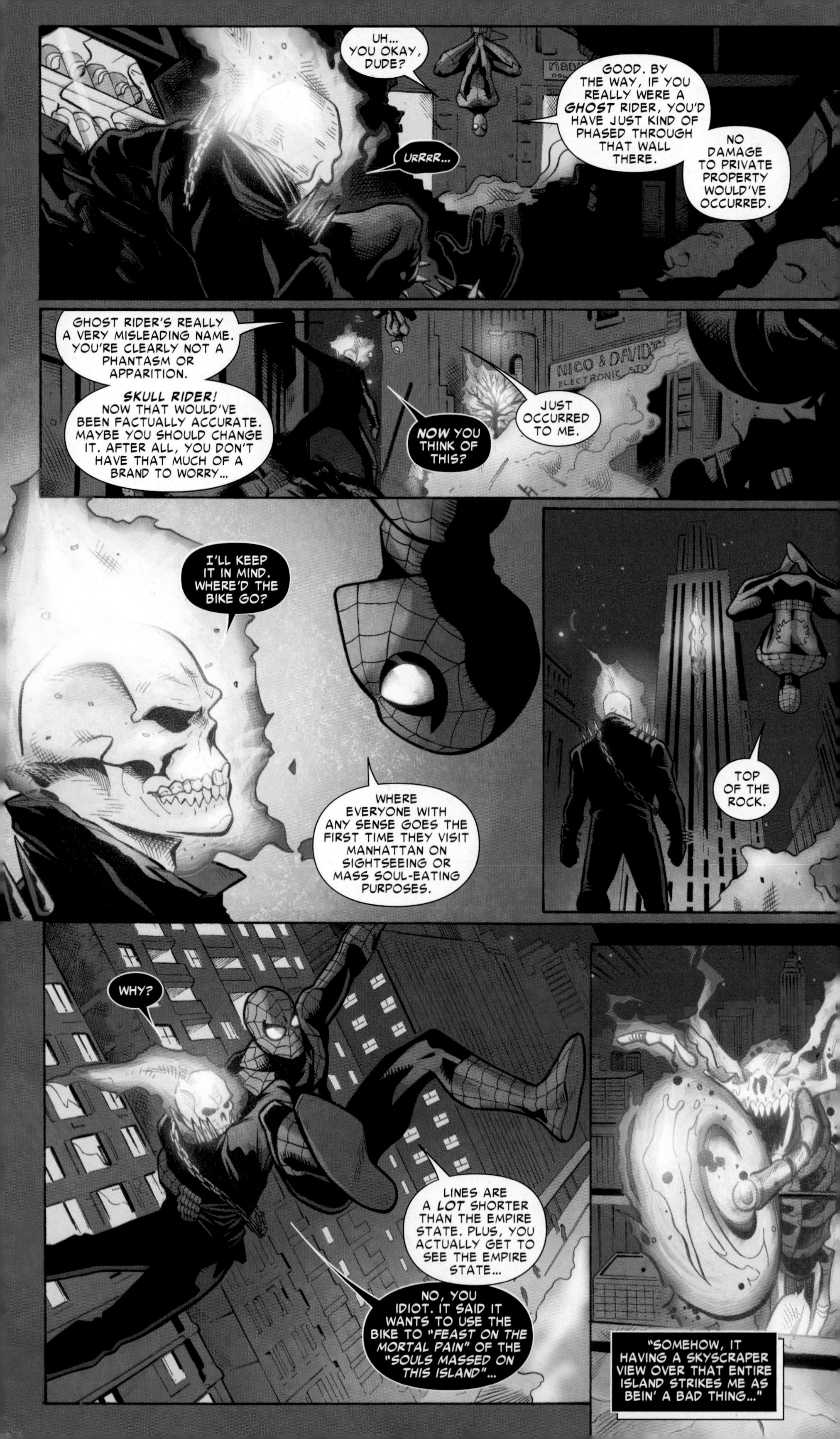
UH... YOU OKAY, DUDE?
URRRR...
GOOD. BY THE WAY, IF YOU REALLY WERE A *GHOST* RIDER, YOU'D HAVE JUST KIND OF PHASED THROUGH THAT WALL THERE.
NO DAMAGE TO PRIVATE PROPERTY WOULD'VE OCCURRED.
GHOST RIDER'S REALLY A VERY MISLEADING NAME. YOU'RE CLEARLY NOT A PHANTASM OR APPARITION.
SKULL RIDER! NOW THAT WOULD'VE BEEN FACTUALLY ACCURATE. MAYBE YOU SHOULD CHANGE IT. AFTER ALL, YOU DON'T HAVE THAT MUCH OF A BRAND TO WORRY...
NICO & DAVID'S
ELECTRONIC STO
NOW YOU THINK OF THIS?
JUST OCCURRED TO ME.
I'LL KEEP IT IN MIND. WHERE'D THE BIKE GO?
WHERE EVERYONE WITH ANY SENSE GOES THE FIRST TIME THEY VISIT MANHATTAN ON SIGHTSEEING OR MASS SOUL-EATING PURPOSES.
TOP OF THE ROCK.
WHY?
LINES ARE A *LOT* SHORTER THAN THE EMPIRE STATE. PLUS, YOU ACTUALLY GET TO SEE THE EMPIRE STATE...
NO, YOU IDIOT. IT SAID IT WANTS TO USE THE BIKE TO *"FEAST ON THE MORTAL PAIN"* OF THE *"SOULS MASSED ON THIS ISLAND"*...
"SOMEHOW, IT HAVING A SKYSCRAPER VIEW OVER THAT ENTIRE ISLAND STRIKES ME AS BEIN' A BAD THING..."

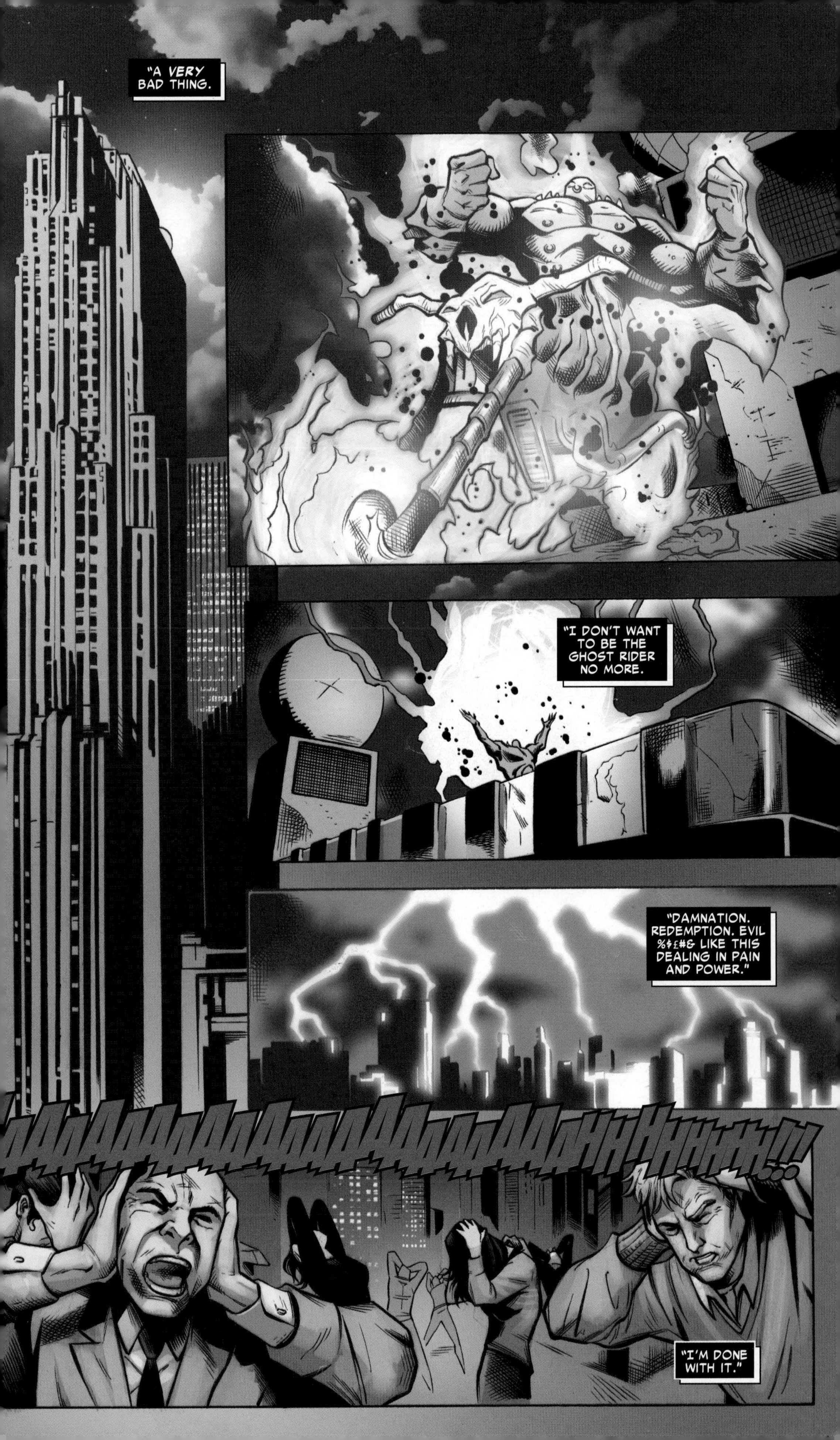
"A VERY BAD THING.
"I DON'T WANT TO BE THE GHOST RIDER NO MORE.
"DAMNATION. REDEMPTION. EVIL %$£#& LIKE THIS DEALING IN PAIN AND POWER."
AAAAAAAAAAAAAAAAAAAAAAAAAAAHHHHHHH!!
"I'M DONE WITH IT."

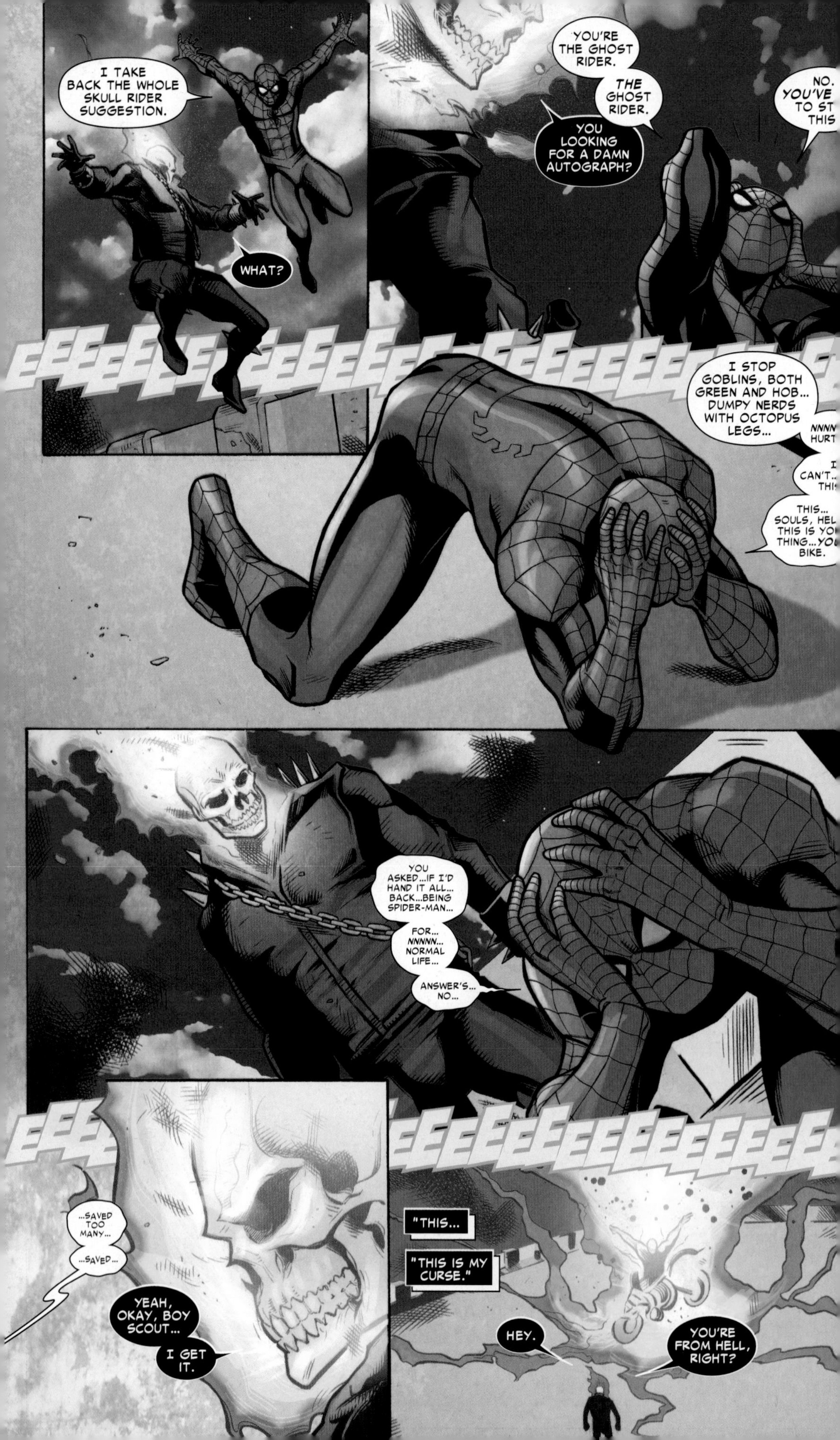
I TAKE BACK THE WHOLE SKULL RIDER SUGGESTION.
WHAT?
YOU'RE THE GHOST RIDER.
THE GHOST RIDER.
YOU LOOKING FOR A DAMN AUTOGRAPH?
NO. YOU'VE TO ST THIS
EEEEEEEEEEEEEEEEEEEEEE
I STOP GOBLINS, BOTH GREEN AND HOB... DUMPY NERDS WITH OCTOPUS LEGS...
NNNN HURT
I CAN'T... THIS
THIS... SOULS, HEL THIS IS YO THING...YO BIKE.
YOU ASKED...IF I'D HAND IT ALL... BACK...BEING SPIDER-MAN...
FOR... NNNNN... NORMAL LIFE...
ANSWER'S... NO...
EEEEEEEEEEEEEEEEEEEE
...SAVED TOO MANY...
...SAVED...
YEAH, OKAY, BOY SCOUT...
I GET IT.
"THIS...
"THIS IS MY CURSE."
HEY.
YOU'RE FROM HELL, RIGHT?

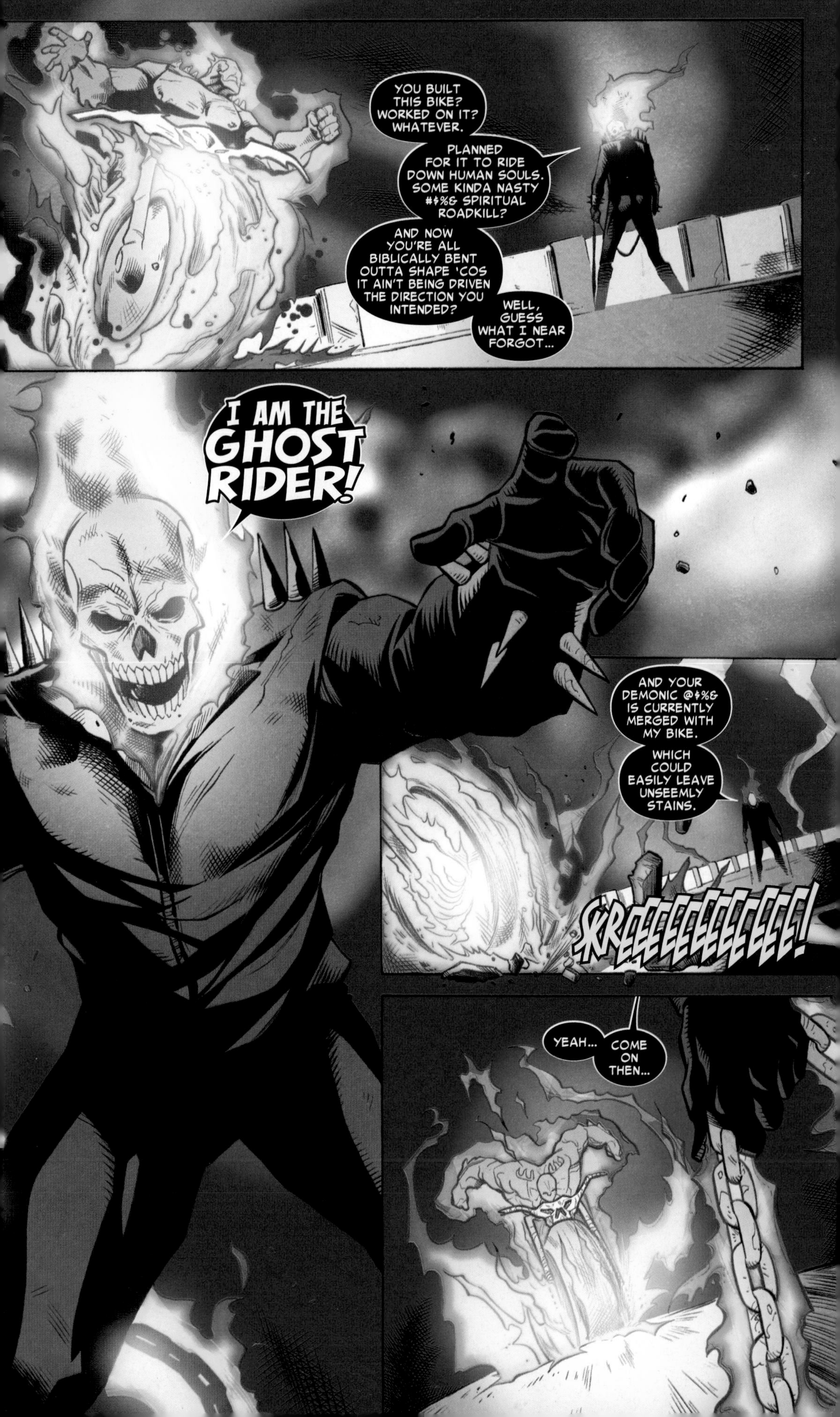
YOU BUILT THIS BIKE? WORKED ON IT? WHATEVER.
PLANNED FOR IT TO RIDE DOWN HUMAN SOULS. SOME KINDA NASTY #$%& SPIRITUAL ROADKILL?
AND NOW YOU'RE ALL BIBLICALLY BENT OUTTA SHAPE 'COS IT AIN'T BEING DRIVEN THE DIRECTION YOU INTENDED?
WELL, GUESS WHAT I NEAR FORGOT...
I AM THE GHOST RIDER!
AND YOUR DEMONIC @$%& IS CURRENTLY MERGED WITH MY BIKE.
WHICH COULD EASILY LEAVE UNSEEMLY STAINS.
SKREEEEEEEEEEEEE!
YEAH...
COME ON THEN...

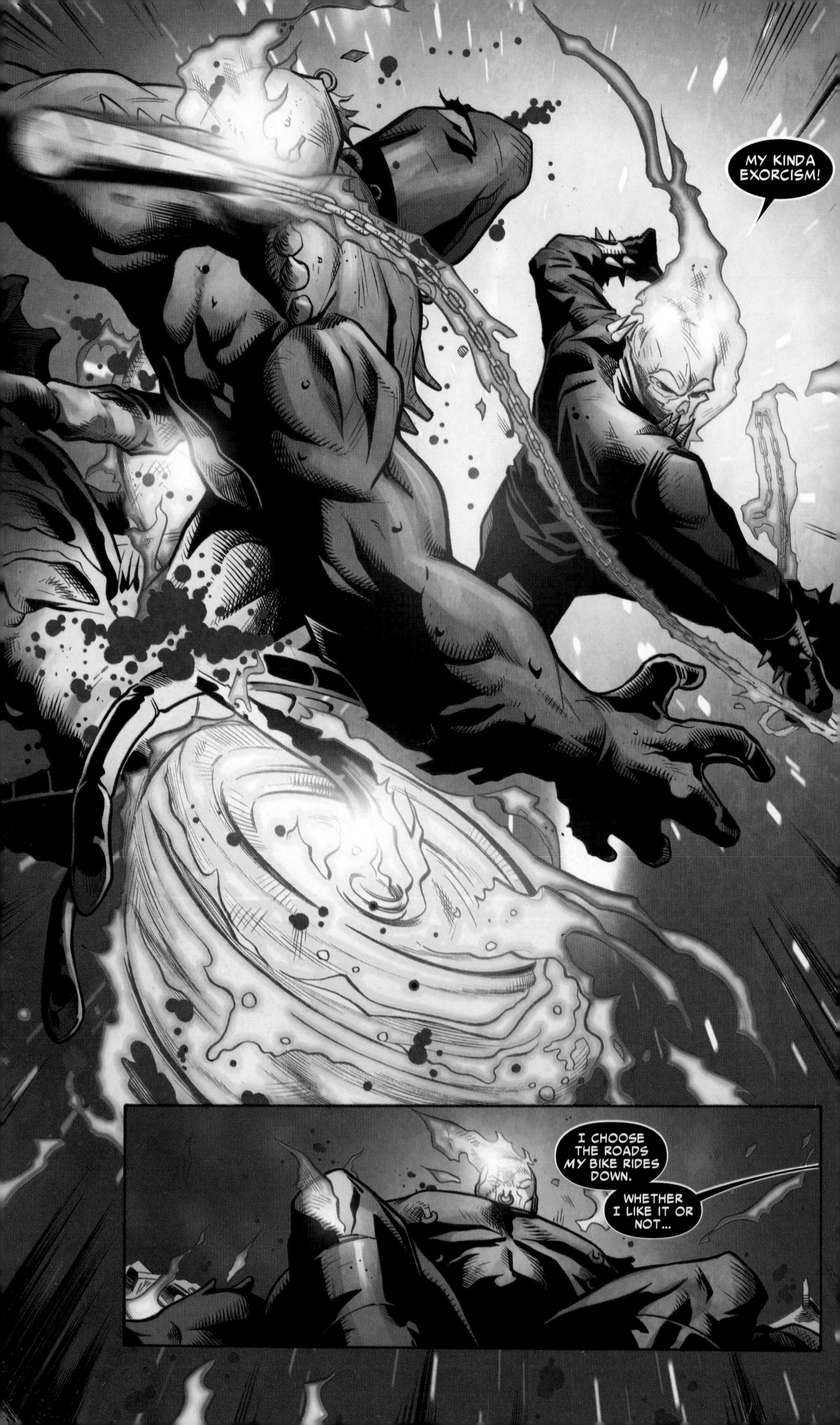
MY KINDA EXORCISM!
I CHOOSE THE ROADS MY BIKE RIDES DOWN.
WHETHER I LIKE IT OR NOT...

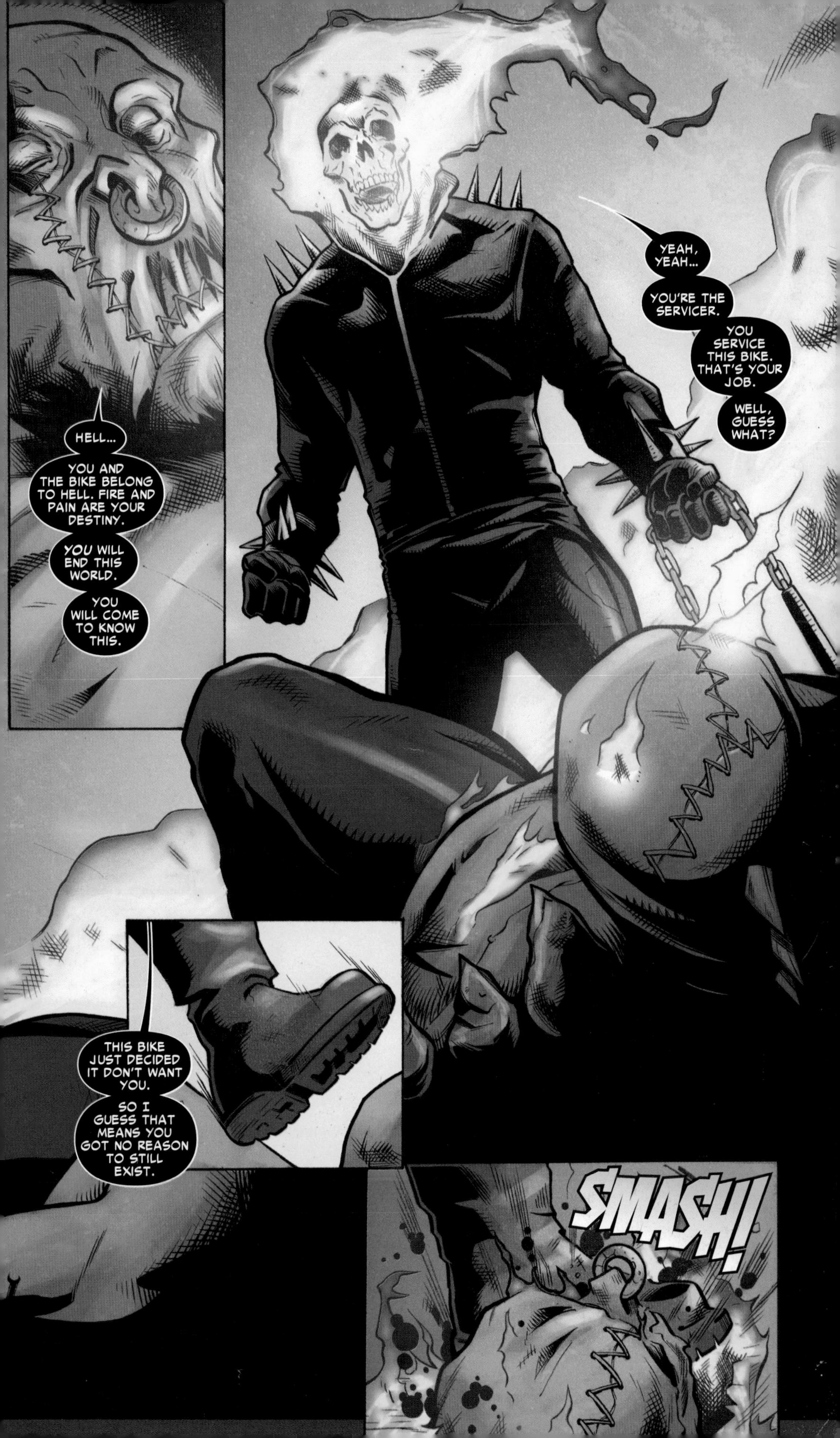
HELL...
YOU AND THE BIKE BELONG TO HELL. FIRE AND PAIN ARE YOUR DESTINY.
YOU WILL END THIS WORLD.
YOU WILL COME TO KNOW THIS.
YEAH, YEAH...
YOU'RE THE SERVICER.
YOU SERVICE THIS BIKE. THAT'S YOUR JOB.
WELL, GUESS WHAT?
THIS BIKE JUST DECIDED IT DON'T WANT YOU.
SO I GUESS THAT MEANS YOU GOT NO REASON TO STILL EXIST.
SMASH!

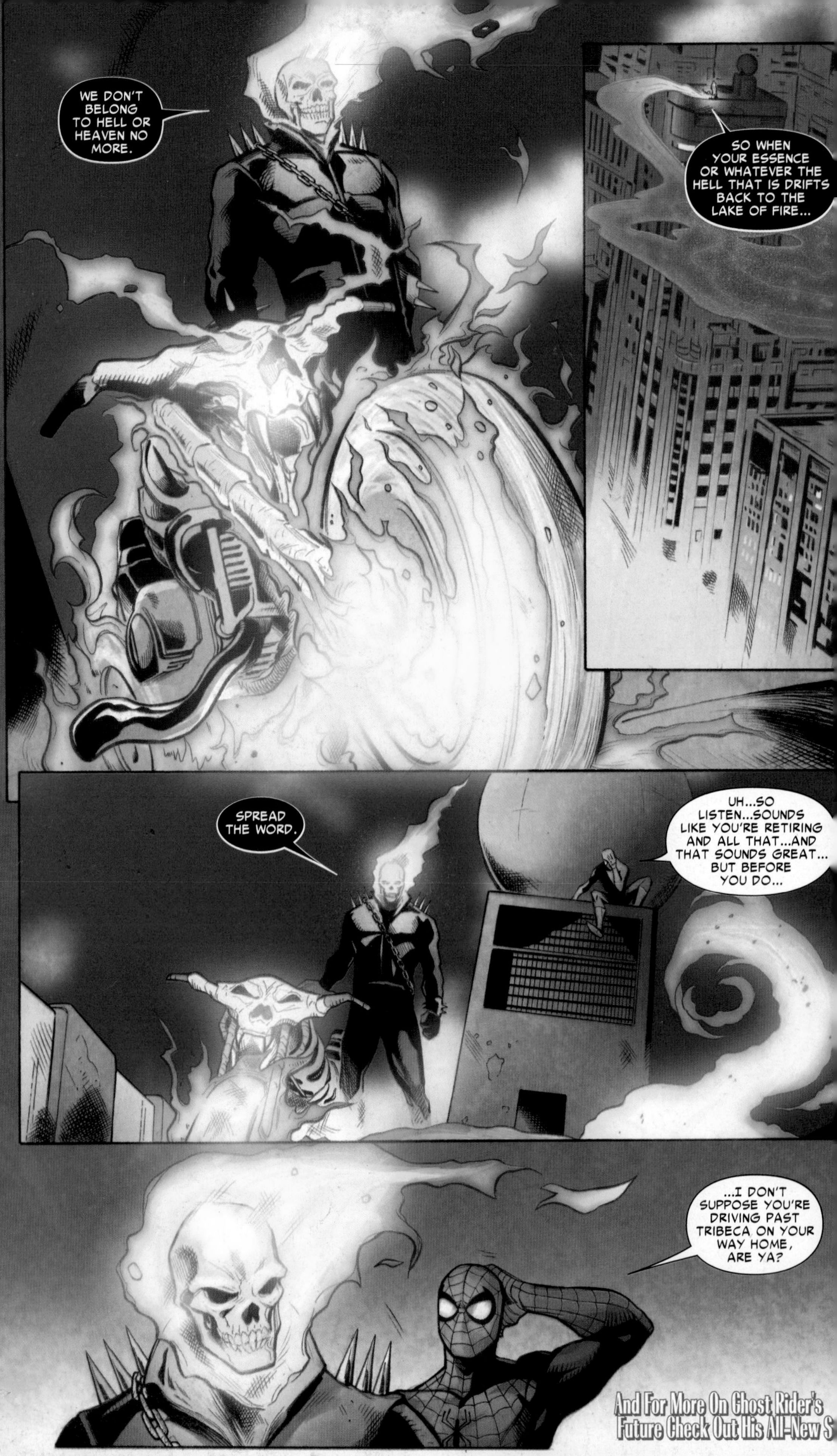

WE DON'T BELONG TO HELL OR HEAVEN NO MORE.
SO WHEN YOUR ESSENCE OR WHATEVER THE HELL THAT IS DRIFTS BACK TO THE LAKE OF FIRE...
SPREAD THE WORD.
UH...SO LISTEN...SOUNDS LIKE YOU'RE RETIRING AND ALL THAT...AND THAT SOUNDS GREAT... BUT BEFORE YOU DO...
...I DON'T SUPPOSE YOU'RE DRIVING PAST TRIBECA ON YOUR WAY HOME, ARE YA?
And For More On Ghost Rider's Future Check Out His All-New S

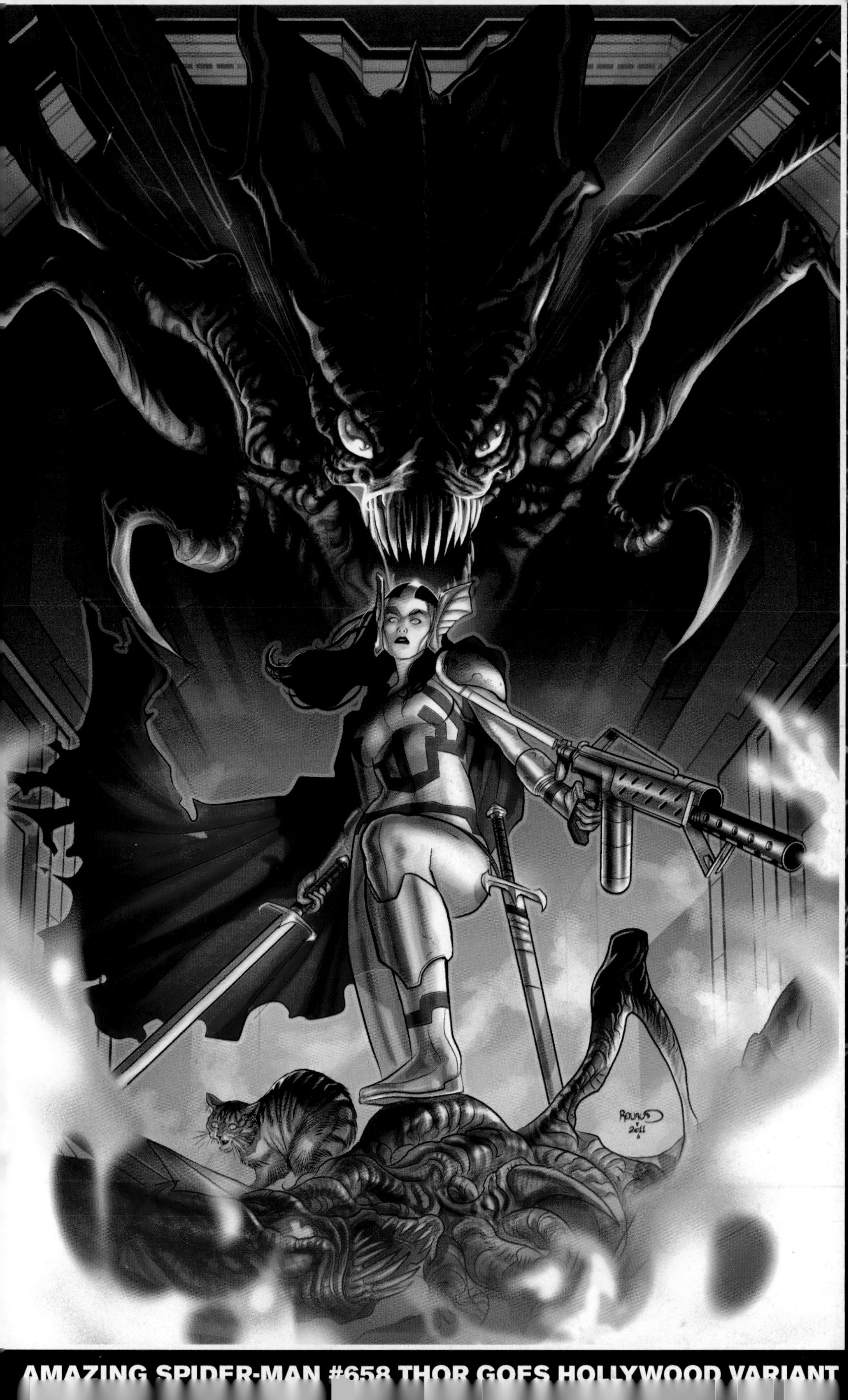

AMAZING SPIDER-MAN #658 THOR GOES HOLLYWOOD VARIANT

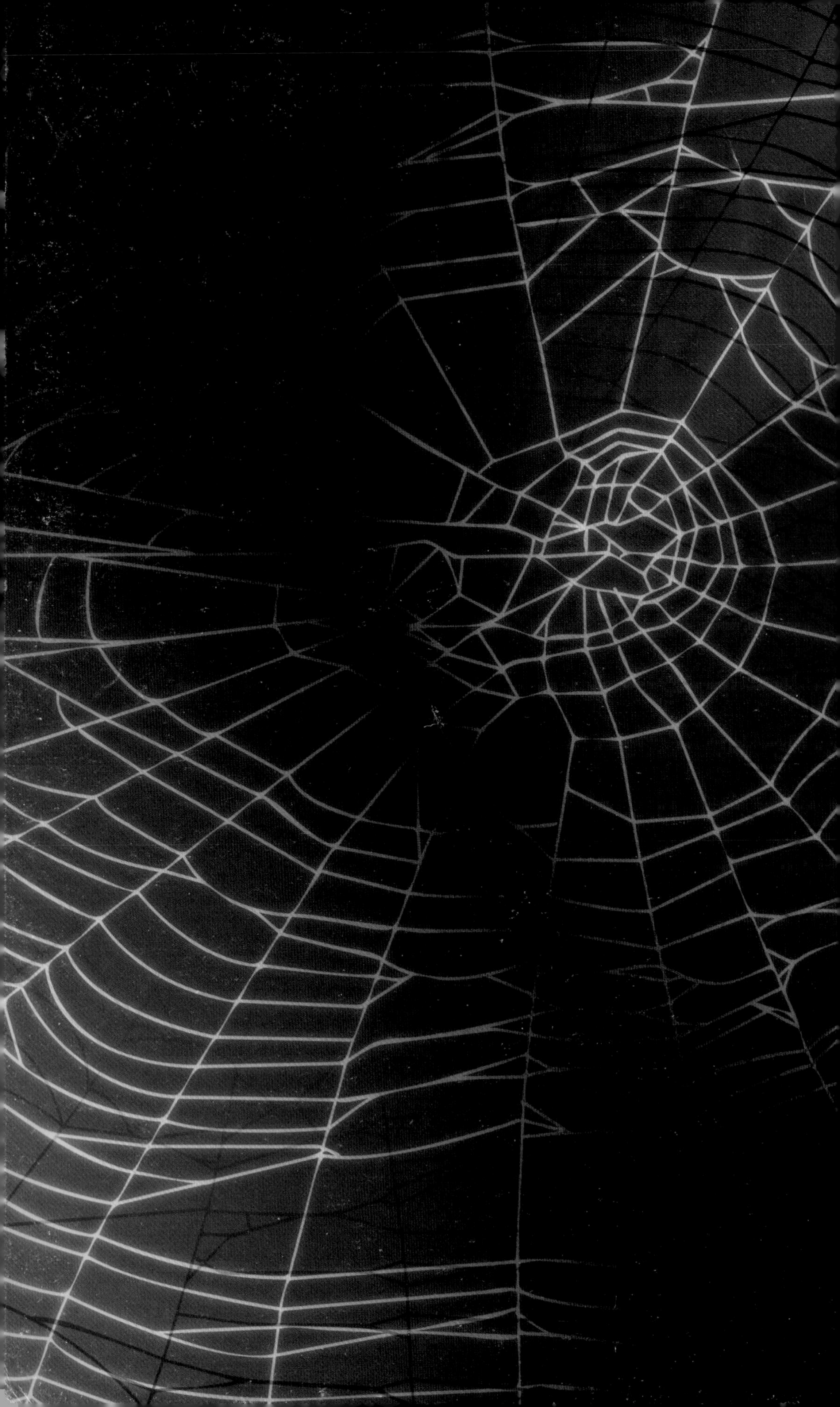